SNAKES AND LADDERS

SNAKES AND LADDERS

The Great British Social Mobility Myth

SELINA TODD

Chatto & Windus
LONDON

1 3 5 7 9 10 8 6 4 2

Chatto & Windus, an imprint of Vintage

Chatto & Windus is part of the Penguin Random House group of companies
whose addresses can be found at global.penguinrandomhouse.com.

Penguin
Random House
UK

First published by Chatto & Windus in 2021

penguin.co.uk/vintage

A CIP catalogue record for this book is available from the British Library

ISBN 9781784740818

Typeset in 10.5/15.5 pt Mercury Text G1
by Integra Software Services Pvt. Ltd, Pondicherry

Printed and bound in Great Britain by Clays Ltd, Elcograf S.p.A.

The authorised representative in the EEA is Penguin Random House Ireland,
Morrison Chambers, 32 Nassau Street, Dublin D02 YH68.

Penguin Random House is committed to a sustainable future for
our business, our readers and our planet. This book is made from
Forest Stewardship Council® certified paper.

MIX
Paper from
responsible sources
FSC
www.fsc.org   FSC® C018179

For Sheila Forbes

Experience isn't only what's happened to us. It's also what we wanted to happen.

RAYMOND WILLIAMS, *BORDER COUNTRY* (1960)

CONTENTS

INTRODUCTION

That our hard work, talent and ambition will make us rich, powerful and happy is an alluring story. It's one that generations of politicians, employers and teachers have encouraged us to believe. Without that promise, the inequality inherent in capitalist societies – where a few people at the top of the ladder hold wealth and power, while most people have very little – looks unfair. But if the rung we are on is determined by our efforts, then those at the top deserve reward. Everyone benefits, because the chance to climb the ladder encourages ambition, competition to do so makes people work harder, and this increases productivity. Even the idle and feckless on the lowest rungs gain from the ideas and innovations that the talented and hardworking produce, and from the economic growth that their ventures create.

But this is a myth. Those men and women born between 1880 and the end of the nineteenth century were the first generation of whom a majority moved up or down the ladder. That's been true of every generation since. Yet despite this, over the past 140 years, birth and wealth have exercised a far greater influence on a person's social position than talent, effort or ambition.

This book explains why. It tells the story of those who lived through these decades, revealing who created and reformed the social ladder; how and why people sought to change their lives and, sometimes, to transform the society they lived in; and the experience of those who climbed or slid down the ladder.

'Social mobility' measures how far a person travels from their parents' social class (although in this book, I also explore people's mobility across their own lives). Measurements of social mobility, whether used by politicians or social scientists, invite us to see society as a ladder, with each rung defined by social and economic status. Most researchers of social mobility use occupation as the basis for defining a person's social class (though income and sometimes 'taste' also play a part). Their ladder usually comprises five or seven rungs, from unskilled work at the bottom to senior professionals and the owners of big businesses at the top.[1]

Unlike most studies of social mobility, this book is more concerned with people's experience than amassing statistics (though I draw on these to provide context). I describe people as travelling up or down a ladder, because this made sense to most of those whose stories appear here. They often used this metaphor to talk about their own mobility. But the people in this book were more ambivalent than most researchers of social mobility about what climbing or falling down the ladder meant. Most spoke of entering a different occupation and social group, and experienced this as a change in status – how they were seen and treated in everyday life. But not all of them thought that they joined a different social class. To many people, across all of the generations this book covers, changing social class required a transformation not only in their wealth, but in the amount of political and social power they held.

Most of those who experienced mobility talked of leaving the working class for the middle class, or vice versa. But they tended to see the middle class as a group defined by cultural tastes and affluence, by education and by certain kinds of work – clerical work earlier in our period, managerial and professional from the mid-twentieth century onwards. Many people associated being middle-class with having greater autonomy and choice over how to live and work, and it was this which made becoming middle class so desirable. But most identified a wider social chasm in Britain: between those who had to work for a living and those who did not. Many spoke of the aristocracy, with their huge tracts of land and family wealth, as symbolising the limits on how far you could rise. None of them joined the wealthy, powerful elite, and very few believed this was possible. Most believed that the actions of this elite had consequences for their own lives and ability to be socially mobile. Those who controlled access to education, and the kind of work that was available, were and are extremely powerful.

This is a more Marxist definition of class than that used by most social mobility researchers, and it is one that I share. This understanding of class sees the most fundamental division in society as that between the tiny minority who live off other people's labour, and the vast majority who do the work. Accepting this definition does not mean disregarding important differences in living standards, status and opportunities between, say, factory workers and their managers. Much of this book is concerned with those distinctions and what they meant to those who experienced them. But it does draw our attention to the limits on mobility; and to the important question of who benefits from the preservation of a class-based society.

Understanding class as a set of unequal power relations, rather than simply a difference in income or occupation, reminds us that inequality is neither natural nor inevitable. Social mobility has not created a fairer society – instead it has helped those at the top to justify their position. By allowing a tiny minority to ascend to the highest rungs, the wealthy and powerful elite have claimed that Britain is a place where merit is rewarded. But because they are the ones who determine membership of these prized perches, they are able to specify what skills and personal qualities are required. Competitiveness, selfishness and the acquisition of personal wealth at the expense of everyone else have been lauded. These practices have impoverished millions of people – most conspicuously by causing the financial crashes of 1929 and 2007–08 and the recessions that followed – and denied opportunities to many more. The myth of social mobility has resulted in most of us having very limited access to advanced education or fulfilling work, and few chances to exercise political and economic power in ways that might reshape society and our own lives.

Most people have achieved social mobility through work. But there is nothing scientific or objective about some jobs being paid more than others. The social ladder is based on a very subjective view of whose work matters most. Modern views about the occupational hierarchy owe a great deal to the work of the Registrar General – the office of government responsible for the decennial census – in 1911. At that time, thousands of British workers were striking for more rights and better pay; the new Labour Party was an increasingly powerful political force; the aristocratic House of Lords was questioning the more middle-class Commons' right to rule; and militant suffragettes were agitating for women's enfranchisement. Established ideas about who should possess wealth and power were being challenged.

It was no coincidence that the Liberal government decided to cat-egorise the population by social class in an apparently 'scientific' docu-ment – the census – that would outlast their administration. By using the 'culture' of occupations to determine class position, this hierarchy placed professionals and industrialists at the top alongside (often far wealthier) aristocratic landowners. Manual workers and domestic servants were at the bottom, despite the fact that British industry and most middle-class households depended utterly on their labour.[2] And hugely vital but unpaid tasks, like mothering, were ignored.

This classification of people's work – updated but not much changed over the past century – continues to shape policymakers' understandings of valuable and less-valuable work. The Covid-19 pan-demic has exposed just how flawed this hierarchy is. Cleaners, carers, shop workers and delivery drivers have played vital roles in keeping society going. The pandemic has made clear to many what these work-ers already knew: that all these jobs require skill. Cleaning – to take just one example – requires attention to detail, stamina, speed and care. If cleaners don't do a good job, the consequences for public health can be disastrous. These are essential tasks – but they have been hugely undervalued.

In this book, talk about those at the bottom and those at the top does not imply that the former are failures and the latter worthy of esteem. The wealthy elite have managed to create a climate catastrophe and wreck our economy more than once. I use these terms because the hierarchy they point to has become embedded in political and social debate and is used by most of those whose stories appear here. That this hierarchy has been made to appear neutral, and even natural, points to the endurance of inequality in both wealth and political power.

The history of social mobility reveals how subjective the social ladder was and is. At various points in the past, the value of jobs changed, and new kinds of work appeared. Before the First World War, clerking was a man's job and considered highly skilled – it was well paid as a result. After the war, clerking became women's work. Because, under capitalism, women are treated as primarily concerned with reproducing the workforce by mothering them, most employers – and many male trade unionists – relegated them to a secondary role in the workforce. After the First World War, it suited many employers to employ a large number of female clerks on tasks considered skilled twenty years earlier, but increasingly defined as routine, and therefore paid less.

By contrast, after the Second World War, Labour's establishment of a comprehensive welfare state demanded thousands more teachers and health workers. The war – like the Covid-19 pandemic of the twenty-first century – demonstrated that nurses, social workers, ambulance drivers and home helps were vital to society. In 1945, voters, and the Labour government they elected, took seriously the need to rebuild Britain. They recognised that only the state could undertake such an enormous task, and that prioritising education, healthcare, housing and work, was the best response to the upheaval and destruction caused by the war. The aim was to create a strong foundation on which a new society could be built, and improve the opportunities of the younger generation whose early lives and education had been hugely disrupted by a global crisis.

Because caring for others was recognised as an essential and responsible job, and strong trade unions had bargaining power, these workers enjoyed relatively high earnings and good conditions. But by the twenty-first century, government and big business focused on rewarding wealth acquisition and little else, and so the value of these jobs declined. Not only did those doing them see their share of the national income fall relative to that of the wealthiest, but they also lost some of their political power due to rising job insecurity and the weakening of trade unions.

Snakes and Ladders scrutinises seven generations born between the 1880s and the 1990s. Their experiences of these generations undermine the claim that inequality is a necessary incentive to hard work. More people climbed the ladder in periods when trade unions were strong – allowing workers to bargain for decent wages and prospects – education was free, and good jobs were available. Innovation was greatest when people knew that a welfare state would prevent them falling into poverty if taking a risk didn't succeed. No single generation enjoyed all of these benefits, but those who came closest were the breakthrough generation (born between 1920 and 1934) and the golden generation (born between 1935 and 1955). The golden generation enjoyed far greater upward mobility than any before or since.

The experiences of two generations: Thatcher's children (born between 1972 and 1985) and the millennials (born between 1986 and 1999), shared some striking similarities that reveal how the ladder, and people's ability to climb it, have changed since 1979. These generations were less likely to be upwardly mobile than any born since the 1920s. Their experiences were framed by an individualistic sense of their place in the world and how they might improve it. Considered in tandem, they demonstrate how the championing of free-market global capitalism, and the decimation of the British welfare state since 1979, have affected the mobility of those who have grown up in this era.

They show that a lack of state involvement in the labour market, and cuts to the welfare state, restricted opportunities to climb the ladder.

I draw on hundreds of stories from archives, published and unpublished memoirs, and interviews conducted specifically for this book.[3] Many were gathered by Mass Observation, a social research organisation established in 1936 by left-wing intellectuals keen to undertake 'an anthropology of ourselves'. During the Second World War, the government commissioned Mass Observation to document morale and behaviour. The organisation disbanded in the early 1950s, but the project was revived in the 1980s and today 800 volunteer writers respond to quarterly 'directives' issued by the Mass Observation Archive. The testimonies used here include 200 replies to a directive on social mobility issued in 2016 for this book.[4]

Snakes and Ladders is about how social mobility has affected British society as a whole – as a shared experience, a political promise and a widely held aspiration. Some readers will be disappointed not to see more famous names. Until the 1940s, most of those who climbed the ladder began life as factory or office workers (or the children of such workers) and ended up as clerks, teachers, nurses or managers. From the breakthrough generation onwards, more went into management and the professions, thanks to the wartime and post-war expansion of room at the top. But very few sought or found fame or fortune.

Their experiences reveal that social mobility rarely brought unalloyed joy. Many of the upwardly mobile did not set out to ascend the ladder, but found that this was necessary to realise their aspirations – for financial security and a modicum of control over their future; for an education and fulfilling work; and, sometimes, for the power to change their society. Most of those who succeeded were proud of their achievements and relished the affluence and status they were able to enjoy. But many also felt guilty about the sacrifices that parents or siblings had made for them; disappointment in how slight an ascent their unending hard work had afforded; and ambivalence about the kudos attached to climbing a ladder that classified their relatives and friends as 'beneath' them.

The experiences of the upwardly mobile illuminate the obstacles that prevented more people from following them. Many felt ashamed of their background, or experienced social unease, when confronted with colleagues or friends who had been born on the rung of the ladder that they had struggled to reach. Their inability to feel fully comfortable on their new perch was provoked by the attitudes of those already there. As we shall see, when there is limited room at the top, those on the higher rungs are understandably wary of outsiders who might displace them or their children.

Downward mobility is an important part of this story. Most politicians have preferred to ignore that, in an unequal society with limited room at the top, the upward mobility of some will necessitate others sliding down the ladder. The fear of social descent has clung to successive generations, encouraging caution and conservatism at points when Britain needed innovation and change. In fact, though, most of the downwardly mobile were not dislodged by newcomers from lower rungs. Instead, politicians' decisions have at times reduced room at the top, with disastrous effects. In the 1930s, governments and employers created a decline in skilled manual work, and a cut in manual workers' wages, sending millions down the ladder. In the 1980s, the erosion of the job security and conditions of many public-sector workers meant that many found their future disintegrating. The downwardly mobile were rarely responsible for their fate. But falling down the ladder often caused shame, regardless of whether descent caused hardship (as it often did). This was true not only for those directly affected, but also for their children and even grandchildren.

Social mobility has often been treated as an exclusively male experience. Most measurements of social mobility ignore or under-count women. Social scientists have tended to assume that women's social position is determined by that of their husband or their father – many married women gave up paid work until the recent past, and those who remained in employment tended to earn less than men. But women's work mattered to them and their families rather more than many social mobility researchers assume. The experiences of women clerks and teachers in the early twentieth century show that many families relied on the earnings of ambitious daughters, whose efforts have been overlooked by statisticians who record only a father's or husband's occupation. And women were central to this history in other ways. Upwardly mobile men were rarely entirely self-made. Mothers often used their earnings to support a son's climb up the ladder; wives sometimes assisted a husband in this way. Sisters and wives often had to put their own dreams aside because a family could only afford to support one ambitious member, and that was generally a man. The achievement of a son or brother often relied on the thwarted opportunities of several women.

Women's unpaid labour was also essential. While social mobility studies tend to take a snapshot – usually by comparing a father's occupation in his mid-thirties with where a son is at the same age – women's experiences remind us that social mobility was a lifelong process. Climbing the ladder, and then surviving on a higher rung, always involved huge but hidden efforts to fit in socially. Wives and mothers were chiefly responsible for negotiating this. Women's appearance, accent and home decoration were all markers by which newly upwardly mobile couples were judged by their neighbours and colleagues. In downwardly mobile households, women were responsible for 'keeping up appearances', and striving to ensure that children ascended the ladder once more. Women's stories are therefore as central to this history as men's, and reveal the hidden costs and effort that mobility demanded.

Snakes and Ladders tells a British story, albeit one that includes the experiences of migrants. The comparative studies we have suggest that the picture I offer here applies in general terms to most Western European countries, North America, Australia and New Zealand. Most significantly, upward mobility rose dramatically after the Second World War when all these countries increased room at the top, by investing public money in job creation and welfare measures like free education.[5] Britain did not offer fewer opportunities to be upwardly mobile than societies that are popularly assumed to be less class-bound, such as the United States. Since the 1980s, upward mobility has declined in both Britain and the USA, due to the destruction of many secure, reasonably well-paid jobs and the decimation of welfare provision and social security.[6]

My focus on Britain reflects the aim of this book. This is not to construct a statistical 'model' of social mobility that enables measurements of and between large populations – as many valuable studies have already done. Rather, I explore the historically specific circumstances that made it possible and desirable for some people to climb the ladder, and caused others to slide down it. This book provides some clues as to what might explain rises and falls in upward and downward mobility elsewhere in the Western world. But *Snakes and Ladders* is primarily concerned to delve into the experiences behind the statistics. I ask why people wanted to be socially mobile, and what helped or hindered them in achieving their dreams; as well as what happened to those who unwillingly tumbled down the ladder.

Much of this book is concerned with those people who climbed the ladder or aspired to do so, and those who descended it. But there were some who questioned whether society should really be structured as a ladder at all, and they are part of this history, too. In the early twentieth century, socialists of the pioneer generation (1880–99) argued that greater economic and political equality would give everyone more chances to make a meaningful contribution to society. That argument reverberated through the next century, finding new force in the 1970s, by which time the post-war welfare state proved that the socialists had a point. As the golden generation came of age, many of them demanded more than the chance to scale a few rungs of the ladder. They wanted to change Britain into a place where opportunities for all were more important than generating profits for a few. In both generations, campaigners believed that most people's potential was thwarted by a system that offered only limited room at the top, and that everyone was the poorer for that.

Their demands and achievements remind us that political discussion of how to increase social mobility – ongoing since the early twentieth century, and especially intense since the 1940s – are conducted within very narrow parameters. It is a debate that betrays a paucity of ambition – not among those constantly cajoled to climb the ladder, but among the politicians who accept that most people should live on the lowest rungs. By looking beyond their blinkered vision to learn from the experiences of our predecessors, we find that inequality is only one way to organise a society – there were, and are, better alternatives.

PART I

THE PIONEERS
1880–1899

Chapter One

THE FIGHT FOR OPPORTUNITY

Victorian Britain was a land of boundless opportunity – at least according to Samuel Smiles. In 1859 his bestselling self-improvement manual, *Self-Help*, declared that 'Great men of science, literature, and art' had come from 'the huts of poor men and the mansions of the rich' alike. According to Smiles, this was because Britons' natural ambition was unfettered by government interference. The 'spirit of self-help is the root of all genuine growth . . . when men are subject to over-guidance and over-government, the inevitable tendency is to render them comparatively helpless'.[1] Allowing people to get rich without restriction, and offering the poor no mercy, encouraged everyone to work hard and allowed the talented to rise to the top.

It was an alluring myth – hence the book's success. But it was untrue. The best social mobility data we have for the mid-nineteenth century come from marriage registers (after 1880 we're able to rely on the decennial censuses for occupation records). These registers show that just one-third of men who married in the 1840s were in a different social class to their father. We have no such information for women, but domestic service and textile work were by far their largest employers, and the registers suggest that these workers married men in manual jobs.[2] In 1880, more than 70 per cent of the workforce were employed in such work, as maids, agricultural labourers, railway porters, hospital cleaners, factory hands, welders, potters, miners and steelworkers.[3]

Those born in the first two-thirds of the nineteenth century had few chances to climb the social ladder, but they did grasp new opportunities to change their lives. Thousands moved from the countryside into the expanding towns and cities. In 1850, almost 40 per cent of the workforce were employed on the land; by 1881 just 13 per cent were. People flocked to the factories: by 1881 more than two-thirds of men were industrial workers. Women, meanwhile, found work as servants in the houses of the expanding middle class – 43 per cent of them were in service in 1881 – but 46 per cent worked in industry, many as mill-workers. Fewer than 20 per cent of workers were in non-manual work: 8 per cent were 'dealers', such as small shopkeepers or street sellers, while 6 per cent were professionals or civil servants.[4]

The generation born between 1880 and 1899 had different opportunities to their parents. In 1870 Parliament passed the Elementary Education Act, which made schooling compulsory for five- to twelve-year-olds in England and Wales; Scotland followed two years later when the Education (Scotland) Act was introduced. The beneficiaries were pioneers. Even more of them took their chances in the urban, industrialised centres than their parents' generation – and many became the first from their working-class families to enter work that required literacy rather than physical strength.

The pioneers were the first generation of which a large proportion could expect to end up on a different rung of the social ladder to their parents. Just over a quarter of men were upwardly mobile and just under a quarter of women. Many of the upwardly mobile became clerks, some became teachers. They entered not only new occupations but a new social world, one that they helped to form.

Far from being the story of a few particularly talented individuals, as Samuel Smiles characterised social mobility, the upward paths of this generation were the result of collective help, from relatives, teachers, trade unions and co-operative societies. Recognising this, some of the pioneers became socialists. They sought positions of influence from which to improve not only their own lives, but those of the class from which they came. The rallying cry of the new Labour

Party – equality of opportunity – is due to them. It is with their struggle to replace the social 'ladder' for a few with a 'highway' for all that our story begins.

*

Ruth Slate, born in 1884, was a factory packer by the age of fifteen. 'I felt the best in me was being starved', she later wrote. She was determined to advance her education, influence politics and contribute to society – 'I want to live.'[5] Many of Ruth's generation shared her aspirations. Better educated than their parents, they determined that if the opportunities to advance did not exist, they would create them. By 1900 Ruth had joined the Independent Labour Party (ILP), one of 35,000 members. She belonged to an expanding, vibrant labour movement committed to increasing access to education and to political power.

By the time Ruth Slate joined the ILP, the labour movement had been modelling collective self-help for decades. Artisans had established the trade union movement in the early nineteenth century.[6] They possessed skills that employers needed, an important bargaining tool in negotiating over wages and conditions. Collectively, they could fund sick and strike pay. And they established co-operative societies, which ran shops owned by their customers – the first was opened in Rochdale in 1844.

Industrialisation, which brought more people into the towns and factories, encouraged the growth of trade unions and socialist societies beyond the skilled workforce. By 1900 2 million workers belonged to trade unions. By 1914 Britain's 1,385 co-operative societies had 3,054,000 members.

Labour activists were never solely focused on raising wages and improving working conditions. Many were committed to giving working-class people a greater share of economic and political power and equipping them to use this wisely. At the very first Trades Union Congress (TUC) in 1869, members unanimously passed a motion

calling for 'a system of national, unsectarian and compulsory education'.[7] In 1870, a national conference of miners declared that their first
priority was not better wages or shorter working hours but 'compulsory education for their children'.[8] Pressure from trade unionists and
employers helped persuade the government to introduce compulsory
elementary education, delivered by 'board schools' (so called because
they were run by locally elected school boards). The government's
Board of Education retained national oversight (in 1944 the Board of
Education would become the Ministry of Education).

But the establishment of compulsory elementary schooling was
not enough for many co-operators, trade unionists and socialists. They
wanted equality of opportunity for their children, not a rudimentary
education inferior to that which wealthier parents could buy. Members
of the Socialist Democratic Federation (SDF), founded in 1884, campaigned for an end to the half-time system, whereby children split
their day between school and factory or mill work. In 1891 the Fabian
Society declared its commitment to 'a national system of education . . .
for all classes alike'.[9] In that year, under pressure from trade unions,
the Liberal government made elementary education free. When the
ILP was formed two years later, its founders immediately called for
the raising of the school-leaving age to fifteen, and thus for the introduction of compulsory secondary education.

During the 1890s, many prominent ILP members focused their
political activism on expanding education. While women were disen-
franchised in parliamentary elections, they could and did stand for
election to school boards. Among them was Mary Bridges Adams, the
daughter of a Welsh engine-fitter, who in 1897 became the sole ILP
member of the Greenwich division of London's school board. She
campaigned for free, secular secondary and adult education. Like
many of her comrades, Mary believed that 'if the people were educated' they would see and destroy the 'wrongs' of capitalism and
inequality.[10]

In the late nineteenth century, neither the Liberals nor the Conservatives showed much interest in expanding access to secondary

or higher education. The Conservatives, with their ties to the aristocracy, believed that hereditary claims to property and privilege were sacrosanct. Many Liberals strongly believed that people should be able to advance on merit – the Liberal Party attracted many of those working men entitled to the vote. But it was led by men like William Gladstone who believed that advanced education was best reserved for a small elite. In 1902 the Conservative government introduced an Education Act that abolished elected school boards and gave their powers to provide education to local councils, which now became local education authorities. The Tories hoped to quash the radical aspirations that some left-wing school boards harboured for free or heavily subsidised secondary education. The 1902 Act allowed councils to support or open secondary schools – but it also embedded the principle of selection into secondary education. Only children whose parents could pay secondary school fees, or who successfully competed for one of the few free places available, were able to attend these schools. Although the Liberals won the subsequent 1906 general election, they did not alter this.

The labour movement therefore did not simply campaign for education – its members sought to provide it. Britain's co-operative societies organised debates, evening classes and Men's and Women's Guilds. The ILP held discussions on everything from religion to feminism, and initiated reading circles. Many activists had a thirst for learning for its own sake, and to equip themselves for the self-government that politicians and employers denied them. Their children attended Socialist Sunday Schools, where they learned about equality and self-help, and co-operative societies' Comrades' Circles, where they debated how to achieve their goals.

Whatever the deficiencies of the board schools they left many pupils yearning for more education, and this led some of them to socialism.[11] Ernest Bevin was born in 1881, the illegitimate youngest son of a large Somerset family of farm labourers. After his mother's death in 1889 he lived with his sister Mary Jane and her husband, George Pope, a railway worker. Although the school-leaving age was twelve, children as young as ten were permitted to leave school if they reached Standard IV (board schools had six standards, or classes; most children left before reaching Standard VI). But Ernest appears to have been a keen scholar. Although he reached Standard IV in 1891, aged ten, he remained at school for almost another year. The Popes lived in a village without a school, so Ernest's studies meant a long journey each day: first to Colebrook Board School, almost an hour's walk from his home, and later to Hayward Boys' School in Crediton, a train journey away (as a railway worker, George Pope was able to secure him free travel).

After leaving school in March 1892, Ernest worked as an agricultural labourer for two years before moving to Bristol, where he joined two of his older brothers and took a series of low-paid manual jobs, including work as a kitchen hand and as a delivery boy. But he clearly hankered after more education. In Bristol he joined the Adult School Movement, an adult education initiative with a strong Christian ethos. A fellow student recalled that 'we met at seven o'clock on a Sunday morning before breakfast, three hundred men or so . . . we broke up into groups and discussed our theme for the day . . . There was one subject fixed for each Sunday . . . women in industry, or Christianity and poverty.'[12] What Bevin learned in these debates led him to join the secular SDF, which advocated the revolutionary overthrow of capitalism.

But others were introduced to what learning could mean when they became involved in trade unionism, co-operative or socialist societies. John Edwards – born in 1888 in a Welsh mining village – had 'hated school' for its 'unsurpassed monotony'. But then, at the age of twelve, he went down the pit, joining a strongly unionised workforce. Among the miners he 'heard the most extraordinary subjects discussed in a most intelligent way . . . rang[ing] quite naturally through Science, Art, Religion, Philosophy and Economics'.[13] He was able to follow up his new interests at the local library, which was funded by the miners themselves.

While John Edwards was beginning his reading, Bessie Braddock, born in 1899 to a socialist bookbinder and trade union organiser, was an unwilling school pupil but an enthusiastic student of Liverpool's Socialist Sunday School, which 'taught me and dozens of other working-class children the Socialist hymns, and the ten commandments', which included: 'Look forward to the day when all men and women will be free citizens of one community and live together as equals in peace and righteousness.'[14]

In their teens, Bessie Braddock and John Edwards both joined the ILP. Bessie 'began to learn the political and economic history I had been denied at elementary school . . . to find out how society evolved, and how trade unions grew up'.[15] John was inspired by his 'longing for a different kind of life where I would not have to work for a living, where all my time could be given to my beloved books' and a world where others could choose that life too, regardless of their background.[16]

Many of John Edwards' generation wanted jobs where they could use their education. Albert Mansbridge was born into a working-class home in Gloucester in 1876, but his parents moved their family of four boys – Albert was the youngest – to London in 1880. Thomas, Albert's father, was a carpenter who rose to become a clerk of works. Albert recalled being 'a normal child in a decent working-class home'.[17] He enjoyed school and won a scholarship to Battersea Grammar School.

Albert's family could not afford to keep him at school for long, even with a scholarship. Like most households they needed their children to earn their living from an early age, and he began work at fourteen. Unlike Ernest Bevin or John Edwards, Albert had the opportunities of a metropolis, and started his working life as a clerk in a City firm.

Albert, however, wanted work that would contribute to society, and to his own learning. Strolling 'enviously' past fee-paying Westminster School pupils on his way to the office, he found his lot wanting.[18] He knew from his own success at school that he was intellectually their equal. Poverty held him back.

Albert Mansbridge was quite prepared to believe Britain rewarded effort and talent, and threw himself into finding the kind of work he wanted. But he discovered that the routes to a more meaningful job were narrow, uncertain, and not to his liking. He failed the Civil Service examinations because he found the set texts dull, preferring to read what he wanted and play cricket in the evenings after long, tiring days at the office. While the boys of Westminster School could combine days of study with friendship, sport and fun, young wage-earners from working-class homes needed to be extremely dedicated and single-minded if they were to advance their education or career prospects. This was highly demanding for a teenager – and Albert was in any case unsure that he wanted a career in administration.

He set his sights on winning a scholarship to Oxford University. He scored high marks but was beaten by a man already studying there. The process showed Albert the deficiencies of his board-school education. Defeated, he found himself at twenty unable to find a job that paid any more than he'd been earning as a school-leaver seven years earlier.

Upward mobility is rarely an individual's achievement alone. Albert Mansbridge's mother, an active member of Battersea Co-operative Society, persuaded her son to refocus his ambition. After he failed to win the scholarship, he was hired as a grocery assistant by the Co-op, and with his mother's encouragement joined the Co-operative Men's Guild to further his education.[19]

Far from such collective endeavour robbing Albert of his ambition, as Samuel Smiles might have presumed, the co-operative debates and classes he attended inspired his brainchild: the Workers' Educational Association (WEA). Albert envisaged a scheme of adult education classes across Britain, building on the discussion circles he'd participated in at Battersea Co-op. More ambitiously still, the WEA would widen access to elite institutions like Oxford, while challenging the narrow conceptions of 'education' and 'culture' found there. Albert Mansbridge determined to destroy the 'educational ladder' that governed access to opportunity in Britain, and replace it with 'a free and open highway'.[20] His own experience had taught him that only by offering equal access to education could everyone's potential be realised.

Albert set about promoting his idea to numerous co-operative societies, trade unions, church groups and political associations of every hue. He met with enthusiastic support, particularly from co-operators and trade unionists. Adult education wasn't new, but Albert Mansbridge suggested a refreshingly different approach. The Adult School Movement and university settlements, where well-heeled university students taught and preached to the urban poor, had a religious ethos. Although Albert was a dedicated Christian, he shared the trade unions' belief that education should be secular, so that students could question all doctrines.

The University Extension Movement, pioneered by Cambridge University in 1873, also offered classes for working-class students. But these were few in number and most were lectures on a subject selected by the university's chosen speaker. The University Extension Movement was born out of universities' fears that nineteenth-century debates about widening educational access might require them to broaden their small, socially elite intake. To ward off any threat to their autonomy, they offered 'extension' classes well away from their own hallowed halls – with the caveat that local partners (often co-operative societies) had to pay for these.

Albert Mansbridge wanted to establish a self-governing organisation. Students would determine their own course of study – 'provided it is non-vocational in aims' – for this was education for life, not a narrow training for work. He envisioned weekly 'tutorial classes' that emphasised group discussion rather than listening to lectures.[21]

In 1904 Albert's vision became reality: the WEA was established. His ambitions struck a chord with thousands of men and women of his generation. By 1907 the WEA had forty-seven branches and 4,343 members. By 1920 5,320 students were attending 229 tutorial classes across England and Wales.[22] They included teachers, typists, pitmen and factory hands. In 1911, the WEA class at Longton in Staffordshire included a miner, a colliery weighman, a potter's engineman, a railway telegraphist, a clerk and an elementary schoolteacher – a typically eclectic mix, all committing hours of their time after long, exhausting days at work.[23] 'We were critical of the existing educational system', recalled one student. 'We felt shut off – "dispossessed" some of us called it – from the means to higher education.'[24]

But whether the WEA – and socialism more broadly – should offer a route up the ladder into elite institutions like Oxford and Cambridge, or create an egalitarian alternative to them, quickly became contentious. Underpinning this controversy was a wider debate: whether the labour movement should strive for equality of opportunity in a competitive, capitalist society (as Fabians like Beatrice and Sidney Webb argued), or to establish full equality in a society based on principles of co-operation and community (as socialists like William Morris believed).[25]

Albert Mansbridge himself worked hard to forge a close relationship between the WEA and Oxford University. He hoped this would allow some working-class men entry to higher education (the WEA was co-educational, but Oxford did not permit women to take degrees until 1920). Ruskin College in Oxford provided the conduit between WEA classes and full university membership. In 1899, three Americans had established Ruskin with the aim of giving working men a taste of university life. Ruskin's founders were the socialists Walter Vrooman and Charles Beard, who had met while studying at Oxford University in 1898, and, crucially, Walter's wife Anne Grafflin, a wealthy heiress.

By 1907, Ruskin's founders had returned to the United States and relinquished their connection with the college. It was taken over by a council of trade unionists, co-operators and sympathetic Oxford dons. The TUC and co-operative societies funded scholarships that enabled up to forty men per year (women were admitted from 1919) to attend residential courses at Ruskin, where they were taught in small groups like Oxford University students, and often by Oxford tutors.

But some WEA classes turned down the offer of scholarships to Ruskin. These students and tutors did not want advanced education to be restricted to only a few students. And they were reluctant to see collaborative learning eroded by preparing for competitive exams.[26] The debate over whether education should provide a meritocratic route up the social ladder, or model a co-operative, socialist society, shaped the development of adult education in Britain.

In 1909, this debate reached the national press when some Ruskin students struck in protest at a curriculum they denounced for its neglect of working-class history and socialist economics. Ruskin, they declared, was no 'avenue to the emancipation of the workers' but rather 'a gloomy archway to the reactionary University' for a select few.[27] This group pointed out that there was a great difference between enabling a few individuals to ascend the social ladder and improving the conditions endured by an entire class. The former accepted the existence of a class hierarchy; the latter sought to destroy it. Some of the strikers and their supporters formed the Plebs' League and the National Labour College in London to address these problems, leading to a further expansion of adult education provision.

Most of those who studied at Ruskin did not go to college hoping to ascend the social ladder. The active support that students received from family and friends reinforced their sense that education was a collective endeavour. Many students relied on their trade unions and relatives to supplement meagre scholarships. Jack Lawson was born in 1882 and went to work down a Durham pit at the age of twelve. He won a place at Ruskin in 1907, but his scholarship was too small to live on. When his wife learned he planned to turn down this chance, she said that she would support him. A former domestic servant, she told her husband that she 'had been in service ten years, and she could always manage another one'.[28] She accompanied Jack to Oxford, but while he lived and studied at Ruskin College, she worked as a maid, bedding down in her employer's attic.

Ruskin's ethos was co-operative rather than competitive. Every student signed a pledge committing them to use their education in their home community, reflecting the fear that they might succumb to Oxford's gentlemanly embrace. Most took this very seriously. John Edwards won a place at Ruskin in 1908. When he arrived at Oxford railway station and met up with the crowd of other students, 'everybody, it seemed, wanted to carry everybody else's bag'. This set the tone for his year there. 'We all secretly found Oxford a dream which had come true', but John and his comrades remained keen to return 'to the pits . . . and to share what Ruskin might give us with our own people'.[29]

These students did not aspire to become middle class but rather, as Jack Lawson said, to show that 'a manual worker might be an educated man'.[30] Despite relishing his time in Oxford – 'every street and every building was alive with historic and literary character' – he refused the offer of a university place, determined to return home and use the knowledge he had gained to improve his community.[31] As one WEA student put it, 'we passionately believed in the emancipating power of education, and that as long as they were deprived of it working people could not exert their rightful influence in political and social affairs'.[32] Education would enable them to do so.

But their education propelled many of these pioneers up the social ladder. Some found it impossible to return to their old jobs because they had been blacklisted by employers convinced that these educated trade unionists were dangerous. John Edwards was among them.[33] He joined a growing number of students entering new careers in the labour movement. Between 1900 and 1915, membership of trade unions doubled from 2 million to 4 million, provoking demand for more union organisers who could write and debate. Jack Lawson and John Edwards were swiftly appointed to full-time trade union posts on their return from Ruskin. Meanwhile, Ernest Bevin's time in the Adult School Movement helped him acquire a reputation as an excellent speaker and debater. In 1911 he became a full-time organiser for the Dockers' Union in Bristol, and never returned to manual work.

By the 1910s, the labour movement was an increasingly important engine of social mobility. The WEA's popularity stimulated demand for tutors, and many of them came from working-class families. They included E. J. Hookway, a young railwayman and active trade unionist, who became secretary of Pontypridd's WEA branch in 1908. In 1910 the WEA made Hookway its full-time district organiser in north-west England, 'one of the first instances', writes the historian Roger Lewis, 'of the WEA's becoming an agency of social mobility'.[34] The Co-op, meanwhile, had become Britain's largest retailer, and one of the few to offer a route from the shop floor to management.

The pioneers also had new opportunities to pursue a political career. Once again, these were created by labour activists. In 1901 the Labour Representation Committee (the forerunner to the Labour Party) was established, and in the general election of 1906 fielded its first parliamentary candidates. By 1910 Labour had forty MPs.

Entering politics looked increasingly attractive. These were volatile times in which some believed that the Labour Party, the trade unions and the wider socialist movement were on the verge of winning power. But Labour movement activists were divided over what 'victory' would look like. Not everyone was convinced that parliamentary representation was the best focus for their energies. In 1909 the socialist and trade unionist Tom Mann wrote *The Way to Win*, a pamphlet that argued trade unions and co-operative societies could kindle a revolutionary challenge to the political and social status quo. British trade unions had traditionally divided skilled workers from the rest: craftsmen were able to enjoy a bargaining power and income that many other workers did not. But Tom Mann and other so-called 'syndicalists' wanted to abolish private property and wage labour. While many other socialists shared these aims, some of them believed in a gradualist approach, which relied on political representation. By contrast, syndicalists believed in the revolutionary overthrow of capitalism through workers' militancy and unionisation. Tom Mann and his comrades argued that trade unions should model the egalitarian society they wished to achieve. They challenged the horizontal organisation of most British unions – which divided workers according to their perceived level of skill – and argued instead for trade unions to which all workers in a particular sector would belong. In this way, the divisions between different segments of the working class would be broken down.[35]

These radicals were inspired by anarchist and syndicalist movements across the United States and Europe. The SDF had disappeared, but many British socialists continued to hold revolutionary aspirations. In 1895, the anarchist and feminist Emma Goldman – born in Lithuania but resident in the United States – had visited Britain and addressed large crowds in London, Glasgow and Edinburgh. She returned to give more talks in 1907. Then in 1910 and 1911, syndicalist uprisings across Europe – notably in Spain, where anarcho-syndicalists established a huge trade union – attracted the interest of Mann and those who shared his views.

In the summer of 1911, Mann led the Liverpool General Transport Strike, which involved thousands of the city's workers. The Home Secretary, Winston Churchill, sent in the troops, but as increasing numbers of strikers and their supporters took to the streets, the government demanded that employers take steps to end the unrest. The strikers won better conditions and trade union recognition. They showed that trade unions could win the support of unskilled and semi-skilled workers and effectively organise civil unrest. Mann was not alone in believing that the dispute suggested Britain was ripe for revolution. Many socialists, Ernest Bevin among them, were convinced that they could enact a major political and social transformation of Britain through rebellion if not reform.[36]

But many British socialists were increasingly interested in parliamentary representation. Some, like Ernest Bevin, thought that they could pursue this alongside more revolutionary ambitions. Others, Jack Lawson among them, believed that legislative reform was the only means of achieving their goals. Both groups were emboldened by parliamentary crises in 1910 and 1911, when the power of the House of Lords – filled entirely with hereditary peers – was seriously weakened. In 1909, the Lords had refused to pass the Liberal government's 'People's Budget', intended to pay for welfare reforms long championed by the labour movement, including old-age pensions and health and unemployment insurance. The Liberals responded by calling a general election, which they narrowly won in January 1910. The Lords reluctantly passed the budget, but then opposed the Parliament Act, which proposed removing their right to veto legislation. Once more, peers' recalcitrance forced a general election, in December 1910; once more, the Liberals won. The Lords capitulated: the hereditary house of Parliament was now subordinate to elected members.

Men were the major beneficiaries of these developments but women were also grasping, and creating, new chances. Teaching provided working-class women with a route into professional work that used their learning. Thanks to the expansion of elementary education, the number of teachers in board schools rose from 119,000 in 1900 to 163,930 in 1920, of whom 75 per cent were women.[37] Among them was Ellen Wilkinson. Born in 1891 in Manchester, she was the daughter of a cotton worker and a dressmaker who, due to complications during Ellen's birth, became a lifelong invalid. Her father, an ardent Methodist, introduced Ellen to the teachings of nonconformist religion. '[I]ts doctrine of the Fatherhood of God and the Brotherhood of man was the assertion of an equality which the next generation [her own] were to find in the socialist movement'.[38]

By her teens Ellen Wilkinson had begun to depart from her father's philosophy, which was 'I have pulled myself out of the gutter, why can't they?' She knew what a difference state assistance could make to ambitious young people like herself. As 'only a girl', she received little encouragement from her schoolteachers, but unlike her parents, she had the chance to go 'straight through the "broad highway of state education"' from board school to a so-called higher-grade school. This was a new type of secondary school established by progressive local authorities like Manchester and London after the 1902 Education Act. Most secondary schools were private establishments and charged fees. In the 1900s fewer than 10 per cent of children in England and Wales, and fewer than 15 per cent in Scotland, remained at school beyond their fourteenth birthday.[39] Ellen was fortunate. She 'won my first scholarship at the age of eleven, and from that time paid for my own education by scholarships'.[40]

Wilkinson got her chance of further education because the increase in school places created more teaching vacancies. From 1907 prospective teachers could get a bursary that allowed them to stay at school and then attend a pupil teaching centre (where they spent half the week in classes, and half the week training in local schools) until the age of eighteen. The cost of remaining at school – in lost earnings aside from the expense of books or meals – and the very limited availability of secondary-school places, explains why so few of Wilkinson's generation got this chance. In 1911, only 8 per cent of fourteen-to-fifteen-year-olds were in secondary education and only 2 per cent of sixteen-year-olds.[41] But family support, and Manchester council's expansion of secondary education, allowed Ellen Wilkinson to join this minority.

Pursuing her ambition took huge determination. Like Albert Mansbridge, Ellen had a strong sense of entitlement to education. She had not been brought up to be deferential to her social 'superiors' and attributed her success to her 'fierce will' to fight the 'waste and extravagance and the poverty' she saw around her. During her years at the pupil teaching centre she became a socialist, influenced by well-read classmates and schoolteachers who encouraged debate about why some people could not help themselves as her father had done.[42] When she was sixteen Ellen joined the ILP. Three years later, in 1910, she won a scholarship to Manchester University to read history.

Ellen's determination was bolstered by her socialism. She did not see her journey as taking her away from her family. Like many Ruskin students, she hoped education would enable her to improve life for the community in which she had grown up and where she still lived 'to remove slums and underfeeding and misery', not to flee from them.[43]

Nevertheless, Ellen sometimes found her journey through education and up the social ladder painful – as many other upwardly mobile people were to do. She lived in fear of failing and tumbling back down the ladder. Aware that she must excel at every stage if her education was to continue, she avoided anything she could not 'do easily . . . I learned all too early that a clear decisive voice and a confident manner could get one through 90 per cent of the difficulties of life. And the awful 10 per cent are thrust down so deep into my thoughts by a fierce will, that the consequent agony of spirit has remained my own. I do not suggest that there is anything particularly wise or followable about all this. It's just the result, as I see it, of an efficient but machine-made education, on a fairly ordinary type of healthy working-class child.'[44]

Many women of Ellen Wilkinson's generation saw socialism and feminism as intertwined battles for equality and justice. Ellen was influenced by 'my mother's protest at . . . those iron conventions which gripped working-class life at that period', such as regularly cleaning the front step. These were time-consuming, wearying activities that she was taught to regard as trivialities.[45] After graduating in 1913, Wilkinson became a full-time paid organiser for the National Union of Women's Suffrage Societies, a non-violent suffragist organisation. Two years later she became the first national women's organiser for the Union of Shop, Distributive and Allied Workers.

Ruth Slate and her friend Eva Slawson – born in 1882 – were brought up in families that strove for 'respectability' rather than ridiculing it. Ruth observed that the church, teachers, employers and working-class mothers themselves often taught working-class girls 'humility', to accept their station in life as servants, mothers and wives. The assumption that many working-class people were dirty, idle and feckless shaped the nineteenth-century Poor Law, which required local Boards of Guardians to discern whether people in poverty were 'deserving' of support. In the 1880s and 1890s, social surveys of the urban poor identified a 'residuum' of beggars, labourers and hawkers who were beyond help; although there were always social investigators and local guardians who pointed out that long years of poverty and squalor might be responsible for the despair that they encountered.[46] And despite the growing incorporation of trade unions into industrial negotiation, and the gradual extension of the franchise over the nineteenth century, neither of the leading political parties was as yet willing to countenance universal enfranchisement for men – let alone women. Ruth Slate blamed this climate for 'the lack of self-confidence which both Eva and I have felt to be the curse of our lives, and which has been unduly and unhealthily fostered in us by religious training and hard circumstances'.[47] Like Ellen Wilkinson, Ruth believed that striving to appear 'respectable' would not change women's lives – only winning political power could do that. She, Eve and Ellen all joined the campaign for women's suffrage.

Women like Ellen Wilkinson who became clerks or teachers would have been ranked as 'middle class' by the Registrar General's 1911 census. Yet many of them had no desire to join the established middle class. They wanted to forge a new way of life. This was also true of many male socialists who left manual work for jobs in the labour movement. But these women believed that this new life would be created by cultural change as much as through political activity or workplace militancy. They railed against the lot of working-class women who lacked birth control or maternity care, and were expected to both earn their living and shoulder childcare and housework. As this left no time for the learning and political activity they relished, they determined to create an entirely different kind of life.

For Ruth Slate and Eva Slawson this meant escaping their jobs – Eva was a domestic servant – for more fulfilling work, or at least for posts where they could use their literacy. By the time Eve and Ruth met at chapel in London in 1902 both women supported the ILP. They attended WEA classes to equip them for white-collar jobs. Both here and at work they debated politics and women's sexual emancipation.

Ruth and Eva were internationalist in their outlook, as many socialists of their generation were. Some women looked to prominent feminists, socialists and anarchists overseas, like Emma Goldman, for inspiration. They were also influenced by avant-garde cultural movements developing in Europe. Ruth and Eva were fans of the 'revolutionary' choreographer Isadora Duncan, an American who spent most of the decade before 1914 working and living in Berlin and Paris: centres of radicalism and bohemianism. Her ideas complemented the socialist convictions that everyone was innately creative, and that their potential could be realised only through collective endeavour. She won a large following among British socialists and feminists. 'Here was dancing expressive of body, mind and soul – my idea of

"redemption" exemplified', Eva wrote. 'Harmony is unity!'[48] Ruth and
Eva both eventually studied at the Woodbrooke Settlement, a Quaker
adult education college in the Midlands. Ruth became a clerk and later
qualified as a social worker, while Eva became a typist.

*

While trade unionists, socialists and feminists clamoured for educational institutions to open their doors wider, even modest attempts to
do so provoked influential opposition. In 1911, parents of fee-paying
boys persuaded University College School in Hampstead to give up
the large annual grant that it received from the London County Council for admitting a few scholarship boys. The school's decision to
exclude pupils from board schools was condemned by the Liberal-
leaning *Manchester Guardian*, which concluded that 'there is only one
explanation possible. There is a fear, no doubt, among the parents that
the "board-school boys" may communicate to the other boys some
taint of faulty pronunciation or inelegant manners.' The *Guardian* regretted that parents did not recognise that 'healthy competition'
would result from allowing 'board-school boys' entry to such schools.[49]

But it was precisely the threat of competition which, understandably, concerned parents. Virulent opposition to any hint of meritocratic selection suggested that middle-class voters would never
accept the broader access to education demanded by the labour movement. But much of this anxiety was caused by the meagre openings
available. In a society where most people lost out, parents were keen
to ensure that their offspring would be among the few winners. In
1914 while about 40 per cent of students at civic universities were
from middle-class homes, less than 2 per cent of eighteen-year-olds
entered higher education. White-collar workers and even professionals could find university fees prohibitive, so there was pressure on
their children to win a scholarship.[50] As the WEA pointed out, the
education system 'cannot accurately be described as a ladder. It is
more like a greasy pole.'[51]

The outbreak of the First World War in 1914 provided new chances for Labour politicians and sympathetic Liberals to campaign for universal secondary education. Before the war, several European countries, including Germany, had opened secondary schools which educated far more of the population than in Britain. These schools prioritised engineering and science, whereas in Britain the classics – central to the curriculum of the expensive public schools – were assumed to provide the 'best' education available. The war, however, highlighted the need for technical, scientific and engineering innovation, both to produce materiel and to increase industrial production.

In 1915, the Liberal prime minister, Herbert Asquith, invited Labour's leader, Arthur Henderson, to join his wartime coalition government. Henderson, an iron-moulder turned politician, became President of the Board of Education. He regularly championed the merits of free, universal secondary education, supported by many Liberals as well as by his own MPs. 'The great tragedy of our system of education', argued John Whitehouse, Liberal MP for Mid-Lanarkshire, '[is] that it has been a class system under which a great section of the community have no education in any real sense at all.' Whitehouse argued that 'education appropriate to a certain rank of life' must be replaced by 'education appropriate to the children of a certain age'.[52] As discussions of post-war reconstruction got underway, trade unionists, co-operators, Labour activists and adult educators argued – in the words of a WEA pamphlet – for 'compensation for the lives which have been sacrificed and the hopes which have been shattered, in the development of the inexhaustible potentialities of a new generation of children'.[53]

The strongest opponents of free and universal education were those who relied on cheap child labour. Farmers and cotton manufacturers presented social mobility as a danger to Britain's economy. In 1915, at a meeting in Castleton, 'Mr J. T. Hedley, a well-known Westerdale farmer, said with regard to the employment of scholars on the land, boys were being over-educated and showed a disinclination for farm work.'[54] Many Tory MPs agreed: 'agricultural work is the

34

healthiest occupation upon which children could possibly be employed', declared Colonel Meysey Thompson, MP for Handsworth.[55] These employers, landowners and politicians believed that people were born into a particular rank and should stay there. From their perspective, the WEA's demands that secondary schools should be free and compulsory, and universities made 'as freely accessible to the sons and daughters of the working classes as to those of the well-to-do', were dangerously radical.[56] When the Armistice came in 1918, the merits of social mobility were still far from widely accepted.

In the immediate aftermath of the war labour and feminist campaigners won some important victories. In 1918 the Representation of the People Act gave the vote to all adult men and to women aged over thirty who owned property. That year's Education Act incorporated watered-down versions of some of Labour's demands, raising the school-leaving age from twelve to fourteen (effective from 1921), with no exemptions – the half-time employment system was abolished. This Act enabled though did not mandate, local authorities to provide more nursery schools, part-time education for young workers aged between fourteen and sixteen, and 'senior' or 'central' schools to provide a free or cheap education for pupils aged between eleven and sixteen. These senior schools were based on the higher-grade schools that men and women like Ellen Wilkinson had attended. They offered a more advanced curriculum than board schools provided, but it was less extensive than that offered by fully fledged secondary schools. The Act also encouraged local authorities to provide more secondary-school scholarships (although most children would have all of their schooling at the board schools or, as they were now officially called, elementary schools).

In Scotland, developments were even more promising. The Education (Scotland) Act of 1918 introduced the principle of universal, free secondary education up to the age of fourteen. In practice, most children were educated in 'advanced divisions' similar to the senior classes of English elementary schools. But by the late 1930s, one-third of Scottish children attended higher-grade schools, which offered a wide-ranging academic curriculum, while just 13 per cent of children in England and Wales went to secondary school.[57]

These two Education Acts of 1918 enshrined the principle that secondary schools should largely still be reserved for an elite. And in England and Wales, secondary education remained chiefly the preserve of those who could pay for it. Nevertheless, these reforms did suggest that more children should receive an education. Labour movement activists were influential in securing this important reform.

The pioneers were well placed to enter institutions and jobs that had been unthinkable a generation earlier. In 1919 Jack Lawson became Labour MP for Chester-le-Street. Observing the careers of his former ILP comrades, he reflected that 'miners, and the sons of miners, became schoolteachers, Headmasters, University professors, managers, ministers, musicians, social workers, and public men and women . . . there grew up men whose fine lives give strength to the working-class communities in which they live'.[58] Jack Lawson attributed this to the debates and activism of their youth. In 1922, Ernest Bevin became a founding leader of the Transport and General Workers' Union, which soon became the country's largest trade union. Two years later, Ellen Wilkinson became Labour MP for Middlesbrough. By the end of the 1920s, Sutton-in-Ashfield's WEA branch had produced three Labour MPs.[59]

Many more entered local government. John Edwards remained active in his trade union and became an ILP councillor. In 1932, twenty-two members of Sheffield City Council were or had been WEA students; in 1935 twenty-two present and former students of Leeds WEA were on local councils.[60] At a time when councils provided elementary schooling and had oversight of secondary and further education, allocated school and university scholarships, had some responsibility for medical care and social welfare, and were increasingly important providers of housing and transport, these councillors had real power. Hundreds more WEA and Ruskin students left manual work to become local government housing officers, welfare workers or senior clerks.[61]

*

The generation born between 1880 and 1899 were among the chief architects of these developments, and the first beneficiaries of them. They used their education – at board schools, WEA classes and labour colleges – to equip themselves for the increasing number of non-manual and professional posts available in clerking, teaching and politics. But they also created more of these jobs. Their campaigns to expand access to education increased the number of teachers and adult education tutors. As labour activists, they created posts in trade unions. Their fight for universal enfranchisement made it easier for working-class men and women to enter politics. They increased upward mobility.

But something was lost. Before the First World War, the labour movement had fostered visions of an entirely different, more egalitarian society – one in which learning, and life, would be organised around co-operation rather than capitalist competition. On this foundation, people would exercise collective economic and political power, first in the co-operative and labour movements, then in the industries where they worked, and ultimately in the country as a whole.

By 1918, fewer people found that vision compelling. Labour's entry to Parliament, universal male enfranchisement and partial female suffrage meant that winning elections became more important than creating an alternative socialist life. Working their way up society as it was, and winning power in the existing political system, was a realistic goal for those who owed their education or their living to the labour movement. Their victories, incomplete though they were, led some to believe they could achieve their aims without overthrowing capitalism.

Looking back in later life, many of the activists who became professional politicians expressed ambivalence about their transformation. 'If I have left the pit', wrote Jack Lawson, 'it is not because I sought to . . . but because events, and my own mates, mastered me.'[62] Bessie Braddock was selected as Labour's parliamentary candidate for

Liverpool's Exchange constituency in 1936. She had been active in labour politics for twenty years by then, and was already established as a larger-than-life champion of the city's poor, with trenchant opinions and a colourful turn of phrase. Yet this tone is missing from her muted description of her route into local government: 'I said I would let my name go forward . . . the constituency committee . . . selected me.' Of her election to Parliament in Labour's landslide victory of 1945, she said simply, 'we were flabbergasted'.[63]

Their ambivalence stemmed partly from the huge social distance that these men and women travelled. Their early lives, and their fight for parliamentary representation, had depended on collective endeavour. Victory, when it came, meant leaving those friends behind for a very different life among the social elite who graced the Palace of Westminster. Some were uncomfortably aware that their entry to those hallowed halls separated them from their left-wing roots, Jack Lawson and Bessie Braddock – both of whom ended up on the right of the Labour Party – among them.

Their diffidence about this 'success' was also due to the crushing disappointments they experienced after 1918. We shall explore these in greater depth in the next part of this book, but their impact on these socialist pioneers is worth outlining here. In 1917, many of them had welcomed the Russian Revolution. Three years later, British communists established the Communist Party of Great Britain – Bessie Braddock was so sure that revolution was imminent that she left the ILP to join up. As the historian Jose Harris has observed, the Revolution encouraged the '"activist" model of socialism' that Tom Mann and others had long advocated, and in the years immediately following 1917 'the language of class war' gained new resonance in the Labour Party and the labour movement.[64]

These socialists welcomed the post-war reforms that occurred in Britain, but they were also attracted by the new and resurgent left-wing movements of continental Europe. In countries that had experienced greater political destabilisation during the First World War than Britain had done – France, Germany and Russia among them

– radicals questioned the very existence of a social hierarchy as well as the inequality of women. 'I shall never recapture now that first ideal- istic approach that some of us felt', wrote Marjory Todd, a boiler- maker's daughter, of the high hopes that she and other ILP activists felt in the early 1920s when the Russian Revolution appeared to be creating an equal society characterised by cultural and artistic innova- tion, while at home the power of Labour and the trade unions grew stronger. Educated at WEA classes, and about to leave domestic ser- vice for a white-collar career, Marjory was confident that both she and Britain were destined for greater things. 'We really did believe in perfectibility.'[65]

But the 1920s brought some grave defeats for the British labour movement: the election of a Conservative government committed to public-spending cuts in 1922; the short-lived and disappointing administration of the country's first Labour government in 1924; and, most significantly, the General Strike of 1926. Called by the TUC to defend miners' pay and conditions, it was defeated by the Conservative government in just nine days. 'All the excitement, all the believing that a new day was dawning, crumbled into bitter resentment and disillu- sionment' recalled Jennie Lee, the daughter of an ILP household in Fife, and a budding Labour politician. 'Our hopes now lay in winning sufficient strength in parliament to be able peacefully and constitu- tionally to carry through basic socialist measures.'[66]

Then in 1929 came the Wall Street Crash, when financial specula- tion in the United States spiralled into a global economic depression. Labour's first majority government voluntarily dissolved itself to form a national government dominated by Conservatives, and on the conti- nent socialist movements were crushed by right-wing dictatorships. Meanwhile, the Soviet Union was increasingly authoritarian, to the dismay of some of its early supporters. Social democratic reform increasingly appeared preferable to a radical, perhaps violent, trans- formation of society.[67]

What many Labour politicians continued to have in common with many comrades in France, the Soviet Union and elsewhere was their faith in establishing a society in which hard work and effort were rewarded. In the Soviet Union, the new regime expanded access to education. By 1927 Soviet politicians could boast that more than half of those Communist Party members who had white-collar jobs had begun their working life as peasants or factory hands. But white-collar workers in the Soviet Union remained far more likely to be the children of professionals or administrators.[68] In 1920s Britain, an educated child from a working-class home stood a far better chance of becoming a clerk than they would in Russia, thanks to the expansion of education and local government. That would have appeared a very partial victory to some of the activists of the 1900s, but the defeats of the 1920s encouraged them to think differently. And the distance some of them had travelled, from pit villages to Parliament, suggested to some that Britain did indeed reward merit.

Those activists who climbed into political and educational posts were propelled by their desire to improve everyone's lives. Their sense of purpose and the solidarity of their comrades gave them strength when faced with the intimidation, fear of failure and sense of isolation that they experienced on their ascent. But they were a minority. Most upwardly mobile clerks and teachers were not motivated by socialism – many were, or became, conservative in their outlook and politics. What explains their rise up the social ladder, and how they fared, is the subject of the next chapter.

Chapter Two

WHITE COLLARS

'Not as courteous as the average rich man, nor as intelligent, nor as healthy, nor as lovable', declared E. M. Forster of Leonard Bast, the clerk in his 1910 novel *Howard's End*.[1] 'By far the most numerous and important' section of the lower middle class, clerks' ambitions caused consternation among those higher up the social ladder.[2] The snobbish clerk set the tone for twentieth-century parodies of lower-middle-class lifestyles and aspirations – but misrepresented many of these white-collar workers. Their fight for desk space was a struggle to grasp more than their so-called social superiors would willingly give them.

What made it possible for these clerks to climb the ladder? Contrary to Samuel Smiles, they didn't embody the spirit of self-help any more than earlier generations. Instead, they benefited from an expansion in secure, well-paid work that relied on literacy. The professions, commerce and finance (which included accountants and bank clerks) employed 7 per cent of the workforce in 1881; by 1911 they employed more than 9 per cent and that figure was rising.[3] The increasing number of clerks was particularly striking. There were 224,790 of them in 1881, but by 1911 their numbers had increased more than threefold to 800,080. This growth of room at the top – or at least in the relatively well-paid echelons of white-collar work and the teaching profession – presented opportunities to those born on the lowest rungs of the social ladder.

This expansion of opportunity owed much to the changes wrought by rapid industrialisation, especially in the growing towns and cities. Factory and mill owners, businessmen, merchants and the proprietors of new railway companies wanted banks and insurance companies to protect their wealth, lawyers to defend it and shops to spend it in. The urban sprawl needed efficient sewage systems, proper lighting, and new roads for trolleybuses and trams. Reformers demanded more hospitals, schools and libraries. Some of these amenities were provided by local and national government, others by churches, and still more by philanthropists. Even those who opposed 'handouts' to the poor wanted more policing and workhouses to prevent the beggars, street urchins and flower sellers from becoming an unruly or rebellious mob. They wanted newspapers in which to read of the early signs of unrest or about the state of the empire on which their livelihoods often depended. Workhouses demanded managers, hospitals needed nurses, sewage systems relied on engineers, newspapers required writers. And all these new institutions and offices required clerks.

Until the 1870s, recruitment to the Civil Service, parliament, most of the professions and managerial positions depended on patronage from a director, family friend or a father working for the same company. In the mid-nineteenth century social and political reformers, including the Chartists, challenged 'Old Corruption' as unjustifiable in an expanding democracy. At the same time, the expansion of finance and commerce was encouraging businesses in London and some of Britain's large provincial cities to expand their recruitment. One important result was the Northcote–Trevelyan Report. In 1853, William Gladstone, then Chancellor of the Exchequer, commissioned this report into the organisation of the Civil Service. Gladstone, himself the upwardly mobile son of a merchant, had great sympathy with the argument that government should be in the hands of hard-working men who owed their positions to merit. So did the report's chief author, Charles Trevelyan, permanent secretary at the Treasury, who had climbed several rungs of the social ladder from his childhood as a Cornish clergyman's son, via service with the East India Company. In

1854 the Northcote–Trevelyan Report recommended that Civil Service appointments be recruited on the basis of examination, not patronage. 'It would be natural to expect that so important a profession would attract into its ranks the ablest and the most ambitious youth of the country', wrote its authors. 'Such, however, is by no means the case.' The report condemned the system of patronage, whereby 'the parents and friends' of 'the unambitious and the indolent . . . endeavour to obtain for them employment . . . numerous instances might be given in which personal or political considerations have led to the appointment of very slender ability, and perhaps questionable character.'[4]

The recommendation that entry to the Civil Service be governed by stringent examinations was finally realised in 1870, when Gladstone became prime minister. Many large firms, including railway companies and major banks like Lloyds and the Bank of Scotland, followed suit, and began recruiting entrants on the basis of examinations and interviews. By 1900, the Civil Service, banks and railway companies were admitting a more socially diverse range of clerks.[5]

Far from becoming pale imitations of their managers, these white-collar workers carved out a new life that emphasised their independence both from the poverty they'd escaped and the scrutiny of their employers. Caricatures of them as deferential and snobbish certainly had some basis in truth but such behaviour was provoked by the suspicions and sneers that upwardly mobile clerks faced from those higher up the ladder. In search of affluence, respect and dignity, they often found themselves treated as unwelcome outsiders.

They succeeded in ascending the social ladder but their experience demonstrates the pitfalls of upward mobility. Climbing even just a few rungs required these clerks to show absolute conformity to unfamiliar social rules whose purpose was to exclude newcomers. They also had to field the suspicion and jealousies of wealthier men who feared these upstarts might prevent their own sons from bagging lucrative jobs. Many clerks were caught between rungs of the ladder, simultaneously negotiating their relationship with the milieu they'd joined and the family from which they came.

Male clerks provoked most concern and so became the butt of journalists' jokes and novelists' satire. Those who sat further up the ladder were also affronted by the huge increase in female clerical workers – when the Post Office began to advertise clerical posts in the 1890s (having previously recruited by word of mouth) one correspondent complained to a London newspaper that 'friends of young gentlewomen will shrink from allowing them to work in offices that will practically be open to women of all classes'.[6] But women were employed only at the lowest levels of the Civil Service (of which the Post Office was part) and in most private firms that recruited them. Their realm was distant from the boardrooms and banks where stockbrokers, solicitors and surgeons entrusted their investments.

By contrast, male clerks could find their way into banks and insurance companies, where they dealt with their customers' most private financial matters. They knew how secure or speculative the wealth of their employers or clients was. And their positions gave them, theoretically at least, the chance to become managers, wielding power over people and property.

For working-class boys born between 1880 and the end of the nineteenth century, clerking was the most realisable way of climbing the ladder. One whose life was changed irrevocably by the explosion of office work was John Gray of East Gordon, a small village in Berwickshire in the Scottish Borders. Born in 1882, John Gray grew up as opportunities for education and office work rippled out into the countryside. For young men willing to work hard and leave their family home, new chances beckoned in Britain's smaller towns as well as the larger cities. The impetus to grasp these chances was growing.

John Gray grew up in a small cottage that his family rented from the Hendersons, a local farming family. John's father, James, was the Hendersons' shepherd, and his older brother, twenty-four-year-old William, had left school in his early teens to follow in his father's footsteps. John's sister Janet, a year younger than William, had left home at fourteen to work as a domestic servant. Their mother, Margaret, appeared as a housewife in the census – a strenuous job on a farm.[7]

John's life was to be very different from those of his parents and his siblings. Unlike his older sister and brother, he went to secondary school. At the end of 1898, sixteen-year-old John sat the Bank of Scotland's entrance examination for bank clerks. He passed with a brilliant performance, becoming one of thirty-six apprentice clerks recruited by the bank that year.[8]

His success was unusual. In 1901 almost 60 per cent of male clerks were the sons of white-collar workers or professional men. While this meant that more than 40 per cent were from working-class homes, they tended to find jobs in small offices or shops, not in the Civil Service or major banks.[9] These latter posts were highly sought after, for they offered high salaries (£120 per year at the Bank of Scotland in 1911, when the average clerk's salary was £99) and a promotion structure that could take a man into management.[10]

John got his chance because of what his bank's manager called approvingly 'a superior education'. In Berwickshire almost one-third of fourteen-year-olds were at school in 1901, compared with fewer than 15 per cent in Scotland as a whole, thanks to the number of school places provided by the local school board.[11] John would have been able to attend the new higher-grade classes at Duns Board School, which gave a broad education to children between eleven and fifteen or sixteen at little or no cost. It is also possible that he attended the Berwickshire High School, a secondary school opened in Duns in 1896, which was educating about fifty pupils by 1900, many of whom paid no or very limited fees.

There was more commitment to investing in state education in Scotland than south of the border. Scotland lacked England's large aristocracy, who traditionally educated their children at home or, increasingly by the late nineteenth century, at fee-paying boarding schools. Scotland had fewer private schools than England, and a strong tradition of providing free primary education that pre-dated the 1872 Education (Scotland) Act. From the 1890s, the British government offered grants to help Scottish school boards to establish secondary schools, and many did so.

But Scotland was no meritocracy. Although the country had a smaller upper class than England, larger cities like Aberdeen, Glasgow and especially Edinburgh were home to many wealthy businesspeople, merchants, doctors and lawyers who educated their children at elite private schools. The universities were dominated by the children of the gentry (aristocrats without the very large estates more common south of the border), wealthy farmers and manufacturers. In 1901, just 4 per cent of Scottish seventeen-year-olds were at school or university – double the figure in England, but average for Western European countries.[12]

It was hard for a young man from John Gray's background to get a secondary education, but increasingly important for those who wished to leave the land or escape the factories. Education in itself did not create opportunities to climb the social ladder; the expansion of employment was responsible for that. But secondary school was the conduit to lucrative white-collar work.

The upwardly mobile owed less to their own talent and determination than to family support. Most working-class clerks were the sons of relatively well-paid skilled tradesmen who could afford to keep them at school during their teens. But others, like John Gray, did not fit this mould. He was fortunate in being a younger son. By the time he was fourteen, his older brother and sister had contributed to the family budget for several years. By contrast, Frank Benson, the oldest child of Lancashire factory workers, 'wanted to be a journalist . . . but I hadn't a secondary-school education and that barred me'. Frank's parents couldn't afford to keep him at school and at the age of fourteen he became a messenger boy. But with Frank and his sister out at work, his younger brother had different chances. 'When my brother finished his secondary-school career he became a cub reporter on the *Bolton Evening News* and I used to envy him,' recalled Frank. 'I was really jealous.'[13] Those patterns of support were well established in John Gray's family – both his parents were older siblings who had helped out younger brothers and sisters with lodgings at various times: his mother's younger sister had boarded with them while she trained as a dressmaker.[14]

Family support brought with it a sense of obligation. As Frank Benson suggests, those who made sacrifices experienced envy and rancour. But the chosen one shouldered a heavy responsibility. 'My mother's motto [was] "if you do well for yourself you'll do well for me"', recalled Robert Ferguson, the son of a widowed factory worker, who became a clerk in a Glasgow office in the 1900s.[15] A studious son could carry the ambitions of an entire family on their shoulders, as John Gray did when he began work at the Bank of Scotland.

Newspaper columnists and the heads of private schools lamented that working-class parents' misguided snobbery was turning 'innumerable good artisans and domestic servants into very inferior and wretchedly paid clerks'.[16] But clerks could earn more than many factory workers or apprentices, making it an attractive job for young men from poor homes. Their chances to enter skilled manual work were limited. More than 50 per cent of the workforce was in semi-skilled or unskilled industrial work in 1911. The strong bargaining power of skilled artisans had enabled them to restrict entry to their trades to a limited number of men who had to serve apprenticeships. In this way, they prevented their trades being flooded with workers who employers could hire or fire at will. These apprenticeships were often poorly paid and frequently allocated to the sons of existing tradesmen. In John Gray's generation, fewer than half the sons of labourers entered skilled manual work, compared with two-thirds of those born to men who possessed a trade.[17] White-collar work was a more feasible option for men from poor families.

There were other perks, too. Robert Ferguson relished working in a job where he 'never worked any longer [than] forty hours a week . . . sitting on your bottom'.[18] Clerking was less exhausting and safer than factory work – and cleaner, which was a significant advantage for men whose homes lacked bathrooms or hot water.

But not all clerks were made equal. Those who worked in factories or small businesses had few promotion prospects, and were often expected to leave their desk if more pressing tasks required their attention. James Luke, born into a working-class family in Glasgow in 1891, became a clerk in a tailor's shop after leaving school because this paid more than factory work. His job involved selling clothes as well as desk work 'because book keeping, that wasnae occupying all my time, so sometimes I went into the shop and . . . sold a suit'.[19] But those employed in the Civil Service, large companies and banks could expect not only security, but promotion to senior clerk or even manager – in short, that middle-class invention: a career.

John Gray's outstanding performance in the Bank of Scotland's entrance examination suggests that he knew success depended on outperforming his middle-class peers. Despite the introduction of examinations and interviews, patronage was still very much alive in the clerical labour market. 'It is in many cases not a boy's attainments so much as the influence which he can bring to bear on the directors or managers of banks, insurance offices, etc., that secures him the appointment', one headmaster told Leith Chamber of Commerce in 1900.[20] Even in London, with its multitude of employers, the social investigator Charles Booth reported that 'well-known commercial houses', banks and insurance companies 'commonly give preference to sons of clerks already in their employ'.[21] The men who worked in such places were well aware that they had good jobs – they wanted their sons to have the same advantage.

Employers saw great benefits in patronage. Banks were still a relatively new institution outside the largest financial centres such as London and Edinburgh. Employing the relative of a valued or potential client could build trust and forge important connections. Many of John Gray's fellow recruits owed their place to family. Alister Macbeth McKay failed the entrance examination, but an uncle who owned a company with an account at the bank secured him a second attempt, which he scraped through. Frank Naismith Young failed the arithmetic paper – one of the more crucial elements of the exam – but was taken on anyway after a branch manager pointed out that his father, a well-connected businessman, had a long-standing relationship with the bank.

John Gray knew he would get no second chance. Banks made no secret that they preferred men of independent means. 'Only those that are living with parents or friends will be eligible for appointments', Lloyds Bank warned potential recruits. The initial salary was not, most banks claimed, sufficient to maintain a young man independently.[22] Nevertheless, the relatives of prosperous customers were sometimes subsidised to ensure their families' custom. The Bank of Scotland, for example, paid Alister Macbeth McKay's removal expenses to his first post.

Being a clerk from a poor family therefore had distinct disadvantages – and being from a poor *rural* family was doubly hard. John Gray was assigned to the Bank of Scotland's small branch at Duns. This was the nearest branch to his parents' home, but the long days expected of bank clerks (eight until six and far longer if an audit was due) meant he could not return home each day and had to find digs. The new office jobs were concentrated in towns and cities, so ambitious boys from the countryside had to leave home at an early age. Many, like John Gray, struggled to get by. 'He lives in lodgings in Duns and his father, a shepherd, must find it difficult to assist him', reported John's manager in 1899, but unlike in McKay's case, the bank made no offer of financial help. It was thanks to his family's support that John Gray was able to struggle on.

He had to do well. The effort required of the upwardly mobile did not end when they reached the next rung on the ladder – they had to continually prove themselves deserving of it. This was particularly true of clerks, for many firms recruited large numbers of cheap, juvenile workers only to dismiss most of them when they qualified for adult pay rates at the age of twenty-one.[23]

Like most of its competitors, the Bank of Scotland closely monitored the performance of its staff. Branch managers, agents (regional managers) and inspectors from its Edinburgh headquarters all wrote regular reports on clerks. Their first three years were called an 'apprenticeship' but were really a probationary term, and not all men graduated to a permanent post. To win approval, John Gray had to work hard and show he was good at arithmetic and paperwork. In this he succeeded: at the beginning of 1899 the bank's agent commented that he 'is intelligent and ... writes a good hand'. His manager observed that he 'takes an interest in his work'. All agreed that he 'works hard and promises well'.

A clerk's 'character' also mattered. They had to conform to a social code enforced by employers. 'A good appearance, unobtrusive dress, and neat handwriting, are the most essential qualifications for a clerk', concluded Charles Booth.[24] This could be costly: clerks were obliged to wear white collars and smart suits. Large banks like Lloyds and the Bank of Scotland were still establishing the trust of the middle-class clients – shopkeepers, merchants, mill owners and factory managers – on whom they relied. Clerks had to appeal to this group's social aspirations by showing them deference.[25] But they were also meant to belong to the expanding middle class they served – some were the sons of the clients the bank hoped to attract.

Above all, these clerks were to differentiate themselves completely from manual workers. 'We were encouraged to consider ourselves higher than them', recalled Caradog Ludwig, the son of a working-class family in South Wales, of his years as a railway clerk. 'The company themselves made you feel that way. There was a rule that you had to present yourself at the office "in a clean and tidy manner". You had to wear a black tie with a stiff collar and a bowler hat.'[26] 'Intelligent and smart' was how a Bank of Scotland agent approvingly described one apprentice clerk. Another clerk's 'good appearance and quiet manner' won him praise. These young men, and their employers, were actively engaged in creating a distinctive middle-class sensibility that emphasised discretion and mutual trust, and prized the display of intelligence, effort and affluence.

Revealingly, John Gray's managers were surprised that a shepherd's son could be 'smart' in appearance and manner as well as educated. The parodies of upwardly mobile clerks like George Gissing's Charles Pooter – whose social faux pas regularly appeared in *Punch* – and Forster's Leonard Bast depicted them as gauche and tasteless.[27] It would have discomfited men who stressed the social distance between themselves and manual workers to realise that John Gray's role had striking parallels with his mother's and sister's experiences as domestic servants. The relationship between servants and their masters and mistresses demanded the former's discretion and forbearance. Anwyn Moyle, who worked as a lady's maid in London, soaked up 'everything like a sponge, watching and observing, listening, taking instruction'. She learned to show that she was 'honest, trustworthy, quick-witted, eager to learn, impeccably clean, methodical and patient'. Like many servants, she took advantage of her position to learn about fashion, literature (through her employer's library) and the 'correct' way to speak.[28] Some servants taught these lessons to their children. Caradog Ludwig's mother had worked for 'a well-known shipbuilding family' before she married and 'modelled herself on the people who she'd been living with. And tried to bring us children up the same way.'[29] This stood these servants' children in good stead when they took jobs that brought them into direct contact with middle- and upper-class employers and clients.

Servants taught their children another important lesson: how to negotiate their delicate position as working-class people in middle-class spaces. While clerks were satirised for seeking to escape their background, in reality they were rarely allowed to forget it. Wealthy young men won the praise of their employers for showing 'confidence' and were likely to be earmarked as future managers. But upwardly mobile clerks were expected to be more deferential. John Gray learned to show constant appreciation for his opportunities. 'Willing and obliging in manner', he quickly won favour. His father's 'sacrifice' in keeping him at school and in lodgings was noted as a sign of responsibility. The bank's managers could only have learned of this from John himself. He made sure that they knew of his family's frugality, his own determination to succeed and his gratitude for the chance to do so.[30]

By emphasising his prudence and hard work, John refuted the assumption that the working class was dirty, feckless and idle. Unlike middle-class recruits, John and others like him were expected to be humble – allowing their superiors to take credit for training them in middle-class *mores*, and distancing themselves from the assertive claims of the labour movement. In this, John succeeded. His superiors were impressed by his diligence and quiet manner. 'Agent is very ambitious that he should be taken on the permanent staff on the completion of his apprenticeship', wrote his manager in 1900.

An exception among the bank's staff, John's background helped his managers to bolster their claim to recruit on merit. Nevertheless, the demand he show constant gratitude for his chance made clear that working-class recruits were perceived as risky propositions who could only fit into their new milieu if they transformed themselves.

The Bank of Scotland was more disapproving of other working-class recruits. These 'roughly spoken' clerks with a 'want of polish' hint that many young men did not emulate their middle-class managers. Rather, they were in search of an entirely new way of life. Those in larger towns and cities had more chances to pursue this than John did. Many had had a taste of secondary education that left them wanting more. Victor (V.S.) Pritchett, who reluctantly left school in 1908 to begin clerking at a London leather works, quickly became one of a 'self-important, cracked-voice little race, sheepish, yet cocky', identified by their 'bowler hats' and constant debate.[31] Richard Church, the son of a London postman, was born in 1893. An aspiring artist and writer, he became a Civil Service clerk in 1909 only at his father's insistence. He was pleased to discover that a salary of fifteen shillings per week, with generous lunch breaks and strictly regulated working hours, allowed him to enjoy literary life of a sort. Discussion in the office and trips to bookshops after work 'served me in those first years in lieu of a university'.[32] James McBey, born in 1883 to a poor family in Aberdeenshire, became a bank clerk thanks to his grandmother's friendship with the local branch manager. Once established in Aberdeen, he used his free time and salary to pursue his love of art. He was also able to use work trips to visit galleries – on one occasion, curtailing his business at a London bank to take a quick excursion to Paris in his employer's time.[33]

Others used their leisure time to pursue political ambitions. Far from being snobbish and deferential, many clerks sympathised with the labour movement's demand for educational opportunity. Herbert Morrison was born in Lambeth in 1888, the son of a Tory police constable. His father wanted to see Herbert established as a respectable shopkeeper and his first job – as a grocer's assistant – set him on this path. But 'without any exact idea of where it would lead me, from my teen years I knew that an active life in socialist politics was the only one which would satisfy me', he later wrote. After a short period in the SDF, Herbert joined the ILP. 'My job with the grocery shop, eminently representing a system I was anxious to change, also took up so much time that I really had to confine my activities to weekends.'[34] Thanks to a word from his brother, a clerk at the Whitbread works near King's Cross, Herbert got a lowlier position there. To his father's chagrin, this job offered few promotion prospects – but plenty of time for political debate after work.

By the 1900s these 'fast young men', relatively affluent bachelors with time and money on their hands, had become new targets of disapproval. 'Servile' office workers by day, they were 'gaudy butterflies' who swaggered around the city streets by night.[35] They wanted a taste of life and learning, not social climbing per se.

But those like John Gray, who were in probationary positions with prospects, had to curb their spirits to secure a permanent job. It must have been a cause for celebration in the Gray household when, in 1901, John's hard work was rewarded with a secure job as bank teller – a cashier who dealt directly with customers.

This brought fresh challenges. Promotion meant moving to the bank's Blairgowrie branch, more than a hundred miles north of his family's home. Middle-class clerks could negotiate posts in places where they had family contacts who might prove useful to the bank. Working-class men had no such bargaining power. For those living outside Britain's largest cities in particular, climbing the social ladder often meant migrating. They had to set aside the ties of home to establish their career.

Getting a permanent post, even one as secure and prestigious as John Gray's, did not mean a working-class clerk was now equal to his middle-class peers. Most clerks had very limited promotion prospects since managerial jobs were few and far between. Openings were increasing by the time John joined the permanent staff, for successful banks and firms expanded in the 1900s, swallowing up smaller competitors.[36] But wealthier, well-connected young men leapfrogged working-class clerks to senior positions. In John's intake at the Bank of Scotland, the sons of farmers and businessmen were most likely to end up in lucrative posts at the bank's headquarters or in expanding city-centre branches with good promotion prospects.

The few working-class recruits who were offered these choice openings often had to turn them down. Large cities like London and Edinburgh were prohibitively expensive for young migrants who needed to help their families rather than being able to rely on them for support. When John Ramsay, the son of a hard-up widow, was offered a highly prized promotion to the Bank of Scotland's London office, he regretfully declined because he feared he wouldn't be able to support his mother. Ramsay's lack of commitment was duly noted: he was transferred to the bank's Airdrie branch and received no further pay rises or promotions.

The salaries of clerks from working-class backgrounds remained far lower than those of their counterparts from middle-class homes throughout their careers.[37] When John Gray celebrated his twenty-first birthday in 1903 he was earning £70 per year; a skilled manual worker of the same age could expect to earn about £99.[38] His salary offered little spending money to a man who had to keep himself in the style his employer expected.

This explains why some men in their early twenties left clerking for manual work. Many commentators worried that young men became clerks with the unrealistic hope of becoming a prosperous manager – 'the eminence of a small minority dazzles the eyes of a large number whose talents might perhaps have been more profitably directed elsewhere', lamented Charles Booth ('elsewhere' meant domestic service and factory work).[39] But clerks from working-class backgrounds were realistic about their prospects. Those who exchanged office work for a manual job did so because some trades paid higher wages than routine clerical posts. In the 1900s James Luke, the Glaswegian clerk who worked in a tailors' shop, decided to marry and 'had to get more money' to support his wife and the children they hoped for. James's father, a furnaceman, got him a job in the same trade. 'See that was a good job. You did earn some money.' His new job offered James overtime and the protection of a trade union. In the 1930s his employer offered him a desk job, 'but I refused because I was making more money than the manager'.[40]

John Gray was fortunate: his family did not require his financial assistance though he did need to support himself. In 1904 he was promoted to senior bank teller, which brought a move to Forfar. But as John crept up the bank's hierarchy, he became prey to anxieties that commonly plagued the upwardly mobile. He won less favour at Forfar than he had done earlier in his career. His new managers described him as 'shy' and 'gawky-looking', and wished him to 'be franker and freer in manner'.

James McBey's experience of promotion to a similar post provides a clue as to what was going on. His new responsibilities provoked sleepless nights, for promotion brought new chances to fail. One mistake might incur charges of fraud or theft – and this was particularly threatening for clerks from working-class backgrounds. 'Without influential friends or relations in the bank I was, I knew, a natural scapegoat', wrote McBey. 'I saw myself as the defenceless victim of the whims and jealousies of my superiors, holding precariously a position of dour respectability . . . in a constant state of anxiety lest by an involuntary slip or an error of judgement I might endanger both my chances of advancement and, at the tail end of a lifetime of faithful subservience, a small pension.'[41]

The higher he climbed, the further a socially mobile clerk had to fall. For John Gray this fear of tumbling down the ladder became very real in 1907. He was jointly responsible for an error in calculating interest rates – a mistake that cost the bank £100 (the equivalent of more than £10,000 today). This kind of slip not only cost his employer money, but threatened the integrity and reliability on which the bank's reputation – and therefore its profits – depended.

In many businesses, John Gray would have been sacked. An unemployed clerk could easily slide into poorly paid, insecure, unskilled manual work – 'those who drop out, drop under', as Charles Booth put it.[42] Alan Rees worked as a shipping clerk in Liverpool after leaving school in the 1900s. In his early twenties he was dismissed for failing to post some important letters. His working-class origins did not help: 'economically, my background didn't fit with the highly respectable clerical white-collared types'.[43] After failing to get apprenticed to a draughtsman – men in their twenties were too old for these sought-after posts – Rees became a door-to-door salesman. When this failed to make ends meet he ended up as a hospital porter. Unlike skilled tradesmen, clerks had no certificated skills they could take with them to a different firm. Most employers placed high value on loyalty and knowledge of the particularities of their business, and recruited senior clerks or managers from within their ranks.

John Gray was lucky. He kept his job though he was denied any increase in pay for two years. While he received a rise of £10 in 1909 his branch manager later admitted that this 'would not have been given had [the] fact of his being responsible for above error not been overlooked'.

John worked even harder to please his employers, and this paid off. 'Have the highest opinion of him', recorded the agent at Forfar in 1909. As a result, in 1910 he was transferred to a bigger branch at Port Glasgow, twenty-three miles west of Glasgow city, and did well. 'Very accurate and expert', wrote the branch manager. 'Has a fine personal appearance.'

But while this makes John sound like the kind of highly deferential clerk satirised by novelists, he was not snobbish about working-class life. On beginning work at Port Glasgow he found lodgings in a tenement where his neighbours ranged from labourers to journalists. His street accommodated many other clerks as well. John's choice of lodgings was dictated by cost – whether they wanted to admit it or not, clerks had more in common with manual workers than they did with their employers. Many clerks refused to join a trade union, citing 'respectability' and a horror of being associated with 'working-class activity'.[44] But by the 1900s, some socially mobile men used the lessons learned by fathers and older brothers in manual work to their advantage. In 1907, the National Union of Clerks (NUC), which had just 160 members, affiliated to the Trades Union Congress and the Labour Party. Its demands for better pay and more security for clerks, for sick pay and enhanced promotion prospects, and the union's provision of education, proved increasingly popular as more working-class young men entered clerking. By 1910 the NUC's membership had risen to 20,860.[45]

We don't know if John Gray joined a union, but we do know that the insecurity and uncertain prospects highlighted by the National Union of Clerks took a toll on his health. He was diagnosed with neurasthenia, a nervous condition caused by stress, and then in 1911 contracted appendicitis, which can be provoked or aggravated by acute anxiety.[46] Working-class clerks were particularly likely to leave the Bank of Scotland as a result of illness.

Sickness brought its own problems. John was clearly desperate to keep his job, and prevent his medical bills sending him deep into debt. Many clerks were members of friendly societies and life-insurance schemes, but long or severe illnesses could still be expensive.[47] John returned to work after only a brief convalescence for appendicitis – a concerned inspector suggested that he was 'not quite recovered'. He soon made another serious error in counting the branch takings.

Some working-class clerks managed to escape from what V. S. Pritchett called this 'dulling routine'.[48] Pritchett himself fled to Paris in his early twenties, where he combined office work with his first attempts at writing – the beginning of a distinguished literary career. Richard Church published his first book of poems in 1917, and eventually left the Civil Service to become a full-time writer in his forties. James McBey made a quicker exit. In 1915 he decided to forego the security and boredom of bank life to try his luck as an artist, and eventually had a highly successful career.[49] For a few clerks, the glimpse of middle-class respectability, and awareness of their own limited prospects, provoked flight into a completely different way of life. Their escape was assisted by the literary, debating or artistic skills they'd devoted their leisure hours to cultivating.

John Gray stayed put – but his life was about to take a more hopeful turn. Like James McBey, Richard Church and most of that faceless 'crowd' of clerks who 'flowed over London Bridge' in T. S. Eliot's *The Waste Land*, he had a private life unknown to his employers.[50] By 1910 he was courting Isabella Donald, the daughter of a house painter in Blairgowrie, where John had worked in the early 1900s. Isabella's father was doing well: he had established a small shop where Isabella worked while John was in Blairgowrie. By 1911, however, Isabella's brother had entered her father's trade, and her services were no longer required. Isabella and her sister took the routes pursued by so many women of their generation who had just enough family support to escape domestic service, factory or shop work. 'Bella' as she now called herself – the fashionable abbreviation denoting her new financial and social independence – became a junior bank clerk in nearby Pitlochry, and her sister became a teacher. The Donalds' neighbours included shopkeepers and master tradesmen. Bella's family were a little better off than John Gray's, and their social status was slightly higher.

It was not unusual for male clerks to marry 'up'. Throughout the twentieth century, about half of all marriages were between men and women from the same social class. But a quarter of men in John Gray's generation married women from a higher social class – a rarer occurrence later in the century.[51] In the early twentieth century, clerks very often married other white-collar workers if they could.[52] Most clerks were female, and those from working-class backgrounds rarely got the few plum posts available to women in banking or the Civil Service. With fewer male clerks to go round, most of these women married manual workers. But male clerks were more likely to marry female clerks and sometimes this took them into more affluent families.

Marrying into a more prosperous household could have obvious financial benefits. But John and Bella were also drawn together as members of the first generation of working-class children to get an education. Climbing the social ladder was a gruelling experience, and it helped if each spouse knew the gains and the strains involved.

Before 1939, employers expected to be kept informed – and often to intervene in – their clerks' marital aspirations. Since the late nineteenth century, many large institutions – banks and the civil service among them – had imposed a marriage bar on female clerks. Female office workers had to leave their jobs as soon as they married. This rule, which many local authorities also imposed on teachers, was designed to restrict women's prospects as their numbers in the workforce grew. The marriage bar ensured that men retained positions of seniority.

Men were not subject to a marriage bar. But male clerks in most of Britain's major banks, including the Bank of Scotland, were not allowed to marry without the permission of their branch manager. This was rarely granted before they reached their late twenties and were earning a salary that their employer considered commensurate with keeping a family. This strategy, like that of appointing wealthy men, enabled banks to keep salaries relatively low – there was no need to pay a young man enough to support a family.[53] As national or multinational institutions, banks liked to have at their disposal a large pool of young male clerks who would accept without demur regular relocations to different branches. And making clerks' right to marry conditional on their salary and age increased the pressure on young men to work hard and attain promotion.[54]

In practice, banks did not always strictly enforce this marriage rule for men. But clerks who had not yet achieved the acceptable age or salary level were obliged to negotiate with their employer.[55] In January 1911 twenty-eight-year-old John Gray asked his branch manager's permission to marry Bella. 'Bank has no objection', wrote the agent, but there appears to have been an understanding that he would wait some months.

John, however, had other ideas. In April 1911 he took more time off to fully recover from appendicitis. Two weeks later he sent his employer a telegram, informing them that he had married Bella while staying at the Pitlochry Hydropathic Clinic, prior to convalescing abroad. It isn't clear whether John's family travelled the long distance for this ceremony – the couple's marriage was witnessed by Joseph Bone, a clerk who lived in Blairgowrie, and possibly a former colleague of John's, and Mary Falconer, the unmarried daughter of an architect who lived close to the Donald family. Mary did not work for a living while Bella did, but skilled tradesmen, small shopkeepers, professionals and their families often mixed together in small towns and villages.

Perhaps the knowledge that John Gray was making a favourable marriage explains his employer's reaction. His managers clearly suspected that the trip overseas might be a honeymoon and telegraphed John demanding that he 'send explanations'. John must have contacted the bank, for his staff record shows that they grudgingly accepted his proffered apology and allowed him to travel abroad, his first trip outside Scotland.

Marriage changed John's attitude to work. In 1912 he requested a demotion from his job as teller: 'of nervous temperament', noted an inspector, 'which no doubt accounts for his desire to be relieved from [his role]'. From being a clerk who 'promised well' he had apparently resigned himself to progressing no further. He subsequently asked for, and was granted, an overdraft of £10, not to further any grandiose social ambitions, but to 'settle [his] doctor's bill'. Paying off debts and establishing a secure niche for himself appeared to be his priorities.

This may have been a sign of new-found confidence and contentment. Sixty years later, the sociologist John Goldthorpe found that many of the upwardly mobile men he interviewed – some of them born just a decade later than John Gray – decided not to seek further promotion once they became husbands or fathers, preferring to devote their time to family life.[56] In John Gray's case, the confidence to take that step may well have come from his marriage into a family with considerably more capital than the Grays possessed.

Edwardian caricatures of clerks showed them graduating from feckless young men into henpecked husbands. They were dominated by socially ambitious and snobbish women like George Gissing's creation, Carrie Pooter, who insisted her husband Charles live beyond his financial means and social station.[57] Many women, denied the education and careers open to men, certainly channelled their ambitions into their husbands' careers. Female clerks and teachers of John Gray's generation valued a man with the determination to 'make something of himself'. Their own occupation having offered them a glimpse of middle-class life, they hoped for a husband who would help them secure this. Ann Hodges was born in 1887 to a lower-middle-class family and became a teacher. In her twenties, she married a clerk who 'also has a good education'.[58]

But often these women discovered that their husbands' ambitions did not match their own, and they lacked the economic or social power to do anything about this. 'My husband lacks something – gumption or pushfulness, common sense', wrote Ann Hodges in the 1930s. She wanted 'a fur coat and a villa and a cat and a maid' – all those accoutrements of bourgeois life that the clerks' detractors sneered at, despite possessing such luxuries themselves. But these women were not superficial, snobbish philistines. As well as regretting her lack of a suburban 'semi-detached', Ann Hodges was disappointed that her husband did not share 'my desire for intellectual life'. She saw no contradiction between wanting material comfort and intellectual stimulation, and many of her female contemporaries agreed. 'Unmarried I'd have got on', Ann concluded.[59]

We don't know if John's wife Bella suffered these same disappointments, but she did get a villa – she and John eventually settled in a Victorian suburb in Glasgow. Clerks and their families congregated in the expanding suburbs, a move often seen as a snobbish flight from their working-class roots 'to imitate middle-class standards'.[60] But they were creating a new kind of lifestyle, which offered them comforts their parents had never known but did not necessarily mean aping their employers. During the first two decades of the twentieth century, many wealthy businessmen – the directors of banks, large manufacturing enterprises and railway companies, for example – moved out of urban areas into the countryside.[61] The aspirations of women like Ann Hodges did not suggest that they wanted to do likewise. Far from desiring social exclusivity above all else, many white-collar workers and teachers sought housing that offered easy access to town and city centres. The neighbourhood in which the Grays lived had been built with this in mind – it was no great distance from working-class tenements, and was within easy reach of Glasgow's banks, theatres, galleries and department stores.[62]

In 1914 Bella had a son, Patrick, the Grays' only child. As the number of manual-workers' children who entered white-collar work increased, the size of families headed by white-collar workers and professionals fell.[63] The growing demand for well-educated clerks meant that investing money and time in a child's upbringing was increasingly important. Upwardly mobile parents were particularly conscious that smaller families could offer children a better start in life. They knew from personal experience the expense that larger families entailed, and had no inherited wealth to pass on to their own sons and daughters.

Women whose aspirations had been thwarted by a lack of education, few jobs or the marriage bar took particular pleasure in helping a son to 'get on'. Nella Last was born in Cumbria in 1889, the daughter of a railway clerk. She married a self-employed joiner whose family 'did not like me for what they called "my fine lady ways"'. Failing in her attempt to make her husband's small business a success, Nella Last invested her hopes in her two sons, Arthur and Cliff – 'I craved the best for them in every way.'[64] Her savings helped to put them both through secondary school. Both boys fulfilled their mother's aspirations: Arthur became a tax inspector; Clifford initially worked in the family business, but after active service in the Second World War he emigrated to Australia, where he became a noted sculptor.[65]

Once she got the vote in 1918, Nella Last voted Tory. So did many male clerks and their wives. They were often caricatured as doing so out of deference to the upper middle class they allegedly wished to join. But their support for the Conservative Party was kindled by fear of falling back down the social ladder as much as by their desire to climb higher (or, more usually, to see their children do so). Between 1915 and 1917 the need for high productivity in the war factories had helped the unions win greater bargaining power with employers and the government. As a result, thousands more manual workers joined trade unions. In 1918 the Representation of the People Act appeared to further increase the labour movement's power.

The 1918 election resulted in victory for a Liberal and Conservative coalition, headed by the Liberal prime minister David Lloyd George. But Labour gained fifteen MPs. With an eye to Labour's growing strength, the government passed not only the 1918 Education Act, but also the 1919 Housing Act, which set out an ambitious plan for 500,000 council houses.

The assertive labour movement, and the public-spending commitments of the post-war government, worried many of the lower middle class. By the early 1920s they had begun to describe themselves as the 'new poor', a term coined in the press. 'Labour today has only to open its mouth and it receives practically what it asks for', complained *Daily Mail* columnist E. Phillips Oppenheim in 1919. 'The aristocracy have taken to selling their land . . . There is scarcely a merchant or manufacturer in the kingdom who has not made money by the war . . . The only class left absolutely without compensation or consolation is the class on whose behalf I write.'[66]

Clerks and their families were among the members of new ratepayers' associations like the Anti-Waste League and the Middle Classes' Union, which campaigned for lower taxes and against expenditure on council housing and medical provision for the poor. The Anti-Waste League scored some notable successes in by-elections in 1921 and 1922, testifying to the popularity of its ideas among a swathe of the middle-class electorate. In 1922, the Conservative Party swept to power on a manifesto pledging to cut public spending. Clerks were becoming an increasingly visible and important political interest group.

But not all clerks took this stance. Increasing numbers of them joined trade unions during and after the First World War. And white-collar workers were among those who swelled the ranks of the WEA. In the 1920s the WEA attracted 'engineers, miners, textile workers, teachers, building-trade workers, clerks, postal workers, railway workers, pottery workers, housewives and domestic workers'.[67] Clerks' appetite for learning and debate had not diminished, and they were not inevitably eager to distance themselves from manual workers.

We don't know John Gray's political views, but in common with many of his generation he continued to ascend the social ladder after the First World War. He did not serve during the war, possibly because of his history of poor health. But after 1918 he had to adapt to changes in banking and clerical careers. Successful banks and large businesses expanded once more, and recruited more junior clerks in new branches and plants. But these younger clerks faced uncertain prospects. Although managerial posts increased, they did not do so at the same rate as entry-level jobs. During the war, many banks had replaced their conscripted male workers with women, and continued to rely on them in the 1920s – they were cheaper to employ than men, and the marriage bar (suspended during the war, but reimposed afterwards) created a young, disposable, female workforce for routine clerical posts.

This may explain why, in the 1920s, John Gray once more began to scale the ranks of the bank's hierarchy. His job as senior clerk lacked the status and security it had offered before the war. As an experienced male employee, he was able to compete for the growing number of managerial and accountancy posts that large firms and banks created to staff their growing number of branches and to manage the increasingly complex finances of their national and international operations.[68]

By 1930 John Gray had become branch accountant at Ayr, forty miles south of Glasgow. This may have appealed to him more than the rapid calculations and daily balancing of the books required of tellers. He was, in any case, a very different person by now – a married man and homeowner, rather than a young upwardly mobile clerk seeking to justify his place in the world. By the time he retired in 1939 he was accountant and agent at the larger Paisley branch.

In John Gray's youth, newspaper commentators and businessmen had feared that scholarship boys like him would rob middle-class sons of their rightful positions. Their concerns had made the climb up the ladder tougher for working-class men, who had to prove themselves at every turn. But their detractors had no reason to worry. The upwardly mobile men and women of the pioneer generation owed their chance to the creation of new jobs in clerking and teaching. They did not knock middle-class boys off their rung on the ladder – rather, that rung broadened. Just as John Gray's entry to banking had depended on the creation of new posts, so his eventual promotions were due not to displacing middle-class men, but to the expansion of middle-management. The top jobs continued to go to those who had started life in the middle class.

The supposed deference and snobbery of the Edwardian clerk set the tone for a further century of sneers at the lower middle class: their suburban aspirations, their petty status distinctions, their social and political conservatism. But white-collar work had strong material attractions for men and women who knew the dangers and poverty that manual work could entail. Clerical work also provided an outlet for this generation's intellectual ambitions, which were fired by compulsory schooling but dampened by the cost of secondary and higher education. These benefits compensated for the hostility and suspicion that many upwardly mobile young people had to encounter from those who feared that their own position was threatened. This hostility, and the insecurity of their position, explains the anxiety, deference and status-consciousness that some of them exhibited.

Clerks like John Gray were popularly represented as desperate to escape their social background. Many clerks certainly relished creating a life imbued with comforts unknown to their parents. They pursued higher wages, but also expected respect for their skills and experience, and the ability to live with a dignity too often denied to the poor. They sought to fulfil ambitions formed in childhood that their parents and siblings (and particularly their mothers) often shared.

John Gray maintained strong family ties. In 1927 his only son, Patrick, was killed in an accident while staying with Isabella's brother, who helped to arrange the boy's funeral. Patrick was buried in a churchyard close to John Gray's own birthplace, in the village of East Denholm where the Grays chose to settle after John's retirement.

This preference for the rural life was evident among many white-collar workers, thousands of whom chose to live in the quiet semi-rural suburbs springing up on the edges of Britain's towns and cities. Their neighbourhoods were frequently denigrated as vulgar by wealthier people: Vita Sackville West condemned suburban growth as the 'great uneasy heave of the uneducated'.[69] But many white-collar workers came from country families and their new homes connected them to their roots. In East Denholm, the Grays were within easy travelling distance of John's sister Janet and her husband James Murdie, a groom. When John died in 1948 he was buried in the village churchyard alongside Bella, who had predeceased him. James Murdie registered John's death. When Janet and her husband died, they too were buried in the churchyard close to her brother, his wife and their son. John Gray never severed his ties to a family that connected him to servants, farm labourers, and to the land.

PART II

THE PRECARIOUS
GENERATION
1900–1919

Chapter Three

CRASHING DOWN THE LADDER

The precarious generation's fortunes were superficially better than those of the pioneers. Statistical studies suggest that about 30 per cent of both men and women experienced downward mobility, but the same proportions were upwardly mobile. This movement occurred between the two world wars. However, as we shall see, the jobs that defined this generation's upward mobility – including clerical work – lacked the security and prospects that some of John Gray's generation had enjoyed. And because studies of social mobility assess people towards the end of their working lives, they miss the impact that mass unemployment had on people's working lives, and their aspirations, during the 1920s and 1930s. Many of the precarious generation were able to recover from this during or after the Second World War. But the consequences of unemployment and poverty on their early lives, education and aspirations were significant. This was true not only for those whose families relied on the dole, but also for those whose parents, a rung or two higher on the ladder, feared for their ability to remain there. They imbibed that anxiety; it shaped their desire to get on in the world.

The pioneers' upward mobility was caused by the expansion of employment and education. The precarious generation's downward mobility resulted from the reduction of these. During the First World War, the Liberal government promised 'homes fit for heroes', and jobs too. But by 1921, 17 per cent of the workforce was unemployed. During the 1920s, unemployment remained above 10 per cent.[1]

Manual workers were the hardest hit by unemployment. Several key industries, including shipbuilding, had been over-producing goods in the uncertain final years of the war, and continued to do so in the early post-war years. Other industries, like textiles, faced competition from overseas. During the war, textiles could no longer be exported and the countries affected – including Japan – set up their own factories. Demand for British cotton did not pick up after the war – in fact, it was further decimated when, in 1920, Mahatma Gandhi and his comrades in the struggle for Indian Independence announced a boycott of all British goods. As India was the recipient of half of Britain's cotton exports, the highly successful boycott had shattering consequences. By 1933 Japan was the world's largest cotton manufacturer. In Britain, steelworkers, miners and textile workers were among those most likely to be unemployed.

Many Liberal, Conservative, and some Labour politicians blamed unemployment on women taking men's jobs during the Great War, or on people's idleness. Neither explanation was true: most of the million women who entered the workforce between 1914 and 1918 took up entirely new jobs, while returning servicemen were eager to find work when the Armistice came. The fault lay with employers and with post-war Liberal and Conservative governments' failure to rebuild Britain after 1918. There was no plan to integrate ex-servicemen into the workforce, and no strategy for returning industry to a peacetime footing. In 1920 the government consigned thousands of British textile workers to poverty by refusing to negotiate with the Indian Independence Movement.

Unemployment rose again after the Wall Street Crash of 1929. This precipitated a global financial crisis that Britain was in no fit state to face. Unemployment peaked in 1932, when 22 per cent of the workforce was unemployed. Just as in the 1920s, workers in heavy industry were the most vulnerable group when it came to job losses. Once again, the government did little to intervene. The number of unemployed fell from the mid-1930s, thanks largely to an expansion of light manufacturing in England's Midlands and south-east. But 11 per cent of the workforce was still unemployed in 1938.

Unemployment was the chief cause of poverty, but the death or illness of a family's chief breadwinner were also important – more so than before the Great War. The social investigator Arthur Bowley investigated poverty in 1912 and in 1924: he found that old age was a persistent cause of hardship. But the causes of poverty among adults of working age and their children changed between the 1910s and the 1920s. Before the war, low wages were chiefly to blame, but the poor of the 1920s owed their state to unemployment, bereavement, or sickness.[2] Many families had lost their chief breadwinner in the Great War: the government made scant provision for war widows and their children. Others suffered in the influenza epidemic of 1918 and 1919, which killed 228,000 people in Britain. When the flu pandemic arrived in Britain in the spring of 1918, the government initially denied its significance. Only after the prime minister, David Lloyd George, was infected in September that year did the government acknowledge that the flu was contagious. Even then, their approach was characterised by 'much talk but very little "do"', as one journalist put it.[3] Hospitals and general practitioners, already short-staffed because so many medical workers were still serving in the military, were left to manage as best they could. Meanwhile, many of the sick could not afford to pay for a doctor.

The precarious generation were among the unemployed. But far more of them were affected by their family's poverty. Many were obliged to leave school as soon as possible to help their household survive. Young workers were not as vulnerable to unemployment as older workers – they were cheaper to employ and had fewer rights. But the industrial and economic crisis that threatened their parents' livelihoods diminished their own prospects. They discovered that skilled manual work was becoming harder to find. In 1911 31 per cent of workers were in skilled jobs; by 1931 just 27 per cent were, and most of them were older men. An army of young, unskilled workers – often poorly paid, with no promotion prospects and vulnerable to being laid off – grew significantly. They became delivery boys and factory hands. In 1911 10 per cent of workers had relied on unskilled manual work, but 15 per cent did so by 1931.

But far more than 15 per cent of workers found themselves reliant on poorly paid, insecure jobs. The precarious generation became dependent on so-called 'blind-alley' jobs. These included the kind of unskilled manual jobs that had occupied working-class young people like Ernest Bevin before the war. But by the late 1920s, 'blind-alley' workers also comprised many young shop assistants, waitresses, usherettes at new cinemas and dance halls, and even clerks. Nineteen per cent of workers were employed in non-manual jobs in 1911, but this had risen to 23 per cent twenty years later, and that figure continued to grow during the 1930s. The numbers of clerks and shop workers grew most rapidly of all. Yet not all of them experienced their work as a step up from manual labour. Employers, emboldened by high unemployment and successive interwar governments' disdain for trade unionism, cut wages and invested little in working conditions. Mass production, which had become popular in wartime industry, was used in peacetime to deskill workers. In factories, assembly-line workers undertook repetitive tasks and were paid by how much they produced each hour. While this method was particularly popular in the manufacture of domestic appliances, food and clothing, many large shops and some clerical employers adapted it to cut costs. The wages of shop assistants and salesmen depended on how many sales they made in a day. Most had no prospect of promotion – only the looming threat of the dole queue. The expansion in clerical workers was greatest for typists and junior staff. Before the war, promotion and salary increases had created clear career ladders in institutions like banks and the civil service. Newer enterprises did not adopt these, while in older establishments only a minority of staff could hope to climb from the lowest rung to the far narrower rungs above.

Politicians' decisions made more difference to people's prospects than their own ambitions or efforts. Interwar governments made little effort to solve unemployment. The Conservatives dominated government in the 1920s and 30s, but many senior Labour politicians shared their view that the best response to economic crisis was to cut wages and sustain a benefits system that was set up only to deal with short-term unemployment. As a result, the unemployed and the low paid often slid down the ladder into poverty. Anti-trade union laws, and a reduction in skilled work, meant that for many of the unemployed their descent was permanent.

Getting a secure job with prospects increasingly depended on having a secondary education. Before the war, many professions had administered their own entrance tests, just as banks and the Civil Service had done. But it cost less money and time to use educational qualifications as a means of selection, and during the war professional associations and trade unions lobbied government for uniform assessments to assist their selection of recruits.[4] The Board of Education was receptive to their wishes, which chimed with the recommendations of the Board's own Consultative Committee. Before the war, this committee, established in 1900 to advise on policy, had recommended a national system of secondary school examinations. In 1918, the first national secondary-school examination, the School Certificate, was introduced for sixteen- and eighteen-year-olds.

A university degree was increasingly desirable for those aspiring to enter the professions. By 1918 teaching was among those professions that required entrants to have some higher education. Some expanding industries such as chemical manufacture were also keen that entrants had an advanced scientific education. In the 1920s new universities and university colleges – including Keele and Leicester – opened to meet demand.[5]

But educational achievement remained closely connected to class background. Although the number of secondary-school places increased, working-class families were frequently too poor to take these up. Fewer than 10 per cent of twelve-to-fourteen-year-olds attended a secondary school in 1931, and only 6 per cent of fifteen-to-eighteen-year-olds. Most were the children of professionals, managers and senior white-collar workers.[6] Two per cent of eighteen-year-olds went to university in 1919, and fewer than 5 per cent by 1939. Although the proportion of working-class children getting an advanced education did rise, the increase in university students was largely composed of the children of shopkeepers, senior clerks, teachers, managers, and small businessmen.[7]

At the same time, universal enfranchisement and the expansion of education sparked new aspirations among this generation. Some became a new type of public-sector professional, among them newly educated women from middle-class families and the upwardly mobile. Many of them were keen to enter the technical, scientific and welfare jobs created by the First World War, new manufacturing industries and by the more ambitious municipal councils (often under Labour control). These new opportunities weren't governed by older patronage and social networks, and offered the chance to modernise Britain through science and social welfare.

These new professionals and administrators wanted to make Britain a fairer place, but they did not share the pioneers' faith in the labour movement as a means to do so. Instead, they believed that technical and social scientific expertise provided the answer. This conviction, coupled with their own sense of precarity, fuelled their desire for a meritocratic society where education and training, not family background, would determine a person's social position. Their development of a new kind of middle-class identity, based on scientific and social scientific expertise, would have repercussions into and beyond the Second World War.

*

After the war, many women were forced out of their clerical or factory jobs. The coalition of Liberals and Conservatives who won the general election of 1918 blamed rising male unemployment on women. They received energetic support from some Labour politicians as well. Manchester's first Labour lord mayor, Tom Fox, declared that '"pin money" girls – those who were merely working to provide themselves with pocket money – would have to leave the Town Hall departments so that their places could be filled by ex-servicemen'.[8] These men blithely ignored the fact that most female war workers had been recruited to entirely new clerical and factory roles – and that many of them had parents and siblings to keep.[9]

In 1922 the newly elected Conservative government introduced an Unemployment Act that obliged all unemployed unmarried women to accept a job as a servant if they were offered one, even if this meant moving away from their home. But this did nothing to solve unemployment, which was highest in heavy industries like steel and coal mining, not in jobs where women worked.

Older, skilled male manual workers were most vulnerable to long-term unemployment. But many younger people, especially young men employed in heavy industry, were out of work for shorter spells. In 1932 the unemployment rate was 22 per cent, but more than half of all workers experienced some unemployment that year.

Women's unemployment, and that of their relatives, made many of them downwardly mobile. The number of women servants rose from 552,337 in 1921 to 639,057 in 1931. Among them was Emma Cleary. Born to a working-class Manchester family, she left school aged fourteen in 1922. Emma became an apprentice confectioner, a skilled trade. But illness forced her to curtail her training, and when she recovered she found her post had been filled and there were no similar ones available. 'There was nothing for women like me after the war', she thought; she was 'forced' to become a maid.[10] While domestic service had not been particularly popular before 1914, its status diminished further during the war when many young women experienced better pay and conditions in the munitions factories.

The number of the unemployed grew, and just as significantly, so did the duration of unemployment. As a result, many skilled workers who lost their jobs also lost their trade, and the status this gave them. They experienced this as downward mobility. In the 1930s, skilled manual workers were likely to remain unemployed for more than a year. While seasonal and short-term unemployment had been common among unskilled men before 1914, skilled men had had greater security. Their skills were often in demand, and their trade unions offered them some protection when sickness or unemployment hit.

Among those affected by the downturn in their prospects in the 1930s was Arthur Rigg. Born in Derbyshire in 1900, he had been a skilled wire drawer – making steel and copper wire – before being made redundant in 1930. 'Before the present depression it was possible to go after work in another district', he wrote in 1933, still unemployed. One of the advantages of having a skilled trade had been that a man could take it with him, wherever he went – 'but all wire firms are in the same state today'. Three years after losing his job, Arthur was constantly disappointed in his attempts to get labouring work, since he was 'competing with thousands of others who are at least as skilled as I'.[11]

This marked a huge change in the conditions and status of skilled workers. Before 1918 they had enjoyed a modicum of independence from both employers and the state. Their collective power had already been weakened after the General Strike of 1926, and the anti-trade union laws that Stanley Baldwin's Conservative government subsequently rushed through. Trade-union membership fell by half a million in 1927, and continued to fall until 1933, decimated by unemployment.[12]

The government called on the unemployed to help themselves, but their policies denied skilled men the chance. When Arthur Rigg lost his job he initially 'received unemployment benefit . . . from my trade union . . . but this was reduced over time' because so many men were out of work that the union's funds dried up. 'I am healthy and strong, but my health and strength will procure me nothing beyond the allowance which the State makes to me in charity', he wrote.[13] Many skilled workers shared his horror at becoming 'a pauper'.[14] These men's loss of collective power hit them as hard as material hardship.

White-collar and professional workers were less likely to be made unemployed, but those who were also descended into poverty. In 1932 an investigation by the philanthropic Pilgrim Trust found that unemployed men who had had 'middle-class' jobs possessed more savings to draw on than a manual worker like Arthur Rigg. But they lacked the support of friends and former workmates that unemployed manual workers relied upon. A clerk or salesman tended to conceal 'the fact of being out of work from all his friends . . . and from his neighbours'. Such men feared that the stigma attached to unemployment would make it impossible for them to climb back into white-collar work. Without capital or connections, concluded the Pilgrim Trust, 'there is nothing save this last straw to which they cling, their respectability'. This understandably meant a great deal to men whose livelihood and status depended on being smarter in appearance and more prosperous than manual workers. But they also concealed their unemployment because they and their families had built such high hopes upon their salaried positions. One unemployed clerk concealed his state from his nine-year-old son, who was 'dreaming of the day when he goes to College!'[15]

The families of the unemployed also suffered the descent into hardship. By 1933 Arthur Rigg was receiving just three shillings a week – less than 5 per cent of the income a skilled manual worker might bring home. In districts where unemployment was high, so too were malnutrition and infant mortality.[16] Households headed by an unemployed man became poor very quickly – social surveys of cities as disparate as Bristol, Liverpool, London and York found that these families were least likely to afford suitable housing and sufficient food and clothes.[17]

The government's treatment of the unemployed exacerbated this. Before the 1930s unemployment insurance was the main recourse for the unemployed. In return for contributions from employers and workers, an unemployed man received 17s per week and a married couple 26s per week. This was less than a third of what a skilled male manual worker could bring home, but it was a great deal more generous than the provision made for uninsured workers (including many women workers in, for example, domestic service or shop work). They had to rely on unemployment benefit, and so too did the increasing numbers of long-term unemployed who had exhausted their claim to insurance. The 1922 Unemployment Act obliged claimants of unemployment benefit to submit to a means test, which in 1931 was extended to their entire household. Claimants had to submit to Poor Law officials visiting their homes to see if they were living above their means, or had anything saleable.[18] As Wal Hannington, secretary of the National Unemployed Workers' Movement (NUWM), pointed out, 'the charity approach' of the benefits system caused shame, demoralisation and depression for men who had prided themselves on their independence.[19]

Walter Brierley experienced this first hand. Born in 1900, he had been a miner before attending Nottingham University College on a trade union scholarship in 1929. He'd hoped to become a lecturer or journalist, but after the Wall Street Crash he couldn't find work, even back down the pit. In the early 1930s his wife bore the brunt of making ends meet and of trying to 'shield our son as much as possible from the bitterness and frustration of our position'.[20] But she could not completely hide her humiliation and despair. Their son, John, later recalled that 'I saw my mother cry bitterly once, because of the Means Test inquisition'. The marriage bar prevented Mrs Brierley, a trained teacher, from getting a secure job. The stigma of being an unemployed man's wife meant the local parish council refused to consider her for supply teaching. 'She was perhaps ashamed of our plight', thought her son, 'and depression sometimes made her keep to the house.'[21]

Many unemployed men tried to help themselves. Between 1918 and 1939, the proportion of self-employed people grew slightly, from 5 per cent to 6 per cent of the workforce, precisely because it 'was a frequent recourse for the unemployed'.[22] These figures don't capture the many people who started a small business only for it to close just a few months later. Before the war, mutual help – of the kind practised by many skilled manual workers – had funded trade unions, friendly societies, co-ops and the WEA. But individual self-help was not a practicable route out of poverty. For those with no savings or property, starting a business was hard and sustaining it even harder.[23] Competition from larger businesses and shops increased during and after the First World War. In London alone, the number of bankruptcies rose from 1,345 in 1923 to 1924 to 2,542 in 1934 to 1935. Small business proprietors and workers reliant on such enterprises composed an increasing majority of bankrupts – up to 86 per cent in the mid-1930s.[24]

Many of the unemployed fell permanently down the ladder. Those who lost a skilled job had little hope of finding a new one. A survey of more than 200 workers at a Tyneside shipyard conducted in the late 1960s revealed that those old enough to have experienced the 1930s Depression were most likely to have fallen out of skilled work. Harry Atkinson of Wallsend was among them. Born in 1910, he followed his father into the local shipyard as an apprentice boilermaker. But after completing his apprenticeship in 1931 Harry was dismissed. After several years on the dole, including a stint travelling the country to find work elsewhere, he was eventually hired as a shipyard labourer in the late 1930s – the 'only job available at the time'. He stayed in that line of work for the next thirty years. He'd have preferred to remain in his trade because it paid more, was 'inside work' and not as exhausting as labouring.[25]

Whether members of the precarious generation experienced upward or downward mobility depended on their families' circumstances, their ability to get an education, and, crucially, on where they grew up. There were huge regional disparities in the work available. In 1936 the unemployment rate stood at 32 per cent in Wales and 17 per cent in Scotland and north-west England. But just 5 per cent of workers in south-east England were unemployed. Here, new manufacturing industries producing consumer goods like wirelesses and tinned foodstuffs were expanding. The difference this made was evident in the employment prospects of teenage girls – the cheapest group of workers and therefore least likely to be unemployed. In 1931 office work was the largest employer of girls in London – but in Northumberland they most commonly found work as poorly paid servants.

Those born from 1910 were less vulnerable to unemployment than older workers. But the impact of recession affected them too. Social investigators revealed that between 20 and 30 per cent of manual-workers' families lived in poverty, and men's unemployment was often to blame.[26] Even in relatively affluent Bristol, during the economic recovery of the late 1930s, 7 per cent of households headed by a manual worker lacked the basic means of subsistence.[27] Children in these families had to leave school at the earliest opportunity and take whatever work they could get. 'Unemployment appears to call out the children to assist in supporting the family', concluded a study of Greenwich in south London.[28] Secondary education was increasingly important for those who wanted clerical or shop work, but the children of unemployed men were least likely to go to secondary school.[29]

Interwar governments encouraged the unemployed to migrate to where the work was. Geographic mobility was to make them upwardly mobile – or at least prevent them falling into poverty. In 1927, Stanley Baldwin's Conservative government introduced an official migration scheme, which placed unemployed men and women from north-east and north-west England, Scotland's industrial belt and South Wales in training programmes and jobs in the Midlands and south-east England. Between 1928 and 1938, 339,843 workers took part.[30]

The majority of these migrants were young men and women, not the older men who formed the core of the long-term unemployed. Employers in light manufacturing industries in south-east England demanded cheap workers with no trade union experience. While the government refused to countenance more generous benefits for the unemployed, these new manufacturers received considerable state help in the form of low business taxes and cheap land on which to situate their plants. Employers wanted to be close to London, and industrial estates sprang up on the edge of the capital and in south-east towns like Slough.[31] They kept costs low by paying wages that were inadequate for supporting a family. Many migrant workers were accommodated in government-provided hostels because they were unable to afford rent and food.[32] Emboldened by weak trade unions, employers increasingly categorised new jobs on production lines as 'unskilled' or 'semi-skilled', offering less pay than 'skilled' work. By 1951 Britain had a million more unskilled workers than in 1911, while the proportion of skilled workers fell from 31 to 25 per cent of the workforce.[33]

The government's anti-trade union laws, and their subsidy of new manufacturing employers' low wages, emboldened other employers to cut wages and erode working conditions. In this situation, welfare agencies placed the onus on young people to select their jobs wisely. 'It does not follow that a job is a good one because you are going to start at a high wage', warned Manchester's juvenile employment bureaux (labour exchanges), in a pamphlet aimed at school leavers. 'IT WILL PAY TO LOOK AHEAD AND BE CONTENT WITH A SMALL WAGE AT FIRST IF THE PROSPECTS ARE GOOD.'[34] But very few jobs offered 'good' prospects.

Nevertheless, young people – and especially young women – were receptive to such messages. Many of those from working-class families ardently wanted to climb the ladder. Escaping poverty was a widely shared dream among those who witnessed first-hand the effect of male death and invalidity in the First World War, and later of unemployment and low pay, upon their families.[35]

For women of the pioneer generation, school teaching had been the surest route up the social ladder. By 1914, it was women's largest professional employer, employing 202,076 of them compared with 76,680 men.[36] A sizeable minority of female teachers were from working-class families. Most learned on the job as pupil teachers.[37]

But for the precarious generation, teaching was neither so accessible nor desirable. After the First World War teachers were obliged to take a college diploma or a university degree. University students who pledged to teach for five years after graduation were eligible for a Board of Education bursary, and in the interwar years this became the most common route by which working-class men and women got a university degree.[38] But most working-class families could not afford the cost of higher education.[39] The largest group of female teachers, whether they trained at university or college, were the daughters of clerks and administrators, as had been true before the war; but whereas the daughters of manual workers had formerly been the second-largest group, they had been displaced by the daughters of professionals and businessmen.[40]

The rewards of a teaching career were also increasingly uncertain. Just as some politicians blamed women for men's unemployment after the First World War, so some male professionals argued that professional women prevented former servicemen from having a career. Male surgeons succeeded in excluding women from those London medical schools to which they had won entry by 1914.[41] A marriage bar for women was instituted in the Civil Service and teaching. By 1926 two-thirds of local education authorities had introduced a marriage bar for teachers – while women were dismissed from the police force.[42] The Sex Disqualification (Removal) Act, passed in 1919 to give women the legal right to enter all the professions, should have prevented these moves. But policymakers and the judiciary proved reluctant to enforce it.[43] Meanwhile, the 1918 Education Act increased demand for teachers by expanding the number of secondary-school places. But local education authorities responded by merging single-sex institutions into coeducational establishments, or establishing new coeducational schools. This obliged women to compete directly with men for posts. Many male teachers refused to work under women, and local authorities supported them. Between 1930 and 1937 women lost 894 school headships.[44] And in the straitened circumstances of the 1920s and 30s, female teachers from working-class backgrounds found that teaching did not offer the social and financial freedoms they might have hoped for. In the mid-1930s, a survey of more than 1,000 female secondary schoolteachers found that one-third of them regularly gave their parents financial help, a figure that rose to more than 60 per cent in north-east England where unemployment was particularly high.[45] Many, especially those who lived with their parents, complained 'that the life is too narrow and restricted for them, and that it does not give them varied enough social contacts'.[46]

Teaching remained graduate women's largest employer, as it would be until the end of the twentieth century. But working-class women were less likely to achieve upward mobility this way. Older teachers – members of the pioneer generation – cited sex discrimination as a reason for their choice of career, acknowledging that many professions were barred to them before 1914.[47] Those born since 1900 were aware that, in theory at least, they were legally entitled to enter any profession.[48] They were more likely to cite family hardship as an impediment. Many said 'the expense of training' for their preferred career pushed them into teaching; almost a quarter would have liked to have been doctors and others architects or scientists.[49]

Family hardship helps to explain why middle-class women experienced downward mobility during the interwar years. Measuring the social distance between a parent and a daughter is fraught with difficulty, because many women (especially in the middle class) did not work once they got married and became mothers. Because men's occupational choices were always different and broader than women's, women were always less likely than their fathers and brothers to enter the most lucrative professions. But it's clear that middle-class women of the precarious generation had fewer options than women slightly older than them. While their access to medical schools was reinstated in the 1930s, strict quotas for women were introduced, to ensure they remained a small minority of students. Very few women entered the law. And while the number of university students grew, the proportion who were women dropped from almost 30 per cent in the mid-1920s to 23 per cent in the mid-1930s. A daughter's higher education could feel like a luxury too far for middle-class fathers who were made unemployed, or feared the effect that the Depression would have on their business or industry.[50]

The nursing profession was open to women without a degree. Nursing had not been a profession before 1918. After the war, nursing leaders capitalised on the crucial role nurses had played in the conflict by pushing for the occupation to become a profession, with central-ised regulation of recruitment and training. They were successful: in 1919 the Royal College of Nursing (RCN) and the General Nursing Council (GNC) were established. But many nursing leaders believed that raising the status of nursing also depended on recruiting middle-class women. The new scheme required applicants to be 'educated' and of 'of good character'.[51] Many senior nurses were open about the fact that this meant recruits from middle-class families. In 1920 the matron of a large London hospital declared that nursing should be 'the profession of women of education, of good social standing to enter.'[52] In the 1930s, despite an ongoing shortage of recruits, the RCN advised the government that 'the payment of high salaries to student nurses is not recommended, as it is believed that this does not tend to attract the most suitable type of candidate'.[53]

As a result, middle-class girls found it easier to enter nursing than their working-class peers. When sixteen-year-old Freda Knowles, the oldest girl in a middle-class family of four, decided to train as a nurse in 1928, the hospital of her choice invited her to send 'references' and evidence of 'my ability to learn'. This was no problem for Freda: 'the doctor and minister were approached and proved happy to vouch for me', and their reports, together with her School Certificate, won her a place as probationer nurse.[54] But she was unusual. Many middle-class girls, and their parents, were horrified at the long hours, dirty work and poor pay. To them, the occupation felt like a step down the ladder, and throughout the 1930s the RCN complained at their inability to recruit the 'right' type of nurse.[55]

By contrast, Edith Hall, born into a working-class home in 1909, found nursing both more attractive and more difficult to enter. After many rejections, 'I realised that there was little chance of my becom-ing a probationer if I kept revealing that I had been a factory girl and a housemaid'. Edith attended evening classes and, in 1929, assisted by a 'glowing reference' from her WEA tutor, she rewrote her application letter. This time she gave 'no information as to any previous employ-ment except to say that my parents didn't believe in young women going out to work with the exception of nursing . . . With this white lie I obtained the first post I then applied for.'[56] But examination fees and the cost of uniform and breakages dissuaded working-class recruits from staying the course. Edith Hall reluctantly left her job after less than a year. She became a poorly paid hospital orderly: a step down the ladder from her parents' secure factory jobs.[57]

In these circumstances, white-collar work became a more realistic route for both working- and middle-class women than a professional career. As successful manufacturers' businesses grew, they required more clerical workers to deal with paperwork. In more prosperous towns and cities, chain stores and department stores proliferated to sell the furniture and fashions that the manufacturers were producing. Meanwhile, many local council bureaucracies grew in size, first to deal with the increase in council housing and secondary-school places legislated for in the immediate post-war years, and then, in the 1930s, to provide better social welfare, leisure and recreation. These developments offered young women with some secondary education new jobs that paid more than factory work or the hated domestic service, as clerks, library assistants, and shop workers. Smart, clean work in venues that appealed to a middle-class clientele were particularly popular. 'I like my work because it brings me into contact with a different class', one shop assistant told a social investigator.[58] For this generation, employment, contacts, appearance and accent were all important in the struggle to climb the ladder. Fashion and permanent waves allowed them to escape the confines of their background, fleetingly at least. 'It is hard to say what class people are in today', observed the manager of a Liverpool dance hall in 1939; he was describing his predominantly young, female clientele, who 'work at Littlewoods, Vernons and Ogdens Pools' as clerks and typists.[59] By 1939, clerical work was women's chief employer in large cities like Manchester and London.

But young women themselves quickly came to believe that clerical work alone would not take them into a different social class.[60] The erroneous justification that women were only out to earn 'pin money' allowed employers to pay them low wages, usually with the trade unions' approval; it was rare for women to earn more than 70 per cent of a man's salary in clerical and professional posts.[61] And there were very few clerical jobs that offered women progression to senior roles.

This was particularly true for women born in the 1910s. The majority of the downwardly mobile women in the precarious generation were born in that decade. They grew up as secondary and university education were expanding and often had high ambitions focused on educational achievement. But they came of age during periods of high unemployment, and family hardship was more likely to curtail their education than that of women born just a few years earlier.

The contrast is evident among those women who worked at one of the newest and most exciting ventures in interwar Britain. The British Broadcasting Corporation was founded in 1922. In 1928, the BBC featured in *Women's Work in Modern England*, a careers manual authored by the feminist Vera Brittain, born in 1893 to a successful, upwardly mobile businessman and his wife. Brittain had had an Oxford education and by 1928 was making her living as a writer and journalist in London. Her book advised younger women to seek out new jobs and fields where they could establish a career free of the male hierarchies that dogged older professions. 'Where no traditions and few precedents have been established, the energy which is too often spent in combating prejudice in the ancient fields may be applied directly to the work on hand', she concluded.[62]

In the 1920s, the BBC bore out Vera Brittain's argument. John Reith, the BBC's first Director General, had hoped to recruit his creative staff and managers from the upper-middle-class, Oxbridge-educated men that the established professions had long relied upon. But men who could take up lucrative and prestigious careers in the law, medicine or the Civil Service considered the BBC a risky proposition. Reith had to look elsewhere, and this gave a chance to numerous middle-class female graduates who used their qualifications and, sometimes, their family connections to secure posts at the BBC. Mary Somerville was recruited while studying at Oxford University in 1924;

she became an assistant to the BBC's Director of Education. Isa Benzie, who had studied German at Oxford, entered the BBC's new Foreign Department in 1927 as a secretary, with the help of her father, an old friend of Reith's. She was promoted to Foreign Director in 1933. In 1930, Janet Quigley, another Oxford graduate, joined Isa in the Foreign Department. She went on to produce *Woman's Hour* after the Second World War.[63]

But by the mid-1930s, the routes that these women had carved out for themselves were closing. As the BBC became an attractive workplace for highly educated men, Reith introduced a marriage bar, which effectively consigned most women to junior roles. Slightly younger women faced a more uncertain future at the Corporation. Among them was Fiona Markham. Born into a 'lower-middle-class' family in 1912, Markham attended a state secondary school before winning a scholarship to Oxford University. While women like Isa Benzie accrued glowing testimonials from their tutors and sporting and social positions, Fiona Markham found the elite environment challenging to her sense of her family's social status. 'From thinking we were immensely superior, I became convinced we were immeasurably inferior', she recalled. 'I was miserable and offensive at home, and, because I had no social experience and not much money, uneasy in my Oxford life'. She became so ill that she had to give up her studies for a time.[64]

When Fiona Markham graduated in 1934, she joined the BBC. She aspired to join the older, more senior women like Isa Benzie. 'I get thoroughly tired of clothes-talk, which takes up most of the time of the secretarial staff', she wrote in 1939. 'The [professional women's] more interesting jobs and wider interests prevent them from having as much time for it'; and Fiona wanted those 'interesting jobs' and 'wider interests'.[65] But it was hard for women to graduate from clerical posts to senior positions at a time when male competition for prestigious posts at the Corporation was growing. By 1939, Fiona Markham relished the independence that her job gave her, but felt that 'I'm not sufficiently established in my job to call myself a "professional woman".[66]

In sociological terms, Fiona Markham, as a clerical worker, had remained in the lower-middle-class. But many daughters of professional men and businessmen also found clerking was the only work open to them in the 1930s, and this helps to explain why one-third of this generation of women experienced downward mobility.[67] These young women were frustrated and disappointed to find that despite having the vote and more education than their mothers, they were unable to achieve financial independence. Fiona Markham measured her trajectory against her male peers: 'I'd earn more if I was a man'.[68] She found her situation wanting.

In the 1930s, a handful of unemployed men – Walter Brierley among them – were able to achieve upward mobility. Aspiring writers had the time to pick up their pen. They were encouraged to do so by a left-wing movement that championed working-class writing, emanating from the Communist Party of Great Britain (CPGB) but not confined to it. In the 1930s, many socialists and communists set out to wage war on fascism culturally as well as politically, by drawing attention to the common experiences of workers under capitalism and offering co-operative and socialist alternatives, an approach which had its roots in those pre-1914 attempts to create a socialist press, co-operative workplaces and educational opportunities.

In the early 1930s, Victor Gollancz's eponymous publishing house and the left-leaning *Adelphi* magazine were among the best-known outlets for working-class writers, though not the only ones. Walter Greenwood was an intermittently employed clerk, warehouseman and salesman before finding fame with his novel *Love on the Dole* in 1933. This appealed to the reading public's growing interest in unemployment, and the *Times Literary Supplement* praised it as a valuable but rare 'social document'.[69] Jack Hilton, an unemployed plasterer from Oldham, joined the NUWM and the WEA in the early 1930s, receiving encouragement from both to publish a series of essays in the *Adelphi*. He later published a novel and travelogue. In 1933, Walter Brierley himself responded to a call by the *Listener* magazine for the unemployed to write about their experiences. His piece appealed to the successful novelist John Hampson. The son of a bankrupt businessman, Hampson sympathised with Brierley's tale of coming down in the world; Walter Brierley's son, John, said that Hampson 'put father's feet on the literary ladder'.[70] Hampson helped to find a publisher for Brierley's autobiographical novel *Means Test Man*, which sold well when it appeared in 1935.

Only rarely could a man write his way out of poverty. Even the few who had a breakthrough found it an insecure and poorly paid trade – many successful writers had a prosperous family to fall back on. Walter Greenwood's future was secured because he married a wealthy American actress, Pearl Osgood; Walter Brierley had to rely on his wife to make ends meet: by 1935 she was working as a dressmaker.

What made a permanent difference to Walter Brierley's life was not his brush with literary fame, but state investment in jobs. In 1936 he was appointed to a new role as welfare officer for Derbyshire local education authority. Posts like his were beginning to appear in numerous municipal councils seeking to alleviate the impact of unemployment and poverty. For a small group of men and women, they also provided a route out of unemployment. Walter Brierley was able to join the ranks of a new kind of white-collar worker, concerned with planning and administering the welfare of newly enfranchised citizens. His own experiences – especially his regret that poverty had cost him an education – found a new form of expression. 'At the highest official level he could achieve', recalled his son, 'he tried to stop a downwards spiral for an individual child.'[71]

Walter Brierley's experience demonstrated that it was not individual ambition or self-help, but state investment and strategy that determined a person's mobility or lack of it. By the end of the 1930s, this miner's son was upwardly mobile. But for many of his generation unemployment ended any hope of climbing the ladder. Robbed of their economic independence, collective power, and ability to plan their own and their children's futures, they testified that unemployment cast a long shadow.

While long-term unemployment primarily affected male manual workers, women's prospects were also gravely affected by the economic crisis. Those whose parents experienced poverty and unemployment were less likely to get an education. And even those who began life higher up the social ladder found their opportunities constrained. The policies designed to combat male unemployment often targeted women. This lent support to those men who preferred to restrict opportunities to their own sex.

By the 1930s, the pioneers' dream that miners and steelworkers would use their education and experience to play a greater role in the running of industry and the country was crushed. The precarious generation could no longer aspire to skilled manual work and the independence it had offered. Leaving manual work looked like the only route to financial security. The impetus to climb the ladder was greater than ever.

Chapter Four

THE TECHNOCRATS

The lives of those born between 1900 and 1919 were shaped by the vote. Ten years after the Representation of the People Act in 1918 enfranchised all adult men and some women, women won the vote on the same terms as men. The era of mass democracy had arrived.

This provoked new concerns about an assertive working class. The fear of downward mobility that plagued some clerks after the First World War helps to explain why the Conservatives won the general election of 1922. The 'new poor's' desire for lower public spending on the working class provided a point of agreement with many wealthier voters who wanted low taxation and no regulation of business. They included the press baron Lord Rothermere, proprietor of the *Daily Mirror*, who established the Anti-Waste League. Pressure from the League encouraged the new Conservative government to cut public spending, including axing the post-war coalition's commitment to increasing council housing and reducing secondary-school scholarships. Anxiety about organised labour, and the Conservatives' success in presenting socialism as a 'foreign' import from communist Russia, helps to explain why they held power for most of the interwar years.[1]

This anxiety was evident among the 'new poor', and even more so among the aristocracy and the grandees of the Tory Party. Aristocrats and big businessmen benefited from relatively low taxes after the war, and aristocrats remained among the wealthiest 5 per cent of the population. Businessmen, financiers and large landowners continued to exert great power both in politics, via the Conservative Party, and in the business world.[2] But they increasingly greeted the aspirations to upward mobility expressed by those lower down the ladder with contempt and suspicion. In 1925 the Conservative minister of education, Lord Percy, declared publicly that 'the worship of the scholarship boy was the great curse of education' which encouraged 'everyone to use the school as an escape from his normal job' – an attack he directed at white-collar workers' children as well as those of manual workers.[3]

The rise of the labour movement, the ambitions of the expanding army of clerks and teachers, and the power of fascism and communism in continental Europe caused those at the top of the ladder to fear for the future. Diana Athill was born into a 'gentry' family who owned a small agricultural estate in Norfolk, in 1917. In her teens she perceived that her grandparents' confidence in the survival of their way of life was faltering. Her grandmother was beset with 'anxiety' that was, Athill judged, 'an acknowledgement of the forces threatening their position . . . Wars and rumours of war; communists abroad and socialists at home . . . falling respect for tradition. She, a conservative, a gentlewoman, a devout Protestant Christian and an owner of property, was automatically on the defensive against powers outside her control.'[4]

The precarious generation took little notice of those who declared they should know their place and stay there. Many were encouraged by their parents to work hard to get out of the insecurity into which they were born or grew up. Even the more conservative sections of the lower middle class were unwilling to accept that their children should defer to the social orthodoxy and remain content with their lowly rung on the ladder. As the 'new poor' epithet suggested, they often saw themselves as downwardly mobile, and taught their children that it was their duty to ascend to their rightful place on the social ladder.

Those who could do so grasped new chances to enter technical and welfare work. Enterprises like ICI, established in 1926, demanded industrial chemists and technicians. In the same year, Labour began to win control of an increasing number of local authorities, including the West Riding of Yorkshire – Britain's largest municipality. These authorities created new jobs aimed at helping the poor and the unemployed. Those who managed to get a secondary-school education were well placed to become the planners and technicians these councils needed.

*

In 1934, Labour won control of London County Council (LCC), promising 'clean, efficient, progressive and public-spirited local government'.[5] The leader of the LCC was Herbert Morrison. The First World War had ended his days as a clerk. As a conscientious objector, Morrison spent the war working as a gardener and involving himself in Labour Party politics. Afterwards he devoted himself to campaigning for Labour in London, surviving on freelance journalism. In 1919, Labour increased its number of council seats in London from forty-five to an astonishing 550. Morrison was given much of the credit. In 1920 he became mayor of Labour-controlled Brixton, and in 1923 was elected to parliament as a Labour MP.

Like many prominent Labour politicians, Morrison shifted to the right in the 1920s in response to mass unemployment and the General Strike. As transport minister in Ramsay MacDonald's government of 1929, he established London Transport, but refused to allow trade union representatives on to the board, arguing that it must be run 'exclusively by men of a business turn of mind'.[6] Morrison no longer believed that economic inequality could or should be overcome. He was convinced that Labour must focus on solving the social problems that inequality caused. His version of social democracy was a top-down one in which scientists, surveyors, engineers, technicians, welfare workers and teachers planned and delivered a better life for the common people.

In the years between 1934 and 1939, London County Council improved the capital's schools and hospitals, opened neighbourhood health centres, built spacious housing estates, created the green belt, and established swimming pools and sports grounds. Morrison attributed the LCC's success to 'the useful classes': those with a secondary or higher education who had administrative or technical expertise.[7]

By the mid-1930s, Morrison's 'useful classes' were to be found across the public and private sectors. Often in their twenties or early thirties, many came from lower-middle-class families who had been able to afford to keep them at school until sixteen or eighteen. They shared Morrison's conviction that scientific, social scientific and technical expertise were the foundations on which modern social democracy must be built. Some were teachers, while others found work with local authorities keen on scientific and social planning. More still were engineers, draughtsmen and industrial scientists.

*

In 1939, Mass Observation – the social research organisation established in 1936 – appealed for respondents to a survey about social class.[8] This attracted many of the upwardly mobile who were making sense of their journey up the ladder and of their new social position.[9] Conspicuous among the hundreds of respondents were educated members of the precarious generation; most had attended secondary school and some were graduates. These Mass Observers defined themselves as the 'educated middle class' or, in the words of participant Bill Ramsgate, 'the technologically educated class'.[10] Bill, a twenty-four-year-old analytic chemist, was the son of a small businessman.[11] Others included Philip Jennings, an engineering draughtsman born to a small-business owner in Yorkshire in 1907. Peter Kemp, a teacher, was born in Scotland in 1914. His father had been a grocer but died shortly after Peter's birth, and Peter's widowed mother took on a variety of jobs to make ends meet. Hazel Royd, born in Kent in 1910, was also the child of a shopkeeper. She had left secondary school aged sixteen to work for a gas company. As a 'demonstrator', Hazel was responsible for selling new kitchen appliances like gas cookers, and helping customers to use them once they were installed.

This group shared a powerful sense of their entitlement to an easier life than their parents had known. They were very clear that they wanted to ascend the ladder into the middle class. Many believed that in doing so they would restore their family's rightful social position. They had grown up being told that their families were downwardly mobile. Bill Ramsgate believed that his grandfather 'came of [sic] one of the chief families of a small provincial town' but 'his early demise and lazy habits' led Bill's grandmother to 'descend into the lower classes with a wallop' when her husband died.[12] Philip Jennings was brought up on similar stories. He considered the lower middle class to be defined by downward mobility: 'The class I belong to ... might be more well off but for bad luck.'[13] This was not of course the case. Many clerks and teachers hailed from working-class homes. But parents, especially mothers, told their children stories that focused on the few relations who had 'done well for themselves', in family lore if not in reality. In the precarious 1920s and 30s, a period when the Conservatives still championed heredity as the determinant of career and social position, this was a means by which the 'new poor' could claim a higher status for themselves. It also allowed mothers like Ann Hodges and Nella Last to register their own discontent at the way life had treated them.

Education was the precarious generation's best means of climbing the ladder. But getting to secondary school remained a struggle for the children of manual workers. Against the labour movement's calls for equality of opportunity, the political right argued that family background *should* determine people's prospects. In 1931, the National Government decreed that further public-spending cuts were required to solve the economic crisis. Investment in secondary schools was among the cuts, and the number of free places was reduced. Instead, a sliding scale of means-tested fees was introduced. The government justified this by arguing that 'the standard of education, elementary and secondary, that is being given to the child of poor parents is already in very many cases superior to that which the middle-class parent is providing for his own child'.[14]

Many Conservative-controlled councils prevented working-class children from taking up secondary-school scholarships. In the 1930s, one-third of scholarship holders in Middlesex – a Tory council – were not awarded a place at secondary school. The education committee encouraged those who lived on council estates to accept places at 'central' schools – a new hybrid establishment which did not offer academic qualifications.[15] Fewer than 14 per cent of secondary-school pupils came from elementary schools in the 1930s.[16] In Conservative strongholds like Hertfordshire, fewer than 8 per cent of elementary-school children were admitted to secondary schools.[17]

The fears of the 'new poor' that working-class children would usurp their children's secondary-school places was unfounded. The expansion in secondary-school places disproportionately benefited the children of clerks, shopkeepers and small businessmen. They were well represented among the Mass Observers. Once at secondary school, they focused on science or technical subjects. Unlike private schools, state secondaries rarely offered an education based exclusively on classics and the humanities. Instead they emphasised science and technology for boys and teaching for girls. In the words of the educational historian Brian Simon, 'higher, truly educational, concerns belonged only to schools which had no such vulgar connection with occupation'.[18]

The question of where education would lead was made more urgent by economic depression. As one WEA student observed in the mid-1930s, 'the emotion of fear, intensified since the peak of prosperous capitalism has been passed, accounts for the diversion of education into the channels where it will serve best to get a living. Children are given the idea that it is only through the perspicacity, vision, or acumen of their parents or guardians that they are going to be allowed to survive at all . . . Mothers whose husbands were painters or bricklayers want their sons to be bank clerks, or accountants . . . they don't want their children to go through the hardship that they went through!'[19]

An increasing number of secondary-school leavers found jobs related to science and technology, while others went into administrative work. The Mass Observers were acutely aware that the social status of their work was ambiguous. They were not professionals, but neither were they manual workers. Hazel Royd was keen that her job was not conflated either with domestic service or with shop work, though it had similarities to both. On visiting customers' homes she experienced 'annoyance . . . on not being received by the lady of the house, but being conducted by the maid straight to the kitchen. This type of embarrassment seems to belong to my work.'[20] Philip Jennings, an engineering draughtsman, lived on a private estate in suburban Surrey. 'As an educated individual I am as good as any in this neighbourhood', he wrote, 'but there is no doubt my salary is less than most householders here.'[21]

A few of the Mass Observers had got to university. Most students who were the children of clerks, teachers, shopkeepers or small businesspeople relied heavily on parental help to get through. Mothers were often particularly influential; women like Ann Hodges and Nella Last focused their own thwarted ambitions on their children. By 1939, Ann's daughter Marjorie was sixteen. She had had a secondary-school education and looked forward to training as a teacher; her mother was determined to support her. '[S]he is ambitious like me', Ann Hodges reported, distancing herself and Marjorie from Ann's unambitious husband, a clerk.[22] Many women whose children got to university took in lodgers, others worked as dressmakers or charladies, while still more begged and borrowed from their extended family.[23] Peter Kemp owed his education to 'my mother's efforts and . . . a small legacy she received'.[24]

The need to make education pay could narrow upwardly mobile students' ambitions and cloud their enjoyment of studying for its own sake. Parents' sacrifices often weighed heavily on the recipients' minds. The National Union of Students found that anxiety about getting a good degree and a job was heightened by 'economic and political insecurity'.[25]

These students' worries were exacerbated by the snobbery some of them encountered at university. The only 'class of people . . . I cannot feel at ease with [are] people of the upper-middle and aristocratic classes', wrote Peter Kemp. At university, 'the aristocrats never spoke to us (by [us] I mean the scholarship students of whom I was one). They had their own sports, cliques, amusements, tables in dining room.'[26]

The Mass Observers' hostility was underpinned by an awareness of these wealthy, well-connected students' advantages. The exclusive 'cliques' that Peter Kemp resented were powerful networks that helped their members enter the most lucrative professions. By contrast, the vast majority of graduates from working- and lower-middle-class backgrounds became teachers, industrial managers or engineers.[27] Class background still made a difference, even to those with a higher education. Many of this group shared Philip Jennings' opposition to 'the old school tie idea of an elite class who are to be themselves regardless of ability'.[28]

Very often these children of shopkeepers and clerks were keen to securely ensconce themselves in the middle class. By stressing their middle-class identity this group consciously set themselves apart from the working class. Most described themselves as left wing, and many were incensed at the plight of the unemployed (some, like Philip Jennings, undertook voluntary social work). Yet they did not believe manual workers were able to provide any leadership or vision for a socialist future. Peter Kemp was typical in describing his set as 'people of education and intelligence', distinguished from 'the very low, ignorant, poverty-stricken classes – labourers etc.'[29]

But they did not want to become part of the established middle or upper classes. They saw themselves as a new group, defined by their social conscience and their education as much as by their work. Hazel Royd considered herself 'middle class' primarily because 'my father is a shopkeeper'. But in common with many of her peers, she also attributed her middle-class status to her education. 'I attended secondary school – the first in my family to do so', she wrote.[30] Philip Jennings considered himself of a superior class to his 'lower-middle-class' parents because 'I am less snobbish and more highly educated'.[31] Many shared Bill Ramsgate's contempt for the social anxieties of parents or lower-middle-class neighbours, and for their preoccupation with material comforts and 'respectability'.[32]

They disagreed with the stress placed on 'accent', etiquette and family background by the established middle class (although many did set great store by their own families' stories of downward mobility). They shared a pride in their own rationality, derived from their training in science or social science. Most agreed with Bill Ramsgate that theirs was an 'emotionally and intellectually detached class', motivated by analysis of facts, not by sentiment or tradition.[33] This set them apart both from the uneducated working class and from the 'hunting, fishing and shooting brigade', as Philip Jennings called them.[34]

They had very definite views on education. Many of their parents had identified as the 'new poor' and opposed the expansion of state welfare and free education for working-class children. But their sons and daughters thought differently. For many of them, winning a secondary-school scholarship at eleven was a proud achievement, and they regarded their careers as the result of their own intelligence. Their encounters with upper-middle-class and upper-class students or employers reinforced their belief that family background should bring no favours. Some wanted private schools to be abolished. Most were educating their own children at ordinary secondary schools or said they would do so if they became parents. They agreed with Hazel Royd that 'the education is better' at secondary schools and that 'if all children had the same kind of education the "class war" would cease'.[35]

Many of this group had witnessed poverty. Some encountered this at work, as teachers in state schools, welfare workers or as clerks in council offices dealing with those in need of housing or unemployment benefit. Others were youth club leaders or welfare workers in their spare time. Many joined the Labour Party.[36] They saw widening access to secondary education as the way to achieve what Philip Jennings called 'a great levelling up of the classes'.[37] But they did not envisage the kind of socialist, egalitarian future that some of the pioneers had hoped for. Instead, they wanted a meritocracy – one that offered a special role to the educated middle class.

Many of these young technocrats stressed the need for social harmony, rather than a wholesale redistribution of wealth and power. They distanced themselves from both the punitive treatment of the unemployed and from the militant trade unionism that had followed the First World War. The lack of understanding between the social classes often aggrieved them more than the inequalities that underpinned this. 'It was remarkable how the [social] classes kept apart,' Peter Kemp remarked of his university days.[38] Like his peers he thought education should encourage people to mix, not reinforce social segregation. Hazel Royd explained that 'I sometimes feel embarrassment when I have to interview maid and mistress together . . . due to the difficulty of deciding whom to address, and how far a friendly attitude towards the maid will antagonise the mistress (I have experienced this).'[39] Like many of the Mass Observers, Hazel believed she was well equipped to diffuse class tensions because of her education and her willingness to judge people on merit, rather than according to their family background. And in common with her peers, she presented her job as invaluable in this regard by replacing outdated social hierarchies – such as the relationship between mistresses and maids – with a more democratic order, shaped by technology and science.

Many placed their faith in social science to eradicate unemployment and poverty, and ease social tensions. Most read psychology and sociology for pleasure. They were not alone: by the 1930s, economics, civics and sociology were among the WEA's most popular subjects.[40] Many of them would have known about the psychologist Alfred Adler's bestselling book *What Life Should Mean to You*. In this book, published in 1931, Adler coined the phrase 'inferiority complex'. 'Behind everyone who behaves as if he were superior to others, we can suspect a feeling of inferiority which calls for very special efforts of concealment', he wrote. 'The greater the feeling of inferiority, the more powerful is the urge to conquest and the more violent the emotional agitation'.[41] It was no accident that this book appeared, and became highly popular, in the middle of a grave economic crisis. Adler proposed that people who lived in highly unequal societies were more likely to suffer inferiority complexes than those in more equal societies, because the social gradations were so numerous and so significant. Many of the Mass Observers were open about the emotional and psychological stress they experienced as they sought to climb the social ladder. Bill Ramsgate spoke for many when he wrote that 'I am not at ease with rich people, even if they are quite friendly; I definitely feel inferior, although I despise myself for this attitude.'[42] Many acknowledged they were 'sensitive on the subject of accent'.[43]

The aspirations of these Mass Observers were more widely shared. A survey of WEA students found that by the 1930s, most had 'a motive already tinctured with vocational ambitions'. Many wanted a political career. 'I saw in my trade union well-meaning men hampered by their inability to marshal their thoughts', said one student. 'I felt that some day I might be called to leadership. I wished to fit myself for it.' Another had more specific goals: 'obtaining a better job as a result of a course at Ruskin College . . . becoming a Labour Agent, perhaps an MP'. This student wanted, he said candidly, 'to use my class as a stepping stone'. Others wished to enter the Civil Service or local government.[44] Many shared a confidence that educated people could make Britain a fairer place, through social, economic and political planning.

Some were more radical. Bill Ramsgate wanted a social revolution. But even he thought that 'no matter how numerous or well organised the working class is, in the modern world it can do little or nothing to influence government policy *by itself*, without the support of the technologists.' He cited the Spanish Civil War, where despite immense popular support, socialist and anarchist Republicans had recently been defeated by 'German and Italian technical materiel'.[45]

In 1939, some of this group were beginning to believe that they might achieve their ambitions. The international outlook was bleak – defeat in Spain and Prime Minister Neville Chamberlain's appeasement of Hitler both suggested fascism was inexorably on the rise. Yet at home the expansion of state welfare and technical work offered hope. And much as they disliked the thought of war, the prospect of attacking fascism provided scope for enacting their vision for society. The 'technologically educated class', thought Bill Ramsgate, 'has more opportunities for power than any other class in the modern world . . . just imagine what a revolutionary international composed of chemists and engineers could accomplish if war came about'.[46] They did not have long to wait.

PART III

THE BREAKTHROUGH GENERATION 1920-1934

Chapter Five

THE MERITOCRATIC WAR

In October 1940, as Britain's cities bore the brunt of the Blitz, Ernest Bevin – now Minister of Labour and National Service – set out his plan for victory. 'Individualism is bound to give place to social action, competition and scramble to order', he told a meeting of trade unionists. 'The individual worker has to be evaluated on a new basis. Skill, ability and energy become the great vital forces for success. Thus will we defeat Hitler.'[1] Hereditary privilege was dead; merit was now all-important.

Bevin was right to predict that this would be a meritocratic war. The dire need for labour, especially in technical jobs, meant that the military and the war industries had to recruit and train men – and to a lesser extent, women – who would never otherwise have got the chance. The war also broadened many people's horizons and provided new educational opportunities, especially for those in the forces.

While several generations benefited from this, those born in the 1920s and the early 30s – the breakthrough generation – were best placed to make the most of new opportunities in education, training, skilled and technical work in the forces and on the home front. Back in 1859 Samuel Smiles had declared that upward mobility relied on the state keeping out of welfare and industrial life. The breakthrough generation proved him wrong. Almost 40 per cent of men and 30 per cent of women were upwardly mobile.

They were not just more likely to climb the ladder than their parents or grandparents, but to climb higher. Most of the upwardly mobile members of the breakthrough generation were the children of manual workers, and the majority of them moved into white-collar work. Some travelled further up the ladder. By the time they had been in work for a decade, more than 10 per cent of manual workers' children and about a quarter of the sons and daughters of clerks were professionals or managers. In 1931, 5 per cent of the workforce were employed in professional jobs and 4 per cent as managers and administrators. By 1951 professionals accounted for 7 per cent of the workforce and managers and administrators for 6 per cent. This increase continued during the 1950s and 60s – by 1971 11 per cent of workers were professionals and 8 per cent were managers or administrators.

*

In September 1939, many of this generation feared that war would dash their hopes of climbing the ladder. The youngest, those still at school or college, had their education curtailed or disrupted. By January 1940 735,000 children had been evacuated from areas deemed vulnerable to invasion or bombing. Few went to wealthy homes – upper-class and upper-middle-class families were unwilling to host evacuees – but some did experience a different kind of life that had enduring consequences.[2] Walter Garnett, the son of a bus driver, was evacuated from Essex to a farming family in Cumbria. He quickly 'developed ideas of a career' in agriculture, an aspiration that his hosts encouraged. When Walter returned home in 1945 he infected his father with his enthusiasm. The family moved to Kent to run a smallholding and later a shop.[3]

But far more children missed opportunities. Ten-year-old Alec Turner from Dagenham was evacuated to Lowestoft and then to Halesworth, where he lived happily enough with a police officer's family. But like thousands of other children his schooling was badly affected – the evacuees were taught in wooden huts and had to share teachers with the village children, which meant schooling in shifts: 'country walks were frequent'. The government gave no extra funding to schools in the reception areas, and made no plans for the allocation of school places. In April 1940 Alec sat the secondary-school scholar- ship exam, but 'great confusion followed as the evacuees took the Essex paper with the local children taking the Suffolk paper – and shortly after the Dagenham children left Halesworth . . . it was eventu- ally revealed to my parents that the exam papers I had taken had been lost. It was highly probable that I would have failed, as there had been a substantial loss of academic work over the previous eight months.' Alec missed out on a secondary-school place.[4]

Slightly older men feared that their chance of professional train- ing would disappear forever. Albert Halsey, the son of a railway signal- man, was a sixteen-year-old scholarship boy at Kettering Grammar School when war broke out. Knowing that his parents could not afford to send him to university, he had set his sights on the annual entrance examination for the Civil Service, due to be held in January 1940. But in September 1939, 'these exams were cancelled because of the war' and his hopes 'collapsed'. Like other boys of his age, Albert Halsey had to find 'a job of some sort' while waiting for his eighteenth birthday when he would be conscripted into the armed services. He became a sanitary-inspector's boy – 'the dull fact is that it was either that or employment as a sorting clerk at the Post Office'. Albert kicked his heels, counting the days until he was called up in 1941.[5]

The men who were conscripted or volunteered in the first three years of the war found that none of the armed forces offered much to ordinary recruits. The military was intensely hierarchical and con- servative. 'The Navy is the most respected of the services, the RAF the most admired', found Mass Observation in 1941.[6] Their status depended on longevity and social elitism: the centuries-old navy, with its tradition of aristocratic officers, was more established than the RAF, founded at the end of the First World War. But equity also affected perceptions of the forces: while the navy and the RAF were thought to offer training and promotion, the army was considered to be more hierarchical and less fair. 'The soldier's status compares most unfavourably with that of the man in the navy or RAF, who on the average is treated much more as a human being with a modicum of intellect', reported a government informer in the Black Watch regiment. 'Also, in the latter two Services, there appears to be . . . more opportunities for promotion by merit rather than favour.'[7] This hierarchy was mirrored in the women's auxiliary services: the Women's Royal Naval Service (WRNS), the Women's Auxiliary Air Force (WAAF) and the Auxiliary Territorial Service (ATS), which was the largest and least popular.

Officers were drawn from the public schools and Oxbridge.[8] In 1938, twenty-two-year-old J. C. Banks, realising war was on the horizon, enlisted in the army. The son of a small businessman, Banks had taken a degree in economics and worked as a WEA tutor in Kent. He hoped that his qualifications and experience might get him a commission, but '[t]he CO [commanding officer] asked: "Public school?" "No, grammar school but also London University." "Doesn't count," he said, "Must be public school." So I became Gunner Banks.'[9] Little had changed by 1941 when Albert Halsey turned eighteen and joined the RAF. His training camp was 'like a boarding school' with officers 'who had or faked public-school accents'.[10]

Professional men and their sons were far less affected by the outbreak of war. Mass Observers found that they were fairly sanguine about their futures. A trainee solicitor said that he and his friends, mostly 'students who eventually hope to go in for one of the professions – law, accountancy, medicine – assume that the status quo or something very much like it will be restored after the war'.[11]

They were right not to worry. During the war, upwardly mobile men and women benefited from an expansion in opportunity – they did not knock large numbers of privileged people off their perch. The relative likelihood of people from different classes ending up in white-collar, managerial or professional positions did not change. In other words, a boy from a middle-class family remained far more likely to end up in a managerial or professional job than a manual-worker's son.

Social background counted in the civilian workforce as well as the armed forces. In September 1939 the government introduced conscription for able-bodied men aged between eighteen and forty-five, and the law required that those unable to serve in the military report to their local labour exchange to be directed into necessary work. But 'educated and professional' men were relieved of this obligation.[12] They were permitted to sign up to a Central Register, noting where their services might be most useful. Government intelligence and the new, top-secret codebreaking centre at Bletchley Park immediately began to recruit from Britain's elite universities – the playgrounds of the upper and upper-middle classes. 'Young men with first-class brains are wanted', wrote one civil servant of Bletchley Park. 'I should imagine that the men required would all be available from Oxford or Cambridge.'[13]

But by the summer of 1940 the political landscape was shifting. In May the ignominious retreat of Britain's troops from Dunkirk emphasised the need for better military leaders, better equipment and better organisation of the war effort – at home and abroad. Britain now stood alone against the Nazi threat, and the urgent need for munitions and tanks meant drastically increasing productivity. In June, the escalating threat of invasion led to the collapse of Chamberlain's government and its replacement by a coalition led by Winston Churchill. His Cabinet included several Labour ministers. Clement Attlee, Labour's leader, became deputy prime minister. Ernest Bevin, who by 1939 was general secretary of Britain's largest trade union, the Transport and General Workers' Union (TGWU), became Minister of Labour, taking charge of productivity and employment. Herbert Morrison became Home Secretary.

These senior Labour politicians shared a vision of social democracy. It owed less to the popular participation and egalitarianism espoused by early labour-movement activists than to the technical expertise and top-down planning that Morrison had championed at

London County Council. It was their vision of society – one that championed equality of opportunity and battled poverty – which would triumph during the war.

The summer and autumn of 1940 gave credence to these Labour ministers' arguments. The Battle of Britain in July and August made clear that productivity would only be increased if greater direction was given to industry, and more consideration given to the workforce. Workers were required to devote increasingly long hours to meet demanding targets. Their paid holidays were suspended 'for the duration', but they received little in return. In the factories, productivity rose in the weeks following Dunkirk but by high summer workers' enthusiasm for the war effort was flagging and so was production.

These circumstances allowed Bevin to achieve centralised direction of essential industries – and to give trade unions a guaranteed seat at the negotiating table. Chief among the unions' concerns was a huge expansion in semi-skilled factory work. In order to replace skilled men, industrial employers, especially in engineering, broke down skilled jobs into repetitive tasks, which could be undertaken by workers with little or no training. This helps to explain why, within the breakthrough generation, the sons of skilled workers were just as likely to enter semi-skilled or unskilled work as to follow their fathers into a craft. Mass Observation found that many experienced this as downward mobility.[14]

The unions, wary of allowing employers to recruit large numbers of cheap, untrained workers, focused their efforts on maintaining the difference in earnings that existed between these new recruits and the skilled workforce. In doing so they missed a chance to contest the grading of workers as 'semi-skilled' or 'unskilled'. The engineering unions had a long tradition of jealously guarding the privileges of their members and ensuring that workers were recruited from a narrow pool – the Amalgamated Engineering Union refused to admit women until 1942. They made no attempt to argue that assembly line work and repetitive tasks themselves required skill; nor did they argue, as Tom Mann had in the 1900s, for the reorganisation of work along lines that might have diminished the division between skilled, semi-skilled and unskilled work.

Nevertheless, trade unions slowly recognised that they could only gain by recruiting unskilled and semi-skilled workers. Union membership increased by more than 1.5 million during the war, and rose fastest in engineering.[15] Demand for manual-workers' labour, and trade union representation, meant that their earnings more than trebled during the war, with unskilled and semi-skilled workers seeing the biggest gains of all.[16]

While for skilled workers' sons semi-skilled or unskilled work was a step down the ladder, those whose parents had done such jobs before 1939 often experienced war work as a step up. These unskilled and semi-skilled workers were conscious of their indispensability, for Bevin's Ministry of Labour designated engineering a reserved occupation. Those who had worked in factories before the war appreciated the increase in wages and welcomed trade union recognition. Mass Observers recorded 'terrific enthusiasm for the job' among Manchester's semi-skilled engineering workers; even after a ten- or twelve-hour shift, 'in pubs or canteens they talk shop'. Their enthusiasm revealed 'a long-denied form of self-expression' and 'a new sense of self-importance [that] goes with higher wages and essential work'.[17] Jobs that had been near the bottom of the ladder before the war were now made into worthy occupations by pay rises, trade union involvement and a political commitment to workers' welfare.

By contrast, clerical work was losing its cachet, for few office workers outside the Civil Service felt they were assisting the war effort in any way. 'The war has affected them but slightly', reported one Mass Observer of women clerks, and 'they gave me an impression of "feeling out of it"'.[18] Phyllis Willmott agreed. The daughter of a working-class family in south London, she had won a scholarship to secondary school, and at sixteen became an assistant librarian. Her parents tried to persuade her to get a job at her local municipal library, but she took a post at a private establishment in central London despite the tiring and costly commute. 'I could hardly admit to them – and, in fact, could only half admit it to myself – that I was trying to escape from them, or anyway from the tensions between their way of life and the style I aspired to' she later wrote.[19] In the summer of 1939, nineteen-year-old Phyllis left this job to become a bank clerk in the City of London. She hoped for 'more interesting' and varied work, but soon realised that while 'young men . . . could expect to become supervisors, cashiers or managers in the fullness of time, the prospects for women were virtually nil'.[20] Before the war, Phyllis had been bent on climbing the social ladder. But within just a couple of years her ambitions had changed. Impatient for adventure, 'dramatic events' like America's entry to the war in December 1941 'served to increase my discontent with the dull part I was playing in them'.[21]

By 1941, many people shared Phyllis Willmott's dissatisfaction. Government intelligence officers and Mass Observers reported unhappiness at the persistence of older hierarchies in the workplace and beyond. The media tried to suggest this was a war of 'fair shares' – *Woman's Own* declared in 1942 that 'there is no such thing as a typical factory girl these days', listing ballet dancers and society girls among the workforce of one munitions factory.[22] But in reality the vast majority of factory workers came from working-class families.[23] Even after conscription for single women was introduced at the end of 1941, Home Intelligence officers found 'considerable resentment among women who are already working that the middle and upper classes are still being allowed to "get away" with voluntary war-jobs'.[24] Productivity declined once more, while absenteeism rose.[25]

By now it was clear that the war would not be won by relying on the social status quo. The shortage of men was taking its toll on Britain's workforce. Technical workers, scientists and engineers were badly needed. But the Ministry of Labour reported that those men who signed the Central Register lacked this expertise. Indeed, 'older men, many of them retired army officers . . . with no previous experience of civilian employment tended to over-assess both their capabilities and the salaries which they would expect to receive'. Even the most diplomatic civil servants found that 'the correction of these impressions was neither easy nor palatable'. Many of these men 'insisted on . . . waiting for the chance of what they regarded as a suitable job turning up'. Used to commanding high salaries and prestige as managers and military officers, they found it impossible to believe that they were now no more valuable than labourers or factory hands.[26]

In tackling this problem, Bevin's Ministry of Labour created new routes up the ladder for young men. In 1941 Bevin launched a recruitment drive for scientists and technicians led by Lord Hankey, a Conservative minister who had previously been a senior civil servant, assisted by Charles Percy (C. P.) Snow. Born in Leicester in 1904 to a self-employed-businessman-turned-music-teacher and a dressmaker, Snow had attended secondary school as a fee-paying pupil, read science at Leicester University College and then completed a PhD at Cambridge University, where by 1938 he was a science don. Now he took full-time secondment to the Civil Service to assist in recruiting men to scientific work.

The scheme became a pillar of wartime meritocracy – though this was not what Hankey and Snow initially intended. They had assumed that they'd follow the lead of other government departments and recruit from Oxbridge. But those students could have their pick of jobs elsewhere, and with other universities' graduates also in demand, Hankey and Snow eventually concluded they were better off training up the scientists they required. With Bevin's encouragement, they devised a bursary scheme which offered full university fees and a maintenance grant to young men with a School Certificate who were willing to study radio, engineering or chemistry on an intensive two-year university course. Two thousand bursaries were offered for October 1941. By the end of the war 6,000 students had received one.[27]

In 1942, Bevin approved a scheme for engineering cadetships, which offered the equivalent of a university degree to young men aged between sixteen and nineteen with a School Certificate and some relevant employment experience. By the spring of 1943, 3,172 cadets had begun their training. Most of them were young men who could not have envisaged a higher education before the war.[28]

The success of these schemes helped to convince civil servants and politicians that recruiters of senior or skilled roles should also fish in a wider pool. In 1942 the Select Committee on National Expenditure advised the government that in grappling with the shortage of industrial managers and technicians, 'the convenient, but frequently erroneous, practice of regarding academic qualifications as a measure of suitability should not be allowed to overshadow the less easily assessable, but great practical, value of men who have graduated through the workshops'.[29] In the mid-1950s, a study of British managers found that this wartime recruitment drive had been pivotal in taking working-class men from the factory floor into senior roles. Like the science and technology trainees, most had a secondary education, and many had only recently left school.[30]

The ranks of the Civil Service itself were increasingly accessible to men with a secondary education. By 1942, a shortage of university graduates necessitated the recruitment of thousands of 'temporary' civil servants. Only 7 per cent of senior civil servants recruited before the war had come from working-class backgrounds, almost all of them graduates. But 13 per cent of the wartime recruits were from working-class families and some had only a School Certificate.[31] Almost all of these new recruits went into brand-new posts focused on scientific and technical development.

Few women benefited from these initiatives. In 1941 Mass Observation conducted an extensive survey titled *People in Production*. 'When we started out . . . to make this investigation, it never occurred to us that from beginning to end we should never encounter a single woman anywhere in the higher grades of industry', wrote the authors. 'We have seen literally hundreds of managerial staffs, Trade Unionists, experts, Government officials. Nowhere a woman above the status of Welfare Manager or minor Trades Union official or subsidiary staff in one of the Supply Ministries . . . The atmosphere is . . . that the women are helping the men and *temporarily* taking over for the men to do something more important.'[32]

Secondary-school girls were barred from the wartime technical and engineering training schemes. In 1943 a shortage of male labour did prompt a recruitment drive for young women in engineering and draughtsmanship, but there were few applicants. It wasn't that women weren't interested, but female entrants were required to have more advanced qualifications in maths and science than male recruits, and employers proved unwilling to take them on. The Ministry of Labour received 'very widespread complaints that women who had been through a course of training were put on to the same jobs as those who went straight into the factory'.[33] By 1942 a secondary education opened many new doors for young men, but it did not have the same value for women.

Women did best where they didn't compete with men. In 1941 Mass Observation reported that the war was affecting young people's ambitions. Most of them wanted an interesting job that helped people – and nursing was women's most popular choice.[34] As demand for nurses increased, entry requirements were relaxed.[35] Strength in numbers, and the fact that some new, working-class recruits came from homes with a history of trade unionism, led nurses to challenge the privations and discipline they endured. Brenda McBryde was among several disgruntled young nurses working at Newcastle upon Tyne's Royal Victoria Infirmary in 1940 where 'it was considered bad form to mention money or the fact we were under-nourished'. Brenda and her friends, none of whom could rely on financial help from their families, were delighted when a strike by hospital porters 'drew attention to the poor working conditions of nurses'.[36] With the advice of the unionised porters, and to the chagrin of the hospital's matron and managers, Brenda and her colleagues established a trade union branch. The same was happening all over the country. As a result, nurses' working hours fell, and their annual pay doubled from £20 in 1939 to £40 by 1943.[37]

Higher education still only provided a tiny minority of women with a step up the ladder. Although the number of university students rose during the war, women composed only 23 per cent of them – the same level as in 1938, and fewer than before the Wall Street Crash.[38] Graduate women's career choices, which had slowly expanded during the past two decades, contracted in wartime. The hopes of aspiring 'architects, actors [and] academics' who studied at Girton College, Cambridge were 'destroyed by the war'.[39] Even before conscription for single women was introduced (after which women graduates were obliged to choose between teaching, nursing and the Civil Service) they found it hard to get professional or technical jobs in the conservative, cautious atmosphere of the early war years. Women graduates were recruited to Bletchley Park only as 'linguists' and 'temporary assistants', on pay grades lower than the men, though many of them played a pivotal role in codebreaking.[40] Fewer women than men were recruited to the higher grades of the Civil Service, and those who were appointed had 'slightly "superior" social origins to those of the men' and were better qualified than their male counterparts.[41]

Nevertheless, women's recruitment into the Civil Service did increase from its low pre-war level. And those women who *were* taken on tended to stay in the Civil Service after the war and attain senior positions, to a far greater extent than was true of those recruited either before or after the war.[42] Their success was due to their recruitment into relatively senior grades – so they had less far to travel – and the absence of male competition.

As Mass Observation's *People in Production* noted, women's most senior role in industry was as welfare managers. In July 1940, Ernest Bevin, who recognised that workers' morale and welfare were key to raising productivity, introduced the Factory and Welfare Services Order, which gave factory inspectors the power to direct large establishments to appoint welfare officers. By 1941 the increasing number of female factory workers led the Ministry of Labour to introduce training courses for women interested in personnel management. Membership of the Institute of Personnel Management rose from 812 in 1940 to 2,881 by 1945 and many of the entrants were women.[43]

By 1941 the government acknowledged the state must do more to help those in need. Charities and voluntary groups couldn't cope with the chaos of evacuation, the necessity of food rationing and the home-lessness caused by bombing in the autumn and winter of 1940. This strengthened the case of those left-wingers who had long argued for more expert social planning. In June 1941 a top-secret memorandum on 'social welfare and the blitzed towns', produced for the govern-ment by an unnamed Mass Observer, recommended that each local authority employ a 'welfare officer, a well-paid person with high rank-ing', that every region be equipped with 'a unit of skilled social work-ers', and that 'a mobile Citizen's Advice Bureau' be funded.[44] By 1942 most city and town councils had adopted at least some of these recom-mendations. In 1931 there had been 7,248 social welfare workers in England and Wales; by 1951 there were 22,153. Women composed 46 per cent of welfare workers in 1931 and 57 per cent of them twenty years later. This was partly due to men moving into the military or reserved war occupations and partly to the creation of new jobs.

Those men and women who experienced a swift ascent into the professions in wartime tended to be slightly older than the break-through generation. This was particularly true of women. While some men with a secondary education could get new technical and scien-tific jobs, women seeking to enter these welfare roles usually required a degree, and some employment experience. Many of them were teachers whose expertise proved useful for new wartime roles in child welfare.[45] Joan Cooper was a twenty-five-year-old elementary school-teacher when war broke out. The daughter of a Manchester salesman who was too poor to fund the university education she aspired to, Joan had signed the Board of Education 'pledge' in order to get a scholar-ship to Manchester University. After graduating in 1935 she taught in the city's working-class districts before helping to organise the evacu-ation of Manchester's children to Derbyshire in 1939. In 1941 she was appointed to the new post of evacuation officer at Derbyshire Council. For Joan Cooper, this was the beginning of a long and successful career in social policy.[46]

Other women pursued their interest in scientific or social scien-tific planning by entering adult education. The need for adult education tutors expanded during the war. Bevin's emphasis on workers' welfare and entertainment – actively supported by the major trade unions – increased demand for adult education in the towns and factories to which war workers were sent. Universities and the WEA were charged with providing this. They offered jobs to some upwardly mobile graduates, but also to middle-class women who otherwise faced the prospect of clerical work.

In 1944 Margaret Stacey, a recent LSE graduate and the daughter of a prosperous London businessman, persuaded the Ministry of Labour to allow her to become an adult education tutor in Oxford University's extramural (adult education) department. Some universities had established these departments between the wars, inspired by the WEA. In the changed climate of wartime Britain, adult education was able to count on some influential support in Whitehall – just enough to help it to flourish. Margaret got her way because 'a long-standing supporter of the WEA was working in the [Ministry of Labour] and she thought it was very important and said "release this woman"'.[47]

Margaret Stacey was charged with offering adult education classes to war workers in Banbury. With their involvement, she embarked on a major social study of 'how "ordinary people" lived'.[48] Her scrutiny of Banbury's new manufacturing workforce, and the upwardly mobile clerks and managers who were also moving into the town, marked a departure from interwar social studies, which had focused primarily on poverty and unemployment. Adult education became a route into advanced research and teaching in new subjects that weren't dominated by well-connected male academics. Margaret's experience influenced her decision to become a sociologist after the war, focusing on the effects of geographic and social mobility on individuals and communities.

Although the wartime expansion of scientific, technical and managerial jobs was significant for those who got these new posts, it did not transform class relations in Britain. In 1931 9 per cent of male and female workers were managers, professionals or senior administrators. By 1951 these occupations employed 13 per cent of men but only 11 per cent of women – a lot of people were affected, but those recruited during or immediately after the war accounted for only 4 per cent of male workers and 2 per cent of female workers. And women were less likely to get jobs in science and technology than men. The increase in women's professional employment during the war was largely due to the rise in female teachers who returned to work during the war to cover men's jobs. These women were members of the pioneer or precarious generations, who had been obliged to leave work when they married.

The most common destination of upwardly mobile men and women of the breakthrough generation was clerical work, and this was particularly true of women. The downwardly mobile, who comprised 28 per cent of women in this generation compared with fewer than 20 per cent of men, were also likely to find themselves in clerical work. Just as had been true of the precarious generation, these daughters of professionals and managers had no chance to enter work of an equivalent level. The war made little difference to their prospects.

*

By 1943 unemployment had virtually ceased to exist, productivity was increasing, workers' incomes were rising and the living standards of working-class people had improved.[49] Men with a secondary education, and women with a university degree, were able to get new jobs making an important contribution to the war effort and, longer term, the development of science, technology and welfare. The difference between factory workers', clerks' and professionals' earnings narrowed. Manual-workers' earnings rose by 141 per cent between 1937 and 1949, and much of this increase took place in the early 1940s.[50] Britain was a more equal place and offered greater opportunity – on the home front at least.

The crucial role played by manual workers shifted attitudes towards social mobility and inequality. The crucial contributions of munitions workers, lorry, tank and train drivers, farm labourers and, of course, soldiers, sailors and airmen, led many people to reassess their view of who fitted where on the social ladder. Some of those who were required to descend to a lower rung as a result of wartime conscription found the experience liberating. 'As a clerk I was obliged to appear respectably dressed', explained an agricultural worker, who enjoyed wearing 'overalls [and] heavy boots'.[51] Mass Observation detected 'a small but significant trend of feeling which wants to get away from indoor work and from towns and cities to simple country and outdoor work'.[52]

The view from the battle front was less positive. A 'very frequent source of resentment', found a Mass Observer in the RAF, 'is the reservation by the ruling classes of practically all the flying jobs for themselves. Most of the volunteers . . . are deeply disappointed when they find, either owing to the lack of a public school or secondary education, or through some accident about the time and place of volunteering, that this is denied to them.'[53] Government intelligence officers were increasingly concerned by the 'social chasm' that existed between officers and men. The former's outright contempt for the rank and file, and unwillingness to nominate them for officer commissions, was hampering the war effort. The War Office noted in top-secret documents that 'misplacement of potential tradesmen [is] a potential source of discontent', and severely impeded efficiency and productivity.[54]

The effect of the Soviet Union's entry to the war in June 1941 fuelled Whitehall's concerns. 'It is evident from the men's letters', reported a government censor, that the rigid military hierarchy 'gives rise to political reflections and leanings towards Russia'.[55] 'The following type of discussion is heard quite often', reported an intelligence source in the Black Watch: '"When this war's over, there'll be revolution in this country." "Yes, and the boys who've been in the Services will start it."'[56]

The RAF was the first of the forces to reluctantly grasp the need for reform. The air force had a particularly high fatality rate and an especially urgent need for technicians and engineers. In 1941 it introduced new training courses for both. Edward Smithies was among the benefi- ciaries. Having watched his father – a Middlesbrough steelworker – spend much of his adult life in dole queues, Edward applied to join RAF aircrew after leaving secondary school in 1937, but was turned down by a 'toffee-nosed' selection board. In 1942, however, the crea- tion of a new category of flight crew in the new heavy bombers – the flight engineer – enabled him to both learn a trade and fly.[57] The RAF began to gain a reputation as the most meritocratic of the services.

The army soon followed suit, under the command of General Sir Ronald Forbes Adam. In June 1941 Adam became adjutant general of the army, with responsibility for personnel. An Old Etonian and grad- uate of the Royal Military Academy, he was an unlikely reformer. But he believed that the army must become meritocratic if it was to win the war. 'The British Army is wasting its manpower', he declared on his appointment. 'The only way to obtain an efficient and contented army is to place the right man, as far as is humanly possible, in the right place. This is particularly important as manpower is short.'[58] Adam introduced a personnel department, which proved 'able to find a very large number of potential tradesmen from the ordinary army class intake . . . [who] had considerable relevant experience'.[59] All new army recruits would now be assigned to the General Service Corps for their first six weeks, so that their subsequent posting could take account of their skills. Adam also overhauled the selection of army officers, which had previously been left to commandants, by introduc- ing psychological testing of recruits' leadership potential.

This major reform had significant repercussions for military and civilian society during and beyond the war. Adam's reforms gave cre- dence to the relatively new science of psychology. The Civil Service quickly followed the army's lead by using these tests for recruitment and promotion. Even more crucially, so did the Ministry of Education as it developed proposals for free and universal secondary education after the war. By 1943 the ministry's civil servants agreed that an eleven-plus exam, derived from psychological testing, should deter- mine which type of secondary school each child would attend. The majority would go to secondary modern schools, offering a very basic education, while a minority would attend grammar schools, where they would be educated for university and the professions. This system of secondary education was endorsed by the 1944 Education Act and came into being on 1 April 1945.

Becoming an officer gave some men a permanent step up the ladder. In the late 1960s the social scientists Jan and Ray Pahl interviewed eighty-six managers across British industry and in the Civil Service. They discovered that 'the army or other service experience was often the crucial stimulant to a managerial career' for upwardly mobile men, who gained 'in confidence as a result of a series of almost fortuitous circumstances, which teach them that they can cope with new situations'.[60] They were men like David Jackson, the son of an Islington shopkeeper. In 1941 twenty-year-old David was conscripted into the army, where he 'crossed the social divide' after being selected for officer training. He 'had to learn new rules of behaviour and acquire the "right" accent' to fit into the officers' mess. These lessons proved important after the war, when Peter 'rose from office boy to managing director' of the firm he worked for.[61]

But Adam's reforms did not eradicate class bias and the forces did not become meritocratic. Psychological testing turned out to be more subjective than its proponents suggested. In 1944 eighteen-year-old Peter Gorb, the son of a businessman, entered the army fresh from public school. He was swiftly invited to train as a radio operator alongside other 'middle-class boys who had stayed at school until eighteen . . . the overwhelming reason for choosing us was that we spoke with received pronunciation'. Peter and his fellow trainees were then sent to a War Office Selection Board for potential officers – held, as was usual, in a stately home. They found the psychological 'intelligence' tests 'an easy challenge to young men used to written examinations'. Other assessments included 'being watched at very formal meals. We supposed it was to see if we held our knives and forks in a manner befitting an officer and a gentleman.'[62] It was the expansion of the officer class that provided more men with the chance of a commission, not psychological testing, which too often simply reflected established ideas about what constituted 'intelligence' (the ability to sit timed examinations) and 'leadership' (familiarity with upper-middle-class life). As a result, the former pupils of Britain's expensive public schools continued to dominate the officer class. In the 1930s they had comprised 60 per cent of new army officers; in 1941, as conscription was imposed on a wider age group and new selection procedures were introduced, they won only a quarter of new officer commissions. But in 1945, one-third of new officers came from public schools, despite these establishments educating less than 1 per cent of the population.[63]

Many women voluntarily joined the auxiliary services, and more were directed to these once female conscription was introduced. Mass Observation found that those who joined up were 'seeking an adventurous touch to mundane lives; trying to assert their emancipated position; [and] looking for a chance to satisfy the soul-craving to "do something worthwhile"'.[64] This was certainly borne out by those who joined up. Women recruited in the first few years of the war complained, as men did, about the lack of training and the stuffy hierarchy. But by 1942, the auxiliary forces provided more options to learn a trade or undertake training – demand for men at the front meant women were needed for the jobs they left. In 1943 Phyllis Willmott finally received permission to leave bank work and join the WAAF. She could choose between becoming a mechanic or a meteorological observer and opted for the latter. 'For the first time since I had left school five years earlier I had a job I liked and believed to be suited to my abilities.' Stationed on a rural airbase, 'both the work and the surroundings were wonderfully different from anything I had known before'. She had achieved an independence and a training that she could not have hoped for in peacetime. Nevertheless, she knew that her sex meant she had no prospects of promotion or advanced training. 'We were very junior as women: our role was to document changes in the weather for the senior meteorologists – who were all men'.[65]

Army education was a great catalyst to social mobility within the forces. The Army Education Corps (AEC), which had been established at the end of the First World War, was chiefly responsible for providing education to the troops. Staffed almost entirely by graduates, the AEC was predominantly middle class but more liberal than many other military units. In 1943 the former grammar-school boy and London University graduate J. C. Banks managed to transfer to the AEC and finally gain his commission. But also influential was the Army Bureau for Current Affairs (ABCA), established in 1941 by William Emrys Williams – a tradesman's son, former WEA tutor, and editor of the WEA's *Highway* magazine. ABCA's scheme of adult education focused on discussing war aims and the post-war future. Churchill was strongly opposed to this, fearing that it would encourage divisive political debate, and sought to outlaw the scheme. But with General Forbes Adam's support, Williams succeeded in having it made mandatory for all army units.[66]

ABCA allowed some men and women to take their first step towards a university degree or a professional career. Provision was patchy: some units did little or nothing, and many relied on volunteers to lead educational work in their spare time. But the haphazard nature of the scheme allowed all sorts of projects to flourish. Richard Hoggart was born in 1923, the son of a factory worker in Leeds. By dint of scholarships he had graduated in English from Leeds University before joining the army in 1940. In 1945, while stationed in Naples, he 'fell into becoming, half unofficially, our resettlement and education officer'. He initiated 'an army education club', essentially an arts and literature society where jazz was played, current novels discussed and politics debated. This fuelled Hoggart's 'rapidly growing' interest 'in adult education and its post-war importance'.[67] Meanwhile, on an airfield outside Manchester, twenty-one-year-old Albert Halsey had become an unofficial ABCA lecturer: 'I often made political speeches in the Nissen hut and the crew room, in effect to a seminar audience'. This stimulated his new desire to go to university, an idea 'clarified and strengthened by mixing with the aircrew classes'.[68]

The wider effect of ABCA on its students is less easy to assess, but at the very least it provided the chance to discuss visions of post-war

Britain. By 1942, support was growing for greater equality, especially equality of opportunity. In June 1941 respondents to a Mass Observation survey on 'things people feel bode worst for the future' had ranked 'restrictions on liberty' highest. But when the survey was repeated in the autumn of 1942, this was only tenth in importance. Highest now was 'the power of vested interests', by which people meant 'big business, conservative leaders . . . and the "old gang"'.[69] Before the war, wealth had been hailed as a sign of personal success, and upward mobility a widely shared ambition. In wartime 'fair shares' Britain, the wealthy were increasingly viewed as self-interested rather than successful.

By 1942 it was clear that state intervention in the form of rationing, co-ordination of welfare services and full employment had not stymied people's liberty, but led to greater social equality, and more chances for some to climb the ladder. Increasingly, people defined equality of opportunity as central to 'democracy' – what Britain was fighting for. When Mass Observation asked people what they wanted from post-war education 'greater equality' was their single greatest aspiration. Mass Observation noted that while some considered equality to mean social and economic levelling, most had more meritocratic ambitions. 'British people want to make excursions up the side of the [social] pyramid', concluded Tom Harrisson, one of Mass Observation's founders. 'They do not so far consider that there is any law of nature or justice which should make it *certain* that they can do so, though there is a growing feeling that their children should be able to do so, if they have the ability and wish.'[70] 'Children should be promoted on merit', as one semi-skilled manual worker put it.[71]

Labour was the party that captured these ambitions. Labour ministers were instrumental in commissioning the Liberal William Beveridge to write his report on *Social Insurance and Allied Services*, published in 1942. The Beveridge Report, as it quickly became known, recommended that the post-war state should provide cradle-to-grave support in order to destroy the 'five giants' of want, disease, ignorance, squalor and idleness. Labour publicly supported Beveridge's conclusion that the state should be responsible for ensuring that its citizens had the basic means to live (a 'national minimum'). The Party also upheld his belief that the state must also enable everyone to fulfil their potential in order to contribute to democracy. Against the inter-war Conservative orthodoxy, Beveridge suggested that state assis-tance was essential to foster the 'freedom and enterprise and responsibility' required to improve one's own life and for 'human pro-gress'.[72] He envisaged a state where people would be assisted to help themselves, not through trade unions or friendly societies as some of the pioneers had envisaged, but by a welfare state managed by national government. This would not be an equal society, so much as one in which people's skills and talents would be fostered and rewarded.

In the remaining years of the war, Labour championed both this meritocratic vision, and more egalitarian aspirations. Labour politi-cians chose not to distinguish between equality and meritocracy, terms that few of them used. Instead they preferred 'fairness' and 'democracy', terms whose precise meaning was ambiguous. For some MPs, the bright new future was clearly egalitarian. 'Our human qual-ity at the end of the war is perhaps the thing that matters most, and . . . we have to do whatever we can for its development', argued Labour MP Arthur Greenwood in 1944. '[I]t is clear that if democracy carries any meaning in men's minds, it must mean the abolition of class dis-tinction'.[73] Others were less sure, but few were entirely committed to meritocracy. Michael Young, the head of Labour's research depart-ment, and largely responsible for the Party's 1945 manifesto, *Let Us Face the Future*, was not a champion of complete equality, but he was resolutely opposed to meritocracy. As the historian Pat Thane has written, his hostility was 'rooted in his belief in the capacity of all to participate in decision making and his conviction that the central role of education was to facilitate this rather than to select out a privileged elite'. Young did believe that people had different 'skills and talents that they should be encouraged to use for the public good.'[74] But pre-serving power in the hands of just a few people was, he thought, dan-gerous to democracy.

In July 1945 voters cast their ballot in the first general election since 1935. They chose between Winston Churchill's Conservative Party – committed to 'free enterprise' and 'the small man in business'[75] – and Clement Attlee's Labour Party, which promised 'Jobs for All', fair shares ('no more dole queues in order to let the Czars of Big Business remain kings in their own castles'), social security, council housing for all who needed it, a National Health Service, and free secondary education 'to give us individual citizens capable of thinking for themselves'. *Let Us Face The Future* placed great emphasis on 'fairness', which at times appeared to mean social and economic equality (though 'equality' was never mentioned). But in other areas, a stress on respecting people as individuals could equally lend itself to meritocratic ideas. This was most clear in education, where Labour promised reforms that would 'give every boy and girl a chance to develop the best that is in them.'[76]

Labour's version of social democracy was, therefore, an evolving and ambiguous one, which could appeal to egalitarian visions and meritocratic ambitions. It was also entirely new to Britain. The innovations of wartime – increased welfare, the expansion of scientific and technical jobs and training, full employment and higher wages – had been pioneered by the public sector, or assisted by state regulation of private enterprise. Now Labour argued that only social welfare provided by the state, public ownership of key industries and full employment could give 'the people ... the means of living full, happy, healthy lives'.[77]

On 26 July 1945 Clement Attlee's Labour Party swept to power with a landslide victory. The new government's jubilant supporters included many of those who had benefited from the meritocratic reforms of the war. 'We voted', said Albert Halsey, casting his first ballot as a twenty-two-year-old RAF pilot, 'with joy and confidence in a future without fascism, with democracy and decency, and free of class inequality.'[78] It remained to be seen whether Labour could fulfil such high hopes.

Chapter Six

ROOM AT THE TOP

In August 1945, Phyllis Willmott, fresh from the WAAF, met up with an old friend, Meg, to talk about their post-war plans. They shared a working-class background; so too did Meg's fiancé, Jake, a soldier who was about to be demobbed:

> There was plenty for us to talk about. For one thing there was the new Labour government which we, voting for the first time, felt we had helped to bring into being. Then there were all the exciting post-war plans for education, health and social security . . . Above all, of course, we were interested in discussing where our own future lay, and how we could avoid being trapped once again in the boring office jobs from which the war had released us. Jake's friends in the [Army] Education Corps were urging him to try for a place at Oxford University, and Meg was thinking about training for some kind of career in social welfare. Under the schemes for the resettlement of service personnel these were all realistic ambitions. I was certain . . . that I had to find 'something worthwhile'.[1]

Phyllis's hopes were shared by millions. In 1944 Mass Observation revealed that many male manual workers, but particularly demobbed servicemen, possessed 'a determination to occupy a position in "civvy life" higher both in the social and financial scale than before [the war]'. Women 'expressed revulsion at the thought of returning to their pre-war life'. Their ambitions were more inchoate than men's and yet broader: 'a desire for escape pure and simple'.[2]

The post-war Labour government, elected in July 1945, created many jobs staffing and shaping the new welfare state. Free secondary education (introduced in 1947), the National Health Service and the new social services (launched in 1948) required millions of new professional, technical and white-collar workers. And winning the peace depended on skilled and professional workers to devise and enact ambitious town-planning schemes, to manage industry, and to deliver Labour's promise of full employment.

The breakthrough generation were well prepared to take advantage of the new post-war chances. Some of them had experienced upward mobility during the early 1940s, but even more did so after the war ended. By the time the breakthrough generation were in their forties, 17 per cent of manual-workers' sons and 33 per cent of the sons of white-collar workers were professionals or managers. While we don't have comparable figures for women, they went into clerical and professional work in increasing numbers: by 1960, office work was their largest employer.

In the years following 1945, some of this generation climbed the ladder via industrial management – we'll meet them in Chapter Eight. Others benefited directly from Labour's expansion of the welfare state. They used the education and training that the post-war Labour government introduced to embark on careers as administrators, planners, researchers and teachers. They became a new kind of professional and white-collar group who depended on the kind of social democracy Labour espoused.

*

In 1949 the sociologist David Glass undertook the first comprehensive survey of social mobility in Britain. Glass's conclusions were flawed:

he erroneously suggested that the children of professionals and managers were increasingly likely to descend into white-collar or manual work. His error was due to his comparison between fathers' last occupations with their sons' first job; he failed to recognise that it often took children several years to achieve the same position as their parents.[3] But David Glass made a significant discovery about people's attitudes to social class. He revealed that two groups of workers attracted unusually high esteem in Britain: skilled manual workers and professionals.[4]

Labour prioritised investment in industry after the war. While the social welfare programme is remembered as the legacy of 1945, Attlee's government was most concerned to establish full employment and industrial recovery.[5] In 1951 25 per cent of men were in skilled manual work. But demand for these jobs outstripped supply. In 1945 Labour introduced training courses and apprenticeships for war workers and service personnel who could prove they had intended to enter a skilled trade before the war. The schemes were swamped with applications. Half of the thousands who applied had to be turned away.[6] Many more people could not even afford to consider this option, for the training offered was as low paid as pre-war apprenticeships had been. John Stafford, born in Scunthorpe in 1920, had been an apprentice baker before joining the army in 1939. By the time he was demobbed in 1946 he was married with a baby and reluctantly decided that he could not afford to complete his apprenticeship. 'I didn't want to go to the steelworks, but it was the biggest-paid job that counted at that time, and you could get a bit of overtime up there. So that was it. I went there.'[7] John Stafford became a semi-skilled factory worker. They composed 32 per cent of the workforce in 1951.

Yet many skilled manual workers wanted more than security and a decent pay packet. Trade union membership continued to increase after the Second World War, and Labour granted the unions significant bargaining rights over pay and conditions. Nevertheless, the power of shop-floor workers remained very limited. Strikes had been made illegal in wartime, and remained so until 1951. And high-handed management remained the norm, even in the industries that Labour nationalised: coal, iron, steel and road haulage. 'Some days were Red Letter days: the day they nationalised the mines was one', recalled Eddie Jackson, a Yorkshire collier born in the 1920s. But he soon concluded 'that nationalisation wasn't making all that much difference . . . the management were still there managing in exactly the same way'.[8] These men and women hoped their children would have more chances to control their work and their lives. Many of them focused their aspirations on their sons' and daughters' education – and a sizeable minority also sought a new life overseas.

*

The educated men and women of Phyllis Willmott's generation aspired to enter the professions. Very often this desire was entwined with their appetite for study. Labour's Further Education and Training Scheme offered a place at university or in further education to any demobbed serviceman or woman who had planned to follow this path before the war. Albert Halsey had previously considered university unimaginably expensive, but one morning in 1945, shortly before the war ended, 'a couple of officers came round to the crew room to say that . . . If we were prepared to perjure ourselves with the declaration that our university careers had been interrupted "for the duration" . . . and if we could find a place, the government would pay both the fees and a maintenance grant'. Albert 'overcame any moral scruples about the complete non-existence in my own case . . . of a university education' and 'resolved to take the entrance examination to the London School of Economics.' In 1947 he became one of 43,000 former servicemen and women to take up a university place. Between 1946 and 1950 they swelled the student body by two-thirds.[9]

But just one in a hundred returning servicemen and women entered the universities. Most former service personnel were ineligible for a scheme that was far less ambitious than the USA's famous 'GI Bill' – the Servicemen's Readjustment Act of 1944 – which granted 15.5 million veterans the right to a free higher education.[10] In Britain, applicants had to prove that they had the requisite qualifications for the education or training they wished to enter. Labour's policies did not aim to give Halsey's generation a leg up the social ladder. Instead, they were intended to prevent the mass unemployment that had followed the Armistice in 1918, and to help people return to the rung of the ladder they'd occupied before the war, wherever possible.

This caused some disgruntlement among those whose ambitions were greater than the government's. Some were already deemed to have received sufficient training. Andrew Norris was born to a working-class family in the early 1920s. He had won a scholarship to secondary school, but his family could not afford to send him to university. Instead, he trained as an engineer at the Post Office, before enlisting in the army in the Second World War. After being demobbed he was 'very bitter' to discover that he wasn't eligible for the higher-education scheme because of his training.[11] Andrew returned to his pre-war job at the GPO.

Far more accessible than university was the Emergency Teacher Training Scheme, which became the major vehicle for upward mobility in the immediate post-war years. The 1944 Education Act made secondary education free and compulsory for all eleven-to-fifteen-year-olds. Labour pledged to increase the school-leaving age from fourteen to fifteen in 1947, but doing so required more than 30,000 new teachers. In 1946, the government established a scheme to train thousands of them in just one year, their fees and maintenance paid by the state.

The expansion of teaching provided an opening for men and women who wouldn't previously have considered entering a profession. 'What is wanted is to tap sources of recruitment among folk who have not hitherto looked to teaching', declared the government committee responsible. 'We need to work some new seams in our society.'[12] Five thousand people applied to join the Emergency Teacher Training Scheme each month during its first year. When the scheme came to an end in 1951 (by which time sufficient new teachers had been trained), 23,000 men and 12,000 women had qualified.[13]

These new teachers came from a wide range of backgrounds. More than 10 per cent had attended only an elementary school. Most had some secondary education, but had left school by sixteen.[14] They included members of the precarious generation who had experienced unemployment before the war, as well as younger men and women. In 1947, a journalist visited one of the new training colleges and met some of the recruits. They included 'Dan' who 'still wears the battle-dress of the RAF. He wears also the invisible chevrons of 16 years of patient sacrifice. Orphaned at the age of 14, he had to become the breadwinner for his younger brother and sister ... he had always wanted to become a teacher.'[15]

The scheme's success relied on recruits putting their faith in the welfare state that Labour promised to build – an entirely new venture with no guaranteed outcomes. Among those who signed up was Richard Pye. Born into a working-class home in Essex, he had won a scholarship to secondary school and then worked as a junior clerk for Essex County Council before joining the army in 1940, where he was granted a commission. While preparing to be demobbed in 1944, Richard accepted the offer of a clerical post at West Riding County Council. But then 'news had reached us in the army about ... a huge need for teachers, something which I felt I might be suited for and would enjoy'. In 1946 'full of apprehension', he left his heavily pregnant wife to take up a place at a residential college in Staffordshire. 'They really were worrying times as the only income we had was my maintenance grant for the course. However it was an opportunity as well and I was determined to make a success of it, and everyone else there was of the same mind.'[16]

Unlike holders of pre-war Board of Education university bursaries, recruits to this post-war scheme weren't compelled to enter teaching. But the vast majority did become teachers and remained so until retirement. Their career options were not as broad as those of graduates. The Ministry of Education assumed that the new trainees would staff primary schools and the lower forms of non-selective secondary modern schools. Very few found employment in the academically selective grammar schools.[17]

Before the war, teachers from working-class backgrounds had most commonly been found in elementary schools, and this trend continued after the war. In 1955 42 per cent of primary-school teachers were the children of manual workers, compared to 26 per cent of teachers in the grammar schools.[18] Richard Pye's first job was at a secondary modern school in Essex, but after ten years of teaching he decided to become a primary-school teacher because 'I was aware that promotion went to the graduates and I was not one.' He eventually became a head teacher in Malvern, and found 'enormous satisfaction' in teaching children to fulfil their potential, not only academically but in sport and arts and crafts.[19]

A smaller group of returning veterans found jobs in adult education. Labour's election in 1945 resulted in 'a big boost' for adult education provision and funding.[20] Richard Hoggart, who took up a post in Hull University's extramural department in 1947, knew that 'many in the Labour government were grateful for the opportunities it had long provided in the provinces – especially in the Welsh valleys, Lancashire, Yorkshire and parts of Scotland.' Hoggart joined a group of upwardly mobile men motivated by 'a sense of the many and major injustices in the lives of working people and so a deep suspicion of the power of class in Britain'.[21] Among the recruits was Raymond Williams, born in 1921 in South Wales, the only child of a railway worker and his wife. Williams had secured scholarships from secondary school to Cambridge University before joining the army in 1941. A committed socialist, Raymond Williams saw the war as a fight against fascism and for a more equal society. After a distinguished war career he graduated from Cambridge in 1946 and became an extramural tutor at Oxford University. Margaret Stacey, the LSE graduate who had been recruited into adult education during the war, was among his colleagues. Many adult education tutors shared Raymond Williams' desire to assist in 'the creation of an educated and participating democracy'.[22] Like Labour's Michael Young, many of them did not believe in meritocracy as much as in fostering greater social equality, and finding new ways to allow everyone to be an active and valued citizen.

Other men and women joined the Civil Service. The excellent work done by the wartime civil servants helped to precipitate a change in recruitment practices, away from entrance examination and interviews – which tended to favour applicants from the public schools and Oxbridge – and towards promotion from the lower ranks. As a result, almost 40 per cent of senior civil servants recruited between 1951 and 1955 had fathers in manual or white-collar work. Most had several years' employment experience in the clerical or technical branches of the Civil Service.[23]

Women's chances to join the professions or management remained more restricted. Those who joined the Emergency Teachers Training Scheme tended to have more educational qualifications than male recruits. Given that the number of applications far exceeded the places available, this suggests that selectors were more amenable to giving men a chance of professional work than extending this to working-class women.[24] Fewer women than men were recruited into the post-war Civil Service. In 1967 women composed just 8 per cent of senior civil servants. More than half of these had been recruited during the war.[25] Often these women were older than the breakthrough generation and had gained some employment experience before 1939. They included Joan Cooper, who had left teaching to take charge of evacuation in Derbyshire during the war. By the late 1940s she was a civil servant, and helped to establish a new approach to social services. Before the war, social work and children's homes had been the remit of voluntary bodies like Barnardo's. In 1948 Labour made local government responsible for the care of vulnerable children. Joan herself became head of one of the new local-authority Children's Departments, in East Sussex. She would go on to become a senior civil servant in the Home Office before the end of the 1960s.

By the end of the war, the results achieved by older women like Joan Cooper had persuaded seventy local authorities to employ social workers. Some of the breakthrough generation were the beneficiaries of this expansion of welfare work. Phyllis Willmott was among them. Her desire to do 'something worthwhile' led her to become an almoner (medical social worker) in 1947. Under pressure from older women who had begun to establish welfare work as a profession before and during the war, the government funded special courses to train legions of social and welfare workers. Among those who pioneered these university courses were Eileen Younghusband and Kit Russell. Born in the 1900s both came from prosperous middle-class families, and had worked as voluntary welfare workers before the war. Both had spent the war years lobbying government for greater support of welfare work. After the war they established a social work training course at the London School of Economics. By 1959 Kit Russell was able to tell a national conference of social workers that 'the profession of social work is growing . . . fast and people from many different backgrounds are coming into it'. She and her colleagues argued that life experience was more valuable than a formal education – 'it may be better for a social worker to have an illegitimate child or an unconventional sex life and be a warm-hearted person capable of real concern for people'.[26] These older, middle-class women opened up new opportunities for younger women from working-class backgrounds.

*

While young, ambitious people like Phyllis Willmott found the late 1940s brought new opportunities, many of the established middle class feared that Labour's reforms would send them sliding down the ladder. Some professionals, managers, small shopkeepers and clerks had experienced a decline in living standards since the 1930s. The social scientist Mark Abrams calculated that they had experienced a 20 per cent cut in real income between 1938 and 1947 due to prices rising faster than salaries and higher taxation under Labour. Meanwhile, the richest people in Britain – those in the most lucrative professions like doctors and lawyers, and those who relied on landowning, property or inherited wealth and had an income in excess of £1,000 per year (about £40,000 in 2020) – experienced a drop in real income of one-third. Abrams deduced that those affected spent almost the same amount of money on food, fuel and light 'but the amount left over for "other" items – house-furnishings, books and periodicals, theatres, education, laundry, doctors, and domestic service' had fallen dramatically.[27]

Labour lost the general election of 1951 to the Conservatives, who held power for the next thirteen years. One reason was housing, which was a major concern for people of all income levels. Before the war, much of Britain's working-class housing was in poor repair, and bomb damage made building an even more urgent priority. In 1945 Aneurin Bevan – a former miner and now Labour's Minister of Health and Housing – promised to build 240,000 houses each year. By 1951 he'd managed 900,000 – an impressive achievement, but not enough for those thousands still living in bomb-damaged homes, condemned slums, or overcrowded conditions with parents and siblings because they had nowhere else to go.[28] Voters thought that Labour's greatest failure was being 'too slow with housing'.[29]

But middle-class anxiety about downward mobility also helps to explain why Labour lost the 1951 election. In 1948 Mass Observation asked those of its respondents who thought of themselves as middle class to explain why they described themselves as such. 'Income' was men's primary reason. 'I am forced to spend an ever-increasing percentage of my total income upon the necessities for a basic existence that does not include the distinction between man the animal and man the social being', complained a male civil servant in his fifties.[30]

Many of Labour's opponents came from families that had worked in business or the professions for two generations or more. Among the Mass Observers, women thought that 'family background' was the most important defining characteristic of the middle class, and were concerned about being unable to maintain the standard of living their parents had experienced. 'My family and my home are getting more and more moth-eaten and patched up', complained one housewife.[31]

Taken together, men and women thought that education was the most important criterion for membership of the middle class. Many agreed with the woman who thought a middle-class person should possess 'a certain amount of leisure and culture . . . for such things as books, music and social activities', and concurred that they were unable to achieve this in the late 1940s.[32]

These years were in fact ones in which working-class people experienced a leisure boom. Rising wages meant that cinema nights, fish and chip takeaways and football matches became staples of many working-class people's lives.[33] And overall, most middle-class people had more disposable income than these working-class households. But the increased affluence of manual workers and their families robbed this section of the middle class of their sense of social distinction. They could afford leisure, books and outings, but these luxuries no longer set them apart from manual workers. Among the discontented was Nella Last, the Cumbrian housewife who had imbued her sons with her own social aspirations. In 1950 Nella and her husband were able to live comfortably on the profits of his small business. But she compared herself to manual workers and found her situation wanting. One Saturday in June 1950, she and her husband drove to Ambleside to picnic by Lake Windermere. Instead of the peace Nella had expected, the Lasts found themselves in 'a throng of milling people . . . decanted from coaches.' She contrasted 'well-to-do types picnicking' with 'the definitely working-class types' from the coaches who were 'eating in the top class hotels'.[34]

Older middle-class people feared falling into poverty. Downward mobility in old age had long been a legitimate concern of those who had only a small pension to live on, including many clerks and shopkeepers. After the war, Labour increased the old-age pension, but many former white-collar workers still found retirement brought a substantial drop in their income. Some of this group now found themselves caught in dilapidated city centres, which had grown poorer before the war and were then shattered by the Blitz. In the early 1950s researchers in Liverpool described the 'genteel poverty' of older people who had lived in the city's grand Georgian quarter since the early twentieth century and watched as businesspeople, then clerks, moved out of the city centre – to be followed, after the war, by factory workers rehoused on new, suburban council estates. The investigators were fascinated by streets where lodging houses for recent immigrants, 'shebeens and clubs stood next door to the houses of prim old ladies'.[35] They met 'two sisters, probably in their eighties, who rarely leave their flat . . . reminders of the time when professional families owned these houses, but they are now strangers in the neighbourhood. They are terrified to go out, but can't face moving away and won't countenance a modern council flat.'[36]

Labour was keen to win middle-class support. Herbert Morrison, now the Deputy Prime Minister, insisted that 'We need the so-called middle class', adding that Labour 'must try to understand their problems'.[37] Increasingly, in the late 1940s, some members of the government and other prominent Labour MPs talked of 'fairness' as best served by a form of meritocracy rather than equality. Attlee's government did not attempt to abolish private education or healthcare. Some senior Labour politicians argued that these were just rewards for effort and enterprise. Labour's Attorney General, Sir Hartley Shawcross, declared that the middle class had 'supplied many of the best brains in the professions often because parents have been prepared to make great sacrifices in order to give their children the best possible education'.[38] Attlee himself believed that Labour's most vital post-war task was to take Britain 'from a capitalism based on private property to a socialist economy based on the control and direction of the wealth and resources of this country in the interests of all the people'. But the prime minister – himself an alumnus of the expensive Haileybury School – believed that this was best effected through economic and industrial reform.[39] In the social realm, Labour's focus was on providing good health, educational and social services for all, without penalising those who wished to pay for privileged treatment.

But Labour's acceptance that the middle class required special consideration only reinforced this group's sense of entitlement, and their anxiety about Labour's reforms. The Attlee governments of 1945–51 never wholeheartedly championed the idea that universal state services were better than the private provision only a few received. The Conservatives, who were more openly committed to private enterprise, were able to outdo Labour in appealing to voters' aspirations to buy the best, and to those who feared that state welfare would mean a levelling down of their conditions.

But although some professionals and businesspeople disliked Labour's reforms, others, and many white-collar workers, were highly supportive. Not all of them experienced the 1940s as a period of downward mobility or rising financial insecurity. While Labour increased taxation on the very wealthiest, most teachers, shopkeepers and clerks did not pay more tax. As Abrams noted in 1947, 'the average middle-class family is still 50 per cent better off than the average working-class family, and the 4 per cent rich[est] people are three or four times better off'.[40]

Even those whose economic interests were not best served by Labour's reforms often approved of them. Opinion polls showed that most people, regardless of occupation or income, approved of social security, the National Health Service and free secondary education.[41] 'The biggest factor liked about the [NHS] is its cheapness to the individual', Mass Observation reported in 1949. 'This is followed by the creation of equality among all people.'[42]

Upwardly mobile people who owed their position to the state – either by receiving a free education, or by being employed in the public sector – were among the most enthusiastic. Philip Jennings became an increasingly ardent supporter of Labour through the 1940s. He had 'the greatest respect' for Clement Attlee and fully supported the continuation of food and clothes rationing (it finally ended in 1954) and state planning of industry because of 'a real necessity for controls in a world of shortages'.[43] Philip wanted to see a world where everyone could benefit from the education he had enjoyed, and in which his own skills were valued. The Conservatives recognised that meritocracy had strong popular appeal. 'We are for the ladder. Let all try their best to climb', declared Winston Churchill in a radio election broadcast. 'They [Labour] are for the queue. Let each wait in his place till his turn comes.'[44] But many voters were sceptical of the Tories' commitment to merit. Men and women like Philip Jennings help to explain why Labour increased its share of the popular vote in the 1951 general election – the party won more votes than the Conservatives, although fewer parliamentary seats.

These educated, upwardly mobile young professionals were united by a belief that the post-war welfare state was the foundation on which modern social democracy could be built. For many of them, this meant a society more equal than the one in which they had grown up, with universal provision of healthcare and education and scope for everyone to develop their talents. Many, including Phyllis Willmott, were less preoccupied with climbing the social ladder than they had been before the war. For them, the welfare state was a point of connection with the families and communities they came from. It was now possible to find professional work that contributed to improving life for those they'd grown up with. And in the doctor's waiting room, the primary-school classroom or the adult education class, they caught a glimpse of a future in which everyone's talents and skills would be valued.

Chapter Seven

THE MELODRAMA OF SOCIAL MOBILITY

During the 1950s and 60s, some upwardly mobile men of the breakthrough generation carved out a new role for themselves as architects of the evolving welfare state. When Albert Halsey went to the LSE in 1947, he found himself part of a group who hailed from working- or lower-middle-class homes hungry to help the welfare state succeed. They 'ardently wanted to believe' that the new post-war climate would offer 'an important role to the social scientist in the process of social reform'.[1] Over the next twenty years, these men achieved their ambition. In the process, they established social mobility as a focus for research, and a political goal.

By the late 1940s, Halsey and his contemporaries were impatient for change. They had served long years of clerking and war service. The welfare state and the expansion of education gave them the chance to carve out new careers, focused on creating the kind of post-war democracy they wanted to see.

These LSE students were inspired by some older upwardly mobile lecturers, among them Jean Floud. Born in 1915 to a cobbler and a shop assistant, she had won a scholarship to a London secondary school but was expelled at the age of fifteen after flouting school rules. She continued her studies at adult education classes, and enrolled for a social-science degree at the London School of Economics at the age of eighteen. By the late 1930s she had begun postgraduate research on the relationship between social class and educational attainment. In 1940 twenty-five-year-old Jean became assistant to the Director of Education for the city of Oxford. After the war she returned to the LSE as an assistant lecturer in sociology.

Jean Floud's schooling, and her work during the war, sparked her interest in education and social mobility. She was drawn to sociology as 'the study of our outmoded but by no means moribund class structure', and 'fascinated by the spectre of educational institutions struggling to respond to the new purposes of an advanced industrial economy'. In particular, she was intrigued by the 'demand for professional and managerial workers and the creation of the new middle-class of white-collar workers [which] turn education into one of the main avenues of social mobility.'[2]

But Jean Floud not only studied the relationship between education and mobility – she influenced it. Education had broadened her horizons and enriched her life, and she was determined to ensure this was true for her own students. As a junior member of staff at the LSE, and one of the few women in her department, Jean was aware of her inferior status. A senior male colleague would regularly 'breeze into my room, fling a [student's] file on the desk and say . . . "Here, you're a good teacher, see what you can do with this one."' Jean had little patience with such 'abrasive and unhelpful' behaviour.[3]

Albert Halsey greatly respected Jean Floud's 'vivacious intelligence'. But he classed Jean and her few upwardly mobile contemporaries as 'assimilators . . . in dress and speech to the culture of the higher metropolitan professionals.' He didn't realise that Jean Floud's accent and clothing only told part of her story; she was too professional to reveal her battles to have both teaching and the study of education taken seriously. Nevertheless, Albert admired Jean, recognising that upwardly mobile men and women of her age had faced 'strong pressure' to conform to the culture of the social milieu they joined. It was not a pressure he experienced – and this, he felt, showed how rapidly Britain was changing. As members of a large group of upwardly mobile men, imbued with the social democratic vision they had crafted during the war, and buoyed by the establishment of the welfare state, Halsey and his friends believed the social and professional world they were entering was 'no longer to be joined but to be transformed.'[4]

These researchers and planners argued that their background and their experience of upward mobility gave them a particular claim to expertise. John Gray's generation had been aware that their working-class roots were an obstacle to achieving their ambitions. But the war had shown that Britain depended on its manual and clerical workers, while the post-war Labour government declared that the benchmark by which a modern democracy should be judged was the welfare of all of its people.

Halsey and his peers set out to provide a 'sociological expression of autobiographical experience'.[5] They believed that their own experiences were invaluable in assessing and improving on Labour's reforms. Many, including Halsey himself, researched the connections between education and social mobility. Brian Jackson, born in 1932, and Dennis Marsden, born in 1933, both hailed from lower-middle-class families in Huddersfield. After graduating from university, Jackson had become a primary-school teacher, while Marsden became an industrial chemist. Neither knew the other at this point, but both wanted to mould post-war society. Dennis Marsden completed his National Service in 1957 'on a wave of interest in the sociology of working-class life which Richard Hoggart's *Uses of Literacy* [his semi-autobiographical study of working-class life, published in 1957], the Bethnal Green surveys by the Institute of Community Studies, and *New Left Review* [a new left-wing periodical] helped to arouse and disseminate.'[6] In the late 1950s Marsden and Jackson found work at the Institute of Community Studies led by Michael Young and Peter Willmott. In 1962 they jointly authored *Education and the Working Class*, a study of socially mobile grammar-school children. 'In this report we are deliberately mapping out a stretch of life, an initiatory experience, through which we lived ourselves', they wrote.[7]

Albert Halsey, Brian Jackson, Dennis Marsden and Richard Hoggart all benefited from huge interest in the social changes wrought by post-war welfare reform and near-full employment. This interest increased in the late 1950s. Working-class life was changing and opportunities to climb the social ladder appeared to be expanding. Harold Macmillan's Conservative government had committed to a huge house-building programme, speeding up slum clearance. The first generation to have experienced the 1944 Education Act reached maturity and entered a world where white-collar jobs were proliferating. Harold Macmillan claimed people had 'never had it so good'. In reality poverty persisted, especially among the old, the sick, single-parent families and in the slums. But many working-class families *were* enjoying a far higher standard of living than their parents had known before the war. The babies born immediately after the war became teenage consumers, with money and leisure to spend on dancing, fashion, scooters and records.[8] In this climate, Hoggart's *Uses of Literacy* became a bestseller, while Jackson's and Marsden's study of *Education and the Working Class* sold more than 14,000 copies in the year after the paperback edition was published.[9]

Other members of the breakthrough generation were also making their name by writing about working-class life. John Braine, born to a lower-middle-class Bradford family in 1922, published his bestselling novel *Room at the Top* in 1957. Alan Sillitoe's *Saturday Night and Sunday Morning* (1958), Keith Waterhouse's *Billy Liar* (1959), David Storey's *This Sporting Life* (1960) and Raymond Williams' *Border Country* (1960) were among the novels that followed. Their heroes were ambitious young men, desperate to exceed their reach, but fiercely attached to their working-class roots. They struggled against the odds to create new lives for themselves in a world very different from the one their parents had known.

Like other members of the breakthrough generation, many of these writers owed their chances to the war. John Braine and Alan Sillitoe gained writing experience and a pension through their time in the forces. Others got a break because so many men were at the front.

They included Keith Waterhouse, born in Leeds in 1929, who failed to get a scholarship to secondary school but was able to move from clerking to journalism in his teens. Younger men benefited from the post-war expansion of education, like David Storey, a coal-miner's son born in 1933, who funded his studies at the Slade School of Fine Art with a government grant (topped up by his earnings as a rugby league player). Their upward mobility happened in the 1940s and early 1950s. But their experiences gained wider resonance in the late 1950s and early 1960s, as universal, free secondary education and full employment promised to take far more young people up the ladder.

These writers and social scientists presented upward mobility as a heroic struggle against the odds. In their hands it became a melodrama that bound together working-class men coming of age in the post-war world. Many of them, including Jackson, Marsden and Hoggart, argued that social mobility could not simply be measured statistically. It was at least as vital to know how the journey up the ladder affected those concerned. The upwardly mobile man, wrote Hoggart, 'has to be more and more alone, if he is going to "get on". He is heading for a different world, a different sort of job.'[10]

This individualistic account of 'getting on' chimed with the Conservatives' championing of competition and individual acquisition. Successive Tory governments in the 1950s championed private enterprise, ended rationing and price controls, and supported private house building. The fifties, thought the prominent socialist historian Edward Thompson, writing in 1960, was 'a decade which sat for its own portrait in *Room at the Top*, which adopted the motto "Opportunity State", and which allowed the priorities of the salesman . . . and the speculator to override all other needs'.[11]

Whether Britain should become a meritocracy, or a far more egalitarian society, was a matter of lively political debate in the 1950s and early 1960s. In 1956 the Labour politician Tony Crosland had published *The Future of Socialism*, which argued that Labour's survival depended on embracing aspects of the Conservatives' programme. This included upward mobility via a 'status ladder'. 'Conservatives like to claim that this is the doctrine of modern Tory radicalism', wrote Crosland. But 'equal opportunity' should be a Labour goal: it would 'make society more mobile and dynamic, and so less class-bound.' Nevertheless, Crosland stressed, it would be vital to ensure that those who lived on the lowest rungs enjoyed a significant share of 'income, power, and occupational prestige', for 'if inequality of rewards is excessively great, the creation of equal opportunities may give rise to too intense a competition, with a real danger of increased frustration and discontent.'[12]

Other prominent Labour politicians and supporters were less sure that the ladder could work at all. In 1958 Michael Young published his satire *The Rise of the Meritocracy, 1870–2033*. Posing as a social researcher writing in the mid-twenty-first century, he argued that the replacement of hereditary privilege with a social ladder based on talent would only replicate inequality. In his dystopia, the 'five per cent' of the most privileged were chosen 'on merit', but their behaviour was remarkably similar to that of the upper class they had replaced, not least in treating their 'inferiors' as 'unemployable' or as exploitable 'domestic servants'. Technological and industrial progress stalled, as those at the top became increasingly preoccupied with retaining their privileged status and less concerned with fostering talent and imagination.[13]

A year later, Labour suffered its third consecutive general election defeat. Edward Thompson argued that it was vital to recognise 'the permeation of the acquisitive ethic into the centres of working-class life'. Later that year, Thompson helped to launch the New Left – a movement focused on understanding the political and social changes that had occurred since the war. The left, he wrote, must understand and appreciate aspirations and experiences that arose from 'the context of social mobility'.[14]

The New Left debated how modern socialism might offer a humane and compassionate form of community against capitalist competition and the horrors of Stalinism. The socially mobile writers added grist to their mill. While they depicted upward mobility as an individualistic pursuit, and one from which they had benefited, they did not necessarily see this as the best way to distribute opportunity. Richard Hoggart described 'the scholarship boy' as 'ill at ease with the middle classes because with one side of himself he does not want them to accept him; he mistrusts or even a little despises them . . . He wavers between scorn and longing.'[15] Achieving upward mobility, argued these writers, did not necessarily bring happiness or social harmony.

Accounts like Richard Hoggart's had a huge impact on a younger generation. In his semi-autobiographical novel *Border Country*, Raymond Williams explored what communities and individuals lost when 'success' meant leaving one's roots forever. Dai Smith read *Border Country* as an undergraduate in the early 1960s. Born in the Rhondda Valley in 1945, Smith had attended grammar school before reading History at Oxford. He was entranced by *Border Country*: 'the instantly recognisable emotional and intellectual journey of a work-ing-class boy who goes away from his shaping community'. At school and university, Smith had imbibed the notion that upward mobility was 'about successful individuals gratefully climbing ladders. Not so here.'[16] *Border Country* spoke to his own experience, despite him being twenty-four years younger than its author.

Some of the upwardly mobile men of the breakthrough generation went further in their critiques of meritocracy than either Crosland or Young. They used their platform to call for a more equal society, in which people would not face such a struggle to get an education or fulfilling work, nor have to leave their roots in order to lead the life they wanted. By the mid-1950s, Albert Halsey had been awarded a doctorate on social class and educational opportunity, supervised by Jean Floud. His findings supported her own research, which showed that social class determined a child's educational achievements, in particular by shaping his or her chance of passing the eleven-plus examination that determined what kind of secondary school children attended.[17] A growing number of researchers began to argue for non-selective comprehensive schools, which would nurture a multiplicity of talents, rather than educating children differently on the basis of their perceived intelligence. Brian Jackson and Dennis Marsden pointed to a 'dilemma: working-class life – listen to the voices – has strengths we cannot afford to lose; middle-class life transmits within it the high culture of our society, that must be opened freely to all'.[18]

Some argued for the complete eradication of the social ladder. In 1958 Raymond Williams argued that 'the ladder is a perfect symbol of the bourgeois idea of society, because, while undoubtedly it offers the opportunity to climb, it is a device which can only be used individually . . . it weakens the principle of common betterment' and simply replaced 'the hierarchy of money or of birth' with 'the hierarchy of merit'.[19] Brian Jackson and Dennis Marsden agreed that 'merit' was a subjective and questionable means of organising society. They argued that 'society's dominant group knits the schools into standards and values so as to produce a school system which strongly favours its own children whilst appearances of justice and equality are suitably pre-served'. By the early 1960s, both the Conservative government and the Labour opposition argued that Britain required technological innova-tion to remain internationally competitive. But Jackson and Marsden cautioned that creating more room at the top did not necessarily cre-ate a more equal society. '[T]he training of a ruling elite . . . has not collapsed under the new purpose – the training of enough able people to man our technological society' they wrote. The success of some upwardly mobile men did not, Jackson and Marsden argued, legiti-mate social hierarchy; it simply replaced one outdated pecking order with another equally arbitrary one. What was more, they suggested that any form of social and occupational stratification would ulti-mately be dominated by those who were able to use family influence and inherited wealth and status to their advantage. '[A]s Eton builds its science blocks . . . putting the same people into the same places at the same price.'[20]

By the mid-1960s, this group had succeeded in their claim that they were worth listening to. Some were bestselling authors. Others, like Halsey, Hoggart and Williams, worked in universities. They were among the 33 per cent of university lecturers who came from working-class backgrounds by the end of that decade.[21] A few exercised political influence. In 1964, Labour returned to power after thirteen years, committed to 'equality of opportunity' and comprehensive schools. Albert Halsey, by now a lecturer at Oxford University, became advisor to Tony Crosland, the Minister of Education. As Halsey recognised, his influence was limited; Crosland and the Prime Minister, Harold Wilson, were far more committed to a meritocratic version of society and concerned to adapt this to the existing status quo. Both sent their children to private schools. 'The English sin in education, I thought, was inequality', wrote Halsey, 'while [Crosland's] great fear was that we might impose unfreedom on those who wanted to send their children to schools in the private sector.'[22] Tony Crosland himself was clear that where he and the researchers could find common cause was in establishing 'equal opportunity'. It helped his case to be able to point to 'the whole series of studies and reports . . . which showed the effect of selection on children's chances', but the government of which he was part was less concerned about equality per se than some of the sociologists with whom they worked.[23] These differences of opinion highlight that 'meritocracy' remained controversial into the 1960s, with some of the upwardly mobile themselves pointing out its weaknesses and limits.

These upwardly mobile men did not knock more privileged people off their rung of the ladder. Instead, they owed their rise to new opportunities that they helped to create. By the 1960s, the proportion of university lecturers who were upwardly mobile was far higher than among senior civil servants or doctors, of whom fewer than 20 per cent were the children of manual workers.[24] The upwardly mobile lecturers were far less likely to work at Oxbridge than at the civic universities and at newer institutions like Keele, Sussex and Warwick which were established after the war. The largest single group of working-class lecturers (and students) were found in science departments, but an increasing number found their way into the social sciences.[25] Subjects like sociology offered a means of explaining their own trajectory and influencing policy. And these

Some of the first students at Ruskin College, Oxford, established in 1899 with the aim of giving working men a taste of university life

A Workers Educational Association summer school at Durham in 1921. The WEA was formed in 1903 by and for adults who wanted more education than their rudimentary schooling provided

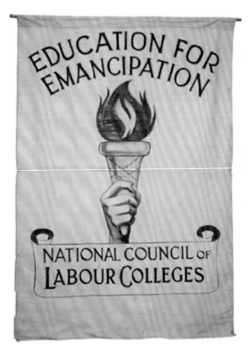

Albert Mansbridge, the founder of the WEA, making a speech in 1913

The Labour colleges were established to provide a socialist education for working-class people

Shop run by the National Union of Women's Suffrage Societies, 1908. The women's movement fought for greater access to education and the professions, as well as for the vote – and provided some women with a livelihood

Labour politician Ellen Wilkinson, who fervently believed in education's ability to 'remove slums and underfeeding and misery'

Clerical work allowed some working-class men – like these clerks in a Sheffield steelworks, c. 1890 – to climb the social ladder by the late nineteenth century

Conservative election poster, 1929–30

While this government poster from c. 1930 presents the servant as similar to a middle-class housewife (albeit in a uniform), most young women found the low wages and long hours unappealing

Teacher and children at Box village school, Wiltshire, c. 1925. Teaching offered a professional career to some working-class girls but usually in poorly resourced and overcrowded elementary schools

THE EDUCATIONAL CRISIS.

London Schoolmasters and Their Salaries.

IS EQUAL PAY FOR MEN & WOMEN TEACHERS JUST?

MASS MEETING OF SCHOOLMASTERS EMPHATICALLY ANSWERS "NO!"

For the first time in the history of the teaching profession, a Mass Meeting of the Schoolmasters of London was held at Kingsway Hall, on Saturday, May 31st, to consider the low rates of salaries now paid to Schoolmasters, and the serious effects likely to be produced thereby on educational progress in this country.

EXISTING TEACHERS' ASSOCIATIONS CAPTURED BY WOMEN!

The situation has been rendered more acute by the adoption of the principle of Equal Pay for Men and Women Teachers by existing teachers' associations. It is important to note that the women members of the existing teachers' associations vastly outnumber the men, and naturally this preponderance is reflected in all resolutions adopted by these organisations. Men now recognise that it is impossible for these associations adequately to express their views.

That intense feeling has been roused among the Schoolmasters is shewn by the extraordinary success of Saturday's meeting; about two thousand Schoolmasters were present, and the proceedings were marked by the greatest enthusiasm and unanimity.

NOT INIMICAL TOWARDS WOMEN.

The President, MR. HERBERT SPRIGGE, opened the meeting by declaring that there was no intention of being inimical towards women. ("Hear! Hear!"). Equal Pay for men and women was, he said, Utopian. Teachers were, by the very nature of their calling, idealists; but by the economic stress of the present abnormal times, they were now driven to a fierce struggle for mundane things, and for the right to live as befitted those whose lives were devoted to the service of the State.

A NATIONAL DISASTER!

Equal Pay in the teaching profession would, MR. SPRIGGE asserted, be based on the wages of the woman, and would therefore conduce to the elimination of men from the teaching profession. This would be a national disaster: for whilst women could impart knowledge, they could not be expected to inspire in boys those manly virtues upon which our great Empire was founded. (Cheers.)

WAGES AND FAMILY NEEDS.

MR. A. E. WARREN then spoke on the effects of "Equal Pay" in the profession. He said that wages should be based on family needs. (Cheers). A single man had greater potential responsibilities than a single woman. A scale of salaries which would satisfy the needs of a woman, with her lesser responsibilities in life, could not possibly satisfy the needs of a married man, and the great majority of the men in the teaching profession were married, whilst the great majority of the women were single.

MEN'S SOCIAL SUPERIORS——?

MR. W. H. THODAY, in moving the formal constitution of the London Schoolmasters' Association, said that women had gone too far. There was a limit, and the women had gone beyond it, and imposed an absolute sex policy on a union which was for the general benefit (Cheers). Give the women equal pay, and they would become the social superiors of the men.

NEW SOCIETY CONSTITUTED.

The motion approving the formation of the London Schoolmasters' Association was carried unanimously, and instructions were given to the provisional committee to frame a constitution.

SECONDARY SCHOOLMASTERS CO-OPERATE.

A request for close co-operation from a representative of the Association of Assistant Masters of Secondary Schools was heartily welcomed.

RESOLUTION OF PROTEST.

The following resolution was carried unanimously and with acclamation :—

"That this Mass Meeting of London Schoolmasters protests against the adoption of the principle of Equal Pay for Men and Women in the Teaching Profession."

Issued by The London Schoolmasters' Association :—

The London Schoolmasters' Association campaigned against equal pay for women teachers in 1919, on the grounds that this would impoverish male teachers' families and make women 'men's social superiors'

Their lives are in your hands.

VOTE – FOR THE
NATIONAL GOVERNMENT
and *PROTECT* their future.

Conservative election poster, 1931–8. The Conservative-led national governments of the 1930s exploited middle-class women's anxieties about their children's prospects

Self-Sacrifice

The key-note of the Nursing Profession is self-sacrifice, the most precious quality in human nature, and one much too precious to waste.

But the appeal to self-sacrifice is too often a cloak which hides injustice, ignorance and inefficiency.

Long hours, unnecessary restrictions, scamped and insufficient meals, "nagging" and bullying and lack of privacy mean ●crifice of self-respect, and, worst of all, inevitably reduce the standard of work.

Be fair to yourself— and you will be fair to your Patients

Here are nurses paying tribute to Florence Nightingale who bravely fought prejudice and ignorance in high places.

Her lamp—which is one of the outstanding symbols in our nation's history—is still alight. Will *you* follow its gleam?

In the 1920s and 1930s successive governments promoted nursing as a genteel profession for women. The reality was very different, as this trade union magazine – encouraging nurses to 'be fair to yourself' and join a union – makes clear

Second World War evacuees from Bristol arrive in Devon, 1940. Evacuation broadened some children's horizons, but disrupted the lives and education of millions

Ernest Bevin, dockworker-turned-Minister for Labour and National Service, 1940

RAF flight-engineering cadets being trained in 1944. Wartime demand for engineers in the armed forces meant more men became skilled workers – a step up the ladder for those who had been unemployed or labourers before the war

new universities and departments were not dominated by estab-lished academic networks and conventions. There was space for upwardly mobile men to colonise.

These men's claim that their upward mobility gave them valuable expertise helped them to establish academic careers. Colin Bell was among those they inspired. He was born in 1942 in Kent; his father was a clerk. After grammar school Colin attended Keele University and then embarked on postgraduate research in sociology at Swansea University. Here he studied geographic and social mobility, influenced by the work of the breakthrough generation. As he suggested, the upwardly mobile social scientists of the 1950s and 60s set out to 'cre-ate the role of sociological research worker' as a respected scholar, whose work informed policy.[26]

But women of the breakthrough generation rarely enjoyed the same success. The upwardly mobile writers and social researchers were almost all men. They gave women only a supporting role in their stories and studies. Typically, Richard Hoggart described them solely as wives and mothers, 'devoted to the family and beyond proud self-regard'.[27] In the 1960s sociologists began developing statistical stud-ies of social mobility. These focused exclusively on men, examining fathers' and sons' occupations, or boys' attainment at school. Diff-erences between the sexes were rarely examined; the focus was almost exclusively on class. Jean Floud's research in the 1950s, and Brian Jackson's and Dennis Marsden's *Education and the Working Class*, were valuable exceptions. They showed that mothers were hugely influential on children's educational performance.[28] Yet this finding was not picked up by subsequent studies of social mobility.

Sociologists relied heavily on women's goodwill as respondents and hosts when they door-stepped interviewees in the communities they studied. Yet these women's roles and experiences were often overlooked. This trend was reinforced by the younger generation of sociologists who were mentored and trained by this group in the 1960s. John Goldthorpe, born in 1935 to a Yorkshire mining clerk and a housewife, was among them. After attending his local grammar school, Goldthorpe studied History at London University, and then trained as a sociologist at Cambridge University. 'It is difficult', he wrote, 'to envisage any factors which . . . would be likely to result in any *sizeable number of women* occupying *markedly* different class positions from those of the male "heads" of their families, or possessing attributes or engaging in activities which would in themselves materially influence the class position of [the] family unit.'[29] This approach ignored the assistance that mothers and wives gave to upwardly mobile men, and the experiences of women who entered 'middle-class' jobs such as clerical work and teaching.

Yet these upwardly mobile writers and scholars depended on women's unpaid labour. Many relied on their wives for vital support. When the ambitious Albert Halsey was appointed to his first lectureship in Liverpool in 1952, he told his wife Margaret 'not to unpack', confident that a more senior post would soon beckon; two years later they left for a post at Birmingham University.[30] An LSE graduate and trained social worker, Margaret became Halsey's chief support through a long and distinguished academic career that took them to the USA and Oxford. Richard Hoggart owed his first job to his wife. In 1946 when her husband was still in the army, Mary Hoggart spent her first pregnancy 'searching for jobs advertised in the educational press, and applying on [Richard's] behalf for any which seemed at all likely'.[31] She won him his interview at Hull University, and she gave up her teaching career to bring up their three children.

These men's claim to professional expertise depended in part on excluding women from their writing, research and departments. Some of them denigrated the expertise of women who had carved out careers as social workers and researchers before and during the war. Here, they were sometimes assisted by older men who had also benefited from the new opportunities that the war, and the post-war welfare state, offered them. In 1950, Richard Titmuss arrived at the LSE to become professor of social administration. Born in 1907 Titmuss himself was 'a splendid example of class mobility – from small farmer's son to grand university professor'. Like so many upwardly mobile men of his generation, he had scaled the ladder via white-collar work, after leaving school at fourteen and training as an actuary. In common with the WEA students of his age, he had a thirst for learning and took a keen interest in social welfare. Self-taught, he published two books on the subject in the late 1930s, and during the war was recruited to the Civil Service to write the official wartime history of social policy. In 1950 he took up his new appointment in an LSE department that had been built up by highly educated women like Kit Russell. Over the next decade, Titmuss edged them out. They went only 'reluctantly', taking with them the principle that trained welfare workers' expertise should inform social policy, and the belief that women's needs should inform social policy just as much as concern over social class.[32]

The focus on male experiences of mobility marginalised those women who did manage to get a foothold in universities. In 1953 Jean Floud moved from the LSE to the more congenial environment of the Institute of Education, from where she was able to conduct her research into the relationship between education and social mobility. But although her work inspired Albert Halsey's, her own contributions were frequently ignored by sociologists and by policymakers. Albert Halsey identified two of his university tutors as influential in his own career: 'men [who] stood out as guides to further ambition – David Glass and Edward Shils'. They 'were indifferent lecturers, but . . . endowed with a compelling charisma'.[33] Edward Shils was an American scholar of intellectual life. He was also the colleague whose 'abrasive and unhelpful' attitude to teaching Jean Floud had found objectionable. Just as he had undervalued her dedication and research, so Albert Halsey's generation often downplayed Jean's contribution to the study of social mobility – and their own experience of it. Charisma and ambition – the hallmarks of self-made men – were lauded; collegiality, nurturing and caring not so much.

Younger women graduates – members of the breakthrough generation – had fewer chances to establish themselves than Floud. Margaret Stacey was one of them. In the 1940s, her ground-breaking research on Banbury provided a rare insight into the lives and motives of the managers, professionals and their wives, often from lower-middle-class backgrounds, who were taking up senior posts in local government and the expanding industries. Stacey focused on the lower-middle class, and on social mobility as a collective experience shaped by employers, influenced by housing and played out in relations between husbands, wives and neighbours.[34] But her approach did not fit the story of the heroic, upwardly mobile man, whose rise from working-class origins was due to his intelligence and education.

Unlike so many of the male social scientists of her generation, Stacey was unable to find a permanent job. Even during the 'sociology explosion' that occurred in higher education during the 1960s, she recalled, universities 'refused to employ [me] because I was married with children'.[35] Stacey succeeded only by finding a role that men didn't want. In the late 1960s she got her first permanent lectureship, in Swansea University's expanding sociology department. The lecturers here 'found they were appointing young men who never came . . . because they got a better job in England, so they scraped the bottom of the barrel and there was me'.[36]

Margaret Stacey's treatment didn't simply reflect wider conservative views about women in post-war Britain. Some male researchers actively marginalised women who had been trying to forge a career since the Second World War. This diminished middle-class women's employment prospects, but also meant that working-class women had little chance of experiencing the ascent that some of their male peers enjoyed. Most women graduates of the breakthrough generation – more than 70 per cent of them – went into teaching.[37] Those who entered the other professions tended to have higher qualifications than men, and were more likely to have attended Oxbridge. Very few working- or lower-middle-class women had those credentials.[38]

Phyllis Willmott was among those women without a degree but keen to help shape the welfare state. By the early 1960s, she had satisfied some, but not all, of the ambitions she'd expressed back in 1945. She became a research assistant to Richard Titmuss, and at the Institute of Community Studies she was given the task of undertaking 'surveys and interviews with Bethnal Greeners about their housing dreams and family life'. This was essential to the work of the Institute of Community Studies, where 'dry statistics were to be brought to life by the human warmth of personal experience in reports that ordinary readers could enjoy as much as, if not more than, the traditional academic audience'. But unlike her husband Peter, Phyllis and the other women at the Institute were employed as temporary assistants and had less input into the institute's analysis and reports.[39]

By the 1960s the breakthrough generation had achieved a great deal. They helped to establish a welfare state focused on improving living standards, and which valued the work of caring for others, whether through social work, teaching, or research. They had created new chances for people to ascend the ladder, by expanding room at the top to include work that made a meaningful contribution to everyone's well-being.

But some men achieved political and social influence by claiming an expertise that was based on their heroic struggle up the ladder. Room at the top remained limited. In order to monopolise it, these men asserted that their expertise was more valuable than that of middle-class educated women, or of working-class women who lacked the chance to ascend the ladder. They stressed the importance of establishing a meritocracy, and of measuring its success by gauging how far men like themselves could succeed. By the 1960s they had succeeded in persuading senior politicians that male upward mobility was the best means to measure Britain's social and economic progress. The great inequality that neither the welfare state nor economic growth resolved – women's limited political power and economic opportunities – was ignored. Women's role was to support the men who planned and maintained this brave new world.

Chapter Eight

A MANAGERIAL REVOLUTION?

In the 1950s the single most important route up the ladder was industrial management. Between 1945 and 1949 British business appointed three times as many managers as during the war, partly due to an increase in managerial jobs in those industries that Labour nationalised (iron, steel, coal, haulage, the railways and electricity).[1] But private sector expansion was more important in the years that followed. Between 1951 and 1964, when the Conservatives were in government, public-sector employment declined for the first time since the 1850s. The Conservatives privatised the steel and haulage industries and chose not to expand the social services as the Beveridge Report had recommended.[2] Instead, they focused on allowing private industry to grow. During the 1950s and 60s the number of managers rose rapidly, to 2,054,000 by 1971 – an increase of 65 per cent since 1951, with an average 40,000 new managers appointed each year.[3]

Those who rose through industry did not take places formerly occupied by men from different social backgrounds; instead they took up entirely new posts. They were middle managers – production managers and personnel managers – whose numbers multiplied as successful firms expanded and multinational corporations moved into Britain. In the late 1960s a study of middle managers concluded that 'during the past twenty-five years there have been more opportunities in this section of the labour force than any other'.[4]

By the mid-1950s more than half of British managers had started out in routine clerical work or manual jobs in their mid-teens.[5] More than a quarter of them were the sons of manual workers.[6] Although few managerial posts were open to women, their lives were also dramatically changed. Many women of the breakthrough generation who experienced lifelong upward mobility did so by marrying a man who became a manager.

In the 1950s, Conservative and Labour politicians alike hailed a 'managerial revolution'. They declared that the rising number of managers was unleashing hitherto untapped talents. After the Conservatives' second consecutive general election win in 1955, Hugh Gaitskell became Labour's leader. Gaitskell, a privately educated former civil servant and WEA lecturer, was on the right of the party. Supported by the Labour politician Tony Crosland, Gaitskell suggested that the party must wholeheartedly embrace capitalism if it was to return to power. In Gaitskell's view, there was no need for strong trade unions or public ownership of industry. The post-war expansion of management in private firms showed that a meritocracy was at work – those with talent and determination were able to rise to the top.[7]

But the lives of these managers and their wives did not testify to a 'managerial revolution'. The routes to promotion were obscure, and few rose from the factory floor as far as the boardroom. British industry was far more hierarchical and less democratic than Gaitskell and Crosland suggested. The new generation of managers possessed little power – they did not supplant those at the top of the ladder. Nevertheless, their ascent into middle management required hard work to achieve and to sustain. And this was a project that relied on the efforts of their wives at least as much as on the managers themselves.

At the end of the war, few men had aspired to become a manager. In 1949 just 5 per cent of manual workers wanted to move into management,[8] and the proportion hadn't changed much fourteen years later when a team of sociologists led by John Goldthorpe interviewed Luton's car workers about their work and aspirations. Goldthorpe was keen to find out if rising earnings had led manual workers to adopt what his team believed to be middle-class aspirations, valuing personal promotion and wealth above trade unionism and pride in craftwork.[9] But few of their interviewees wanted to become foremen, let alone managers. Many shop-floor workers worked hard to acquire material comforts that the researchers considered symbols of middle-class life – a house, a car, a three-piece suite. However, they eschewed any desire to join the middle class, who were widely viewed as pretentious and snobbish – people who, in the words of Bill Ellis, 'think they're better than they are . . . like the managers'.[10]

Many of those who became managers did so reluctantly. They fitted David Glass's conclusion that most people in post-war Britain held skilled workers and professionals in particularly high esteem. Managers from working-class backgrounds had often wanted to go into skilled manual trades. The Depression and then the war had prevented them doing so. Those from lower-middle-class or working-class families who had had a secondary education often hankered after university and a professional career. This was particularly true of those who had served alongside graduates during the war and then had their hopes raised by Labour's post-war education and training schemes. In the mid-1950s the social scientist Roger Clements studied 646 managers in Manchester. He found that 'many regret not going to a university', believing that higher education would have offered them a 'broadening cultural experience'.[11]

These men did not want to settle for unskilled or semi-skilled factory work, or routine clerical jobs. June Abbott's father, a bank clerk conscripted into the RAF, came home in 1946 'unsettled by the war and he wanted to retrain as a doctor'. His wife, a secondary-school teacher who had 'loved' her job (she had left when she married), was willing to return to work to support him through a shorter course, but she judged a lengthy and expensive medical training too impractical and risky given that the National Health Service was very new. Mr Abbott returned to the bank and focused on rising through the ranks there, eventually becoming a branch manager.[12] Having been disappointed in their hopes of a trade or education, men like him looked to improve their position within their firm.

They got their chance because of a new emphasis on production and people management during the war that was then embedded into post-war industry. 'To these men a big helping factor has been the growth of the firms in which they work', observed Roger Clements.[13] Their workplaces had expanded, first to meet wartime production needs, and later to produce the goods on which the post-war consumer society depended: cars, televisions, fridges and three-piece suites. Forty-six per cent of manufacturing workers were employed in enterprises with more than 5,000 employees in 1958, and 17 per cent in firms with more than 20,000 employees.[14] Both the public and private sectors remained very hierarchical. With shop-floor workers allowed little responsibility or power, the only way of coping with expansion was to hire more managers.

Most firms offered no clear route from shop floor to management. Workers complained that 'there is insufficient opportunity for the bright young internal candidate to apply for admission', particularly in privately owned firms.[15] 'You are put in a certain stream and you make certain progress in a certain direction', one worker complained to Clements.[16] Those who did become managers often ascribed their promotion to 'luck' or 'being in the right place at the right time'.[17] They were likely to have received wartime training in technical and engineering jobs, or had attended night classes in these subjects at their own expense – for personal interest as much as in the hope this would benefit their careers.[18] But this meant they were well placed to take advantage of a 'lucky break'.

Their good fortune usually resulted from a crisis. Senior managers were conservative, autocratic, reluctant to innovate and hostile to trade union and shop-floor consultation.[19] They tended to react to emergencies rather than to plan ahead. In a period when firms were rapidly expanding, numerous men were promoted overnight when their boss suddenly realised that a new plant required a production manager.[20]

But even as the number of managerial roles increased, nepotism and social elitism persisted. These men were appointed to completely new roles – most frequently in production management. They were not recruited into established, senior positions, and few reached the directors' boardroom. In family-owned firms, senior managers were often related to the owner. In private firms, men who had attended a private school were most likely to reach managerial positions – more so even than state-educated university graduates.[21] In 1968 50 per cent of senior managers in Britain's largest industrial firms had been privately educated.[22] Frequently, these managers were appointed to senior roles straight from school or university. 'Relationship with a family influential in the firm may . . . assist promotion', observed Clements. And 'less specific "connections" stemming from higher social origins are important . . . implicit in the protest by several managers that "it's not what you know, but who you know that matters", coupled sometimes with a reference to the "right school tie"'.[23]

Employers – themselves often the products of private schools – prioritised '"leadership qualities", supposedly inherent in the public school type'.[24] This was just as true in newer firms as in long-established enterprises. In Banbury, Margaret Stacey observed, a new large aluminium factory included 'among its annual intake a number of public school men, whose qualification is just that they are public school men. They have a "social know-how" that the management consider valuable'.[25] On the whole, directors underrated technical knowledge and production experience. They took little interest in the long-term strategic direction of their firms, preferring to prioritise short-term profit and to support their own sons and wider networks for the top jobs.[26] Far from encouraging innovation, the unequal and rigid hierarchies of private firms led to stagnation as the top men reproduced the status quo.

Among working-class men, only the few who got to university had a good chance of becoming senior managers. It was very rare for a man to work his way up that far from the factory floor. The industries that Labour nationalised after the war had a better record than private firms of recruiting men with a state education. But they did not appoint a greater proportion of working-class men than other industries, because they preferred to recruit university graduates wherever possible. University degrees were beyond the means of most members of the breakthrough generation.[27]

But for male working-class graduates, industrial management was an attractive route. While privately educated senior managers read for a wide range of degrees, these working-class men tended to have scientific qualifications. They included Barry Thompson, the son of a railway worker, who had won a scholarship to secondary school in the late 1930s, then been 'pushed by Dad and the school' to university. Like many upwardly mobile students, Barry was encouraged to specialise in science. He 'worked like hell' and in 1950 graduated with a first-class degree in chemistry. He was headhunted by an international corporation that offered him a middle-management post.[28] University education, which made little difference to the prospects of public schoolboys, could be decisive for working-class men's careers. But they were most likely to get work in the nationalised industries and in multinational companies like Barry's employer, which valued scientific expertise more than most privately owned British firms did.[29]

Working-class men who became managers often claimed their background as a virtue. Those who had started out as shop-floor workers boasted of having come 'the hard way up', resonant of the 'hard-boiled', masculine toughness lauded by older technocrats like Bill Ramsgate in the 1930s.[30] Production managers oversaw shop-floor workers and technical processes. They mingled more with manual workers than with their firm's directors. Many agreed with those on the shop floor that 'the bosses' knew little about production. 'Some argue that they are closer to the ground', observed Clements, 'and so can understand and manage labour the better.'[31]

But the domestic lives of these managers were very different from those of the men they supervised. Family life was fitted around their career. Surveys conducted between the early 1950s and the late 1960s by Clements, the Acton Trust and the social scientists Jan and

Ray Pahl found these men regularly worked more than sixty hours a week (at a time when most manual workers were employed for forty-eight hours per week and, even with overtime, rarely worked more than fifty-five). They often devoted weekends to their work although they professed to find it boring, and said they'd prefer to spend more time with their families. When they did go home, many found it impossible to switch off – their wives expressed concern that they could never relax.[32]

Ambition to ascend into senior management rarely explained their hard work. 'They only appoint above my level from outside, so I'll stick here', reported one manager in his early forties.[33] As a survey of managing directors and senior managers discovered, 'many British managements have a deep-seated prejudice against increasing the number of . . . managerial employees'.[34] They did not want to erode the tight-knit family and social networks from which they had tradition-ally recruited. When expansion in the boardroom was necessary, many firms sought graduates, rather than promoting their own workers. By their late thirties, most middle managers believed that they had ascended as far as they were likely to go, and many were content with this. As a forty-two-year-old engineer explained to the sociologist Colin Bell: 'I've done alright, I started on the shop floor, became fore-man and went to night school' and eventually became a production manager.[35]

For some, hard work was an attempt to assert their individuality. Barry Thompson 'used to think I was a cliché – the working-class boy who made good, a member of the new middle class, the meritocratic technocrat'. But while this had been an attractive thought to some of the precarious generation, Barry, born in the 1930s, worried that it limited his horizons, consigning him to a growing group of technical workers without much power, cogs in the machine of the post-war state – 'the whole question of identity was very difficult for me and my kind'. He'd wanted to do a PhD after graduating, 'as much as anything to avoid going out into the world', but this proved too expensive once he had a wife and a child to support. He wasn't sure how to get the role he wanted for himself: one that offered more power and variety than engineering or teaching in a technical college. But after becoming a manager, and winning several promotions, 'this is no longer a problem because I now think I know where I am going'.[36]

As a senior manager, Barry was unusual among the upwardly mobile men. Those who didn't ascend to his heights had a different motivation for working hard: fear of sliding back down the ladder. Managers from working-class backgrounds, and manual workers who aspired to be managers, prized 'security' more than pay or social prestige.[37] Although Britain enjoyed near-full employment through the 1950s and early 1960s, seasonal lay-offs remained common in some industries, including car manufacture. The Conservatives were unwilling to interfere with the private sector and eager to create mini 'booms' directly before general elections by lowering inflation – but this meant elections were often followed by rises in inflation and unemployment.[38] And smaller firms were increasingly taken over or subject to mergers, as the largest firms expanded and multinationals moved in. 'It is the fear of falling rather than the positive aspiration to climb which pushes these men on', found Jan and Ray Pahl. This was particularly true of 'those who had an experience of downward social mobility in their family history'.[39] Many men of the breakthrough generation had witnessed first-hand the effect of unemployment or bankruptcy on their fathers and families in the 1930s.

Retaining a managerial position increasingly meant being geographically mobile. A study of people who moved house in 1957 found that while most did so to get a home of their own or to acquire a bigger house, 18 per cent moved for work. Most of these were in 'administrative, professional, managerial or proprietary jobs'.[40] In 1968 the sociologist Colin Bell studied two large private housing estates in Swansea where more than half of the inhabitants had moved in during the past five years – and about half expected to have moved on within the next five. More than a third of them were employed in managerial roles.[41]

As they worked their way up, these managers continued to exert little control over their careers. The Pahls found that 'few men were advancing along a clear and structured career line' much to their frus-tration. They were obliged to move because a plant closed or a new one opened, or a boss's favourite wanted their job. Some moved to a different firm in the hope of better prospects, but this was less com-mon among those who'd 'worked their way up' from the shop floor. Those with a degree had a marketable qualification, but most men's expertise relied heavily on their intimate knowledge of a particular firm. Most men continued to talk of 'being in the right place at the right time' and 'luck' as key to further pay rises or an increase in their responsibilities.[42] Most moved between posts simply to secure their managerial status, rather than for a promotion.

Those members of the breakthrough generation who entered aca-demia or welfare work enjoyed not only security but a sense that their education and background entitled them to their position. The man-agers felt far more precarious. Like the clerks of John Gray's genera-tion, most of them relied on working their way up a single firm. Experience and contacts counted for more than qualifications in their rise up the ladder. They often likened their relationship with their employer to a love affair. Barry Thompson spoke of being 'seduced' by his firm, while others were 'courted' by companies. But once ensconced at a firm, they became subordinate partners in an unequal relation-ship. Many saw their greatest asset as their loyalty, describing them-selves as 'faithful' to their company.[43] This affected even those with special assets, like graduates. Barry described his work as 'prostitut-ing' himself.[44] Unlike the technocrats of the 1930s, or the social scien-tists and welfare workers of their own generation, these men did not see their work as offering anything of significance to society. They rarely took much pride in what they did. It was a means to an end – a middle-class standard of living.

These men regularly presented their hard work as a sacrifice they made to acquire affluence and social status which, they implied, were at least as important to their spouses as to themselves. They spoke of their wives as passive beneficiaries of their careers, interspersing 'I' and 'we' as they discussed their ambitions. 'I am as determined as anyone to get on', one manager told Colin Bell, explaining why he was willing to move house so often: 'we will not be here on this estate in five years' time'.[45] Another had decided to stay on the estate: 'I can't get any higher . . . we're going to settle'.[46] Most assumed that their ambitions were in accord with, or took precedence over, their wives' wishes. Barry Thompson had moved to his current firm 'as much as anything because they offered me a job in a part of the country in which I wanted to live: Kent . . . so *we* moved and really liked it, both the place and the job'. He spoke of his first major promotion as 'us' acquiring 'a bit of seniority'.[47]

These managers undervalued the crucial contribution that women made to their social mobility. For the pre-war generations of clerks and technocrats, parents, especially mothers, had played a pivotal role. For men of the breakthrough generation, wives were even more important. These men married women from working-class backgrounds similar to their own. Many of their wives had been secretaries or typists, often meeting their future husbands at work. They understood their husbands' jobs and the organisations they worked for.[48]

A man's rise into management affected both spouses. Mrs George, who was one of those interviewed by Jan and Ray Pahl, had married a factory worker who trained as an engineer during the war. By the 1950s he was a production manager. 'After my husband studied and qualified, he went into bigger and better jobs and after the sort of background we had both had, we needed each other to face the consequences of this'.[49]

Wives acted as hostesses, entertaining their husband's clients or bosses. Some relished this. The Pahls found that women with a secondary-school education and a background in clerical work often aspired 'to leading the gregarious social life traditional in the solid middle class'.[50] Mary Edwards, the daughter of manual workers, had been a bank clerk before she married in the early 1950s. Her husband, also from a working-class background, 'worked his way up' an insurance company, becoming a manager in the late 1950s. Their daughter Tracey recalled that 'my mum's role was to look after my dad and us and to entertain for my dad. She used to do a lot of dinner parties for his work.' This was Mrs Edwards' contribution to their joint effort to 'move up in class'.[51]

But not all wives enjoyed this role. Many of those who had had professional careers found entertaining tiring and tiresome, while those women who had been factory or shop workers were often intimidated by catering for middle-class clients or bosses.[52] Among the professionals was June Abbott's mother, who returned to teaching in the early 1950s. When her husband became a bank manager in the mid-1950s she was required 'to entertain his clients and colleagues, which she did a lot of and was good at', but this required 'enormous energy' on top of her own full-time, demanding job.[53]

Husbands also expected their wives to provide a haven from the workplace. Many upwardly mobile men kept their domestic lives entirely separate from work, entertaining clients only when they had to and avoiding staff parties. 'I don't have any business people to the house', one man told Jan and Ray Pahl. 'I'd prefer to keep business and social life apart.'[54] Meeting clients and senior managers could foster feelings of inferiority. 'Men of working-class origin feel that opportunities to demonstrate their abilities are limited by local peculiarities of speech, too narrow an outlook, or poor conversational powers', reported Clements. 'A haircut and clean clothes would have got me on a bit quicker', said one; others thought that 'accent' was a barrier.[55] In the workplace they could not help being aware of these social differences. At home they could be themselves. Their wife's role was to allow them to relax without worrying about social etiquette. But this could be a lonely life for women, especially for those who regularly moved to a new area for their husband's work. Many complained to the Pahls that their husbands made no effort to be pleasant, help around the home or reciprocate their own work and affection in any way – 'the manager wants a cross between a secretary and a nanny'.[56]

Other women supported their husbands financially. Those managers who'd got their break after studying at night school or university often relied on their spouse's help to do so. In the late 1940s Ann

Davies' mother worked as a draughtswoman (a trade for which she'd trained during the war) while Ann's father studied first for a science degree and then a postgraduate diploma, enabling him to become a senior engineer at the Mars company.[57]

Working wives also provided the family with the furnishings, holidays and children's music lessons that the managerial lifestyle demanded. Upwardly mobile managers' wives were aware of the material difference that class background made. 'There's a lot of what I call real money here, you know, family money', is how one described her neighbourhood to Colin Bell. 'We lived in a two-roomed flat when we started.'[58] Bell found that managers from middle-class families relied on their 'father or father-in-law' for financial help with a deposit on a first home, and subsequently for luxuries like 'central heating . . . regular help in the home' and 'expensive toys' for children like bicycles, riding and ballet lessons.[59] Working wives could compensate for a lack of family money. June Abbott's mother returned to teaching because she loved her work and because 'most of our friends were richer than we were'. Mrs Abbott's salary meant that the family could employ an au pair and take regular holidays.[60] Women without her education turned to that older route for material improvement: self-employment. Roger Clements discovered that many managers of 'lower-middle and skilled working-class origin' aspired to eventually leave their firm and 'expand the business the wife is already looking after', generally 'tobacconist and newsagent shops'.[61] Owning their own business promised a degree of autonomy over their working hours and conditions that social researchers found these men craved, but could not achieve at work.[62]

Just as crucially, managers' wives were responsible for negotiating the family's changing social status. Middle managers occupied an ambiguous social position because their roles were so new. In the absence of ascent to the boardroom, these men often imbued each geographic move with social significance. In Banbury, where the postwar expansion of local firms caused an influx of new managers, Margaret Stacey discovered that many were keen to send their children to private schools 'so that they won't pick up an accent'.[63] But it was their wives and children who had to grapple with the social complexities this posed. Women were responsible for identifying a 'nice' neighbourhood and suitable schools each time their husband's work necessitated a move – tasks, they told the Pahls, that their husbands underestimated.[64]

While long-standing residents of Banbury used family background to discern each other's status, 'it cannot count in the same way for immigrants who do not know each other's background', found Margaret Stacey. 'Furthermore, the upwardly mobile . . . wish that it should not count'.[65] Instead, a man's occupation mattered a great deal, but so too did a woman's behaviour and appearance. Frequently, managers' wives lost their regional accents even if husbands hung onto theirs. Carol Horn's parents both came from working-class homes in northern England; when they followed his firm to Guildford in the 1950s 'my father maintained his short "a" pronunciation and accent, [but] my mother gradually became more southern in her accent – and I think much more middle class in her attitudes and aspirations'.[66]

Upwardly mobile managers often appeared to social researchers as men who were proud of their working-class roots, married to women who were concerned to keep up appearances. But far from being diametrically opposed to each other, these were two complementary approaches to climbing the ladder. As Clements astutely observed, 'prestige means a lot to these men, whether it is in the technical or the social fields'.[67] Men were able to present themselves as 'hard-boiled' types who had 'worked their way up' and were proud of their accent and background, evoking the manual skills and independence of the skilled craftsman. But they relied on their wives to create a lifestyle that fitted their new status and offered the rewards they wanted their hard work to provide – and to reflect that lifestyle too.

But however preoccupied they were with their own social status, these managers and their wives were more anxious about their children's prospects. 'The most important decisions we have to make are those concerning the children and their future', one manager told the

Pahls, echoing the thoughts of many.[68] Some men were in fact persuaded by their wives to climb the ladder in order to help their children 'get on'. Ella Carey, a miner's wife in north-east England, encouraged her husband to get promoted, first to foreman and then to a clerical post, to support their studious son, Malcolm – 'everything had to be the best for him'. She worked to put her husband through night classes and he eventually did gain promotion and earned 'a lot more money'. When Malcolm went to university, 'we kept him . . . and put money in the bank for him . . . It took quite a bit to start him off. To keep him there.'[69]

Many managers did not want their children to follow in their footsteps. This was partly because the opportunities they had enjoyed were disappearing by the 1960s. During the war, firms had had to recruit managers from the shop floor, but twenty years on this impetus had gone. Managers were increasingly poached from competitors, while university graduates were taking the place of those men trained on the job during the 1940s.[70] By the late 1960s the Pahls observed that 'it is becoming proportionately *more* difficult for men from working-class backgrounds to get into managerial positions'.[71]

There was another reason why these men and women wanted their children to do something else. Those manual workers who became managers had mixed feelings about their own success. Most were proud of their achievements. They 'had been, comparative to their origins, very successful, and they doubt whether they could have been equally so in any other walk of life without an extensive and special education', reported Clements.[72] Money, and the ability to keep their family, were important to men who had known poverty.[73] They measured themselves against their fathers: Barry Thompson stressed that his annual salary was 'more money than my father earns now in five years . . . I know that I have come a long way. I notice it especially when I go home.'[74]

But when they compared themselves with their peers, these men were dissatisfied. Many remained disappointed that they had not become craftsmen or gone to university. And while in mid-career they consoled themselves with their managerial status and the affluence it brought, their wives more openly questioned whether the hard work had been worth it. 'I have a nice house, and I can afford things, and I have a nice daughter, and my husband has a nice position, but deep down I have not had the happiness I expected', one woman told the Pahls. 'It always goes back to this thing of my husband seeing me as one of his other possessions.' Jan and Ray Pahl found other women shared her discontent.[75]

These couples wanted their children to enter the professions. They told the Pahls that university lecturers, politicians, lawyers and doctors 'would not be obliged to work long hours but would have the ideal "balance": a high status and respected position, "enough" money and more autonomy in making his important life-plan decisions'.[76] Men who worked long hours themselves secretly 'wanted a quiet life ... there was a strain of non-ambition', judged Ray Pahl.[77] Some echoed June Abbott's father, who had wished to pursue socially useful work, in his case as a doctor. But most important was that professionals had a degree of independence and fulfilment in their work – similar to the skilled craftsmen of an earlier generation.

The experiences of these managers and their wives did not testify to a managerial revolution. They often worked desperately hard to achieve managerial status precisely because ordinary manual workers wielded so little power over their working conditions, pay and the organisation of their work. This was a matter of great frustration to workers in firms that, whether private or nationalised, tended to be extremely hierarchical. Senior managers and company directors pursued short-term profits rather than investing in long-term innovation which might have displaced them in favour of those with technical expertise.

Being a manager was a family project that did not stop when a man gained promotion. It relied as much on women's unpaid labour as on men's paid work. These couples' achievements took them up the social ladder but they endured the fear of falling back down it, reliant as they were on capricious bosses and the financial health of firms that refused to innovate. They aspired to middle-class status for themselves – the accoutrements of affluence meant a great deal to men and women who had grown up in poverty. A house, a car and private school for the children could also be important signs to themselves and others that their hard work had paid off.

But many of them discovered that the stress, striving and boredom that a manager's job entailed, and the loneliness and emotional labour of being a manager's wife, were not entirely satisfying. They wanted their children to experience greater autonomy, enjoy more fulfilling work and, above all, to get an education. They looked to university and the professions to provide chances that they, materially successful as they were, so often regretted the lack of. Unlike those politicians who lauded the 'managerial revolution', they believed the state was more likely than private enterprise to provide the next generation with the chances they yearned for.

Chapter Nine

MOVING ON, BUT NOT MOVING UP

While British born men and women were climbing up the ladder into clerical work, management, the welfare professions and the universities, another group was also on the move. Increasing numbers of migrants arrived in Britain between 1945 and the 1960s. By 1961 there were 500,000 West Indian and Asian migrants in Britain – about 1 per cent of the population – and more than 1 million from Europe and Ireland.[1]

While not all of them were members of the breakthrough generation, they shared the experience of moving away from family and friends to forge new lives for themselves in the aftermath of war. Their ambitions were as high as those of their British-born peers – but their fight to realise them was even harder. Against the backdrop of widespread racism, class background continued to matter, even thousands of miles from home.

Meanwhile, thousands of Britons were starting a new life overseas. At the end of the war, former British colonies like Australia and Canada were desperate for skilled manual workers, and it was cheaper and quicker to import them than train up their own citizens. Emigration schemes like the Australian government's 'Ten Pound Pom' offer targeted those who could not afford to pay the full cost of moving overseas, but could contribute a little. About 125,000 people left Britain for a new life elsewhere every year between 1946 and 1960. Skilled manual workers and their families composed 40 per cent of them. They cited 'problems at work' – boredom, lack of promotion and training – as the most important negative reasons for their decision.[2] These emigrants were tired of the class-bound nature of British life. Australian sociologist Reg Appleyard, who surveyed hundreds of British migrants in Australia in the late 1950s, found that their chief ambitions were to 'purchase a house, educate their children and live in a society free of class-based restrictions on achievement'.[3]

Migrants had always been members of British society. Waves of Irish migrants and those from mainland Europe had made their homes in the towns and cities. Asian and African seamen had settled around the country's ports, and servants, soldiers and aristocrats from all corners of the Empire had made Britain their home. But after the war more people were given new hope that Britain might provide them and their children with a better life. In 1946, less than a year after the end of the war, the government convened a Foreign Labour Committee to 'examine, in the light of existing manpower shortages, the possibility of making increased use of foreign labour, particularly in essential industries which are now finding special difficulty in recruiting labour'.[4] The committee recommended recruiting workers in Jamaica, India and Britain's other former colonies in Asia and the Caribbean.

To speed up the migration process and enhance its attractions, the 1948 Nationality Act made it easier for Commonwealth migrants to get British citizenship. In the same year, the *Empire Windrush* became the most famous emblem of post-war migration when it docked at Tilbury carrying 492 passengers from across the Caribbean.

By 1951 about 80,000 people in Britain hailed from the Caribbean or South Asia. Meanwhile, Britain became home to 300,000 Europeans between 1945 and 1961, many of them refugees, displaced people or former prisoners of war. And young people from Ireland continued to flock to British towns and cities in search of work, composing the largest single group of post-war migrants. More than 900,000 of them arrived between the end of the war and the beginning of the 1960s. All these new arrivals joined another wave of recent migrants – the 70,000 Jewish refugees who had fled Europe to make a home in Britain in the late 1930s.[5] Ten years later, they were just finding their feet in peace-time society.

European migrants often came to Britain to escape political insta-bility or persecution, with no ambition other than to survive.[6] Isaac Cohen had been born to a German Jewish family in 1910. The son of a prosperous farmer, Isaac finished school in the 1920s, by which time agriculture did not offer such a good living but Germany's professions were attractive to educated young men. Like many Central and East European Jews, Isaac's family had a long history of migration. The family farm could not support all the sons of the family, and so they took their chances overseas. Isaac was able to attend university thanks to an uncle 'who had emigrated to the United States in the early twen-tieth century and did well'.[7]

Isaac graduated with a PhD in chemistry in 1933, but the Nazis ruined his hopes of a career in scientific research, and soon threatened his life. By 1938 Isaac was 'desperately trying to get out of Germany'.[8] But doing so depended on having money or contacts. The British gov-ernment, like many others, refused to accept Jewish migrants unless they had a job offer or a financial guarantor. Young men like Isaac, with a scientific education, were in an advantageous position. They had skills that employers wanted, and some had contacts abroad. In 1939 Isaac had a stroke of luck: a friend from student days, who had already emigrated to Britain, offered him a job as an industrial chemist in Manchester. He left Germany just before the outbreak of war closed international borders.

Women had less chance of getting professional or managerial jobs – but a middle-class background could work in their favour. Before the war, some European women from middle-class, Jewish families had come to Britain as domestic servants. In February 1939 the magazine *Housewife* urged its readers to see the European crisis as 'Your Opportunity' to recruit a 'Foreign Maid', more reliable and used to higher standards than a working-class girl from Britain.[9] After the war, the European Voluntary Workers' Scheme recruited the inmates of displaced-persons camps across Europe to jobs in Britain. Men were assessed according to their education and technical qualifications (although most ended up in mills and factories). But government recruiters were more interested in women's social origins. They sent working-class women from the Baltic States to Britain's factories and mills, while middle-class German women were employed as domestic servants or hospital cleaners. 'An exceedingly good type of woman is available for hospital domestic work', reported the Ministry of Labour. 'They would . . . constitute a good and desirable element in our population.'[10]

For many of these women, domestic work was a humiliating descent: some had been used to employing servants back home. Most were treated no differently to the working-class British women they worked alongside.[11] But some employers were keen to help these migrants restore their middle-class status. Milda Black's family had been prosperous professionals in Latvia. When she arrived in Blackburn to work as a hospital cleaner in 1951, she found it difficult to get on with her working-class British workmates. Her employers sympathised: 'the matron, the sisters, they all told us that we are not really lower-class people'. After two years' service, 'Matron said that those of us that want to could start to train as nurses.'[12] This privilege was not extended to most hospital orderlies, but in 1952 the Conservative government ordered that selected European Voluntary Workers should be given the chance.

Civil servants at the Ministry of Labour and many employers believed that a person's social background should influence the kind of work they did. Women from middle-class families were considered deserving of jobs and assistance denied to those with working-class origins. After qualifying as a nurse, Milda left Blackburn, an almost exclusively working-class town, for Oxford, a city she considered more in keeping with her aspirations. There she married a professional man.[13]

European migrants from middle-class backgrounds were more likely than any other group to have the qualifications, skills, contacts and money to re-establish their status in Britain. By 1945 Isaac Cohen had married his employer's secretary, the daughter of Russian Jews. They settled in a semi-detached house in a 'lower-middle-class, Jewish area' in north Manchester. They weren't particularly religiously observant, and nor were their neighbours, but anti-Semitism – prevalent in Manchester, as throughout Britain – encouraged Jewish residents to create their own self-help networks in areas where they could afford to buy housing or rent accommodation from sympathetic landlords.

But in other respects, Isaac Cohen's trajectory was similar to that of a British-born, middle-class educated man. As his daughter Sue recognised, he benefited from the 'economic improvements in the country as a whole . . . and in my father's occupation particularly' that assisted British-born men of the breakthrough generation.[14] Isaac's career as an industrial chemist flourished because Britain's post-war economy relied on the production of consumer goods from synthetic fibres to household cleaners.

The Ministry of Labour reported approvingly that middle-class migrants from Europe would 'assimilate well' in Britain.[15] Certainly, by the late 1950s families like the Cohens who had only arrived in Britain ten or twenty years earlier had much in common with other prosperous, solidly middle-class families. They used the same strategies that had benefited them back home, and enabled them to migrate. Chief among these was education. In 1954 Isaac Cohen's daughter Sue won a free place at the fee-paying Manchester High School for Girls, which had a tradition of accepting Jewish girls. The school was in south Manchester, the more prosperous side of the city, and this was the catalyst for the family's move to the middle-class suburb of Didsbury in 1959. Sue was aware that they were following in the footsteps of many other upwardly mobile Jewish families 'who'd made a lot of money in trade or in other areas'. Isaac encouraged his daughters to fit into the suburban, middle-class lifestyle, as Sue recalled: 'we joined the local tennis club'.[16]

But the Cohens' lives continued to be shaped by their history of migration and by the prejudice they encountered in Britain. Sue and her sisters were brought up with a very strong work ethic. The need to do well 'was always a background anxiety'.[17] Isaac Cohen owed his life to his qualifications, and the need for his daughters to be well educated was made even more acute when, in the late 1940s, he discovered that many of his relatives had been murdered by the Nazis. He always feared that the life he'd worked so hard to create might once more be snatched away, even when the family was settled in well-heeled Didsbury.

Hard work and striving for education did not simply testify to migrants' ambition to climb the social ladder. These were also strategies encouraged by racism and anti-Semitism. The Cohens themselves tried to avoid anti-Semitism by using schools and associations that welcomed, or at least tolerated, Jews. The tennis club Isaac's daughters joined was exclusively Jewish, because the nearby, longer-established one 'didn't allow Jewish members'.[18] Shoring up their social position by using private education, home ownership and hard work was important for those whose grasp on citizenship, let alone their perch on the social ladder, was precarious.

Isaac Cohen was unusual. Most migrants, regardless of their background, did not join the British middle class in less than a generation. After the war, most European migrants ended up in factory work. They were far more likely to slide down the social ladder than to climb it. The poverty, homelessness and desperation that led them to Britain meant most prized security above all else. Zdzislaw Labedz, a Pole, was twenty-three when the war ended. His parents had been clerks and his mother had collaborated with the Nazi occupiers, so Zdzislaw had looked forward to a white-collar career in the German Civil Service. The war ended his hopes. After a spell in the German army, Zdzislaw was captured by the British. In 1943 he was shipped to a camp in Cheshire. At the end of the war, with Poland in the hands of the Soviet Union, 'I could not go back.' Like hundreds of other prisoners of war stationed in Cheshire, Zdzislaw was offered a factory job and a place to live by ICI, a large local employer. 'I got married to an English girl, had four children . . . spent thirty-three years at ICI.'[19] He craved stability, assimilation – in his case through the local Catholic community – and security.

This desire for security encouraged frugality and caution about the future. Nina Kusnir's parents were Ukrainians, born during the 1920s. They arrived in Bradford in 1949, fleeing Soviet occupation and seeking work in the city's mills. Growing up in the 1950s, Nina didn't bring friends home because of 'the enforced poverty . . . you got a lot of English children whose parents didn't bring in a great deal of money and yet they seemed to spend more money on their house . . . we used to have this lino . . . other children's houses, they had carpets . . . I suppose it was because my parents were unsure of their continued income'.[20]

Nina's parents were conscious of their tenuous status in Britain; they had only been able to apply for permanent residency after several years of working in their new home. Throughout her childhood Nina witnessed 'this continued feeling of insecurity in my parents, thinking that if they didn't watch their step they might be sacked'. Cautious and conservative on their own account, they invested heavily in their children's success. 'My parents always rated education very highly because they had such little education, such little opportunity for it, first at home and then here'.[21]

*

The hopes and experiences of British emigrants were very different to those of these European immigrants. Reg Appleyard found that the Ten Pound Poms hoped for a job on the same level as the one they'd had in Britain – and most of them achieved this. But they wanted far more for their children. 'Many families . . . said that their own limited opportunities for a good education and their working-class background had restricted their achievements', and worried 'that the same barriers would restrict their children's achievements' if they stayed in Britain.[22]

This was true of Edward Stoye's family. Edward was born in 1934 in Middlesbrough, the son of a secretary and a painter and decorator. He had been evacuated to Canada during the war, where his foster parents were a prosperous engineer and a schoolteacher. Edward attended a junior high school before returning to Britain in 1945. After failing the scholarship examination for his local grammar school, he 'was relegated to a secondary modern school' with the prospect of a factory job when he left at fifteen. The Canadian offer of an academic schooling to every child 'was the reason we all moved to Canada in 1947'.[23] Edward went to university and became a high school teacher.

The countries to which most Britons emigrated offered them some crucial advantages. Abundant natural resources and cheap land were a boon to those who decided to set up their own business or wanted to buy or build their own home. Societies with expanding populations like Australia had more room at the top, because they needed professionals, such as teachers and doctors, as well as skilled manual workers. Many migrants spoke of a 'can do' philosophy in their adopted country; a pioneering spirit and pride in 'working your way up', a society less fettered by class than Britain.[24] And they moved to countries where racial discrimination was enshrined in law. The indigenous populations of Canada, Australia and New Zealand were excluded from employment and educational opportunities open to white settlers, just as black Africans were in South Africa. British migrants had one immediate advantage: they were white.

But emigrants sometimes over-estimated the differences between Britain and their new homes. By the 1960s, some of the opportunities that children experienced in Australia or Canada were benefiting relatives and friends back home. Working-class children born after 1945 had a longer education than their parents had had. Thirty-six per cent of British people born in the 1950s had some further or higher education, compared with 34 per cent in Australia and 28 per cent in New Zealand. Only in Canada was the figure far higher, at 46 per cent.[25] And British children born between the mid-1940s and the late 1950s were far more likely to experience upward social mobility than previous generations, and no less likely to do so than children who grew up in Australia, New Zealand or North America. By the mid-1960s emigrating was no longer the widespread dream it had been twenty years earlier. As the post-war generation came of age, countries like Australia and Canada no longer needed emigrants, and so ended assisted passage schemes. By this stage, British people were less eager to move – they knew they had as much chance of meeting some of their aspirations in Britain.[26]

*

British emigrants benefited from being white. By contrast, those who arrived in Britain from Asia, Africa and the Caribbean had to grapple with racism. Many came to Britain out of necessity. Most of them came from poor countries and grew up knowing older relatives or friends who'd had to emigrate to find work. By the 1940s Britain's colonies and former colonies – including India, Ireland, Trinidad and Jamaica – had been used for cheap labour or as export markets for the 'mother country' for at least a century. As the sociologist Sheila Patterson observed in a study of African Caribbean people in London, 'overpopulation; economic underdevelopment resulting in large-scale unemployment [and] low wage levels' had sent 'stream after stream of West Indian migrants, particularly Jamaicans, in search of temporary and permanent work' to North America and Europe.[27] South Asians faced similar pressures. Those from relatively affluent families were not immune. The younger sons of wealthier farming families had often had to migrate because their family's land couldn't give them a living. Those who aspired to be teachers, lawyers or doctors often hoped for better training and posts in Britain than they could get at home.[28]

At the end of the Second World War, many migrants continued to leave these countries in search of better work elsewhere. In the late 1940s British voters were experiencing near-full employment and welfare benefits. But the Labour government did not extend these commitments to citizens in the colonies or the Commonwealth. A journalist aboard the *Empire Windrush* found that most of the travellers had left their homes because of lack of work: 'some had been unemployed for two years'.[29]

Most of these migrants were young men, born in the 1920s and 30s. The war and its aftermath had disrupted or closed those emigration routes that were popular with earlier generations. Caribbean workers were also influenced by the McCurran Act of 1952, which imposed new rules on who could enter the United States, and virtually ended black immigration there. On the Indian subcontinent, political and economic upheaval following the war and the partition of India and Pakistan in 1948 made migration more attractive. Indians in search of work had traditionally migrated to African countries, but the growth of independence movements in many African states during the late 1940s and 50s made this route less promising. Political turbulence, and a commitment by new African nations to give work to their own people, led more Indians and Pakistanis to consider Europe as a destination.[30]

Britain looked particularly attractive to colonial subjects who had learned English at school and been brought up to believe that it was their 'mother country'. Some had served in the British armed forces during the war, which strengthened the idea that Britain might welcome them. Others were encouraged by the British government's new post-war recruitment scheme. Carlton Duncan, a Jamaican, was ten when his parents left for Britain in 1954. He saw it as 'a craze, you know, that the place to be was England . . . the invitation came from "the Mother Country"'.[31] But some were less positive. 'When the situation is desperate you take a chance', was how one man aboard the *Empire Windrush* explained his decision to migrate. 'You don't wait until you die.'[32]

Arriving in Britain could mean stepping down the social ladder. Zahoor Ahmed, a young man from a middle-class Pakistani family, arrived in Birmingham in the late 1950s. There he discovered that his grandfather's nephew 'used to sell things along Bull Ring Market'. Zahoor was surprised: 'that was something, below, you know, our expectation'.[33] In 1976 a study of sixty-seven young south Asian men living in Newcastle upon Tyne found that more than 60 per cent of their fathers 'regarded themselves as middle class in Indian or Pakistani terms'. They had been farmers or entrepreneurs before emigrating in the 1950s or early 1960s. On arrival in Newcastle most of these fathers had got factory jobs.[34] The same was true elsewhere. A survey of south Asians living in Oxford found that more than half came from families who owned businesses, farms or smallholdings but in Britain almost half became semi- or unskilled manual workers.[35]

Black migrants did not often receive the warm welcome they'd been led to expect.[36] Many found it hard to get even unskilled factory work. In 1954 the research organisation Political and Economic Planning undertook a major study of racial discrimination experienced by Commonwealth migrants. 'Discrimination in employment is the single biggest criticism in migrants' spontaneous criticisms of life in Britain', the investigators found. Thirty-six per cent of those questioned said they had been denied a job, promotion or training because of the colour of their skin, or had been paid less than a white person doing the same work.[37] The researchers concluded that these claims were entirely justified. Employers were reluctant to recruit 'coloured immigrants', claiming 'that the existing staff will not like it; that customers will not like it, or that the immigrants are under-skilled, indolent or unlikely to stay with the company'.[38]

Many of the new arrivals knew that they would likely get menial jobs. Migrants weren't wanted for the skilled manual work or managerial or professional posts that the British-born breakthrough generation benefited from. They were required for unskilled factory work, producing consumer goods on which the country's economy prospered, or as orderlies and cleaners staffing new hospitals and schools. Carlton Duncan's parents, skilled tradespeople, knew that the jobs available to them would be 'unskilled . . . essentially jobs that the local people would not do'.[39]

But they did believe that this work would be recognised as a valuable contribution to rebuilding post-war Britain, and paid a decent wage. Many expected to stay in Britain for just a few years, saving money before returning home to realise their ambitions there. Nurul Hoque, from Pakistan, decided to migrate after a bad harvest decimated his smallholding. 'When you go to the market, people talk about go to England, have a good earning, you can live prosperously.'[40] Government recruitment material encouraged the migrants to believe that they would be able to save money. Clara Brown and her husband moved to Britain from Barbados in 1952, when they were in their early twenties. Although this meant leaving their daughter, Marcia, at home, they expected that within five years 'we would go back home and build our own business and a fantastic house'.[41]

But the high wages they'd expected were not forthcoming. Saving money proved harder, and took longer, than they'd anticipated. Avtar Singh Jouhl was born in the Punjab in the late 1930s to a farming family. In 1957, having completed a college course, Avtar was keen to go to university. One of his uncles had lived in Britain and now returned home, with the proposal that Avtar should study there. Avtar's brother had recently moved to Smethwick in the West Midlands, and the family decided that Avtar would join him there to get work before beginning his university course. 'My situation was unique', Avtar recalled. 'Most of my contemporaries didn't come for education, they almost all came to work.'[42] He arrived in Smethwick in 1958 and became a moulder's mate in a foundry. The moulder was white. 'None of the Indians' Avtar worked with had a job that was 'considered skilled and which was highly paid . . . all so-called skilled workers were white'.[43]

Not only were migrants' wages low, but housing costs were far higher than they'd expected. After dodging the 'No Blacks, No Irish' signs placed in many private landlords' windows, migrants found themselves with no option but overcrowded and overpriced slum dwellings. In Bradford, Clara Brown and her husband found to their dismay that 'after sending money home for our daughter in Barbados and paying the rent, we had no savings left'.[44] Meanwhile in Smethwick, Avtar Singh Jouhl lived in a 'two up and two down . . . At one time there were twelve of us living there'. White landlords would not rent them accommodation, and estate agents refused to sell houses 'to "coloured people"'. Avtar quickly realised that 'council housing wasn't an option.' Smethwick was one of many local councils that ruled that only those who had lived in the district for several years (a decade, in Smethwick's case) could apply for council accommodation. Avtar recognised this was a racist ploy: 'no black or Asian people had been living in Smethwick for ten years' in 1958.[45]

As it became clearer that their stay in Britain would be longer than they had anticipated, these migrants considered how to improve their conditions. They quickly realised that however ambitious, determined or well educated they were, they could not use many of the strategies that British-born people used to climb the ladder. They did not qualify for university or further-education grants, and racial discrimination blocked many migrants' chance to get managerial or professional work.

Some went into business, serving other migrants at first, often selling goods door to door or on market stalls. These entrepreneurs often came from families that could not afford to support them back home, but did not rely on them financially either. In Manchester, it was farmers' sons who began selling clothing door to door in the early 1950s, graduated to market stalls by the 1960s and eventually became shopkeepers. Building a business was a collective enterprise. One Pakistani migrant who moved to Manchester in 1948 joined his father on what was by then a flourishing market stall. But they 'lived in a shared house' with several other men 'and all shared expenses'.[46] Self-employment was a tough route to take, requiring several family members to live and work together, barely scraping a living for the first few years.

By acting together some migrants did improve their prospects. Many joined trade unions, while others began their own associations to fight for equal pay and an end to racial discrimination. In the 1950s, Punjabi migrants revived the Indian Workers' Association (IWA), first established in the 1930s. Avtar Singh Jouhl was among them. He and his brother began recruiting members at the foundry where they worked in the summer of 1958. Then they sought to join the Amalgamated Union of Foundry Workers, but here they encountered racism. 'When we took in the union forms, the union officials asked us if we had a proposer and seconder with two years' membership in the union', Avtar recalled. 'But there was no union in our workplace so of course we said: "No." They didn't give us union membership, arguing that if you don't have a proposer and seconder you can't become a member.'[47] Eventually, Avtar and his comrades succeeded in joining the union with some assistance from Communist Party members.

But these campaigns and strikes could cost migrants their jobs, and required huge investment of time and energy. Avtar's political activities cost him the chance of a university education. He had wanted to leave work to begin his studies in October 1958, but many of the black foundry workers accused him of 'doing a runner' just as they were beginning to organise. Avtar felt torn, but 'in India getting a tag that you are a "runner" is a label for your whole life, to be held against you'. And in Smethwick, he felt that he needed the solidarity and support of other Indians to survive. 'So I didn't leave work . . . instead of my university education I got my foundry qualifications'.[48] Avtar would eventually become a trade union lecturer in a further education college, and the President of the Indian Workers' Association.

Avtar Singh Jouhl decided to prioritise collective improvement of migrants' conditions over his own chance to climb the ladder. Some other migrants sought to combine both strategies. Educated men were among the leaders of the IWA. Some had found it impossible to get the professional work they'd hoped England would provide. Others combined university studies with manual jobs. In 1965 'a remarkable feat of organisation' by leaders of the Indian Workers' Association at Southall prompted more than 500 Asian workers at a rubber factory to join the Transport and General Workers' Union and then to strike for better wages and union recognition. One of the leaders of this dispute was N. S. Hundal, 'a law graduate of the University of Punjab who is working his way through Gray's Inn'. Despite the TGWU's refusal to pay the workers any strike pay – 'district secretary, Mr F. Howell, said it was a matter of sifting the qualifications of the various strikers before deciding how much they should get' – Hundal and his associates sustained the strike for six months. They persuaded the local Indian community to make generous donations, and Indian landlords to forego rent payments for the duration of the dispute. Their employer eventually agreed to most of their demands.[49]

But many migrants focused their hopes on 'home'. Through frugality and communal living they managed to send money back to their families, albeit at a slower rate than they'd hoped. Abdul Farooq grew up in Pakistan. His father migrated to Britain in 1951 when Abdul was a baby. He 'wrote and sent us money', Abdul recalled. As a result, 'our material circumstances changed because we had a lot more money . . . We had clothes which were made in England of good quality'.[50] By the 1960s some migrants had the satisfaction of knowing that their families had climbed the ladder. Ahmed Hakim migrated from a 'poor' family in rural Pakistan to Oxford. After ten years as a bus driver he had transformed his family's lifestyle. He was 'working class here in England', but in Pakistan his family were now 'upper class' thanks to the money that he and other migrant sons had sent home.[51]

In their dealings with relatives, many Asian and Caribbean migrants cultivated the myth that they'd risen up the social ladder in Britain. 'I would see the photographs of my relations which were sent to us in Pakistan . . . We would look at their jackets, how expensive they were, or their shoes', recalled Ali Said, who grew up in Pakistan and emigrated to Britain in the 1960s. 'When I came to this country I realised that the photographs were – that there was some exaggeration.'[52] 'They thought that we who were in England were living the life of Riley', said Yasmina Khan, who grew up in Britain but whose extended family lived in Pakistan. 'My dad's family didn't realise that we were actually working-class people.'[53]

Many migrants took care to present themselves as wealthy in pictures destined for their relatives. Photographer Tony Walker was the proprietor of the Belle Vue photography studio in Bradford in the

1950s and 60s. Most of his clients were Asian millworkers, transport workers or factory hands, but they asked Tony to help them look like office workers or businessmen. 'Next door to me was a gent's outfitters, and they would buy a shirt, come into my dressing room and change into the shirt', recalled Tony. 'And they'd ask me . . . could they have my tie, and they'd even ask for my jacket.' Briefcases and pens were popular accoutrements, and one young man posed on a scooter. But not everyone wished to conform to the British, middle-class image of success, with its understated symbols of wealth. Some required more ostentatious displays. Some of Tony's clients came in 'with three wristwatches, which must be shown, on the same arm! I photographed a couple from Birmingham with fistfuls of fivers on the table, in their hands.'[54]

These photographs had some striking similarities with the painted portraits commissioned by European merchants and manufacturers in the eighteenth and nineteenth centuries, in which jewellery, fashionable clothing and ornate furniture were conspicuous.[55] But those earlier oil paintings had glorified success, whereas the migrants' photographs and letters were more often signs of thwarted ambition. They expressed what their subjects could have become, given the chance. Their senders also hoped to reassure loved ones and conceal the sacrifices that sending money and gifts home required. Jay Singh grew up in India while his father worked in Britain. The family benefited enormously from his wages but still 'missed him' badly. That 'he sent pictures of himself and he looked very healthy and he looked very smart' was an important consolation for them.[56]

Other migrants found it too painful to acknowledge the reality and the racism of the 'Mother Country', even to themselves. After nine years of separation from his parents, nineteen-year-old Carlton Duncan, back home in Jamaica, had set his heart on becoming a teacher. In 1963 his parents wrote to him 'saying "Look, you come to England, the place is riddled with teacher training colleges, with universities, you are going to have it so much easier getting into one of these places." ' Carlton 'jumped at' the chance. But England was 'a disappointment . . . my qualifications weren't recognised.' Having been told by his parents 'about this wonderful "Mother Country" . . . I took it a little bit hard'.[57] Carlton's parents had managed to convince themselves that the discrimination they faced was because of their own lack of schooling. Like many migrants, they were confident that their well-educated son would fare better. As Sheila Patterson observed, many migrants were 'unwilling to admit to disillusionment and failure'.[58]

Very few migrants climbed the social ladder. Those who were white and hailed from middle-class families were best placed to reproduce their privileges in Britain. This was particularly true if they had contacts, skills and qualifications in expanding sectors such as industrial science and nursing. Migrants whose families were not desperate for their financial assistance were more likely to be able to start their own business. Background mattered, even when their families were thousands of miles away.

But all migrants, and particularly the poorest, were at the mercy of governments and employers with little interest in the newcomers' aspirations. Their job was to take those menial jobs on which the post-war welfare state and industry relied. In doing so, they helped to create new opportunities for the next generation – both by providing for their own families back home, and by staffing Britain's new and expanding schools, hospitals, and industries. Those British children born between the mid-1930s and mid-1950s were to build their lives on those foundations. For them, the golden age of social mobility had arrived.

PART IV

THE GOLDEN GENERATION 1935–1955

Chapter Ten

BUT ONLY SOME SHALL HAVE
PRIZES

The children born between the mid-1930s and mid-1950s were more likely to be upwardly mobile than any generation before or since. More than 50 per cent of men and 40 per cent of women reached a higher social class than their parents, and fewer than 20 per cent of them experienced downward mobility.[1] They ascended because the middle and upper rungs of the ladder widened after the Second World War. The post-war Labour government's introduction of full employment, and its expansion of the welfare state – policies upheld by the Conservative governments of 1951–64 – was partly responsible. So too was the growth of private industry in the 1950s. Public-employment expanded further when Labour held power once more between 1964 and 1970. The upwardly mobile members of the golden generation went into clerical, engineering, technical and managerial work just as the breakthrough generation had done. But they were also increasingly likely to enter the public-sector professions, especially teaching and nursing.[2]

The golden generation benefited from the expansion of certain types of jobs. But they and the political reformers who shaped their chances saw education as the major catalyst to improving their lives. Some were able to take advantage of the educational innovations of the post-war years: free, academically selective grammar schools, expanding universities, and technical and teaching colleges. These were the children who held the post-war state's golden tickets, and many of them did experience upward mobility. But, as we shall see, grasping their new opportunities involved loss as well as gain. Meanwhile, the majority – those who didn't enter these hallowed institutions – were consigned to the lowest rungs of the ladder.

*

In April 1945 every child in England and Wales became entitled to free secondary education, thanks to the 1944 Education Act. In Scotland that right had been granted in 1918, but the Education (Scotland) Act of 1945 now strengthened it. Free and universal secondary schooling was extremely popular with parents and teachers alike. Most parents, regardless of their social class, wanted their children to have a wide-ranging but primarily academic schooling until their mid-teens.[3] Many teachers agreed that all children could benefit from this. Their largest union, the National Union of Teachers, had proposed that comprehensive, non-selective secondary schools would be the best means to achieve it.

But the 1944 Education Act did not introduce comprehensive schools. Instead, the secondary school that a child attended would be determined wholly or largely on the basis of their results in the 'eleven-plus' examination, which all ten-year-olds would sit. About 35 per cent of children would attend selective secondary schools: 20 per cent of them would go to academic grammar schools, and 15 per cent to technical schools. The rest would attend secondary moderns, where they would receive a basic academic and vocational education until the age of fifteen.

Labour inherited this so-called 'tripartite' system of secondary education when the party swept to power in July 1945. But many educationalists hoped that the new government would ditch it. More than half of local councils wanted to introduce comprehensive schools.

Alec Clegg, director of Britain's largest educational authority, the West Riding of Yorkshire – and an experienced teacher himself – was among the advocates for comprehensive schools. Clegg was influenced by the example of Scotland, where more children had attended state secondary school before the war than in England and Wales. Those who did so were at least as successful at winning university scholarships as those who attended private and selective schools south of the border.[4] Clegg was convinced that comprehensive schools would best achieve what he and many others saw as the purpose of post-war education: assisting children 'to earn their living along lines in which they will make the best contribution and which afford them the best hope of self-fulfilment'.[5]

Clegg and those who agreed with him were quickly disappointed. Labour's Minister for Education was Ellen Wilkinson. She hoped that the different kinds of school – grammar, technical and secondary modern – would achieve parity of esteem. But she was primarily concerned with establishing a meritocracy, and believed that selective schools were the best means to help bright working-class children to climb the ladder. Her conviction was strongly influenced by her own experience as a scholarship girl who 'had to fight my own way through to the university'. Wilkinson had benefited from the expansion of secondary education in the 1900s. But she had been unable to attend a grammar school. Labour's commitment to the tripartite system would, she declared, ensure that 'no boy or girl is debarred by lack of means from taking the course of education for which he or she is qualified'.[6]

It took some time for local education authorities to expand existing secondary schools and to build new ones, but by the end of the 1940s the vast majority of children in England and Wales were educated under the tripartite system. Provision was never uniform between local authorities. Rural areas quickly jettisoned technical schools as too expensive. Some local authorities offered grammar-school places for almost a third of children (Merthyr Tydfil in South Wales was one), while grammars in other areas could accommodate fewer than 10 per cent of children. In Scotland, compulsory free secondary education also brought reform. Children went to either junior or senior secondary schools. Entry to the senior secondaries depended on passing the 'qualifying examination'. This was similar to the eleven-plus, but there were more places available in senior secondary schools than in the English and Welsh grammars. While politicians and civil servants often claimed that selection for secondary school was 'scientific', based on children's intelligence, it was in significant part a postcode lottery.

The chief architects of this system did not believe that it would increase upward mobility, nor did they want it to. Ellen Wilkinson cited her own history as a scholarship girl in support of selective education, but she was also strongly influenced by her civil servants. The Ministry of Education was staffed by appointees of the interwar Conservative governments. In the 1930s they had assisted with the Spens Committee, appointed in 1933 to consider the future of secondary education. The Spens Report, published in 1938, recommended raising the school-leaving age to fifteen, and establishing the tripartite system. It also advocated that children be granted a place at grammar school if 'family circumstances and tradition' meant they were likely to work 'with tongue and pen'.[7] During the war the Conservative Minister for Education, Rab Butler, appointed Cyril Norwood as chair of a commission to design the post-war curriculum. Norwood taught in the private sector. In 1943 the Norwood Commission endorsed selection at eleven. It also recommended that 'parents' wishes should be given due consideration' in allocating children to secondary schools, upholding the Spens Report's advice that social background should influence a child's education. Norwood also proposed that universities should admit candidates not simply on the grounds of 'intellectual merit' but also 'of strong personality and character' and ability 'to take the lead'.[8] But characteristics like 'strong personality' were highly subjective.

After the war, the Ministry of Education's civil servants continued to argue that the role of education was to reproduce the status quo, not to increase social mobility. In 1949 they dismissed Alec Clegg's proposal for comprehensive schools on the grounds that 'some whose interests are in schools with long and tried traditions' opposed his suggestions.[9] Clegg's most vociferous opponents were landowners, grammar-school headmasters, doctors, solicitors and clerics, whose letters to the Ministry were logged and carefully read by civil servants.[10] They received more serious consideration than those working-class parents who were dismayed that their children weren't guaranteed an academic education. The Ministry of Education dismissed this as misplaced snobbery about the 'supposed superiority of the black-coated [clerical] occupations' which was 'deep-seated in the minds of parents'.[11]

But the Ministry's claim that there was no real 'superiority' to a grammar-school education or non-manual job was disingenuous. We have seen that many members of older generations hankered after more education precisely because non-manual workers had more pay and prospects than most of those in manual jobs. Similarly, grammar schools were viewed as 'superior' because they were better resourced than secondary modern schools and technical schools. Although Ellen Wilkinson had hoped that different kinds of schools would achieve parity of esteem, neither she nor her successors did much to assist this. The Ministry of Education denied secondary modern schools the right to enter their pupils for formal qualifications until 1953. Even then they were not expected to offer O levels (which had replaced the School Certificate in 1952) but the inferior Certificate of Secondary Education.

Local authorities were encouraged to allocate more money to grammar schools than to secondary moderns. Ministry of Education officials contested plans to introduce comprehensive schools as 'expensive', but were sanguine about Conservative-controlled Northumberland's lavish investment in a handful of grammar schools, paid for by maintaining pre-war elementary 'all-age schools' for everyone else.[12] In 1951 628 schools in England and Wales were still housed in buildings that had been condemned as 'unfit for use' in 1920 – the vast majority were secondary moderns.[13] Twelve years later, more than a quarter of secondary moderns had no library.[14] The tripartite system did not provide room for a range of talents and interests to be equally valued – far from it. And the 'elite' status of some schools relied on the rest being highly inferior.

Education certainly determined who got the opportunities available. Unlike the breakthrough generation, many of those born between 1935 and 1955 *began* their working lives in professional or white-collar work, demonstrating that schooling and qualifications made a discernible difference. Those who attended grammar school were far more likely to enter the professions, technical work or clerical jobs. Boys who attended grammar school were more likely to get apprenticeships in skilled manual trades than their counterparts at secondary moderns. The 80 per cent of children who attended secondary modern schools were more likely to become unskilled or semi-skilled factory workers, shop assistants or clerks in jobs offering few prospects for promotion.

By the early 1950s it was clear that selective education was not creating a more meritocratic Britain. In the 1930s fewer than 10 per cent of working-class boys entered selective secondary schools. By 1952 this had risen to just 12 per cent. By contrast, more than 60 per cent of professionals' children passed the eleven-plus.[15] Supporters of selective education argued that intelligence was inherited. In 1948 Eric James, headmaster of Manchester Grammar School (a fee-paying school), argued against greater social mobility. 'We must recognise with greater frankness the facts of human inequality', he wrote in the *Manchester Guardian*. James admitted that children at academically selective and private schools were likely to come from wealthier families, but he insisted that this only showed that 'brilliance' was hereditary. In any case, James concluded, children from such backgrounds 'would probably become leaders in every branch of national life', and therefore required an education that fitted them for this.[16]

But some upwardly mobile social scientists, most prominently Jean Floud and Albert Halsey, powerfully challenged this view. By the mid-1950s, they proved that middle-class children benefited from private tuition for the eleven-plus. The exam used middle-class reference points, such as questions about travel or classical music, which were easier to answer for those whose parents had money for holidays and music lessons.[17] Middle-class children were often identified by primary-school teachers as more likely to pass the exam, and given additional help to do so. So were those children thought to belong to what social researchers Brian Jackson and Dennis Marsden called 'the sunken middle class'. This group, whose grandparents or parents had experienced downward social mobility as a result of the Depression or war, were the working-class children most likely to pass the eleven-plus, partly because of parental pressure and partly because they benefited from teachers' help and sympathy.[18] They included Lorna Sage, born in 1943. She was the daughter of a mechanic, but her maternal grandfather was the vicar of their Shropshire village. As a result, she later acknowledged, the village school's headmaster 'graciously cheated me through' the eleven-plus and into a place at Whitchurch Girls' High School.[19] Lorna went on to become a university professor.

But many experts believed that intelligence testing was a failed experiment. As early as the mid-1940s, psychologists had concluded that such tests were 'unreliable'.[20] These assessments had had indifferent results in the wartime selection of officers, and also in the Civil Service, which had adopted intelligence testing during the war. Some critics questioned whether 'intelligence' could be narrowly defined and assessed. Others noted that test results had little bearing on a person's subsequent performance of the tasks they were being assessed for.[21] As a result of these flaws, the Civil Service began to phase out intelligence tests in the late 1940s 'except for lower grades where there are far more applicants than we can assess any other way'. In other words, intelligence tests were only useful as an entirely arbitrary means of filtering a large group of applicants. The Ministry of Education, however, remained impervious. As one of the staff involved with phasing out intelligence tests in the Civil Service observed, the 'real problem' was their 'use at the transfer stage' between primary and secondary education.[22]

Where comprehensive schools were established, they proved popular. The first purpose-built comprehensive opened on Anglesey in 1949. In 1952 Anglesey Council announced plans to abolish the eleven-plus altogether. A highly positive report on this decision in *The Times* concluded that it 'will cheer many parents and children on the island – and doubtless raise feelings of envy elsewhere. For the "11-Plus" ... in too many cases casts a long shadow of apprehension before and leaves a long trail of disappointment behind it.'[23] As *The Times* presciently suggested, many parents would have preferred their children to receive a good education whichever school they attended.

Arguments against the eleven-plus gained more popularity in the late 1950s when children born immediately after the war reached secondary-school age. The birth rate had risen in the late 1940s, but no new grammar-school places had been created. As competition for the existing schools increased, parents began to call for non-selective schools. By this stage, numerous authorities had established comprehensives, and children there were performing as well as or better than children in the grammars. In 1959 parents in Leicester campaigned against tripartite education by pointing to the well-resourced comprehensive community colleges pioneered in neighbouring Leicestershire. Those who could afford to were increasingly moving into the catchment areas of these new schools.[24] When Jan and Ray Pahl interviewed upwardly mobile managers and their wives, they met some who saw new, well-resourced comprehensives as their child's best route to a promising future. 'Having studied comprehensive education we decided that that was what we wanted for our children, if for no other reason than to cut the heartbreak of eleven-plus failure', the wife of a manager in the private sector told them. 'My husband's transfer offered us the chance we needed. We found that Wetherby had just built a brand-new comprehensive school so we decided to look for a house in Wetherby.'[25]

When the Conservatives had returned to government in 1951, they had ruled out any new comprehensive schools. But by the late 1950s politicians on both the left and the right were becoming more sympathetic to comprehensive education. This was not always for meritocratic reasons – financial and logistical considerations were also important. As the post-war baby boomers reached secondary-school age, it was clear to local-government planners that comprehensive schools could cope with demographic change far more easily than a selective system that offered a fixed number of places in each type of school. In 1955 Oxfordshire education authority suggested opening a technical school in a rural area to cope with the shortage of school places. But a senior civil servant at the Ministry of Education, Helen Asquith, dismissed this as 'hare-brained'. 'It would be far better', she said, 'to open a good, all-round secondary school'.[26] By now, the Conservative government had quietly dropped its ban on new comprehensives, and Oxfordshire took Helen Asquith's advice. In the same year, the Labour Party conference adopted comprehensive education as Party policy.

By the late 1950s, it was evident that selective education underrated most children's prospects. British firms and politicians were casting a nervous eye at West Germany, where growth and innovation in the motor and engineering industries threatened the dominance Britain had enjoyed in these fields since the war. Employers and educators observed that most West Germans received a much broader secondary education than their British counterparts. Only at the age of fifteen did they decide on either advanced academic study or robust vocational training combined with college tuition.[27] It was increasingly evident that British children could benefit from non-selective, high-quality education.

But most children born between 1935 and 1955 were educated under the tripartite (or more commonly bipartite) system. Those from upper-class and upper-middle-class families were immune – they tended to go to private schools. The fee-paying establishments remained the pinnacle of the educational hierarchy. The social kudos of the most expensive public schools survived the post-war reforms. But the fortunes of those private schools that relied on middle-class parents were less certain during the 1940s. During the war many had been in danger of closing, due to the uncertain economic climate and public opinion shifting in favour of 'fair shares'.[28] They needn't have worried. In the late 1940s, Labour allowed struggling private schools to become 'direct grant' establishments. These schools continued to admit a majority of pupils based on their ability to pay, in return for opening a quarter of their places to 'scholarship' entrants – usually the children who got the best eleven-plus results in the district. The private schools lost nothing, since local authorities were obliged to pay them generous compensation for these places. These schools' social cachet remained intact and their academic kudos grew.

Meanwhile, those private schools that remained more detached from the state (all of them received state subsidies, as charitable organisations) boomed. Mass Observation found that professionals, businesspeople and landowners were least enthused by Labour's extension of secondary education, fearing that this might hinder the chances of their own sons and daughters.[29] Concern about the fate of their children led to a 'sharp demand' for private education after the war.[30] Preparatory (private primary) schools were popular because they trained children for the eleven-plus exam.[31] The junior departments of direct-grant schools were particularly prized as they trained pupils for the senior school's 'scholarship' exam.

Meanwhile, fully private secondary schools educated middle-class children who had failed the eleven-plus. Roy Todd grew up in Northumberland in the 1950s. He failed the eleven-plus but 'my father was a farmer and was able to afford to send me to a modest boarding school'. This meant that Roy 'was able to have an education that allowed me to gain seven O levels' and become a teacher.[32]

About 80 per cent of children were educated in state schools. But free secondary education did not overcome the influence of family background – even among those who got to grammar school. Those children of managers and professionals who attended grammar school were more likely to start their working life in these occupations than other children who passed the eleven-plus. Middle-class children who were educated at secondary modern schools were far more likely to go into clerical work than secondary modern pupils from working-class backgrounds. Although attending a secondary modern might hamper these middle-class children's initial chances, after ten years at work they were likely to have moved into managerial, professional and senior administrative posts, regardless of their schooling.[33]

Selective schooling filtered which working-class children got the golden tickets, but had little effect on middle-class children's prospects. The downwardly mobile members of the golden generation included those manual-workers' children who attended secondary modern schools and then entered unskilled or semi-skilled factory work, rather than pursuing a skilled trade as their fathers did. Others tumbled down the ladder later, in the 1980s, as a result of rising unemployment – particularly men. As we shall see in later chapters, those most at risk of this were manual workers – the vast majority of whom had parents in similar work and had attended secondary modern schools.

Selective education also reinforced inequalities in the opportunities available to boys and girls. Less than 20 per cent of men and women in the golden generation were downwardly mobile, but there was a difference in *when* they experienced downward mobility. Men tended not to slide down the ladder until mid-life, when they were affected by the recessions of the 1980s. But women were likely to be downwardly mobile in their twenties, during the 1950s and 1960s. This testified to the limited job opportunities for women. By the 1960s clerical work was their largest employer. This allowed many daughters of manual workers to climb into white-collar work, but also meant that the daughters of professionals were likely to end up in jobs that paid less and offered fewer prospects than their fathers' occupations did. Other downwardly mobile women were the daughters of skilled manual workers, who ended up in unskilled or semi-skilled manual work.

These women's likelihood of experiencing downward mobility was increased if they failed the eleven-plus exam. Middle-class girls who failed the eleven-plus were more likely to experience downward mobility than middle-class boys, and far less likely to climb the ladder. Those professions that recruited large numbers of women – predominantly teaching – required a higher education. Girls who attended secondary modern schools did not have this option. They were also far less likely than girls who attended grammar schools to get a clerical job with prospects of promotion. And while middle-class boys who ended up at a secondary modern sometimes progressed to further and then higher education, parents were less willing to invest in a girl's education. Barely any girls left a secondary modern school for college or training.[34]

Ann Davies was among those who failed their eleven-plus. She was born in 1944. Her parents were from working-class families but were both able to take advantage of wartime changes. Her mother continued her work as a draughtswoman after the war to enable her husband, Ann's father, to take a university degree. As a qualified chemist, he was able to become a senior manager at the Mars company. In the early 1950s, the family moved from inner London to an outer London suburb. Ann, who was at primary school, knew the move was in part 'for the good schools' that her parents hoped she and her younger sister would attend. But in 1955 Ann failed the eleven-plus, to her own and her family's disappointment. After she left her secondary modern school at fifteen she got a clerical job in local government. This was considered a very 'good' job for a girl who had attended secondary modern school, but Ann compared it unfavourably with her younger sister's opportunities. She did pass the eleven-plus, was able to go from grammar school to university, and to become a librarian. Although Ann eventually went to university as a mature student in the 1970s, the stigma of failing the eleven-plus remained a burden. After she achieved a first-class degree, her tutors encouraged her to consider postgraduate research, but despite very much wanting to do so she decided to return to secretarial work. 'My self-confidence has always been extremely low and even getting a first-class degree didn't change that (I felt I'd only got it by working really hard, not by being clever!)'.[35]

Brian Jackson and Dennis Marsden found that mothers were often the strongest influence on those working-class children ambitious to pass the eleven-plus. Frequently these women had been denied an education in the 1920s and 30s due to their family's poverty. While their husbands often saw skilled manual work as a worthy aspiration for their sons, mothers wanted their children to escape the hardship and limited horizons they themselves had experienced. Often these women had been clerks or shop assistants in workplaces where they'd glimpsed a more affluent life – one they wanted for their own children.[36] They were right to see grammar school as the means to realise this aspiration: working-class children who passed the eleven-plus had a far greater chance of going into skilled manual work, clerical jobs with prospects, management and even the professions.[37]

These mothers' aspirations were often echoed by the minority of working-class children who went to grammar school. They arrived at grammar school full of ambition – the vast majority wanted to stay at school until they were eighteen and possibly go to university.[38] Some – particularly boys – had specific career ambitions. Most – especially girls – had the kind of hopes expressed by Maureen Thomas. She was born in Barnsley in 1941, the daughter of a subpostmistress and a miner. Like many of those who attended grammar school, Maureen was influenced by her mother, whose family were slightly better-off than her father's and whose white-collar job often paid more than he earned down the pit. She taught Maureen that her family had been 'better-off in the past', thanks to women who combined 'intelligence' with 'resourcefulness'. Maureen enrolled at a girls' grammar school in 1955. She hoped that school was going to help her to achieve her ambitions, which were not fully formed, but were nevertheless strong. Maureen 'wanted a life. Not lots of foreign travel, not loads of money, just a bit of freedom somewhere away from grimy old Barnsley.'[39]

But during their time at grammar school, most of these children became disenchanted. They discovered that passing the eleven-plus was only the first of many hurdles they would have to leap to achieve educational success. They had to work harder and from a lower rung than middle-class pupils. When school inspectors questioned the poor results obtained by pupils at Cockburn High (a grammar school) in Leeds – Richard Hoggart's alma mater – the school's representative retorted that these were 'the fault of the children's homes and not of the teachers'.[40] Working-class children were likely to find themselves relegated to the lowest streams of grammar schools, regardless of their eleven-plus results.[41] This meant they were denied the support and attention that the higher streams received. Brian Simon, who taught at Salford Grammar School during the 1950s, learned that 'the grammar school is geared to the university and the professions. It prides itself chiefly on that small proportion of its pupils . . . who are selected for higher education', and tended to see middle-class children as more fitted to that route.[42]

Negotiating between the worlds of home and school was another challenge, one that the schools' snobbery made harder. Maureen Thomas was aware of being very different from her older sister, Gillian, 'a home bird' who 'couldn't understand' why her younger sister wanted to leave home. At the same time, Maureen was 'always a bit frightened' of her grammar-school teachers: their world seemed so different from her own, and they were both powerful and remote.[43] At times it felt she did not fit in anywhere, and Jackson and Marsden revealed that Maureen was far from alone. They found that children at grammar school had too much homework to keep up with old neighbourhood friends who had gone to the secondary modern. Their school uniforms were objects of ridicule and envy. And they found the social distance between their school's expectations and those of their family very hard to bridge.[44]

Those who adapted most easily were children with a strong desire to escape their background. Many of them were brought up to believe their family had been downwardly mobile and their job was to restore its rightful social status.[45] Barry Dobson passed the eleven-plus in 1956. His father had owned a small garage in the 1930s, but when his business was requisitioned as part of a wartime airfield he became 'a jobbing carpenter'. Barry's parents told him that 'the war sent us right down the socio-economic pile'. He grew up conscious of his parents' acute disappointment and frustration, and was taught to see 'education as the means of getting on'. Barry enjoyed grammar school, where 'they treated us all as if we were middle class, presumably because they were too polite to ask if anyone wasn't'.[46]

Many more were influenced by their mothers' experiences. Jean Floud and Albert Halsey found that a working-class grammar-school pupil was likely to have a mother who had 'received something more than an elementary schooling, and, before marriage, to have followed an occupation "superior" to that of his father'.[47] Their children's education provided some of these women with a means of rectifying their own downward mobility – or the dashing of their hope to ascend the ladder – due to marriage to a manual worker, a husband who had been made unemployed, or a clerk who failed to rise.

Brian Jackson and Dennis Marsden observed that these children often studied intensively and anxiously, the pressure to both fit in and to succeed exacerbated by '"guilt"' and "obligation" to parents, or to the school itself for permitting them entry'.[48] Melvyn Bragg, born into a working-class Cumbrian family, suffered a breakdown shortly after he joined Nelson Thomlinson Grammar School in 1950, a 'private, locked-in desperation' in which he endured visions of himself 'shrinking' – surely connected to a sense of losing himself as he adapted to this new way of life.[49] A study of working-class children in the Midlands concluded that 'good grammar-school material tends to be characterised by introversion [and] a tendency to self-blame'.[50]

Melvyn Bragg excelled at grammar school and progressed to Oxbridge and a professional career. But very few working-class children followed his trajectory. In 1957 fewer than a quarter of fifteen-to-seventeen-year-olds were in full-time education, and fewer than 10 per cent of manual-workers' children.[51] 'The traditionally middle-class schools are evidently failing to assimilate huge numbers of the able working-class children who win their way into them', concluded Floud and Halsey.[52]

Those children who managed to enter the sixth form entered an even more exclusive elite. Yet those who did so – particularly the boys – could find it a more congenial environment than the lower forms had provided. These working-class children who had succeeded in following the rules were now 'rewarded for it'.[53] Pupils considered worthy of Oxbridge were given huge amounts of help, regardless of their background.[54] Those from working-class families were more likely to be made prefects and offered support with their studies and future plans than their middle-class peers. They were the golden examples who proved that grammar schools were meritocratic.[55]

Boys were encouraged to broaden their horizons. Barry Dobson 'had been planning to get a job straight after A Levels, for my family needed the money I would bring in'. But when he was turned down for a job as a bank clerk on health grounds, 'I didn't know what to do.' He approached a schoolteacher, who told him about university grants and advised him to apply to one of the newly established universities, 'and then teach. Which is what I did.' Barry became the first in his family to attend university.[56] Like the clerks of John Gray's generation, these upwardly mobile young men were rewarded for their conformity.

But girls received less support. It was in sixth form that many realised how limited their prospects were. Many girls' grammar schools had a strict sense of the educational hierarchy: highly academic girls were encouraged to apply to Oxbridge, the next tier to teaching college, while the majority were expected to find jobs as clerks or nurses before becoming full-time wives and mothers. Working-class women who aspired to university were often cautioned against it. Maureen Thomas, who studied arts and languages in the sixth form 'would have loved to be able to do art, drama . . . sociology'. However, her Barnsley grammar school made clear that teaching college was her only option. When Maureen's A level results arrived her teachers were 'surprised' that she'd achieved very good grades, 'but I didn't think of waiting a year [to apply to university]', and no one suggested that she should. Maureen went to teaching college, became a teacher 'and hated it'.[57]

Girls' schools were not responsible for their pupils' limited prospects. There were far fewer university places for women than men. Women were barred from most of the colleges of Cambridge, Durham and Oxford universities, and subject to strict quotas at medical schools.[58] More than 70 per cent of women graduates in the golden generation became teachers. In 1969, a nationwide study of educated women's employment prospects revealed that sex discrimination was rife in business and the professions.[59]

But the schools failed to embrace the changes that did occur. By the beginning of the 1960s, many Conservative politicians were committed to meritocracy for its own sake, and many more saw the virtue in expanding higher education as demand for professionals, managers and technical workers continued to grow. In 1961, the prime minister, Harold Macmillan, commissioned a Committee on Higher Education under the chairmanship of the Conservative peer Lord Robbins. Robbins was charged with thinking about the future of higher education at a time when universities and training colleges could only accommodate 4 per cent of eighteen-year-olds, yet the proportion taking A levels was rising above 20 per cent. Robbins' Report, published in 1963, argued for a huge expansion in university places. Robbins saw that societies committed to economic and technological progress must make 'the most of the talents of their citizens'.[60] Twenty years of the welfare state had made clear that the creation of more room at the top had great social benefits for society as a whole. Robbins also argued that the labour market should not dictate who received an education: university courses should be available 'for all those who are qualified by ability and attainment to pursue them and who wish to do so'. A wealthy society could and should invest in developing people's interests and nurturing their ability to play a full and active part in society. 'This is an age that has set for itself the ideal of equality of opportunity', wrote Robbins. 'Equality of opportunity for its citizens to become not only good producers but also good men and women.'[61]

Robbins caught the political mood. Macmillan's Conservative government welcomed the report. They had already initiated an expansion of higher education – by 1965 the universities of Sussex, York, Lancaster, East Anglia, Essex and Warwick had opened their doors, while older colleges like Keele gained university status.

But many grammar schools remained immune to the social and political changes that Robbins testified to. Already, by the late 1950s, educationalists were beginning to question the value of rote learning and social conformity – the cornerstones of grammar-school education. In the West Riding of Yorkshire, Alec Clegg was increasingly exorcised by 'the problem of teaching grammar-school pupils to be independent learners'.[62] In 1956, as the first cohort to enter secondary school under the 1944 Education Act reached their late teens, Clegg expressed disappointment in those who had been most successful at the West Riding's grammar schools. It was Clegg's job to interview those sixth formers applying for a financial award for their university studies (between 1948 and 1962 university grants were made at the discretion of local authorities). He was dismayed that they saw examinations 'as a goal not a gateway', had 'a complete lack of curiosity' and a very narrow range of interests – 'incredible'.[63] Brian Jackson and Dennis Marsden agreed. As the Robbins Report was being written, they were concluding that those who left grammar school by sixteen included 'the most questioning students, whose nonconformity did not endear them to the school, nor the school to them'.[64]

Britain was changing rapidly. Industry was expanding, the welfare state was still in its infancy, slum clearance was accelerating and the appetite for technicians, planners and researchers seemed insatiable. At the same time, problems like poor housing and poverty continued to blight millions of people's lives. In these circumstances, educators like Clegg wondered if innovation and imagination weren't worthier skills to teach than an adherence to what Jackson and Marsden described as 'Latin mottoes, gowned prefects [and] the race for Oxbridge awards'.[65]

Meanwhile, the girls' schools remained wedded to an older idea of middle-class womanhood, seeing all but the brilliant few as destined for paid or unpaid care work, as nurses, teachers or mothers.

Sue Cohen, the oldest daughter of Isaac Cohen, who had migrated from Germany to become an industrial chemist in Manchester, got three A levels at her direct grant girls' school, but 'no one suggested university ... my parents were disappointed, they'd set their sights on Oxbridge'. Sue's treatment may have been due in part to her Jewishness: she 'was made to feel different' by some of her teachers, and by the school's practice of excluding Jewish girls from assembly.[66] Religion and whiteness, as well as family background, determined who won approval in these conservative, conformist, hierarchical institutions.[67] But her route – becoming a secretary, despite getting A levels that were more than satisfactory for the university degree she pursued several years later – was one that many similarly educated girls took on their school's advice.[68] The belief that advanced education was best reserved for an elite meant these girls' schools were ill-prepared both for the new emphasis on equality of opportunity that became stronger in the late 1950s and 60s, and for the slow increase in university places. Although the proportion of girls staying on at school rose faster than boys between the late 1940s and mid-1950s, they were *less* likely to go to university than they had been in the 1920s.[69] In the early 1960s women constituted just 23 per cent of the student population, compared with almost 30 per cent forty years earlier.[70] They were, however, more likely to go to teacher-training colleges, which had five times as many students as they had done before the Second World War.[71]

Among those who reluctantly went to teaching college was Anthea Samson. She was born in Lancashire in 1943 to a pharmacist and a nurse. Her parents sent her to the fee-paying junior department of a girls' direct grant school 'as a springboard' for the school's own entrance test. Anthea subsequently passed this and qualified for a local-authority scholarship for her secondary education there. By the time she was sixteen Anthea was keen to go to university and perhaps pursue a career as a university lecturer, but her teachers told her that she 'wasn't good enough' for Oxbridge. She reluctantly followed their advice to apply to study physical education at a teacher-training college. But when Anthea stumbled on a prospectus for the brand-new Keele University she 'put an application in to do chemistry and geology'. While she was waiting to hear from Keele, her headmistress told her that 'we've heard that you can go to the PE college'. Anthea explained that she'd rather go to Keele, but her headmistress told her '"Oh, you can't do that. They've gone to all this trouble to get you"'. Anthea 'just did what the headmistress said' and in 1962 she began her course at a teaching college. She 'hated the college' and the teaching career she took up. But brought up to believe that she had been 'extremely fortunate' to attend a 'good' school, it was virtually impossible for her to challenge its judgement.[72]

Many students who attended college or, especially, university, experienced this as a step up the ladder, materially and socially. Unlike members of the precarious generation, they did not have to worry about funding. Labour had introduced university grants in 1948, to be awarded at the discretion of local education authorities. In 1962 Macmillan's Conservative government went further, by compelling local education authorities to provide grants for all those holding a university place. Barry Dobson went to Keele University in 1962. He was housed in a Nissen hut that had been used by the army in the Second World War, but 'there was a *bathroom with a bath*! Both of these were luxuries I had not previously experienced.'[73]

But at elite universities in particular, these students could feel like outsiders. In 1962, Ferdynand Zweig found that wealthy university students deliberately excluded those from working-class and lower-middle-class families from influential social and career networks. At Oxford University, he observed that the upper- and upper-middle-class students 'keep together', their cliques defined by 'expensive sports' and knowledge of public schools. Few of them countenanced having a relationship with someone from a lower social class.[74] And working- and lower-middle-class students were anxious that their hard work would not lead to success. Many told Zweig about recurring nightmares in which they were stuck on a tightrope, teetering on a cliff edge, or suspended in space: all of these dreams ended with them falling from a great height.[75]

What 'success' meant was a moot point. For most working-class and lower-middle-class students, university or college was a stepping stone into industrial management or teaching. They entered occupations that their parents could not have dreamed of entering in the 1930s. But many were conscious that their options were far narrower than those of students from more affluent backgrounds. For all the talk of equality of opportunity that permeated politics, those on the higher rungs of the ladder had great power to prevent newcomers from displacing them or their children. The social networks identified by Zweig were crucial conduits to the most powerful professions. A study of seventy-seven judges who graduated between 1959 and 1979 found that almost half got their first job directly via friends or family. Others benefited from the advice and contacts of university tutors at the elite institutions they attended. 'Pupillages [traineeships for barristers] were done partly on the old-boy network', reported a former public schoolboy, born in the late 1940s; 'the father of a friend . . . placed me as a pupil'.[76] In the 1960s, successive investigations showed that the most lucrative and powerful professions, including law, medicine and the Civil Service, gave preferential treatment to applicants from professional backgrounds.[77] Leading medical schools acknowledged that the children of doctors 'would [automatically] be included in the list for interviews', while having parents in the professions 'would not be a disadvantage'.[78]

Upwardly mobile students were aware that the state's provision of higher education was directly linked to the need for more workers in professions like teaching. 'It is education which enabled me to change social class, first winning a place at grammar school in 1955 and then being able to go to university in 1963', reflected Barry Dobson. He valued 'the fact that the state believed in me, which made it possible for me to study and become a socially useful teacher.' But he quickly realised that 'there is a difference between being able to do something and enjoying doing it'; and he didn't much enjoy teaching.[79] He had 'loved' his university days, but regarded his subsequent career with a degree of disappointment.

These upwardly mobile graduates were a minority. Most of the golden generation left school by the age of sixteen. While most went into manual work, a sizeable minority became clerks, engineers and technicians. Arthur Moon was born in Clerkenwell, London, in 1943, the younger son of struggling shopkeepers; his father also worked nightshift at a telephone exchange to make ends meet. Keen for their two sons to escape this precarious position, Mr and Mrs Moon were delighted when first Arthur's older brother, and then Arthur himself, passed the eleven-plus and attended the local grammar school, seeing this as a passport to, in Arthur's words, 'a job with a guaranteed pension at the end of it'. Arthur had 'wanted to be a teacher' from an early age, but at grammar school he was relegated to a low stream and offered no careers advice. He decided that this was a sign that he 'couldn't keep up with the competition' and left school at sixteen. 'My parents said you can go into a bank or the Civil Service', he recalled. 'I didn't fully realise how many opportunities the Civil Service could offer, so I went into a bank.'[80] Despite the growth of the public sector, large private enterprises often provided secure employment with good promotion prospects (especially for men). Douglas Yates was born in Sussex in 1947 to a lower-middle-class family. Like Arthur Moon, he grew up in a household acutely conscious that working for oneself brought great risk: his grandparents on both sides had owned small businesses that failed in the 1930s. Douglas's parents, who were clerical workers, encouraged him to work his way up a large organisation that was unlikely to fail. After leaving his local grammar school at the age of eighteen he joined a bank. 'It was secure and it had a pension', he recalled. 'My parents told me that was very important.'[81]

Those who attended secondary modern schools showed that, given the chance, they were just as capable of doing these kinds of jobs as the minority who got to grammar school. Joan Robinson was born in London in 1941 to factory workers. In 1951 she failed the eleven-plus and went to her local secondary modern. She was 'very jealous' of her younger sister who got to grammar school and was able 'to learn music and foreign languages'. When Joan left school in 1956 she was able to get work at the Post Office, and finally realise her ambition to learn French. She eventually became a bilingual telephonist there. Two years later, her grammar-school-educated sister joined her at the GPO.[82] The experience of young people like Joan strengthened the argument made by a growing number of social scientists, including Jean Floud and Albert Halsey, that intelligence was neither hereditary nor fixed at the age of eleven.[83]

That those consigned to secondary modern schools were capable of more than a basic education became even clearer from the mid-1960s. In 1964, Harold Wilson's Labour Party won the general election, promising 'the ending of economic privilege, the abolition of poverty in the midst of plenty, and the creation of real equality of opportunity'.[84] Wilson, a grammar-school boy from Huddersfield, presented himself as a modern meritocrat determined to help others to get on in life as he had done and a champion of new ways of doing so, from pop stardom to the 'white heat' of technology.

The new government committed to a huge expansion in further and higher education. Harold Macmillan had accepted Robbins' recommendations, and Labour upheld this. Wilson's government also established new higher education institutions – polytechnics – that focused on scientific and technical education. By 1970 polytechnics were educating 215,000 students, almost half of all those in higher education.[85]

To eradicate poverty, Labour embarked on a dramatic expansion of the welfare state. The golden generation were well placed to enter the growing welfare state professions and the increasing number of clerical and administrative jobs. Between 1966 and 1976, the proportion of workers employed in the public sector grew from 23 per cent to 31 per cent, most notably in education and healthcare. The number of clerks, teachers and nurses grew most spectacularly.[86] In 1951, 6 per cent of male workers and 9 per cent of female workers had been professionals. By 1971, 11 per cent of male workers and 12 per cent of female workers were employed in such posts, and the increase was concentrated in nursing, teaching and technical work. A higher proportion of people from working-class and lower-middle-class homes were getting these jobs than had been the case a generation earlier.

At the same time, manual workers and these public-sector white-collar workers and professionals benefited from a narrowing in the gap between their earnings and those of managers and higher-paid professionals like lawyers and doctors. This was partly because Labour raised the tax paid by the highest earners. Full employment enabled trade unions to negotiate favourable settlements for their members, and Labour proved receptive to their claims.[87]

But while upward mobility increased for the golden generation, the children of managers and professionals remained far more likely to end up in similar work themselves than the children of clerks or factory workers were to climb into such jobs. And the legacy of failure at eleven continued to define the lives of the 80 per cent who did not get to grammar school, especially the large majority of children from working-class backgrounds. Managerial and professional jobs were usually out of their reach. And some were left with a lifelong sense of failure and self-doubt.

In 1966, Labour returned to power with an increased majority, firmly committed to equality of opportunity. Tony Crosland, the Education Minister, requested local authorities in England to submit plans for the reorganisation of secondary education into comprehensive schools. Opinion polls suggested that by 1967 a majority of voters supported comprehensive education.[88]

Expanding opportunity for all had become more important than deciding which few children got the golden tickets. Far from encouraging upward mobility, selective schooling was an obstacle to working-class children. The restriction of advanced education to a small minority required people to compete against each other, rather than using their experiences to enrich and change society for the better. Selection induced fear of failure, encouraging conformity to the existing rules rather than imagination and risk-taking.

By the end of the 1960s, the value of giving everyone greater opportunity – both for personal fulfilment and economic progress – was more widely understood, particularly when it came to education. But this lesson was learned at the expense of thousands of children defined as 'failures' at eleven years of age. They paid a high price for the illusion of meritocracy.

Chapter Eleven

THE LADDER SHAKEN

'Angry demonstrations in the streets. Protest after protest, strike after strike. In Britain's once ordered society disruption grows almost daily.' That was the *Daily Mirror*'s take on 1971 following three years of demonstrations against the Vietnam War, a wave of strikes by workers demanding not only more pay but greater say over their working conditions, feminist rallies for equal rights, rent strikes by council tenants, and student rebellions in Britain's universities.[1]

Among the agitators both on and off campus, journalists identified a new group: upwardly mobile young people apparently biting the hand that fed them. When the periodical *New Society* interviewed demonstrators against the Vietnam War, the tabloids leapt on its conclusion that 'working-class students were much more opposed to capitalism in general than any other group, even than workers'.[2]

Many students agreed with this assessment. 'I am one of the lucky few, also one of the "mindless militants" so often reported in the press', wrote Chris Jones, an undergraduate at Lancaster University, to the *Mirror*. 'I don't come from a rich background and have always lived in the working-class part of Merseyside. Because of this background I can't help but reflect on why it was me and not the others around me, that "got on". I'm no better than them, I merely had the right kind of parents and a lucky passage to a "good" school . . . You may ask why I am militant? It is precisely because I am privileged.'[3]

Chris was one of the 457,000 students in higher education by 1970.[4] Students from a working-class background were a small minority, and so too were those engaged in left-wing activism, not all of whom hailed from working-class families. But the activities and outlook of young working-class radicals had a huge impact on their own lives and on wider society.

Born in the decade from the mid-1940s, Chris Jones and his contemporaries formed a particularly distinctive group within the golden generation. They were even more likely to experience upward mobility than those children born just nine years earlier, with 60 per cent of men and 43 per cent of women ascending the ladder, often into white-collar work but increasingly into those professions on which the welfare state depended: teaching, nursing, social work and technical work.

But many of them were highly critical of the meritocratic rhetoric of the welfare state, arguing instead for political and economic equality. They grasped the chance to leave manual and routine clerical work behind, but were fuelled by the conviction that they were making the world a better, more egalitarian place. They became socialists as students and as workers in an expanding welfare state. They argued that equality meant levelling up, not levelling down. They created new openings for people to participate in education, welfare work and in some of those professions most impenetrable by the upwardly mobile, like law. They helped to ensure that the 1970s was the decade when Britain became more equal than at any point in modern history, thanks to significant improvements in ordinary people's daily lives, education and future prospects. They wanted not only economic equality but a redistribution of political power. They argued for the replacement of a social ladder with broader horizons for everyone, in a society where the divisions between professionals and unskilled workers, welfare experts and their clients, and between workers and carers were broken down. They wanted a society focused on human fulfilment not profit.

*

The golden generation, and especially those born from the mid-1940s, were far more likely to experience upward mobility as a collective experience than members of earlier generations, for whom it had often been a lonely ascent. So many of them travelled up the ladder that they felt one of a crowd. Also, they were highly conscious that they owed their chances to the welfare state, not simply to their own 'intelligence' or 'talent'. Many described themselves as 'a post-war-generation person', in the words of June Hannam.[5] She was born in 1947, the only child of a wages clerk at the Southampton docks and a dinner lady. Don Milligan, born in 1945 to a cleaner and an engineering worker in Kilburn, fleshed out what this meant: 'I was socially mobile because I got educated and . . . we experienced a long boom . . . an expanding economy, new jobs.'[6] Lyn O'Reilly was born in 1949 in Bristol, the middle of three sisters. Her father was a docker, her mother a cleaner. She believed that 'we were very lucky [to be] born after the war' because of 'free education . . . full employment . . . and opportunities to make a useful contribution to society'.[7]

But for many of those who later became socialists, the gap between their living standards and the 'never had it so good' rhetoric of the 1950s was also formative. Ruth Hirst was born in 1944 in Hunslet, the same district of Leeds where Richard Hoggart had grown up. She was one of six children in a family that relied on her father's wages as a welder and her mother's part-time work in the local fish and chip shop. 'I saw poverty all around me while people worked long hours, often in physically demanding and filthy jobs.'[8] Lyn O'Reilly's father, a casual worker hired by the day, did not enjoy the benefits of secure employment and overtime that some factory workers had – 'if my dad didn't have work then we'd be hungry'.[9] And many families better off than the O'Reilly's endured housing poverty in the 1950s. Although the Conservatives built more council accommodation in the 1950s, they relied heavily on the private sector to solve the housing crisis. Their refusal to implement rent controls helped a few slum landlords – most famously London's Peter Rachman – to make their fortune, but left thousands of families languishing in overcrowded, dilapidated rented housing. Don Milligan, his parents and his older brother 'lived in three rooms . . . it wasn't a flat; there were three separate rooms in a tenement house . . . no bath'. For many of these children, the contrast with other people's way of life was stark, for they grew up in inner-city neighbourhoods that were cheek by jowl with more affluent districts. 'My mother, as a cleaner, used to work for very, very posh people in Hampstead', recalled Don, 'so we were very well aware of the enormous differences in wealth.'[10]

But they did not aspire to join the wealthy elite. Many of this group of budding left-wing activists grew up in families or neighbourhoods where politics was, if not ever-present, certainly considered important. Diane Reay, the daughter of a miner, described 'growing up in a tough, fiercely oppositional working-class culture, anti-monarchist, nonconformist and strongly trade unionist. There was always a potent sense of righteous indignation about the way things were, and that "the bosses and the aristocrats were to blame for our deprivations".'[11]

Post-war writers and sociologists preoccupied with documenting 'working-class community', or measuring upward mobility, missed this aspect of working-class life. For Ruth Hirst, 'election-day in Hunslet [was] when the place seemed to come alive with [Labour Party] canvassers and campaigning'.[12] This influenced her own ideas about who might be interested in changing life for the better. Diane Reay's father encouraged her to 'become a political researcher' or an MP – an early clue that climbing out of manual and clerical work might be a means of changing other people's lives as well as her own.[13] The existence of the USSR and the Eastern bloc provided a highly visible reminder that capitalism wasn't the only way to organise society. June Hannam's family were socialists, who 'cheered for the Soviet Union when the Olympics were on'.[14] Many of those who went on to become left-wing radicals grew up believing that their prospects would only improve if society became more equal.

Crucially, they grew up in a welfare state that, despite its deficiencies, suggested that everyone mattered enough to enjoy free healthcare and education, a roof over their heads and the safety net of social security. This provoked not gratitude, but an empowering sense of entitlement. Encouraged by the sense that change was in the air, many children, particularly girls, recalled early rebellions against parents' or teachers' limited expectations. On her first day at primary school, Diane Reay 'was placed on a table with the other children from my estate. It was assumed that we could not read. But I could read, and said so. The teacher ignored me but . . . I persisted, and eventually I was moved.'[15] Ruth Hirst was the only girl in her large family. Her conviction 'that the world was an unfair place for working-class people and women . . . always seemed to have been with me. As a five- or six-year-old I had refused to touch my parents' birthday present of a doll with a pram, sensing the restriction such a role-defined toy would place on me. My brothers would never have been offered such a present. I wanted a bike and after months of rejecting them, the doll and pram were sold and I got my bike. Action paid off.'[16]

Parents, conscious that the golden generation would have a life very different from their own, often encouraged them to make their own decisions – and were sympathetic to their desire for more than just a steady job. Andrew Dewdney was born in 1948 in Cheltenham. His father was a semi-skilled engineering worker and his mother was 'a housewife, not a happy one . . . she gave us the sense of a wider world, she loved books, she played the piano'. Andrew had two brothers, Alec and Steve, who were almost a decade older than he was. But between their adolescence and his, horizons broadened. 'Alec and Steve grew up in the 1950s and the assumption was you left school and went to work', Andrew recalled. 'My father was very clear that they were going to go into apprenticeships like he had.' After failing the eleven-plus exam in 1957, Andrew was concerned he'd be expected to do the same. But by the time he left school in the early 1960s his family was better off thanks to manual-workers' wage rises. Further and higher education were expanding. When a sympathetic art teacher encouraged Andrew to go to Cheltenham School of Art, 'the message from [my parents] to me was, "well, whatever you want to do"'. The world had changed so much since their youth that they felt they could not advise their son, and while his father was ambivalent about Andrew's desire to study art, he did not stand in his way.[17]

The experience of education was often radicalising. Andrew Dewdney's 'failure' to get to grammar school was 'the big, big breaking ground' that divided his Conservative-voting mother's aspirations – she was determined that her children 'should be upwardly mobile' – from his own growing commitment to equality. Andrew 'felt a failure', but the chasm between the expectations that his secondary modern school had for him and his own artistic ambitions gradually provoked his anger and defiance. His headmaster 'had no expectations for the kids other than that the boys would become at best skilled apprentices'. But full employment, the safety net of the welfare state and the growth of a new kind of youth culture led Andrew to believe this was outdated. His school's expectations jarred with 'this sense you could do anything'.[18]

The same was true of Don Milligan, who quickly became aware that his secondary modern school 'was definitely for the hewers of wood and the drawers of water'. As he recalled, 'the kind of working-class culture I grew up in was all about . . . making your way and improving yourself'.[19] But the poverty of his schooling – in resources and ambition – convinced him that the world would need to change radically before anyone could make a life on merit alone.

The few who got to grammar school found they were outsiders there. 'There was a real awakening there of my being different', said Lyn O'Reilly of her grammar school. 'I was like a fish out of water, I didn't feel posh enough to be there.'[20] This was not an uncommon experience, but this group – some influenced by a socialist upbringing, most by belonging to an oppositional, working-class community, and all by the sense of entitlement bred by the welfare state – were quick to question why they did not fit in. Far from feeling ashamed of their working-class families, these pupils quickly diagnosed the root of their problems as others' snobbery and discrimination. June Hannam found herself surrounded by 'all these middle-class [girls] and I wasn't used to their way of life'. Her sense of 'being a bit different' was crystallised during council and general elections, when 'I was one of a very small minority who wanted to speak up for the Labour Party.'[21]

They entered their teens in the late 1950s and early 1960s, as Parisian bohemians populated the Left Bank and black American civil rights activists protested against Jim Crow segregation. These movements percolated their consciousness, shaping visions of the future they'd like. Ruth Hirst 'took out all the books about Switzerland in Leeds City Library, because I'd heard of this place, Lausanne, somehow – it was a bit bohemian, like Paris – black polo necks, Sartre. Somewhere you could be different.'[22] An increasing number of families could afford trips abroad. Thirteen-year-old June Hannam spent two weeks in Le Havre on a French exchange. She realised that she 'was European' and the experience 'transformed' her life.[23] Wendy Pettifor, the daughter of a firefighter and a housewife 'who just wanted me to be respectable', caught a glimpse of a more exciting life when she went on a school trip to France in her early teens. 'My first serious boyfriend was French', she recalled. 'I became very fluent, I loved the films and the culture' and aspired to work in Paris.[24] Being bohemian laid claim to a future that wasn't defined by their background, but didn't conform to the middle-class life grammar schools prepared their pupils for, either.

These bohemian dreams starkly contrasted with their daily lives. The majority left school at fifteen or sixteen. As Don Milligan said, they had no fear of unemployment – school-leavers in the late 1950s and 60s could 'walk out of one job on a Friday and into another on Monday'. This encouraged them to kick against the staid hierarchies they found in the workplace. Don became a clerk, which 'was seen as excellent by my parents – a white-collar job! But the firm had a rule that people of a certain rank couldn't ride in the lift. So being a bolshie sixteen-year-old, I insisted on riding in the lift. I was taken aside by the senior clerk, the chief clerk, and hauled over the coals . . . I completely refused to submit to this nonsense.'[25]

Young women chafed at sexism. Wendy Pettifor left grammar school at seventeen and trained to become a bilingual secretary. She'd hoped this might lead to work in France, but found that 'secretaries were very much second-class citizens. Men would come in and dictate and you'd sit there – didn't satisfy my creativity or my intelligence.'[26] Many of this group were sure that they had more to offer the world, if only the world would let them.

Music and art were important outlets for their creativity. Working-class people had won a new prominence and respect in the arts and the media in the 1960s. Many of the most exciting developments happened outside London. Successive governments invested in regional media and supported those entrepreneurs willing to do so. In 1955 the Conservative government launched a third television channel – ITV – run through regional franchises with a local remit. Some of the best openings appeared at Granada Television, which won the franchise to deliver ITV in north-west England. Granada's owner, Sidney Bernstein, was keen to recruit from the same pool of male Oxbridge graduates on which the BBC relied, but he quickly realised that Granada would need to draw on local people who understood the target audience. By 1960 many people in formerly depressed regions could afford a television, a radio and a daily newspaper. When twenty-year-old Leslie Woodhead was interviewed by Granada scouts in 1960 he found that he had two great strengths in their eyes: a Cambridge degree and a father who was a Halifax dance-band leader – the 'perfect credentials' for a production trainee.[27] He went on to have a highly successful career as a documentary film-maker, including on the ground-breaking Granada documentary *Seven Up!*, which followed eleven children born in 1957 from childhood to adult life. The director Michael Apted saw his role as exposing 'class conflict, the difference in opportunity, the unfairness of it all'.[28] Working-class people's opportunities – or the lack of them – was now a subject of great interest for the media.

Other Granada recruits had not gone to university or ever left the north-west. Tony Warren was born in 'the land of sunshine semis' in a lower-middle-class suburb of Salford in 1936 – his mother was a millworker who had married a clerk.[29] Tony himself got a clerical job after leaving school at sixteen before joining Granada. In 1960, twenty-four-year-old Warren devised the hugely popular soap opera *Coronation Street*. One of the very first characters to be introduced was a member of the golden generation – Ken Barlow, the duffel-coated working-class graduate of Manchester University, determined to escape the parochialism of his working-class district, but unsure what he wanted from the future.

The increasing number of educated young working-class men provided new recruits for the provincial press. Britain's largest newspaper groups had begun training schemes for graduates that gave them work on the booming regional newspapers as well as in Fleet Street. Among the recruits was Hunter Davies, born to a working-class family in Carlisle in 1936. After grammar school, a full grant took him to Durham University in 1954. After graduating in 1957, Hunter worked on the *Manchester Evening Chronicle* for a year and then moved to Fleet Street. Like his contemporaries in television, he was interested in showcasing other upwardly mobile young men. When he took over the *Sunday Times'* 'Atticus' gossip column, he 'dumped all interviews and stuff about bishops and establishment figures', focusing instead 'on the new confident cockney photographers, cocky northern actors, young fashion designers, new TV playwrights, working-class novelists and young football stars'.[30]

For young men like Tony Warren and Hunter Davies, hailing from families that relied on factory work and clerking, the media offered an uncertain future in an unknown world. When Hunter was offered his first job his mother was 'apprehensive, thinking journalism was not a proper job, it had no security'. But the safety net provided by the welfare state and the jobs it created encouraged the golden generation to take risks and innovate. As Hunter told his mother, he would always 'have teaching to fall back on.'[31]

By the mid-1960s, being from a working-class background was fashionable, and being upwardly mobile a success to be celebrated. Although few regional accents were yet heard on the television, and it remained hard for working-class people without a higher education to break into the media, politicians and the cultural sector more readily acknowledged that working-class people were the majority of the electorate, their welfare a central concern of the state. In 1965 Prime Minister Harold Wilson made the Beatles MBEs in Queen Elizabeth II's Birthday Honours list. These 'ordinary lads' from Liverpool were, the *Daily Mirror* reminded its readers, 'unknown three years ago'.[32]

These developments influenced and inspired the golden generation. In the early 1960s, Andrew Dewdney 'asked my mother if I could paint a mural on my bedroom wall and she said yes'.[33] A generation earlier, it would have been rare for a working-class boy to have a room of his own. By the 1960s, Andrew not only had that, but felt entitled to stamp his personality onto it. His artistic career began to take shape on the walls of his parents' council house. Paul Salveson was the son of 'respectable' working-class parents in Lancashire, where he attended a deeply conventional Catholic grammar school. As a teenager in the mid-1960s he became 'interested in photography' – mass-produced cameras were within reach of a working-class budget by now. This apparently innocuous hobby took him across the United Kingdom, including to Northern Ireland. The 'discrimination and political action' he witnessed there 'provided a very different message about the world' to what he received 'at home or school'.[34]

Socialism and the peace movement were this generation's most common routes into political activism. The Campaign for Nuclear Disarmament (CND) was established in 1958. Fear of the atomic bomb provoked tens of thousands of people to join its annual Aldermaston marches. In 1963 fourteen-year-old Jo Stanley, the daughter of an insurance salesman, joined Youth CND on Merseyside. She recalled that the debates and the music she was introduced to – jazz and rock and roll – 'taught me far better than speeches that I was connected . . . to US civil rights struggles in Alabama'. She found herself discussing 'the immorality of capital punishment, the connecting egalitarian function of Esperanto, the merits of anarchy versus communism, and the use of unions.'[35] Fifteen-year-old Don Milligan joined the Young Communist League. 'You got an education in some sense', he recalled. 'You went to meetings, somebody turned up with a load of gramophone records of Bessie Smith and played the American blues music, and then gave a little talk about it.'[36]

Left-wing politics introduced these young people to middle-class students, academics and politicians. Don Milligan's branch of the Young Communist League 'was practically entirely working class, but the local Communist Party had some Hampstead intellectuals'. Their participation encouraged 'the idea that you should read, that you should go and see films with subtitles.'[37] In 1963 Ruth Hirst established a branch of the Labour Party's Young Socialists in south Leeds. Meetings 'turned out to be very lively and were well attended, mainly by students'. The 'heated political discussion and activity' were Ruth's 'introduction to a political education.'[38] The vitality of left-wing networks sprang from their social and cultural eclecticism, as well as from the participants' shared desire to create a different world. Paul Salveson believed that 'the Communist Party was a transmission belt for quite a few working-class people into social mobility', because it was 'genuinely rooted in a strong working-class culture' in 'alliance with quite upper-middle-class people, academics'.[39]

University offered a more permanent route to a different life. Those who entered their schools' sixth forms were attracted by the expanding variety of institutions and different courses available. Against the wishes of her headmistress, who explained that 'girls like me didn't go to university' – but with the full support of her father – Diane Reay won a place at Newcastle University to read politics and sociology.[40] June Hannam quietly resisted her teachers' encouragement to apply to Oxbridge. 'I thought, "I don't want to do [that]"', and the increasing number of new universities provided exciting alternatives. June chose to read history at Warwick University, which was just one year old when she began her studies there in 1966. She was attracted by 'the fact they were quite laid-back [and] there was modern history and . . . labour history.'[41] Paul Salveson's love of photography took him to a further-education college. This was, he judged, likely to be far more fun 'than working in a bank. Or being a senior local government [clerk]'.[42] He went on to study sociology and politics at Lancaster University.

By their late teens, many of those who had left school at fifteen or sixteen were thoroughly bored by work. Even though fewer than 8 per cent of this generation went to university, the expansion of higher education, and the introduction of mandatory student grants, meant that it was often on the news, in the press, and a subject of discussion in factories and offices. Young people who had never expected to go into further education were encouraged to do so by workmates or fellow activists. In 1966 sixteen-year-old Ian Beesley left his Bradford grammar school to become a labourer. His workmates were highly influential. 'They said, "You got to better yourself. You can't end up like us, semi-skilled or going from job to job." And they put a lot of value on education, but also – this was a *big* thing – finding something that you really, really want to do and just going for it.' Ian became a keen photographer. One of his workmates 'knew somebody's son who'd gone to art college. And he said, "Why don't you apply to art college?"' Ian did. The aspiration to 'better yourself' wasn't new to Ian's generation, but the chance to follow a dream was far more realistic in an age of expanding, free higher education. 'I didn't think I was better than the people I'd worked with', he recalled. 'I was supported by them. I just had better opportunities.'[43]

Many of Ian's contemporaries shared his understanding of education as offering more than improved job prospects. In 1966 twenty-two-year-old Ruth Hirst was 'looking for some other challenge'. However, she recalled, 'opportunities for someone like me, with few or no qualifications or contacts, were limited. I had toyed with the idea of Voluntary Service Overseas . . . then Ruskin College came to my notice through a piece in the *Leeds Weekly Citizen*, the local Labour Party paper . . . when I discovered I could get a grant to fully support me, this seemed like too good an opportunity to miss.'[44] Labour colleges like Ruskin were still educating hundreds of people each year, usually students recommended by their trade unions, WEA branch or local Labour parties.

Art colleges and labour colleges had existed before the 1960s, but the route Don Milligan took was entirely new. In 1965 Don's middle-class girlfriend, whom he'd met in the Young Communist League, went to Leeds University and Don moved to Leeds with her, working as a window-dresser to make ends meet. He took A levels at a further-education college and then in 1967 applied to Lancaster University, 'because they let in students from so-called "non-traditional" back-grounds'.[45] In fact, the new universities like Lancaster were no less middle class in their intake than any other university (polytechnics were more socially mixed). But the need to appeal to a wider range of students, and their range of new degree courses like sociology, meant these institutions did attract small but significant numbers of mature and working-class students. June Hannam found that 'there were quite a few working-class students because Warwick took people who'd worked before coming to university. And many of them had already been active in trade unions or Labour or the Communist Party.'[46] Whereas earlier generations had relied on scholarships or bursaries, this generation had grants. These grants, and the sense that the universities had been built for them (even if in reality they served few working-class people), gave some of Don Milligan's generation a sense of entitlement to education that their parents and grandparents had not possessed.

Regardless of whether they'd gone straight to university from school, or had worked beforehand, these students rarely considered their future career. Until the 1950s most students had studied science degrees, a choice often shaped by anxiety about finding a job after graduation. But university grants and full employment broadened people's options. By 1970 half of Britain's undergraduates were study-ing the humanities, arts and social sciences.[47] 'I never went into it thinking, I've got this career path in mind', recalled June Hannam. 'There wasn't big unemployment and . . . you assumed you'd get a job somewhere.'[48] In 1968 a survey of students completing courses at Britain's art colleges found that almost three-quarters of them had opted to study art simply because it was their favourite subject.[49] Ian

Beesley went to art college because he 'was always interested in art and film-making and documentaries, and this seemed like the perfect opportunity to do more of that. Didn't think about where it might lead. You got a grant, you could go anywhere and study anything.'[50]

Like the socialists of the pioneer generation, these young people arrived at university or college hopeful that their education would help them to transform society, not simply improve their place within it. 'I saw doing sociology as my political education', said Paul Salveson. 'I didn't see it as about getting a career. I wasn't interested at all in that.'[51] History and the social sciences were popular courses for those who hoped they were going to create a better, more equal world focused on human fulfilment rather than profit.

This group was not interested in conforming to middle-class conventions. Those at college or polytechnic often found themselves in socially mixed institutions, like Ian Beesley who studied at the 'predominantly working class' Bradford College of Art. Ian's tutors encouraged him to connect his own experience of working-class life to wider political and cultural movements. 'They had fantastic guest lecturers', he recalled. 'Champion Jack Dupree, who was one of the last blues men [and] Brendan Behan's brother – Brendan Behan who wrote *Borstal Boy*.' His time there 'transformed' Ian and convinced him that 'everyone should have this chance'.[52]

Those who went to university found themselves in more socially elite environments. Some deliberately sought out life beyond campus. This became easier in 1970 when the age of majority was lowered from twenty-one to eighteen. Universities were no longer *in loco parentis* and students could live where they chose. Paul Salveson chose to live in digs rather than on Lancaster University's campus. 'I didn't really see my social world as determined by the university', he recalled. Paul's fellow activists included 'people who were from Lancaster and Morecambe, who were from working-class backgrounds'.[53] At Warwick, June Hannam 'gravitated to left-wing groups' where she made friends 'from working-class backgrounds, and mature students with life experience'.[54]

Most of the golden generation experienced the eleven-plus as a pivotal moment, regardless of whether they went on to university or college. But for this group, higher education stood out as more important. In part this was because it allowed them to confound the expectations of teachers and parents, at a safe distance from home. The debates, research and political activism Paul Salveson experienced at Lancaster were a world away from the 'rather mean conformism of the grammar school'.[55] In 1971 a survey revealed that almost 30 per cent of nineteen-year-olds who had gone to university from grammar schools said what they liked about it was 'no petty rules [and] being treated like an adult' (students from further-education colleges and comprehensive schools did not notice such a difference).[56]

Most of this group did not experience the social anxiety that many other upwardly mobile people endured. Those in the most socially mixed environments experienced least stress and anxiety. When Ruth Hirst arrived at Ruskin College, 'I couldn't believe all this space was just for me. It was amazing. And I had money to enjoy Oxford . . . second-hand bookshops, access to university facilities and student societies, teashops and restaurants, old pubs and beautiful buildings'. Working-class students at more socially elite institutions could have said the same. But Ruth was experiencing this 'totally different world' with the trade unionists and socialists who composed Ruskin's student body. This helps to explain why she 'embraced' her new life, 'including drinking wine for the first time.'[57]

Others found it harder to adjust, especially if they lacked friends from similar social backgrounds. At Newcastle University, Diane Reay 'was plunged into a middle-class world that was even more alienating than my school'. She was 'the only female and the only student from a working-class background on the course.' Diane developed anorexia. She graduated 'with a strong sense of being bruised and battered by the whole experience'.[58] When Lyn O'Reilly went to teaching college on Merseyside, she 'was back home within a week'. Her parents' marriage was in trouble, her father could be violent and Lyn felt she 'was needed at home'. As well as these domestic commitments, she found entering 'this new world' daunting; she believed that many of her fellow students 'just would not have understood' her situation. After spending a year back in Bristol, Lyn returned to college, but this formative experience helped her when she became a teacher. 'I could understand why the working-class young people I taught thought university wasn't for them – it isn't low aspiration necessarily; moving away from everything you know does involve loss'.[59]

These students' determination to stay the course sprang from their belief that they were waging a battle against social inequality. At art college, Andrew Dewdney quickly realised that he was one of 'just a trickle of working-class students – one was impatient for greater change and it wasn't happening'. Richard Hoggart had written about the unease and alienation that an interwar 'scholarship boy' could feel on leaving their community, in ways that struck a chord with students just a few years older than Andrew. But by the late 1960s, the growth of left-wing politics in Britain, fuelled by the aspirations and anger of some of Andrew's generation, convinced him that this unease was not inevitable. He 'read a lot of stuff about social class and inequality and post-war schooling doing nothing to change class inequality, against a post-war movement that saw education as being a great lever for social change.'[60] Students like Andrew Dewdney believed that they owed it to themselves, their families and their communities to transform the system.

They were fired by anger as well as optimism. More than 7 million people were still living in poverty in 1970. And while social scientists openly wondered if rising wages would lead Britain's manual workers to experience 'embourgeoisement', trade union membership increased among manual and white-collar workers.[61] These workers became increasingly militant – between 1965 and 1969 Britain experienced, on average, 2,885 industrial disputes per year.[62] Discontent with high-handed management was exacerbated by the government's cap on wage claims from 1967, alongside growing evidence of wealth inequality. While the earnings gap had narrowed during the 1950s and 60s, the value of unearned income from corporate investment and stock-market speculation rose, and Labour took no measures to prevent this.[63] The gap between the rich and the rest began to grow wider.

Across the Western world, civil rights movements and trade unionists were demanding greater political and economic power. Television brought the huge protest marches organised by black American civil rights activists into British living rooms – and, in April 1968, news of Martin Luther King Jr's assassination. Just a month later, in France, thousands of students and factory workers united against de Gaulle's conservative government, tearing up Paris's cobblestones as they rioted against police in the 'May Days' – and almost toppling the administration. Meanwhile in Czechoslovakia, the Prague Spring of 1968 saw workers and students demand greater democratic rights and cultural and social freedoms. Soviet troops crushed their protests in August – but despite the defeats of that year, 1968 became and would remain an emblem of people's shared aspiration for equality, and of their conviction that this could be realised only by greater popular participation in decision-making.

Some of the golden generation found that civil rights movements abroad spoke to their own experience. When Lyn O'Reilly returned to teaching college in 1968, she quickly joined an anti-apartheid group – the first political organisation she'd belonged to – and 'did a lot of anti-racist campaigning'. She was inspired by 'all the civil rights stuff going on in America, the apartheid in South Africa and lots of global issues that we felt part of'.[64] Wendy Pettifor, meanwhile, had not gone to university, but moved to Manchester in her early twenties, where she found work as a clerk. Like Lyn, she was drawn to anti-racist campaigns, a commitment that led her into an activist network where she 'encountered feminism and also socialism'. As Wendy recalled, 'this explained lots of things that I'd felt very frustrated about, like nobody listened to you when you were a woman, and they didn't like you having a broad accent . . . It was wonderful; it was my coming-of-age really; understanding how the world worked.'[65]

Student protests changed the way higher education was run. From 1968 until the mid-1970s, they initiated occupations to demand that universities become more democratic. They won the right of student unions to participate in university governance. They campaigned for curriculum reform, to reflect wider society's concerns and composition and – they hoped – to attract an increasingly diverse student body. At Warwick, June Hannam campaigned to get women's history and black history on the curriculum. This was part of a broader attempt to open up universities to a wider group of people 'by asking "Where are the women? Where are . . . the working class?" . . . the whole thing went together'.[66] As David Adelstein, student union president at the London School of Economics, put it, 'the student who regards his study as a privilege or a means of social mobility is likely to be very passive towards the system . . . the student who takes higher education as a right will respond much more assertively'.[67]

Among these students' lecturers were some of the upwardly mobile men of the breakthrough generation. A number of these were quietly supportive of the protestors. They included Richard Hoggart, who by 1968 was professor of English at Birmingham University. He directed the new Centre for Contemporary Cultural Studies, which pioneered studies that crossed traditional disciplinary boundaries to scrutinise class and race relations in modern Britain. Raymond Williams was by now an English don at Cambridge University. He praised the protestors for reviving the older 'struggle by working men to get an education that answered their needs'. In 1968 he reminded readers of the *Guardian* that this older generation, who had founded the WEA and formed the first cohorts of Ruskin students, 'insisted on sharing in the essential decisions: about what was to be studied', because they believed 'that education for democracy must be democratic in its form and content'. Williams judged that 'the student movement has been right to identify the present educational and administrative structure with the values of the bourgeois society which, in the nineteenth century, created it: the rigid selection and distribution of specialised minority roles, as against the idea of public education, in which the whole society is seen as a learning process, and in which, consequently, access is open, not only for all people but for all their questions, across the arbitrary divisions of quotas and subjects.'[68] Student representation on university committees, the recognition of the right of the National Union of Students to organise on campuses, and the proliferation of courses in social and labour history, sociology, women's studies and women's history, were all significant, lasting achievements.

Some student activities sought alliances with young wage earners. By the late 1960s, many trade unionists were disillusioned with the failure of Wilson's Labour governments to offer people a greater say in the running of their workplaces. Those employed in motor production saw that competitor firms in Japan and West Germany were forging ahead, while British firms failed to innovate and relied on outdated machinery. Younger workers, emboldened by education and job security, were frustrated that their high-handed managers ignored their skills and ideas. Huw Beynon, a sociologist who had grown up in the South Wales industrial town of Ebbw Vale, interviewed workers at Ford's Merseyside plant in the late 1960s. They had, he wrote, 'little respect for authority . . . They thought of themselves as smart, modern men . . . They walked with a slight swagger . . . They were born and brought up in the city that produced the Beatles and had always known near-full employment . . . They . . . respected tradition but seemed to be less bound by it.'[69] They didn't want promotion to management, but rather greater industrial democracy.

In 1968, Harold Wilson initiated the Donovan Commission to examine trade union practices, with an eye to curbing workers' militancy. Donovan in fact discouraged legal constraints on union organisation and recommended extending collective bargaining and workers' representation on management boards. Wilson chose to ignore these recommendations, instead pressing ahead with plans to regulate the trade unions and curb their power (policies eventually passed by Edward Heath's Conservative government in the early 1970s). Among young trade unionists and students, disillusion with the Labour Party fuelled support for the International Socialists, the International

Marxist Group and the Communist Party, organisations that believed in revolutionary, extra-parliamentary change.

British workers' discontent increased after 1970, when Edward Heath's Conservative Party took power. Heath instituted a public-sector pay freeze, while also easing control on financial speculation, enabling the very rich to get richer still. Bankers were now free to borrow and lend money with little regulation, leading to huge speculation by those willing to pay the exorbitant rates of interest that the bankers demanded. With too much money chasing too few goods and services, prices increased and unemployment rose. Workers found their living standards were insecure and their future uncertain. Tension increased, especially when an oil-supply crisis in 1973 (the result of the Yom-Kippur War) increased oil prices globally. This meant the price of petrol rocketed, and obliged governments to pay more for their energy supplies. Inflation rose. Hundreds of thousands of workers struck for higher wages to keep pace with rising prices. Meanwhile, employers demanded more controls on trade union activity.[70]

By the early 1970s, working-class student radicals were leaving higher education for the wider world. Unlike the labour activists who gained an education through the WEA or the labour colleges fifty or sixty years earlier, few of these campaigners had any interest in a parliamentary career. With 1968's 'May Days' in Paris and the Prague Spring still vivid memories, June Hannam was not alone in believing that 'we weren't necessarily heading for revolution but certainly very profound change could be imminent'.[71] As Jo Stanley put it, the activists were drawn together by the fact that they 'expect[ed] and organise[d] for a future full of justice, equal rights, the finest life for all'.[72]

But they had to earn a living. Many were clearer about what they didn't want to do than what they did. Working in business or finance was unattractive. 'I think my generation, especially on the left, you simply thought, "There is no way I would work in the private sector"', said June Hannam. 'I was going to get a job somewhere in the public sector.'[73] Others rejected the idea of 'professional' or 'graduate' jobs in favour of work they could fit around their political commitments. Don Milligan 'taught myself to touch-type with a Remington gramophone record', a skill that proved more important than his Lancaster degree 'because I could always get a job, typing' – and could produce radical newsletters and pamphlets in his free time.[74] Others observed the huge increase in trade union membership and militancy and decided that industrial militancy was the best hope for political change. Paul Salveson 'didn't want to do a middle-class job'. He 'went to work on the railways, and joined the Communist Party'.[75] Paul trained as a guard while becoming increasingly active in his trade union.

Most of this group worked at a distance from the most socially elite and powerful institutions. This was not entirely by choice and many spoke of 'ending up' in unsatisfactory jobs or careers. Most were frustrated by their limited prospects. Sex and sexuality were barriers just as much as class. Don Milligan wanted to become a teacher, but by the time he graduated he'd come out as gay and was conspicuous as an activist in the new Gay Liberation Front. 'You couldn't work as a teacher if you were a gay man', he recalled. 'You'd never get a job. So that was that.' He spent the 1970s in a range of manual jobs, eventually moving to the Netherlands where he'd heard there was less homophobia. However, without understanding Dutch, Don's employment options were limited and he 'ended up being a cleaner.'[76] By contrast, women who didn't wish to become teachers ended up doing so because of a lack of alternatives. Diane Reay was among them. 'Instead of the political researcher both my father and I had aspired to [for me] I became the primary-school teacher my grammar-school teachers had advised me to become', she recalled.[77] June Hannam reluctantly 'ended up in education', teaching teenage apprentices at a 'stuffy' further-education college.[78]

Most of this group found work in the public sector, which had rapidly expanded thanks to investment by Harold Wilson's Labour governments. London and the south-east were the traditional destinations of the upwardly mobile, but those who worked in the expanding educational and health sectors were most attracted by northern England

as well as by the capital. In London and many northern towns and cities, Labour-controlled local authorities invested heavily in the public
sector, and many encouraged innovations like comprehensive education. Lyn O'Reilly moved to Rochdale after she completed her training, accompanied by her husband – also a newly qualified teacher
– 'because housing was cheap and education was quite well funded'.[79]
Lyn and her colleagues pioneered comprehensive education in the
town. By 1970 one-third of children in England and Wales were educated in comprehensives; six years later, more than half attended these
schools.[80] A survey of teachers in Stoke – where the local authority was
just beginning to introduce comprehensives – found that 74 per cent of
them were attracted to work there because it had 'a progressive LEA'.[81]

Because they were drawn to new and expanding institutions and
sectors, many of this group were able to make decisions and enact
reform. By the late 1970s June Hannam had left further education for
a lectureship at Bristol Polytechnic. She was attracted to working at a
polytechnic because 'you had different types of students than you
might have at the very prestigious universities'. They were so new that
there was no long-established hierarchy – at Bristol Poly 'there were
no professors and everyone felt equal'. This allowed June and a group
of like-minded colleagues to design a curriculum in which working-
class and women's history featured prominently. By the end of the
1970s they had established a women's studies degree and were attract-
ing many mature, working-class students. June measured her success
in how far the institution changed, rather than in terms of promotion.
'You felt like it was a very pioneering time and you were changing
things' she recalled. 'You had a lot of freedom . . . And we had a sense
that we were doing what we thought was worthwhile.'[82]

Few of this group considered they were climbing a career or social
ladder. But many wielded responsibility and some held a modicum of
power at a young age. Lyn O'Reilly 'never really sought career progression', being most concerned to find work in schools where she
could 'fight for the rights of working-class kids'. But she quickly found
herself in a senior role, for many older teachers resisted comprehensive

education or retired rather than cope with the challenges it posed. Lyn's aims were similar to those of the student movement in which she'd participated – broadening both access to and the nature of education, by 'having a broad curriculum, and giving the kids good experiences and opening their eyes to the broader world, rather than having a narrow curriculum [focused entirely on] academic assessment'.[83]

Others created alternatives to a public sector that they saw as overly bureaucratic and top-down. In the 1970s optimism about new, egalitarian developments like comprehensive schools coexisted with a growing critique of the high-handed management of industry and welfare provision. Among the radicals of the golden generation were pioneers of social work community projects, founders of law centres, creators of adventure playgrounds and initiators of community arts. In 1970, Britain's first law centre was established in Kensington – then as now a socially polarised district. The founders included Peter Kandler, born in London in 1935 to Jewish parents. His father had begun life as an office boy and the family lived in 'comparative poverty' while Peter was at school, but were doing well enough by the 1950s to allow him to study law. After being radicalised by CND, Peter became interested in law centres as means of 'redressing the wider injustices affecting larger groups of people'. Rather than simply advise clients, law centres would educate communities in how to use the law, and help to campaign for a fairer society. Solicitors would work alongside community groups and campaigners, and centres would be run democratically, with administrative staff and clients participating in governance. In the late 1960s, the idea met with some support in Labour circles, but after the Conservatives won the general election of 1970, hopes of government funding were dashed. Activists like Peter focused on community-led projects that could find support from sympathetic local authorities. Existing on a shoestring, law centres were highly popular, as Peter quickly discovered. 'In the first two weeks we saw 300 people', he recalled.[84]

The upwardly mobile young men of the 1930s and 40s thought that establishing a fairer society was best entrusted to a fairly small group of highly educated people. But by the 1970s, a significant group of left-wing activists were arguing that so-called experts should disseminate knowledge and enable people to speak and act for themselves. They believed that the public sector offered, in Wendy Pettifor's words, a means of 'contributing to society', by which they meant transforming it.[85] Ruth Hirst became a probation officer after leaving Ruskin but 'identified more with the clients than the court and the conflict became too great to continue'. She later became an advice worker at community welfare rights centres and law centres. 'My reasoning was that information is power, and the more information I could impart to people . . . the more power they had in their own lives', she recalled. 'I felt I was able to stand alongside them rather than over them.'[86] The popularity of these initiatives showed that many people did indeed want to participate more actively in the welfare state, rather than be passive consumers of it.

These new developments challenged the elite status of the professions and opened new routes into some of them. Wendy Pettifor worked for Manchester's law centre when it opened in the early 1970s, 'mainly advising on women's issues'. She later moved to London and began work at a new law centre there. 'It was always other people encouraging me', she recalled. 'They said, well, you're doing a lot of legal advice work, why don't you do a law degree?' After graduating she became a solicitor committed to legal-aid work. 'Law centres were the entry into the profession for many, many working-class women', she believed.[87] Such initiatives showed that there was no reason why the professions should be restricted to a few students at elite universities. And workers like Wendy Pettifor suggested that understanding inequality was just as important a skill for a lawyer as being able to talk to a judge.

Andrew Dewdney and Ian Beesley decided not to try to break into what Andrew called 'the elite spaces' of universities and galleries.[88] In the 1970s, Ian became a freelance photographer focusing on poverty and deindustrialisation 'which were not exactly popular topics for photographers, but because there was at least talk about these things, in politics and in the press, you could find an audience and a bit of funding'.[89] Andrew Dewdney became a community artist. By the mid-seventies, the concrete estates and precincts planned so optimistically in the 1940s and 50s were the site of social problems as unemployment rose and problems with the housing – no play space for children, for example – caused discontent. As the sons and daughters of the welfare state grew up, some became councillors, teachers and social workers who argued that residents should be active participants in civic life, not grateful recipients of state beneficence. Council funding enabled Andrew Dewdney, together with a group of artists and local residents, to create an adventure playground in Paddington to alleviate 'the greyness and uniformity' of the neighbouring estate. For Andrew and his collaborators the project provided 'a way of working through these strands of our lives: [we were] this post-war generation who believed in social change and social experimentation, and who saw education and art and media as being a real genuine means of transforming people's relationship to the world.'[90]

Trade union membership rose in the 1970s, most markedly among white-collar and public-sector workers, and especially among women. Forty-four per cent of female workers were trade unionists by 1975.[91] The growth of the trade unions spoke to a spirit of both frustration and optimism. Pay levels were good, and poverty was declining. Millions of people apparently shared a belief that equality worked. This was not confined to those at the bottom of the ladder. Middle-class take-up of comprehensive education was extremely high, showing that universal provision of public services could prove popular if it was well funded and seen to offer good opportunities, equally shared.

But many people were frustrated about the lack of power they had over their lives at work and beyond. Their frustration was exacerbated by a growing sense of insecurity as unemployment rose in the 1970s. That was highest among manual workers, but thousands of other people wanted a bigger say over the direction the country was taking. Professionals joined trade unions at a faster rate than manual workers.

By 1974, prominent Labour politicians, including the senior MP Tony Benn, were arguing that rising unemployment, and constant disputes between workers and employers, could not be solved by the social democratic policies of 1945. While they argued for an increase in spending on the social services, and for the trade unions to play a bigger role in national bargaining on pay and conditions, they also argued for a new form of democratic socialism. Politicians like Benn argued that Labour should not simply commit itself to a redistribution of economic power, but of political power as well. This meant supporting workers' co-operatives, encouraging workers' control of industries, and providing incentives for firms to innovate rather than simply focusing on short-term profit gain. Nationalisation should not solely be used to support failing industries, as had been the case in post-war Britain, but to introduce more grass-roots participation in industrial management. Workers should be provided with technological and managerial training so they could put their ideas into practice. Professionals, such as teachers, nurses and doctors, should be consulted over policy, and the primary aim of economic policy should be providing the health, educational and social services everyone required. That would mean redistributing wealth through taxation and generating wealth through publicly owned enterprises.[92]

In 1974, following a long-running strike by miners and the institution of a three-day week, Edward Health called a general election, asking the country to choose between him and the strikers. The country was sharply divided, but Harold Wilson's Labour Party won the largest number of seats and was able to form a minority government (converted into a tiny majority when Wilson returned to the polls in October that year). Labour's manifesto was more radical than any produced since 1945. It promised 'a fundamental and irreversible shift in the balance of power and wealth in favour of working people and their families'. The new government promised to invest in the public sector, make 'industry genuinely accountable to the workers and the community', and 'enhance the power of British democracy' by increasing the remit of local councils and trade unions.[93]

The general election of February 1974 was the first in which all of the golden generation were eligible to vote. Labour's policies appealed not just to manual workers but also to teachers, nurses, social workers and public-sector administrators, many of whom were the first in their families to enter the professions. These groups did not on the whole want to claw their way further up the ladder; they saw their interests, and those of the communities and families they came from and served, as benefiting from the creation of a more equal society. They wanted a country where power as well as wealth was distributed more fairly.

Britain enjoyed greater equality in the 1970s than ever before or since, and these activists played an important part in achieving this. People had greater negotiating rights at work, largely due to the hard work of trade unionists like Paul Salveson. Like many men before him, he moved into full-time work in trade union education, assisting those who wanted to instigate campaigns for trade union recognition, greater democracy within trade unions, and lead negotiations with employers for better pay. Trade union membership rose among manual, white-collar and professional workers, which helped to increase wages and conditions for all of them. By 1979, more than 13 million workers were trade unionists, manual-workers' earnings had increased and the gap between the rich and poor was narrower than it had been since the Second World War.

Public-sector clerical and professional work expanded further, and so did higher education. The golden generation benefited from this, particularly women. In the 1970s, many of those women who had become clerks or teachers as young adults were able to return to study, rethink their future, retrain, and take the new jobs now available to them. The proportion of women with qualifications increased between 1971 and 1981 by 50 per cent – and many of them were members of the golden generation. The number of married women born in the 1940s who possessed some qualifications more than doubled during the 1970s, and many went on to get teaching and senior administrative posts.[94]

These women benefited from a new feminist movement they helped to initiate. In 1970, the first national Women's Liberation conference was held at Ruskin College. Equal rights at work and in education were among the goals of the 600 participants. Jo Stanley was one of many who initiated trade union 'campaigns against sex discrimination', lobbying government for the Equal Pay Act of 1970, and then the Sex Discrimination Act of 1975.[95] As a result of feminist activism, Labour's 1974 manifesto acknowledged that 'not all of our proposals should be judged on economic tests. It is the duty of Socialists to protect the individual from discrimination on whatever grounds', including 'women and girls'.[96] The Sex Discrimination Act made it illegal for a woman to be barred from employment or education on the grounds of her sex.

Jo Stanley and her colleagues recognised that legislation alone could not solve sex discrimination. Only by giving trade unions the power to enforce it could the Act be a success, so activists like her were crucial. During the 1970s, the sex pay gap narrowed. Female white-collar workers and professionals saw their earnings rise faster than men's. Feminists and trade unionists also helped narrow the gap between the earnings of so-called 'lower' professionals – including teachers, librarians, social workers and nurses, all female-dominated jobs – and those of so-called 'higher' professionals, such as lawyers and company directors, narrowed in favour of the former group.[97]

While parts of the women's movement were dominated by highly educated women from middle-class backgrounds, working-class and socially mobile women also played a vital role, not only in campaigning for change but also ensuring that equal-rights legislation was implemented. Dee Johnson was born in Oldham in 1947; her parents were both millworkers. After attending grammar school Dee went to teacher-training college in Bradford. 'I think my politics until then had been from a very emotional place', she recalled. 'That was when I started thinking about governments, banks, structures and how all those things impact on ordinary people's lives, and how you had to organise to beat that.' Dee joined the Labour Party, but she also began to reflect on her mother's life. 'My dad was very easy-going and happy with his lot. And I think my mum had more ambition . . . she had huge common sense but she'd never been able to get an education.' Dee's life 'was full of opportunities they'd never had' but she had had few options other than teaching so was aware that sex discrimination still mattered. When she became a teacher she joined 'a sort of feminist consciousness-raising group', campaigned for female teachers to have the same promotion prospects as men, and in the 1970s she supported curriculum changes which saw schools and local authorities gradually outlaw the practice of girls being taught domestic science and biology while boys did carpentry, chemistry and physics.[98] Women's chances of gaining a good education and a good job were advanced by feminist campaigns for these goals and, once they had won legal reforms, for the implementation of new laws.

Unlike many upwardly mobile people, these activists rarely felt guilt or anxiety about their trajectories, and experienced little sense of loss. In part this was because they believed society was fundamentally divided between two classes – the wealthy, powerful elite, and the rest. As Wendy Pettifor said, 'I can see why people might ask "how does it feel to be socially mobile?", but I'd never describe myself as that.'[99]

At work, many mixed with other upwardly mobile people – a testament to the huge impact of the post-war welfare and educational reforms. These colleagues shared their commitment to furthering equality. 'You were all working towards the same thing . . . having that network and that framework to move you forward helped', recalled Lyn O'Reilly. Many of the staff she worked with 'were working class'.[100] June Hannam also valued this. 'Most of the members of staff I worked with had come from either working-class or lower-middle-class backgrounds', she recalled. 'We were nearly all first-generation university people, and . . . what we argued for came out of our experience'.[101]

Many saw themselves as part of a changing working class, rather than as joining the established middle class. Don Milligan and Lyn O'

Reilly were among those who spoke of 'learning [their] craft': aligning their work with the practical skills that fathers or brothers had learned in apprenticeships.[102] Diane Reay's disappointment at 'settling for' work as a primary-school teacher was offset by the fact it allowed her to help her family financially and to give her younger sisters a home in London when they chose to study there. In her words, 'I did not want to leave my family behind.'[103] Andrew Dewdney's younger sister and brother 'loved' him being at college; he invited them to visit and was pleased when 'they eventually left home and did their own thing, too'. Like many of this group, he hoped to challenge the notion that certain jobs and pursuits were the preserve of 'a talented elite'.[104] They saw no inherent tension in coming from a working-class background and being interested in art, politics or literature.

In the second half of the 1970s, their sense of being part of a changing working class was reinforced by their neighbours and friends. Private and council tenancies were easy to come by in many city centres, and inner-city housing was cheap to buy, because the most desirable housing was now in the suburbs. As a result, students and professionals like teachers began to move into traditionally working-class districts. In 1979, a survey of Liverpool's inner city found that it was far more socially diverse than fifteen years previously, with lone parents, pensioners, and unemployed dockers living alongside black families and a significant minority of students, hippies, social workers and trainee teachers.[105] Many upwardly mobile professionals agreed with Lyn O'Reilly, who believed that 'we weren't that different to other workers'. Lyn believed she was still 'part of the working class'.[106] Despite improvements in teachers' salaries, in 1978 they earned 137 per cent of average earnings, while male skilled manual workers earned 110 per cent. Male 'higher' professionals, by contrast, earned 209 per cent.[107] And many, including Lyn herself, had no desire to distance themselves from the working-class communities they served. It seemed possible that social divisions that had once appeared hard and fast could be eroded or even eradicated.

The group who helped make this happen were part of a generation who experienced unprecedented upward mobility. They were unusual in their left-wing activism, but their activities had a huge impact. The rise in equality and opportunity in the 1970s wasn't the result of government largesse. It was the achievement of trade unionists, student activists, teachers and welfare workers. Many of them had experienced upward mobility as a result of post-war reforms. They understood that their chances were shaped by the expansion of employment and education and, inspired by this direct evidence of what state intervention could do, they campaigned for even greater change.

They appreciated the state's support, but were impatient with the top-down nature of post-war reform, the limited expectations of their schoolteachers, the hierarchies they'd encountered at work, and the snobbery that still permeated the universities. They questioned why caring for others was worth less than being a banker or a lawyer. They railed against a welfare state that had attended to the concerns of middle-class parents when planning secondary education, but cleared the slums without imagining the inhabitants could design their new communities. They did not want equality of opportunity, nor even greater economic equality. They believed that only by giving ordinary people more political power, and encouraging them to exercise this collectively, could Britain become a true democracy where everyone's talents were unleashed. Cushioned by the safety net of the welfare state, they felt able to create or participate in new ventures: comprehensive schools, law centres, community arts and social activism. They initiated campaigns for equal rights for women and greater democracy in workplaces and communities. They created alternatives to the social ladder.

By the mid-1970s, Britain was a place where ways of working, educating and living were under debate. 'You thought that a really great society was going to come out of all this', recalled Peter Kandler.[108] But in fact the foundations on which they'd begun to build their new society – the welfare state and full employment – were about to be attacked.

Chapter Twelve

MONEY, MONEY, MONEY

The 'golden age' of social mobility ended abruptly thanks to Margaret Thatcher's election as Conservative prime minister in 1979. In 1974 Labour had pledged to expand democratic control of industry and to focus economic policy on creating a more equal society. Investing in people and long-term development, rather than in short-term profits, was the party's strategy to reduce unemployment and refocus industry on the needs and desires of the 1970s. But Labour was divided, and rocked by the ongoing international financial crisis precipitated by the rise in oil prices since 1973. Tension in Wilson's Cabinet mounted when the European Economic Community, of which Britain was a member, and the International Monetary Fund, made it clear that they would not stand for Labour's socialist policies. To join international trade agreements, and to have access to credit (important as oil prices soared), the British government was obliged to agree to public-spending cuts and the curbing of trade unions' rights. Against the wishes of left-wing ministers like Tony Benn, Wilson's Cabinet acquiesced to these demands. After Harold Wilson resigned, in 1976, Jim Callaghan replaced him as prime minister and implemented public spending cuts and wage freezes. This was not what the British electorate had voted for. Anger and anxiety turned into strikes, while the dole queues lengthened.

Yet while Britain's future seemed uncertain, many people believed the gains made since the Second World War – a welfare state, greater equality of educational opportunity, and trade union bargaining – were here to stay. In February 1979 the *Daily Express* predicted that 'Maggie will sweep Jim out with the tide' in the forthcoming general election. Comparing her position with that of Winston Churchill in the crisis of 1940, the *Express* opined that Thatcher would lead Britain out of its crisis. Yet on the same page, readers were assured that 'We're going up in the world!', in a long, optimistic feature that dwelled on the expansion of opportunity since 1945. The article reported on a major study of social mobility conducted by a team led by John Goldthorpe, the sociologist who had begun his career by studying Luton's car workers in the early 1960s. A decade later, his research team had investigated social mobility among 10,000 men born between the 1900s and the 1940s. By 1979 their analysis was complete, and provoked great interest in the press. The newspapers were as taken with John Goldthorpe's own trajectory – from son of a colliery clerk to Oxford University don – as with his statistics. As he said, '"I epitomise the sort of mobility I describe"'.[1] His research highlighted the increase in professionals and managers that had occurred since the Second World War – or, as the *Expess* put it: 'The upper-classes are steadily expanding. More of us are joining more of them.' The *Express* assumed that this '"increasing upward movement"' – Goldthorpe's words – would continue into the 1980s and beyond.[2]

Within months of Margaret Thatcher's election in May 1979 it was clear that the Conservatives planned radical change. The new prime minister declared that those who accumulated great wealth should be encouraged and rewarded. Many of her supporters persisted in believing that this marked a return to post-war meritocratic ideals. 'The Tories will foster social mobility, by creating equality of opportunity', concluded the *Daily Express* six months after Thatcher entered Downing Street. The new government would 'fulfil Churchill's dictum of providing a ladder up which all can climb.'[3] The prime minister certainly drew on her own background – as a grocer's daughter who had got to Oxford and Westminster – to underline her commitment that 'whatever your background, you have a chance to climb to the top'.[4]

But while the government skilfully used nostalgia for the post-war past, they did not wish to return to the 1940s. The post-war drive for equal opportunity had rested on a welfare state and high employment. But Thatcher's government was committed to monetarism, an increasingly fashionable philosophy that argued that state investment was the wrong way to solve a crisis. Instead, people should be encouraged to acquire wealth unfettered by state regulation, the benefits of which would trickle down the social ladder. The taxation that had paid for post-war welfare must be reduced to encourage wealth acquisition. The wealthiest enjoyed tax cuts, and benefited from the government's relaxation of restrictions on currency movements. This made financial speculation more attractive and the use of offshore tax havens easier. In 1986 the government deregulated the London stock market, allowing foreign banks to trade there.

There were certainly some success stories, as we shall see. But upward mobility declined in the 1980s. And among those most badly affected were the golden generation, especially men. Of the 20 per cent of men born between 1935 and 1955 who were downwardly mobile, the majority experienced their descent during the 1980s. Two-thirds of unemployed men and half of all unemployed women were members of the golden generation.[5]

Women's experiences were more mixed. About 20 per cent of those in the golden generation were downwardly mobile, but most of them experienced this before the 1980s. Many of them were the daughters of skilled manual workers who took jobs as unskilled factory hands, or the daughters of male professionals who became clerks. As women, they were unable to find jobs comparable to those of their fathers. The expansion of further and higher education in the 1970s meant that for some women the 1980s was a decade of expanding opportunity. But their horizons were not broadened by free enterprise; rather, they were due to the survival of the welfare state and the public-sector work it provided. The nature of women's work was changing, in ways that challenge the social mobility statistics. Clerical work remained their most common occupation, but it was increasingly insecure. And many women now found that their earnings had to support their family, as male unemployment increased. Those married to unemployed men were just as affected by their husband's worklessness as their spouse was.

The pace of change was rapid. The proportion of people who were unemployed trebled between 1979 and 1985, and for most of the 1980s more than 10 per cent of the workforce was jobless. People in areas where manufacturing had provided the major source of work were particularly vulnerable: 20 per cent of workers in Northern Ireland and more than 15 per cent in north-east England, Scotland and South Wales were out of work in the mid-1980s.[6]

People's prospects depended on their location and the job they did, but the dream of climbing to the top of the ladder had never been less attainable. The opportunities that had provided earlier generations with security and advancement – from skilled industrial work to promotion structures in banks and the professions – were destroyed or drastically reduced. A small number of people certainly did grow very rich in the 1980s, but they tended to be from relatively wealthy backgrounds – and their success did not benefit others. Instead, the gap between Britain's richest people and the rest grew dramatically. The Gini coefficient is the most reliable means of assessing income distribution. It measures the distribution of income on a scale from 0 (if all incomes are equal) to 100 (if all income is concentrated in the hands of a single person). During the 1980s, the Gini coefficient increased in favour of the rich. In 1984, it was 49 per cent for income before tax, but on taxed income it was 30 per cent. By 1990, the Gini coefficient for pre-tax income had risen by 3 percentage points to 51 – but for post-tax income it had risen by 10 percentage points to 40.[7] Conservative tax cuts for Britain's richest people helped them to get richer still.

The seismic nature of these changes was felt as early as 1980. In January of that year, John Goldthorpe's research on social mobility was published, and caused a stir. The *Daily Mail* presented a much bleaker view of Britain than the *Express* had done just a year earlier. '[E]conomic stagnation now seems likely to make it more difficult to climb', acknowledged the *Mail*. John Goldthorpe argued that strikes and unrest had resulted from financial insecurity, fear of downward mobility and frustration at lack of opportunity. The government must invest in improving the lives of those at the bottom of the ladder and in creating 'a more open and equal society', he said, harking back to Clement Attlee.

Just a few years earlier, this would have been an uncontroversial stance, more likely to be criticised from the political left as unsupportive of egalitarianism than from the political right. But by 1980 the landscape had changed. The *Mail* challenged Goldthorpe's view, arguing that the government was right to take 'a firm authoritarian stance' in order to 'put down working-class unrest'. This would find favour with 'those who believe society stands to gain more from encouraging individuals to help themselves get on than from trying to impose greater equality.'[8] In the post-war years, politicians, social scientists and journalists had believed that greater equality could increase upward mobility by creating more educational and job opportunities. Now the political right presented equality as hindering the work ethic and determination that fuelled people's ambition to rise.

Meanwhile, Keith Waterhouse – no friend of Tony Benn and 'polytechnic militant socialism' – used his column in the *Daily Mirror* (broadly left wing in its sympathies) to support John Goldthorpe's conclusions. Pointing to the rise of unemployment, Waterhouse argued that for working-class voters, 1980s Britain 'is definitely not a country where life is going to be appreciably more attractive for their children', due to high unemployment and cuts to education and the welfare state. '[W]hile this deficiency may inspire them more towards part-time mini-cab driving than to Marxism, they are no less angry than the student slogan-chanters', Waterhouse concluded.[9] He was right: the shrinking of opportunity marked a transformation in people's lives and hopes, one that would have powerful personal and political repercussions.

*

Unemployment was a huge shock for the golden generation. They had been brought up to believe that if they worked hard they could find a job for life. Alan Watkins had been born in Coventry in the early 1940s. His father was a labourer but Alan had worked his way from apprentice to skilled engineer to production manager. By 1979, with Britain's manufacturing base shrinking – 40 per cent of workers were in manufacturing when Alan began work in the 1950s, but just 22 per cent by 1981[10] – Alan thought the Tories were the only party who offered a solution. He didn't think Thatcher would make his fortune, just hoped her influential friends in the City would prevent him tumbling down the ladder. '[Y]ou should vote where the money is', he believed. 'If anyone is going to be able to change things, they can because they've got the influence and the power'.[11]

But in the early 1980s Coventry's engineering works closed down. 'If you'd told us, my parents, me, any of us in the 1960s that twenty years later it would all have disappeared we'd have laughed', Alan said. 'In the early 1960s it was just booming.'[12] Most men of Alan's age experienced unemployment as a permanent step down the ladder. 'We've gone to a station lower in life', one middle-aged man, a former manual worker, told researchers after two years on the dole.[13] Manual workers were the hardest hit. In 1983, 2 per cent of unemployed people had previously worked in the professions (compared with 7 per cent of all workers), while 65 per cent had previously been manual workers (who composed 48 per cent of the workforce).[14] Manual workers were also more likely to remain unemployed for longer than two years, after which point few unemployed families were able to keep themselves out of poverty. Forty per cent of those professionals and managers who were unemployed in 1983 found work within fifteen months, but only a quarter of unskilled and semi-skilled manual workers did so.[15]

Unemployment affected an entire family. What most found hardest to cope with was the loss of financial security and the ability to plan ahead. Hardest of all was the fact that their children, far from improving on their parents' standard of living, were now experiencing tougher childhoods than they themselves had had. "'I like to give them what I can'", Mr Black, a former manual worker who had been unemployed for 20 months, told researchers in 1984. He and his wife had three children aged between four and ten. "'I never wanted for anything, not really . . . I don't want to see their standard of living drop.'"[16] Children's clothes, books and toys were the very last things that unemployed families cut back on.[17]

Finding a new job brought relief but also recognition that the old way of life was never to return. It was rare for an unemployed man to find work comparable to his old job. Those who got new jobs tended to go into expanding, low-paid service roles, as salespeople, shop assistants, cleaners or security guards.[18] These jobs did not offer them the trade union protection, wages, security or skill that they had previously experienced. Women were responsible for attempting to make ends meet or, in more fortunate households, to keep up the former standard of living. When Jennifer Agnew's husband, an engineering manager, was made redundant in 1983 she returned to secretarial work to support their young family. They were relieved when her husband found a new, white-collar job, but this paid less than his former role. Jennifer helped to make ends meet by working 'in the evenings at a local nursing home, when my husband arrived home from work and could take over putting the children to bed'.[19] Jennifer was conscious that 'we had a far harder struggle than my mother ever did', which was not what her generation had been led to expect.

The Conservatives believed that it was not the state's role to provide employment; rather, people were encouraged to create it for themselves. Self-employment was lauded: in 1982 the government established 'Enterprise Zones' in areas of high unemployment where hopeful entrepreneurs could receive grants and training. Going it alone appealed to some of the golden generation. During the 1980s the proportion of the workforce who were self-employed rose from 9 per cent to 13 per cent. But most of these entrepreneurs earned a living as window cleaners, taxi drivers, childminders or market traders, jobs that did not offer the security, pay or pension that permanent posts in the declining industries had provided.[20]

The best solutions to unemployment were those that allowed people to help themselves and each other, assisted by the state. Some local authorities – predominantly those under Labour control – allowed unemployed people free access to leisure centres and adult education, and introduced training and public-works schemes. Alan Watkins was able to escape unemployment by getting a job at Coventry City Council where he ran youth training schemes. To his surprise he 'loved it' and remained with the council for the rest of his career.[21] A study in the mid-1980s found that former manual workers who had got off the dole included many beneficiaries of local-authority schemes, including youth workers and community sports leaders.[22]

Sociologically speaking, some of these workers were taking a step 'up' from manual to white-collar work; others, like Alan Watkins, were making a sideways move from middle-management. More than 10 per cent of men born in the 1940s experienced downward mobility in their thirties, most usually because of unemployment, so this group were lucky. But they did not always feel fortunate. Some former skilled manual workers felt the loss of their craft acutely. Alan Watkins, meanwhile, 'felt quite guilty, because . . . the fact that people were unemployed had given me employment'. Living in an affluent suburb, donning a collar and tie, Alan nevertheless regretted that 'Coventry really was a ghost town like the song said'.[23] For him the 1980s was a decade when his living standards declined due to the uncertainty, crime and poverty that increasingly characterised the city he loved.

Women were less vulnerable to unemployment, which was concentrated in male-dominated industrial work. But the jobs open to them rarely offered security or good pay, and were increasingly part-time. While part-time work was widely assumed to suit women with family responsibilities, not all of them were keen on it because of the poor conditions and pay associated with it. In 1984 researchers found that women's 'downward mobility is particularly associated with returning to work part-time rather than full-time', after having children or after a woman's husband was made unemployed.[24]

The treatment of office work as a step up the social ladder by social mobility researchers had never fully resonated with women's own experiences – they'd often found themselves in jobs that offered few prospects and were consistently paid less than male workers. But in the 1980s, the value and status of clerical work fell dramatically, especially for the rising number of part-time employees. Part-time office workers had only slightly better wages and security than part-time cleaners, factory workers and shop assistants.[25]

*

The absence of secure work meant people had to look for other ways to create the lives they wanted (or retain the lifestyle they'd got). Speculating on the stock market was also encouraged. The Conservatives opposed Labour's claim that nationalisation would create more democratic control of industry. Instead they promoted ownership of stocks and shares as a more valuable 'freedom'. In 1986 Margaret Thatcher announced plans to privatise water, electricity, gas and the railways, declaring that this would enable 'millions of people to own shares for the first time in their lives'.[26]

This was a very different version of the social ladder compared to what the golden generation had grown up with. It was quickly embedded into the political and social fabric, helped by the media. In 1984 Rupert Murdoch, one of the world's richest men, removed his News International newspapers from Fleet Street to a new plant at Wapping in order to deskill printers, and later journalists, by placing severe constraints on trade unionism and slashing job security. The government, which refused to countenance support for the declining industries or the workers laid off, authorised the deployment of huge numbers of police to crush the picket lines of printers, journalists and their supporters. Murdoch rewarded them by offering vociferous support to the Conservatives in his tabloid and broadsheet newspapers.

Entrepreneurs were feted for their rags to riches tales, though the most successful were either from very wealthy families, or had accumulated wealth before the 1980s. Alan Sugar, the son of a London market trader, became a millionaire in 1980 by floating his Amstrad computer business on the stock market. But Sugar, who was born in 1947, owed his success to the post-war welfare state and full employment. His education at a comprehensive school allowed him to get a clutch of O levels and launched him into a Civil Service career. Sugar considered this 'the most unbelievable bore going', but it gave him a training in economics that set him in good stead when he started his own business in the early 1970s.[27] Rising wages for manual and clerical workers (thanks to strong trade unions) gave his electrical retail business a large clientele. The safety net of social security meant that Sugar, in common with many of his contemporaries, could afford to take a risk by innovating – in his case by using a new and cheaper form of moulding the plastics used in hi-fi turntable covers. It was in this climate that Sugar amassed considerable capital – enough to take advantage of the stock market in the 1980s without worrying about losing everything.

Richard Branson was rarely out of the newspapers after launching his own airline, Virgin Atlantic, in 1984. 'Capitalism – which in its purest form is entrepreneurism even among the poorest of the poor – does work', he claimed.[28] But Branson's own story offered no clue about how the poor might make their fortune. Branson was helped into business by his education at an elite public school and by his relatives. Bolstered by a hefty offshore investment portfolio managed by the exclusive Coutts bank (his family were long-standing customers), Branson was well placed to take advantage of the Conservatives' relaxation on financial speculation, their privatisation schemes and the ending of British Airways' monopoly in British airports. He also benefited from the state-funded innovations of the 1960s and 70s. Virgin Atlantic was able use the aircraft, airports, air traffic control, and the technology underpinning air travel that had all been produced under post-war governments, and funded by the taxpayer.[29] For ordinary workers, stocks and shares could not alone bring about upward mobility. Those who did buy shares in the newly privatised utilities could not afford to buy enough to make any significant difference to their living standards.[30]

Far more people became home owners than shareholders. The 1982 Housing Act ushered in 'Right to Buy', obliging local authorities to allow tenants to buy their homes and to offer subsidised mortgages to help them do so. 'It will give more of our people that freedom and mobility and that prospect of handing something on to their children and grandchildren', the prime minister said of her scheme.[31] The popularity of Right to Buy suggested many agreed. In 1981, 58 per cent of housing in England and Wales was owner-occupied and 29 per cent was council housing. By 1996, 67 per cent of the housing stock in England and Wales was owner-occupied, and just 18 per cent was council housing.[32]

But a major study of new homeowners revealed that most did not become wealthier by doing so. Fear of downward mobility was as big a motivation as ambition to climb the ladder. Most of those who bought their properties in the first half of the 1980s did so because they were worried about rising rents – the result of government cuts to local-authority budgets. Uncertainty about the future of council housing also made people decide it would be better to go it alone.[33] Among them were the Brown family of Birmingham. Concerned that '"the rents were going up"', the Browns bought their home in the early 1980s. A couple of years later they moved away from the estate where they'd lived, because the tenants of the council houses that remained were changing – '"problem families"' were being moved in as unemployment rose and the council (faced with a housing shortage as more affluent tenants bought their homes) could only accommodate those with very serious needs.[34]

The Browns appeared to be one of Right to Buy's success stories. By the end of the 1980s they lived in an affluent suburb of Birmingham. They'd been able to move there thanks to Mr Brown's 'promotion to a manager'. But their very large mortgage payments required all members of the family to contribute. Mrs Brown found part-time work in a launderette, and they also relied on the earnings of two adult children living at home.[35] Right to Buy returned many families to the strategies for getting by and getting on that had been so common in the 1930s, when the very hard work of several adults had been necessary to buy or rent a home.

*

There were, though, Thatcherite success stories among the golden generation. Among them were those with skills in technology, finance or construction, living in south-east England. Here, just 8 per cent of people were unemployed in the mid-1980s.[36] Those in work were more likely to be in well-paid jobs, as successive governments prioritised investment in London as a global financial centre. In the mid- and late 1980s, the expansion of the financial sector in London, and the Conservatives' relaxation of rules governing mortgage-lending and property speculation, created a housing boom in and around London. Service and construction workers benefited from growing demand from the capital's wealthy elite for housing, office blocks, restaurants and bars. The difference between the earnings and opportunities of workers in the south-east and the rest of the country widened in the former group's favour.[37]

Many of these workers were enthusiastic Tories. The few manual and white-collar workers who bought shares in the newly privatised utility companies were concentrated in skilled and technological jobs in the south-east.[38] Some manual workers were able to retrain for new computing and technical roles as prospering private firms invested in information technology. Among them was Lucy Young's father. Lucy was born in London in the early 1980s; her father was a printer and her mother a secretary. During her childhood her father, whose trade was becoming obsolete, was able to move to a well-paid desk job 'due to the advent of computers'.[39] This was just the start of the Young family's rise up the social ladder. Like thousands of other council tenants, they took advantage of Thatcher's hugely popular right-to-buy initiative. Lucy Young's parents were among those who contributed to this change. She grew up knowing how proud they were of becoming 'homeowners due to being able to buy their council house'. The Youngs' home was in an increasingly desirable part of the capital and its value soared. Lucy was aware that her family 'moved very much to the middle-class strata [sic] from a working-class start.'[40]

Men who had got into management in the financial services, or the more lucrative and prestigious professions, also did well. They benefited from Conservative tax breaks, and were relatively untouched by public-spending cuts and industrial restructuring. Among them was Arthur Moon. By the 1980s Arthur's first job, as a bank clerk, was far behind him. He had left in the early 1960s for work at a newspaper firm. Those of Arthur's peers who had gone into the public sector included some who were very open about their background and upward mobility. For Lyn O'Reilly or June Hannam, for example, the experience of upward mobility shaped their desire to create a more open and egalitarian education system, and proved important in building relationships with likeminded colleagues. Arthur's career, and his life, had been very different. By the time he left grammar school aged sixteen in 1959, he was 'a loner'. This, he explained, was 'partly because as a gay man who couldn't afford to admit it, I lived a life of cover-up.' Over the next four decades, Arthur and his partner (with whom he would spend the next forty-four years) guarded their private life closely. He 'allowed only three colleagues across all those years to know the truth.' But this approach served Arthur well. Constantly on his guard to give nothing away about his private life, he became an astute reader of situations and colleagues. He attributed his success at work to 'knowing when to speak and, as importantly, when not to'; he became valued for his discretion and tact. In the volatile 1980s, as Arthur's company grew, faced mergers and takeover bids, these skills proved to be valuable. Arthur rose to become a senior manager with a large salary, 'plus a company car, BUPA membership, and other fringe benefits'.[41]

The women who did best in the 1980s were very different to Arthur. They achieved what they did in spite of the economic reforms of that decade, not because of them. They tended to be public-sector workers, who benefited from those reforms of the 1960s and 70s that survived the Conservative cuts: the expansion of further and higher education, and of public-sector employment. The gains made by the women's movement of the 1970s, including laws against sex discrimination and raising the value of women as citizens and workers, continued to affect the golden generation. Many women whose teenage aspirations had been thwarted by conservative families, teachers or employers were able to realise these in the 1980s. Pamela Thornton was among them. She had been born in 1943 to a working-class Lancashire family. A 'bookworm' from an early age, Pamela was 'very jealous' of those girls who passed the eleven-plus. She attended a secondary modern school and left at fifteen to become a bakery assistant. By 1973 she was married to a council clerk, had a young daughter starting nursery school and 'was ready for a new challenge'. The local further education college invited her to teach a baking class and she 'loved it'. By the end of the 1970s, Pamela was teaching a number of evening classes. In 1981 her newfound confidence led her to answer a plea for help in establishing a library at her daughter's new comprehensive school. With the school's support, Pamela trained as a library assistant and took up a permanent job with the council-funded schools library service. State-funded education provided Pamela with learning, training and a career. She travelled all the way from shop assistant to a senior clerical worker. More important to Pamela, she had a satisfying career centring on books and young people which she 'loved'.[42]

Pamela Thornton was not alone. Although she and most of her contemporaries left school at fifteen, many returned to education after their children were born, benefiting from the expansion of adult education classes, further education colleges and polytechnics in the 1970s. In the 1980s, these women were well placed to fill professional and white-collar jobs that were essential to the welfare state, and which some local authorities worked hard to support and even expand.

Another was Maureen Thomas. In 1966 she had left her Barnsley grammar school for teaching college. She married in the early 1970s and quickly left her 'hated' teaching job to have two children. Her husband was a town planner who shared her working-class roots. By 1981, he was earning enough to buy the family a house in a 'nice area' of a northern town. Unlike Pamela Thornton, who was 'very proud of being working class', Maureen had always wanted to move into the middle class. By 1981 she thought she was 'halfway to making it'.[43] But 'making it' also meant becoming financially independent of her husband and broadening her education and social circle. In her youth, a lack of money, narrow educational pathways and the need to train for a job had prevented Maureen from pursuing interests such as travel, art and music. Now she had the chance to do so. In 1981 she returned to work, not as a classroom teacher but as a local authority tutor for children who couldn't cope with mainstream schooling. In the 1970s, many local authorities, especially those that were Labour controlled, had expanded welfare state provision, attempting to meet local demands and move away from the top-down, one-size-fits-all approach of 1945. This new role was one of the results. It offered Maureen more scope for 'creativity' and autonomy than teaching.[44]

Maureen discovered that her aspirations were far from unusual. She joined the Housewives' Register, a women's group popular in affluent suburbs, 'where I got to know women who had professions rather than jobs'. She began attending concerts and exhibitions with these new friends. In 1984 Maureen met the man who would eventually become her second husband, an accountant who shared her love of 'what some would consider to be middle-class stuff!': visiting art galleries and stately homes, travel and classical music.[45] Her social life, husband and her work were all important components of what Maureen experienced as an upward trajectory in the 1980s. But what made all of this possible was the expansion of the public sector which offered her first husband a career, and then her the chance to create a new life for herself.

These journeys were not always experienced as changing class. Although Pamela Thornton had moved up the ladder in sociological terms, she saw herself as 'working class', which she defined as needing to work for a living, and relying on effort rather than family money.[46] Pamela saw her work as a librarian as entirely compatible with remaining working class, having loved reading and debate long before she had entered white-collar work and because her own pathway to a new career – further education and her daughter's comprehensive school – did not necessitate escaping from her roots.

By contrast, Maureen Thomas thought she had joined the middle class, but not just by virtue of marrying, first, a town planner, and then an accountant. Her work in the public sector, and the autonomy and financial independence this offered in the 1980s, was very important to her. In sociological terms, there was no difference between schoolteacher and home tutor, but for Maureen the freedom that the latter role gave her, and the feeling that she was making a significant difference to people's lives, were vital distinctions. Her financial independence also enabled her to participate in what she defined as middle-class pursuits. As someone who had been encouraged to believe that success in the eleven-plus marked her departure from the working class, she associated learning, theatre and art with middle-class life (despite her grammar school having discouraged her love of art and drama).

What both women, and many of their contemporaries, shared was the belief that they had moved into what Pamela called 'the professional world'.[47] What united them was a strong generational and gendered sense of themselves as public-sector professionals: a social group who owed everything to the post-war welfare state.[48]

*

By the end of the 1980s, Britain was a radically different country to the one in which the golden generation had grown up. At the end of the Second World War, providing a decent standard of living for all had become the benchmark against which the new welfare state was measured. In the 1960s Labour had suggested that a modern democracy should both provide good living standards for all and equality of opportunity to climb the ladder. By the mid-1970s, increasing numbers of people were calling for greater political and economic power to enact a more radical collective uplift. But in the 1980s the Conservatives, assisted by the media, revised the political narrative. A flourishing society was now one where the talented and ambitious could get rich – allegedly. This entrepreneurial dream attracted many people who had felt helpless and powerless in the face of political and economic turbulence in the late 1970s. But the fear of downward mobility was at least as important as the hope of ascending the ladder in explaining why so many of the chief beneficiaries of the welfare state embraced the new free-market philosophy.

Few of those who experienced downward mobility were concerned about social status per se. In the 1930s, some of those affected by the depression had hoped that claiming middle-class status would elicit government assistance. But the golden generation had grown up in an era when manual work had been valued – albeit often more in political rhetoric than in financial reward. In the 1980s, those who were made unemployed, or whose job security diminished, worried about their inability to make ends meet, to plan for the future and – crucially – to give their children a better life than they had had. Few had expected to end up unable to look after themselves and their own.

Some of the upwardly mobile benefited from the expansion of technological work and the construction boom in south-east England. Many welcomed self-employment and the Right to Buy as an escape from the control of employers, trade unions or the local council housing department. But private enterprise was far less important than the public sector in helping some of the golden generation – especially women – to climb the ladder in the 1980s. They owed this to expanding educational and employment opportunities created by the welfare state. In turn, they helped to ensure that the welfare state, and the chances it provided, survived the 1980s. That was to prove vital to the next generation.

PART V

THE MAGPIE
GENERATION
1956–1971

Chapter Thirteen

DIY SOCIETY

'Most of my generation, we didn't have mentors', said Darren Prior, born in 1962. 'We were like magpies. We picked bits that either spurred us on through anger or attracted us because we wanted to be like that.'[1] The magpie generation were born between 1956 and 1971. They began life anticipating that they would benefit from the welfare state and full employment just as their parents had done. Unlike many of the older generation, they did not have the stress of worrying whether they would be selected for one of the golden tickets at the age of eleven; more than 70 per cent of them attended comprehensive schools. As the first cohorts of children to be educated at comprehensives reached their late teens, increasing numbers of them took A levels.[2] More than 15 per cent went to university, compared with less than 8 per cent of the golden generation.[3] Between 1974 and 1979 they lived under a Labour government committed to harnessing 'the idealism and high intelligence, especially of our young people' to help achieve 'far greater economic equality'.[4]

But this landscape was transformed in the 1980s and so were their prospects. Upward mobility declined. Only 40 per cent of the magpies rose from their parents' rung, and thirty per cent of them were downwardly mobile.

In this chapter we meet the upwardly mobile magpies; in the next, those who did not fare so well. Clearly even those who climbed the ladder were affected by the changes that the new political era brought – and not all considered themselves to have benefited from these. Faced with a very different future to the one they and their parents had anticipated, the magpies mapped out different routes to get what they wanted. The older aspirations for economic security, greater education and socially useful work remained strong in this generation. Many of the upwardly mobile did not set out to climb the social ladder, but their pursuit of education and public-sector work took them up its rungs. Others tried to be entrepreneurial. Many of them drew on the spirit of self-help, and helping each other, that Darren Prior touched upon. They shared the sense of entitlement that the golden generation had imbibed from the welfare state. But they also chafed against the limited ambitions that many of their schools and parents had for them. The spirit of 'do it yourself' took a new form in the countercultural music, art and fanzines of the punk era. But the desire to create one's own future, unfettered by the state, was then embodied in a different form by the Conservatives' championing of free enterprise in the 1980s. As society became a more unequal place, the upwardly mobile magpies could find their own journeys perilous and stressful, their outcome uncertain.

*

Of all the generations featured in this book, the magpies were the least interested in climbing the social ladder. Within this generation was a large minority who were content to replicate the lifestyle their mothers and fathers had created. This was especially true of men born to white-collar workers, skilled manual workers and public-sector professionals. Many of them saw social mobility as something their parents had achieved, and as an irrelevance to their generation. Nick Grier was born in 1963, the son of a senior engineer and a schoolteacher. Both his parents were the first in their working-class families to attend university. 'Social mobility is something we've never talked about in our family', Nick said.[5] He assumed he would enjoy the same educational opportunities and economic security as his parents. Darren Prior had a very different upbringing. His family were 'Gypsies' – a term they preferred to 'travellers', the word more commonly used today – but had long worked as engineers. Darren 'assumed I'd follow my fathers and brothers into that'.[6]

These magpies were very different from those clerks of John Gray's generation who had had to subjugate their personal life to their careers. They were also different from those members of the breakthrough generation who had invested so much time and energy establishing themselves. These younger men grew up believing that secure work and the safety net of social security would allow them to devote most of their energy to family, friendship and, in some cases, contributing to political or civic life. Chris Harris was born in 1966 in Bath. His parents were from working-class backgrounds, but thanks to their education and to the expansion of the public sector, both were civil servants by the time Chris was born. His family and his comprehensive education imbued Chris with the belief that 'if you were able and worked hard enough you could achieve'. As a teenager Chris, like many of his contemporaries, didn't give his career much thought. He recalled his main ambitions were to have 'a loving relationship, with sufficient funds to provide the standard of living you desire'.[7] Medical experts now know that the life Chris and his friends assumed they'd lead – one founded on economic security, with scope to choose and control the work they did, and with plenty of time for a range of satisfying relationships and for rest and relaxation – encourages excellent mental and physical health. It also leads to greater productivity at work.[8]

Women were less satisfied with replicating their parents' lives, even if they grew up in economic security. Most of them grew up before the Women's Liberation Movement, in households where mothers continued to shoulder the burden of household chores and childcare, even while increasing numbers of them held down part-time work. Amanda Hall was born in 1964 in a small town in Lancashire. Her father was a firefighter; her mother had been a school secretary before she married, after which she worked part-time as a shop assistant. Her mother was both a devoted Catholic and focused on shoring up the family's social standing in their street and the wider community. 'She didn't set much store by education, she emphasised respectability', Amanda recalled. But this attitude seemed increasingly outdated by the 1970s as the number of young people going into further education and on to university grew. With new opportunities opening up, Amanda 'started to question a lot of things'. Like many young women of her generation, she was clearer on what she didn't want than what she did. 'I knew "settling" for what the majority of girls and women in my home town were doing wasn't going to be enough for me', she recalled. Her dreams were given some form by family outings to 'museums and galleries', made easier in the 1970s because manual workers' wages had increased.[9]

The singer-songwriter Tracey Thorn agreed. She was born in 1962 in suburban Hertfordshire. Her mother was a secretary; her father 'pulled himself up to get a white-collar job' in accountancy. For some men, these stories of earlier generations' endeavours were the foundation on which their own easier lives and better prospects were constructed. But for young women, the effort and energy of upwardly mobile parents could provide an inspiration. In Tracey's neighbourhood and at her comprehensive school 'no one really expected much' of her or her friends. 'People suggested we learned to type, because that's probably what we'd end up doing'.[10] But if her father had achieved so much, why shouldn't she? For Tracey, the punk era offered some clues as to how she might create a different life without the help of parents, teachers or the state. 'You didn't want or need anyone's help', she recalled, 'the whole point was to Do It Yourself'.[11]

These magpies were at far greater pains than earlier generations to stress that their ambitions were, in Amanda's words, 'not about being a snob'.[12] They stressed utter disinterest in acquiring wealth – most of them had grown up with just enough money, if not in great comfort. They saw a preoccupation with social status and 'respectability' as outdated in an era when hard work and talent were meant to determine your place in life. Family stories of the 1930s means test, or of disapproving welfare workers, were ancient history, where they were told at all. Their parents' confidence that the bad times were behind them meant that these magpies rarely grew up with the family memories of shame, privation or downward mobility that some of the golden generation had imbibed (and which had provided a powerful catalyst to passing the eleven-plus). They grew up in a time of optimism, and often placed great stress on achieving personal independence and intellectual and cultural fulfilment. Nick Grier followed his parents to university. Unlike them, he did not experience this as a momentous decision or one that could be justified only by its vocational benefits. University was a 'natural' next step, which allowed Nick to pursue new interests and learn to live independently. After graduation in the mid-1980s, Nick took a range of jobs focused on improving people's mental and physical health, including working as a counsellor. He described choosing jobs that 'felt right' and that he 'wanted to do – rather than because I wanted "position" or "authority" in society'.[13] Nick considered himself to belong to the same social class as his parents: by their forties he and his civil partner owned their home in rural Staffordshire and Nick could afford the time and money for holidays and further study.

Those magpies who could get the qualifications for secure, non-manual work often did well. Chris Harris got three A levels and then followed his parents into the Civil Service. He recognised that this offered 'a job for life I could work my way up'. He 'meandered through' several roles, enjoying his work without the desperate search for promotion and security that so many post-war managers had experienced, before finding a senior niche where he could make a significant contribution. After Chris married, he and his wife were able to buy a comfortable house in which to bring up their children. He described himself as enjoying 'a similar sort of standard of living to my parents'.[14] For him and many like him, this was success.

By the time they had reached their twenties, the magpies were living in a new political era in which private enterprise was lauded. But most of the upwardly mobile owed their chances to education and the public sector, just like the golden generation before them. More and more of them recognised the value of an education. Student grants, and the expansion of higher education in the 1960s and 70s, allowed increasing numbers of them to realise their dream. By the end of the 1970s girls were as likely as boys to remain in education until the age of eighteen and women composed almost 40 per cent of the student body at Britain's university (rising to 50 per cent by the early 1990s).[15] Tracey Thorn went to Hull University to read English in 1981. She was the first in her family to do so, yet she recalled it as a straightforward decision. 'It never occurred to me not to go to university', she later wrote. '[T]he opportunity to carry on reading . . . while I thought about related possible careers – journalism? Teaching? "Something in the media"? was too good an opportunity to turn down'. Thanks to grants and the expansion of university places, 'it was a readily available opportunity.'[16]

Amanda Hall's journey to university was less straightforward. In 1980 she left school with two O levels, but the Civil Service was a large local employer and she became a clerk there. She quickly realised that without A levels she would not make much progress, but the Civil Service 'offered you the chance of further training and education'.[17] The expansion of further and higher education in the 1960s and 70s was accompanied by new training and day-release courses for public-sector employees. Amanda was one of the beneficiaries. At the age of twenty-two, she won a place on a full-time access course and left home, then progressed to a prestigious university. Amanda was part of a new wave of mature students, many of them women, whose numbers on full-time undergraduate courses doubled during the 1980s and early 1990s.[18] The broadening horizons of the 1970s, the availability of free education and grants, the establishment of better adult and further education and the declining merits of clerical work explain why women like her took this route.

Public-sector work was also important for those who had expected to follow their parents into manual work, only to see this route vanish in the 1980s. As Gypsies, Darren Prior's family travelled around Britain, and as a result his education suffered. He left school at sixteen and, keen to see some of the world, he joined the merchant navy for five years. When he returned home in 1984, the recession had hit. 'I got a job with an engineering firm', he recalled. 'But Thatcher was privatising the steel industry, which collapsed. I was made redundant.' It was a wrench to leave engineering, his family's trade. But Darren had become interested in politics thanks to a teacher at his final comprehensive school. In 1984 this influenced his decision to go into the public sector. 'I was quite active in the Labour Party and I thought, this [redundancy] is going to keep happening so I need to get into a more secure job.'[19] Darren became a nurse in the NHS, and, like Amanda Hall, benefited from education and training. With the support of his NHS employers, he got a degree and became a medical researcher. He later moved into higher education where he eventually became a senior manager.

As a result of government cuts to the public sector, the entrepreneurial routes advocated by Margaret Thatcher's governments appealed to some of this generation. In the private sector, the expansion of finance provided some openings for the magpies. Those in south-east England were best placed to take advantage of the deregulation and expansion of the stock market. Often they came from families with no connection to the public sector, and where older strategies for getting on in life had persisted despite the welfare state. Among them was Nick Leeson. In 1985 eighteen-year-old Nick, the son of a Watford plasterer, got a job as a clerk at Coutts bank. Nick's mother, who worked in factory, cleaning and secretarial work, was a huge influence on him. He felt indebted to her hard work. 'She had fought for us all our lives', he recalled. 'Even if I'd wanted a silly thing like a Pringle sweater because all my friends at school had one, she'd work some extra overtime and manage to buy it.' Her message to 'work hard and the results will look after themselves' ensured Nick got three good

A levels. But while hard work apparently paid off, he already knew the world was an unfair place: his mother had died of cancer when he was in his late teens, leaving him and his dad to look after two younger siblings. And Nick had imbibed his mother's belief that self-reliance was essential. 'The one legacy my mother left me was the clear understanding that I was the ... person in the family who should push hard to get on in life', he recalled. 'She'd pushed me in my exams, she'd helped me type up my application form to Coutts, and she'd always sent me out with ironed shirts and polished shoes.'[20] As in earlier generations, in the Leeson family the oldest boy was expected to look after the rest. Aged twenty, Nick moved from Coutts to Morgan Stanley, one of the American banks that moved into the City after deregulation. These foreign banks were more open to recruiting men (and more rarely women) without public school or Oxbridge credentials.[21] And they were expanding. Those upwardly mobile men who got a foothold in the City usually owed it to the creation of new jobs. Nick Leeson carved out a niche for himself in those branches of speculation that were 'expanding rapidly, and few people really understood how they worked'. This offered some men the chance to scale the ladder.[22]

But rising through the financial hierarchy was far harder for those who began life on a lower rung. Nick Leeson observed that men from public schools or with contacts in the banks quickly became traders on the stock exchange floor, which was where 'the real money was being made'. It took Nick several years and a move to the Far East to achieve this. Like James McBey back in the 1910s, he was aware that he had no support or patronage to rely on. 'I had a clear sense of having to do it all myself', he recalled.[23]

Women, meanwhile, continued to enter business and finance in very small numbers. The City was a macho world where cut-throat competition was strongly encouraged, bolstered by long drinking sessions after work. Nick Leeson, whose idea of a good night out was to 'get out there and behave like an animal', could fit in.[24] Women could not. The few who did well tended to come from well-connected, wealthy families. Nicola Horlick was born in 1960 and educated at private school and Oxford, after which she worked for her family's import firm. She decided to go into the City in 1983 and recalled that 'my business experience became the focal point of most of my interviews'.[25] She won a job with a prestigious firm. All the same, Nicola faced dismissal after becoming a mother when her boss decided that she was no longer committed to the firm. For women facing the additional challenge of climbing the social ladder, the City and the upper echelons of other professions lauded as entrepreneurialism – advertising and accountancy, for example – were almost impenetrable. In the early twenty-first century, by which time the magpies were in the final third of their working lives, the directors, partners and CEOs of major law, finance and advertising firms remained overwhelmingly white and male. Socialising in expensive bars and restaurants in the evenings, and criteria such as a person's social connections and perceived 'gravitas' were hugely influential in determining who got the top jobs.[26]

South Asian migrants were meant to epitomise Tory entrepreneurialism. 'The Asians refute the modern orthodoxy . . . that the despair and hopelessness of our inner cities are the inevitable result of deprivation', declared the *Daily Mail* in 1993. The newspaper claimed that 'a noticeably large percentage of the children of Asian immigrants go on to higher education . . . An extraordinarily high proportion of Asians run businesses . . . they are more eager for promotion . . . they teach us that poverty is not an economic condition but a state of mind.'[27]

In reality, migrants had a harder time climbing the ladder than their white British counterparts. This was particularly true of first-generation migrants, of whom there were significant numbers among the magpies. Like older men and women who had moved to Britain in the 1950s, this group were most likely to end up in unskilled manual work.[28] Second-generation migrants were more likely to be upwardly mobile than their parents. A larger proportion of those from Indian and black African families got a further or higher education than white British magpies.[29] But their likelihood of doing so depended on their family background. A study of Indian and Pakistani migrants in Newcastle found that many young men 'set their expectations on professional careers ... overwhelmingly in the fields of medicine, science and engineering'. Those who achieved this goal were likely to have fathers who had followed similar occupations before emigrating.[30]

Family background was no guarantee of success. Many migrants' children were refused entry to the prestigious medical and dental schools they applied to, regardless of their parents' employment or education. In 1995 a study reported in the *British Medical Journal* found that white British applicants to medical school were significantly more likely to be accepted than other applicants with the same A levels, and white British applicants with the minimum entry grades were twice as likely to be admitted as other applicants with these grades.[31] By 2010, when the magpies had reached middle-age, second-generation migrants who had a degree were as likely as their white counterparts to end up in senior clerical posts and in IT and public-sector professions. But they remained less likely to end up in professional or managerial jobs than their white contemporaries.[32] A far smaller proportion of them were in the most lucrative professions (such as law and finance) than their white peers. Those who did get jobs in these sectors were less likely to reach the top.[33]

For many migrants, self-employment was a consolation rather than a glittering prize. A survey of south Asian small business owners in Oxford found that just 7 per cent wanted their children to follow in their footsteps. They pointed out that self-employment was extremely hard work; shop ownership required far longer hours than were required on the assembly lines in Oxford's car factories, where they or their fathers had started out.[34] The desire for autonomy, and escape from racial discrimination, were important motivations for starting their own business. The closure of factories in the 1980s provided another. Jodha Kaur was born to an Indian businessman's family, who came to Britain from Kenya after racial tensions in their adopted homeland forced them to flee. In Britain her parents took factory work, but by 1980, Jodha had qualified as a teacher. By the mid-1980s she was living with her husband, an engineer, and his parents, who owned a small shop. When her husband's father and brother were made redundant from their engineering jobs in the early 1980s, it became clear that they 'could not afford to live just on the shop business' and so 'we all decided on getting a pub'.[35] This joint venture relied on the extended family living together to save on housing and childcare costs. The arrangement allowed Jodha to work as a teacher while her in-laws cared for her children, and enabled them to buy property in the Punjab, where both Jodha's parents and her husband's family came from.

In terms of income and home ownership, the Kaurs had risen up the ladder. But Jodha had to work a double shift – teaching during the day and helping out in the shop and the pub at night. And it could be claustrophobic – she would have liked to have established a home with her husband and daughter but it was hard to envisage 'being the only one to break away'. Doing so ran the risk of annoying her in-laws so much that she would be forced to 'break with them' entirely, losing the shared income and free childcare she depended on.[36] Nevertheless, self-employment remained important to many migrants. Large numbers took this route because they could not find the professional work or training they had aspired to. Most of the Indian and Pakistani men in Newcastle who were refused entry to the degree courses they wanted became self-employed.[37] And despite the fact that less than 10 per cent of the south Asian small business owners surveyed in the Oxford study wanted their children to follow in their footsteps, by the end of the 1980s almost a quarter had done so because of the lack of opportunity to get what they really wanted: a professional job.[38]

A very different, far more unpredictable route up the ladder was the dole. During the 1980s the magpies comprised about one-third of unemployed men and up to half of unemployed women.[39] For a small number of them, being out of work and able to claim the dole kick-started a new career. Few of them intended this. Some of them became involved in community arts initiatives run by local councils, often Labour controlled. The most ambitious schemes were developed by the Greater London Council, which created a £1 million budget for community arts ventures.[40] At a time of swingeing cuts to the arts, it was these schemes, and the dole, that provided many aspiring artists, musicians and writers with the support they needed as they sought to make their mark. Geoff Dyer, born in 1958, grew up in Cheltenham. The son of a sheet metal worker and a school dinner lady, he got to grammar school and Oxford University. His highly respectable parents 'hoped that after going to Oxford their only child might become middle-class'. Geoff initially hoped to work in advertising or the media. In the 1950s and 60s, an expansion in media and the arts had helped some men from working-class backgrounds take this step, but in the 1980s, with no money and no contacts, Geoff found it impossible to break in. Eventually, he later wrote, he 'moved into a house in Brixton with a whole bunch of people who, like me, were on the dole'. Obliged to confront the fact that he might never have a career, Geoff settled into enjoying himself. 'Thatcherism had ushered in an era of high unemployment but the safety net set up by the post-war commitment to the Welfare State was just about intact. Housing Benefit paid your rent and Social Security gave you money to live on.' This gave him the freedom to pursue other interests that he'd never imagined might pay his way. He 'ended up' becoming a highly successful writer.[41]

Stephen Morrissey was born one year later than Geoff Dyer. He grew up in Stretford, Greater Manchester. Like Geoff Dyer he sat the eleven-plus, but he failed and attended the local secondary modern school. From there he drifted into a series of dead-end factory and office jobs. Being made unemployed in the early 1980s was something of a relief. 'I am removed from the lifelong definition of others', was how he put it.[42] In his case, music and song-writing were his new lifeline. By the mid-1980s, Morrissey and the Smiths were household names. Their songs had none of the optimism of the 1960s pop groups like the Beatles; they sang about despair, anger, and shattered dreams. Those sentiments resonated with their own generation, and younger people, too. But the mass unemployment that corroded many people's futures helped a few, including Morrissey, to realise their dreams.

Labour Party general election poster, 1945, stressing the party's commitment to preventing the poverty and unemployment that had followed the First World War

Aneurin Bevan, the former Welsh miner who founded the NHS, tours a hospital in Lancashire, 1947

Trainee teachers at Wynyard Hall in County Durham, one of the colleges established by the Emergency Teacher Training Scheme of 1946–51. Many trainees had missed out on further education in their teens due to family hardship or the war

After 1945, secondary education was free and compulsory for all, but private education was not abolished. Pupils at the most expensive schools – like these boys at Winchester College in 1952 – continued to enjoy easier access to elite universities and the most lucrative and powerful jobs

Social scientists together in 1958 including Michael Young (middle row, second from left); Phyllis Willmott (sitting below Young); Richard Titmuss (on Willmott's other side) and Peter Willmott (far right corner)

Clerical workers, 1948. After the Second World War, office work became women's largest employer

A Bradford Bangladeshi family, c. 1960. The watches, smart clothes and money pinned to the son's jacket were signs to relatives back home that the family had moved up in the world

Labour Party leader Harold Wilson meets the Beatles in 1964, six months before the general election that made him Prime Minister

Teacher and pupils at Clissold Comprehensive School, London, 1973. The Labour governments of 1964–70 encouraged the replacement of selective schools by comprehensives, in order to give children equal opportunities

Ruth Hirst with her fellow Ruskin College students demonstrating in 1969

Members of the Association of Scientific, Technical and Management Staff hold an equal pay placard at the TUC International Women's Year Rally in London, 1975. Women joined trade unions in increasing numbers during the 1970s, as their employment in clerical and technical work rose

Schoolgirls in Coventry learning to use computers, 1987. The computing revolution of the 1980s was meant to provide their generation with work, but rapid advances in technology meant that technical training like this quickly became obsolete

ONE FORM OF SELF-HELP AND FREE ENTERPRISE
THAT HAS FLOURISHED UNDER THE TORIES.

Labour Party general election leaflet,
1987

Don't just hope for a better life. Vote for one.

VOTE CONSERVATIVE

Conservative Party election poster, 1979

The Patel family outside their corner shop in London, 2004. Politicians and the press often represented South Asian small-business owners as the epitome of Thatcherite entrepreneurship, but many wanted their children to have greater security and less onerous work

Lauded as an engine of social mobility, London in the 2000s in fact became increasingly polarised between those with family wealth, lucrative jobs and their own home, and those struggling to get by

Protests against library closures and public spending cuts were widespread in the 2010s. In 2019 the campaign to Save Our Libraries Essex (SOLE) successfully prevented Essex County Council from closing a third of the county's libraries

These upwardly mobile magpies, like those who climbed the ladder via education and public-sector work, experienced mobility as a collective enterprise. They did not see themselves as competing for scarce opportunities, or on a lonely ascent as some members of earlier generations had done. Like the golden generation, they saw themselves as part of a collective, either by moving through the open doors of education, public-sector work, training and promotion or as creating their own music or arts scene with others on the dole. But they were aware of having to do it themselves: 'we had no mentors' said Darren Prior. Like the golden generation they were entering a very different world than that their parents had known. But many of the golden generation believed the state helped them to get on, or should do. The magpie generation no longer had this expectation. Whereas left-wing activists of the 1970s had focused on reforming or democratising the state, this generation created the DIY culture of the late 1970s and early 1980s, which stood apart from the state, relying on it only for a dole cheque in times of need. In this situation, friends were even more important. Darren Prior was part of a group who met in the merchant navy and recognised that the work their parents had done was disappearing. 'We decided we'd go for it', he recalled, 'try to make something of our lives'.[43] Several of Darren's friends took advantage of further or higher education and became professionals or public-sector managers. Other magpies formed bands on a shoestring, creating their own cassette tapes of music; budding writers produced sport and music fanzines on cheap duplicators. 'Punk groups, like no other groups before them, inspired . . . the conviction and desire to take part in what was happening rather than simply to watch and listen', wrote Tracey Thorn, who joined her first band in 1979.[44]

In the absence of any political commitment to making everyone's lives better, the magpies knew they needed to stand out from the crowd to achieve what they wanted. Tracey Thorn believed that 'escape meant . . . making an impact', by 'being Somebody'.[45] The DIY music culture connected her with like-minded souls. But the stress on self-help and entrepreneurialism could also find an outlet in the Thatcherite values of competition and risk-taking. Like some of the technocrats of the 1930s and the managers of the 1950s, Nick Leeson prided himself on 'never talking about my emotions' or letting them get in the way of his career. His 'tough' persona and 'confidence' brought him great success.[46] But the risks of climbing so high on the basis of gamble and speculation were also huge. In the early 1990s, Nick was convicted of fraud worth millions of pounds, which bankrupted his employer, Barings. The bravado, gambling and ambition that got him to the top was also his undoing. He was jailed for several years.

The golden generation saw state assistance as hugely influential in explaining their mobility and many expressed pride in their working-class roots. By contrast, the magpies grew up at a time when state support was no longer publicly lauded as a central tenet of modern democracy (though it proved very important to many of them). And by the end of the 1980s, the championing of working-class people and working-class communities that had occurred in the media and politics twenty years earlier was a distant memory. Of course the working-class hero had always been male and was never paid as much as doctors or lawyers – but it was a different world than that in which the miners became Margaret Thatcher's 'enemy within' during the 1984–85 strike, and the prime minister could declare that there was 'no such thing as society'.[47] In this new climate, many magpies sought more individualistic explanations for their upward mobility. Amanda Hall suggested that her desire to escape from her roots was somehow innate: 'I find it very difficult to explain because I didn't even really know any [women] who had done it.'[48]

The anxieties and tensions experienced by older upwardly mobile people continued to affect the magpies. 'I am myself', said Darren Prior, and for him – as for many members of the breakthrough and the golden generations – this meant acknowledging his roots. 'I would never change my accent or deny where I come from', he explained; but also acknowledged that 'I don't have a lot in common with my family any more.'[49] Amanda Hall had considered university a realisable goal, but when she got there 'I felt I shouldn't be there, intellectually and socially (because I was working class)'. Only after two years of really hard work did she come to believe that she deserved this chance. She was proud of her subsequent career, but contentment in her settled, happy life with her partner, in an affluent suburb of a prosperous city, was sometimes marred by 'guilt' that not everyone could live this way – and wondering if she really deserved to. Like most of the upwardly mobile magpies, Amanda prided herself on having friends from a wide range of social backgrounds, including those from rich families. Yet differences in education and wealth could rankle, and made her wonder whether she really had done enough to merit the lifestyle she now enjoyed. Many of Amanda's friends and colleagues were in jobs that demanded even more qualifications than her own. 'I do feel comfortable with them', she stressed, but 'I would really like a PhD to go along with theirs!'[50]

Those who climbed furthest tended to feel most guilt and social anxiety. They were also more likely to conceal their origins from their colleagues. The limited kudos attached to a working-class background in the 1960s and 70s had never really permeated some of the elite professions they entered. Despite his macho persona, Nick Leeson was careful to ensure 'nobody knew where I came from or what I did at weekends. I wore my suit and tie and learned fast.'[51] In the cultural sector, Amanda Hall said that she worried 'a great deal about what people think of me . . . I find it difficult to express my own views especially if I know it will contradict others'. She compared herself with 'Eliza Doolittle', the star of George Bernard Shaw's play *Pygmalion*, who is turned into a lady under the tutelage of Professor Henry Higgins. '[S]ometimes when my confidence is low I feel I don't fit in anywhere,' said Amanda. The 'old-school tie' network was still very strong in the cultural sector, and she was well aware that she did not belong to it.[52]

Even in the public sector, where many of the upwardly mobile members of the golden generation had felt very comfortable, the magpies were not always keen to reveal their past. In the late 1980s the Conservative government began to introduce a marketplace into the public sector, first into education – by requiring schools to compete for resources depending on how popular they were – and then into the National Health Service. Ministers claimed this would make services more accountable and, in the words of Kenneth Baker, Margaret Thatcher's Secretary of State for Education, give 'power to the people most directly concerned with decisions'.[53] The Conservatives understood that wielding more control over their lives was an aspiration that many people shared. But budget management, winning customers, pupils or patients, and implementing change led to the creation of new managerial tiers. By the late 1990s, this had permeated many other parts of the public sector. The autonomy of professionals like teachers and nurses was eroded; those who wanted to have some control over their working conditions had to consider going into management.

Darren Prior took this route in the 1990s when he moved from research into higher education administration. He decided not to tell anyone that he came from a Gypsy family. 'I don't think I'd have been treated fairly if it was known where I came from', he judged. Darren's desire to establish more humane and less corporate management strategies in higher education – 'I think if anyone wants to start a redundancy programme, he or she should start with themselves' – provoked hostility from some of his peers, who he knew would pounce on any weakness. 'If people knew my actual background, they'd change', he said. 'They'd think, "You're not as clever as you think you are."'[54] The elitism and practices of exclusion that operated in the older professions and in older businesses were not simply due to outdated traditions, they were effective ways of restricting who got the limited room at the top. As the public sector became more stratified, these practices took root there too. And social scientists found that as managerial structures became more hierarchical, room at the top more limited, and job security waned in both the public and the private sectors, so more elitist recruitment and promotion strategies became more overt. One study of the so-called 'big four' accountancy firms found that technical expertise was less likely to help someone get promotion to partner by the early twenty-first century than had been true thirty years earlier. More emphasis was placed on social connections that might win the firm important clients, or on unde-fined 'leadership' skills that tended to favour white male graduates from middle-class backgrounds.[55]

*

Although the hopeful horizons of their youth soon closed in, many of the magpies benefited from the optimism of the 1960s and 70s. For those whose parents had been upwardly mobile, and for those who were upwardly mobile themselves, Britain appeared a reasonably fair place, with plenty of opportunity. A minority made a career in the ex-panding finance sector, or became entrepreneurs. But most of the up-wardly mobile magpies relied on state education, the support of the welfare state, and public-sector work. While many of the golden gen-eration had been frustrated at the limited options available to them (especially women), the magpies had more choices. A few established careers in music and the arts. Many more went into education, health and the cultural sector. They benefited from continued state invest-ment in these areas, especially at local level in Britain's largest cities. They were able to take advantage of the expansion of further and higher education. And they imbibed a new confidence that they were both entitled and able to create new ways of living. Many of them as-pired to more education and to wielding power over their own lives. As the left-wing activists of the golden generation had showed, this desire could fuel collective attempts to create a more equal world. But it could also fuel more individualistic aspirations: to achieve self-realisation; to become 'somebody', as Tracey Thorn put it. As trade unions declined in the 1980s, and the mantra of free enterprise domi-nated politics, those who wanted to achieve their dreams were often obliged to adopt more individual strategies to get on.

The upwardly mobile magpies were justly proud of their achieve-ments, but many also expressed regret at what they'd lost, guilt that others hadn't had their chances, and sometimes doubt that they themselves had worked hard enough to merit what they had. Mass unemployment, financial insecurity and public-spending cuts meant that the gap between what they had, and what was available to those they'd left behind, had grown immeasurably since their childhood. And these developments, together with the growth of managerialism in the public sector, meant that they were less likely to come across others who shared their background and more likely to feel it was best to keep quiet about where they came from. Their experiences show that ascending the social ladder could be fraught with ambivalence, even when it brought great economic reward.

This group were, however, the fortunate members of their generation – as most of them readily have acknowledged. The dramatic changes they observed and adapted to affected others more directly and sometimes with dire results. It is to the downwardly mobile magpies that we now turn.

Chapter Fourteen

RAT RACE

While most of the magpies remained on the same rung of the ladder as their parents or ascended it, 30 per cent were downwardly mobile. And some of those who appeared to have ascended the ladder, in sociologists' terms, did not feel that they had done so. They shared those expectations of education, secure work, autonomy and broad horizons that those we met in the previous chapter had possessed. But this group's dreams were crushed by a lack of room at the top, and by conflicting information about how to access the opportunities that did exist.

While this generation's prospects were affected by the turbulent changes of the 1980s and 90s, so too were the lives of the golden generation. As we shall see, many members of the golden generation who had experienced upward mobility between the 1960s and the 80s found the late 1980s and 90s brought a reversal in their fortunes. Even if, sociologically speaking, they still appeared to be upwardly mobile, they experienced a decline in their status, security and autonomy.

Many of the downwardly mobile or dissatisfied magpies began life with a strong desire to climb the ladder. Like Amanda Hall and Darren Prior, they were realists: they understood that life had changed since their parents' youth and sought to use their initiative and imagination to make their way in the new world of the 1980s. But growing up, this group's outlook was very different from that of Chris Harris or Nick

Grier. Very often they came from unhappy families that had not enjoyed the fruits of post-war affluence. Many of these children grew up in areas that had not shared much in the boom of the 1950s and 60s: small towns and villages remote from the big cities, often in northern England or rural Scotland and Wales. Their parents worked in unskilled or semi-skilled manual jobs or had poorly paid retail and office posts.

In these families money was tight, and strategies for survival and getting on centred on the different members of the household helping each other. Parents were often bitter about their own thwarted ambitions. Graham Knowles was born in 1962 in a small Lancashire town that had never entirely recovered from the 1930s Depression. His father was a clerk in a dead-end job who drank most of his earnings. His mother had a series of part-time shop jobs. Graham wanted more – to study and to have 'a career'.[1] He wanted the kind of security that Chris Harris and Nick Grier took for granted.

A socially conservative respectability permeated these households, and made small town life more stifling still. Graham's father 'was a special constable in his spare time because he believed this would give him respectability'.[2] Graham's parents encouraged their children to hide the family's poverty and his father's alcoholism from neighbours and teachers. Neil Black's childhood had some striking parallels with Graham's. Born in 1958 in rural Scotland, he described his parents as 'respectable' and 'conservative' people. His father was a fireman and later a lorry driver; his mother was a garage attendant. They emphasised hard work and deference to hierarchy. Neil was taught that a woman who married a doctor was, in his mother's words, 'better than us' because marrying into the professions was a step up. As he reached secondary-school age, Neil became aware that his parents were unable to get jobs that matched their aspirations. He was 'amazed' to discover that his father was a lorry driver, having assumed that he worked as a 'manager' for a company. And he 'was excruciatingly embarrassed' that his mother worked at a petrol station.[3] Like Graham, Neil was taught to prize the family's privacy above all else.

Respectability, privacy and keeping up appearances had long been important strategies for those wishing to 'get on'. In the early twentieth century, deference and cleanliness had helped clerks like John Gray to present themselves as deserving of their chances. But in the changed world of the 1960s and 70s, many magpies knew this kind of respectability wasn't necessary to 'getting on'. Education had always been important, and now the advent of comprehensive schools, student grants and the expansion of higher education meant they did not need to adopt a middle-class persona to prove them-selves deserving of it. Many of the upwardly mobile magpies – Amanda Hall and Tracey Thorn among them – had parents who either recognised this or were content for their children to go their own way. But Graham Knowles had no such support. Although he 'loved learning', his comprehensive school did not offer him any help in pursuing further education.[4] In any case, Graham's father quashed his son's ambition to stay at school beyond the age of sixteen. While some parents dealt with their thwarted aspirations by giving their children the chances they had never had, this was never universally the case. Bitter about his own limited prospects – and possibly dubi-ous about the rewards education might bring – Mr Knowles insisted that sixteen-year-old Graham take his chances in the uncertain labour market of 1980.

A generation earlier, a sixteen-year-old with a handful of exam passes could have hoped for a job in a bank or the Civil Service. In some towns and cities, this was still an option in the 1980s – one that Amanda Hall took advantage of. But these chances were becoming rarer and had never really existed in Graham's birthplace. He became a shop assistant, the beginning of a 'career' made up of a succession of badly paid, often temporary, retail jobs interspersed with periods of unemployment.[5] Researchers found his was a common trajectory among those young people who relied on manual and routine shop work. When they did manage to get off the dole it was often as a result of short-term government training schemes which paid very low wages and rarely led to permanent jobs.[6]

Living in a small town, Graham had no access to the community arts and sports initiatives provided by local authorities in some larger towns and cities.[7] By his late twenties he was stuck in a rut that, in his words, 'I would only be able to leave if I got some qualifications.' But outside the largest banks and corporations, private-sector work rarely offered the training or education opportunities that Darren Prior and Amanda Hall had grasped. While Graham finally 'achieved my dream and enrolled on a History degree', he had to study in his own time. The relative earnings of low-paid workers like him declined during the 1980s, and eventually he had to give up his course 'because I could not afford to continue my studies while also earning my living.'[8]

*

The socially conservative respectability that Graham Knowles grew up with posed particular difficulties to gay men and lesbians. The magpie generation was more willing to talk and write openly about their sexuality than was true of the earlier generations in this book. Gay men in particular won new rights during their lifetimes. Male homosexuality was legalised in 1967, when this generation were very young (lesbianism had never been illegal), and the gay and lesbian rights movement in which Don Milligan had played a role, together with feminist activism, made it easier to live in a homosexual relationship. This generation were therefore more comfortable to talk about their experiences. But homophobia continued to be virulent, stoked by the AIDS crisis of the 1980s and by successive governments' refusal to lower the age of consent for male homosexual sex from twenty-one to eighteen until 1994; only in 2001 was it lowered to sixteen to match the minimum age for heterosexual sex. Gay men and lesbians were often 'out' only in certain contexts.

Moving to the largest cities offered both anonymity and a gay and lesbian social scene. Neil Black was among those desperate to escape to such a place. While Neil had 'never really thought about what social mobility means', he did know by his mid-teens that he was gay. He wanted to leave home for a large city 'where hopefully I could be myself'. Aware that his sexuality was deeply suspect, moving up in the world was also a means of gaining social approval; by then, he was 'aware that you could move up in [the eyes of] people around me by getting a good job'. But Neil's parents refused to allow him to leave home and study at art college. 'They simply tore up the forms.' His second plan, to train as a teacher, was 'shot down in flames too'. Knowing your place, while also knowing that this was slightly superior to the neighbours' place, was important to families like Neil's; a way of keeping control over their tiny piece of the world. Neil got a job as a social care assistant for the NHS, and eventually managed to leave his 'very controlling' parents in his mid-twenties, when he got a similar job in Glasgow. 'This was at a time when you could work your way up on experience', and that security enabled Neil to move into his own flat.[9] He did indeed work his way up to become a care manager ten years later.

But Neil didn't have access to the education and training that Darren Prior and Amanda Hall enjoyed. He was stuck in a job that was increasingly exhausting, due to the rise in unemployment and the health problems this caused, and the Conservative government's replacement of institutional care for the mentally ill with 'care in the community'. Management brought neither autonomy nor security. Neil's job grew more 'boring' as he acquired seniority: meeting government targets obliged him to spend more of his time on administration.[10] By 1991, 60 per cent of male healthcare 'professionals' – including many physiotherapists, nurses and paramedics – were employed on part-time or temporary contracts, compared with just 10 per cent of male corporate managers.[11] Neil Black kept his job, but he could not afford (in money or time) to pursue his ambition of studying art, nor to find 'the bohemian life I'd craved [which] just wasn't available unless you were a student or had money'.[12] Sociologically speaking, he had achieved upward mobility. In reality, his experience fulfilled none of his ambitions.

*

The life Neil aspired to was in some respects that which some of the golden generation had achieved in the 1970s. But by the 1990s, many of them, too, were finding it harder, even impossible, to exercise autonomy at work or to find time for political or social activities in their leisure time. Many public-sector professionals found their working conditions and prospects declined. Maureen Thomas reluctantly returned to classroom teaching in the late 1980s after several years working as a home tutor – a service that fell victim to public-spending cuts. She found that teachers' status had fallen and their autonomy all but disappeared. She blamed 'the constant changes in government policy, changes in [inspection] and pressure from parents' who were endlessly told by government ministers and the media that state schools let down their children.[13]

Few women got the chance to enter the new managerial positions: public-sector managers were disproportionately likely to be male.[14] A study of female teachers concluded that women's likelihood of gaining promotion to headships and other senior roles 'deteriorated' because while '[t]he "headteacher tradition" of headship ... tended to focus on the headteacher's personality, personal authority and teaching experience', the 'managerial model is essentially a technical model, which stresses school organizational problems as technical problems amenable to rational problem-solving techniques. Such a perspective emphasises characteristics which are commonly depicted as "masculine": analytical detachment, strong task direction, "hard-nosed" toughness.'[15]

But even those who got into relatively well-paid managerial roles did not experience this as a step 'up' but rather an unwelcome necessity. June Hannam, by now a senior lecturer at Bristol Polytechnic, 'got drawn into senior management, partly because you wondered who would end up doing it if you didn't. I did end up making decisions my younger self would not have agreed with, and which I found very difficult.'[16]

Those members of the golden generation who had been upwardly mobile in the private sector were less affected by these changes. But

an increasing emphasis on qualifications, and the decline in employers' investment in their workers' training and education, did affect
them. Douglas Yates, who had become a bank clerk in the late 1950s,
had worked his way up to bank manager in the small Sussex town
where he lived. By the 1990s this job was changing as the bank central-
ised more operations in London. Douglas realised that he was unlikely
to be appointed to a more senior role as his employer 'began to target
graduates'. Douglas would have liked to have done a degree, but the
bank wasn't interested in training its own employees. Experience no
longer mattered as much, with many firms investing less in training
their own employees in order to maximise profits. Selecting graduates
was a much cheaper way of appointing managers. By the mid-1990s, 'a
degree became a prerequisite for advancement', and fifty-year-old
Douglas took early retirement. He then did a degree. This, he said, was
for personal fulfilment but also 'a way of putting two fingers up to the
bank to show I had equal ability to the graduates they employed.'[17]

*

The government encouraged young people to go 'into industry, into
commerce, because that's where the money is made', as Margaret
Thatcher put it, decrying the lure of older professions and academic
university degrees.[18] As the 1980s progressed, the government increasingly promoted technology and computing as exciting possibilities for
achieving success. Many of the magpies were aware of Alan Sugar,
who was making his fortune selling home computers. The number of
degree courses in computing and information technology rose. And in
1988 the Conservatives introduced City Technology Colleges – a new
breed of state school funded by private providers and a signal that
technological work offered bright prospects.

One who heeded the call was Paul Cosgrove. Born in Cheshire in
1964, Paul was the son of a travelling salesman and a cleaner. His parents' marriage was unhappy and, like Graham Knowles, Paul felt stifled by their desire to keep up appearances and preoccupation with

social status. At his comprehensive school he met 'kids who appeared "privileged", who lived in bigger homes in leafy roads'. Paul set his sights on achieving 'their lifestyle'.[19]

Paul Cosgrove saw education as his route to achieve this. In 1982 he began his A level course. No one in his family had gone to university, but like many other magpies, Paul didn't see this as an impediment. In fact, he had a huge motivation to leave home: university meant, he said, an escape 'from the toxic atmosphere of the tail end of my parents' marriage.' Paul initially wanted to study a subject he enjoyed – 'history or English'. But 'unemployment was high', and he and his parents thought he should choose a course 'that offered a real possibility of a job in the future'. In 1984 he began a degree course in computing at a polytechnic. He found student life a disappointment. He had hoped, he said, to 'stay up late into the night philosophising and putting the world to rights', as they did 'on 1960s college [television] dramas'. Instead he found himself spending nights completing his work: he found the course both 'hard' and boring, and only completed it 'out of duty'. But when Paul passed, he found that, most disappointingly of all, the hoped-for jobs didn't exist. While he had been studying, 'computing had become ubiquitous'. There was no need for large numbers of highly trained programmers as the home computer revolution began. Basing education on current technology was as short-sighted in the 1980s as it had been in the technical schools of the 1950s. Paul became a support worker in air traffic control, but he found the job unsatisfying and was aware that he 'didn't need a degree to get it.'[20] He remained in this line of work for the rest of his career.

*

While many of the magpie generation agreed with Graham Knowles that they were 'very proud to come from a working-class background', most were keen to be seen to have bettered themselves, too. Those whose parents espoused a socially conservative respectability that emphasised the importance of social status were particularly likely to feel this way. They imbibed the Thatcherite message of the 1980s that anyone successful could and should climb the ladder. Those who had not achieved what they wanted via education or work placed greatest importance on social status. But their lack of qualifications or satisfying work obliged them to acquire this status in some other way. Home ownership – lauded by the Conservative governments of the 1980s and 90s – provided one means of describing themselves as upwardly mobile. Graham himself believed that 'I am on a higher level than my parents because my first rented flat had an indoor bathroom and I later bought my own home.'[21] Paul Cosgrove thought that he and his siblings 'have definitely "gone up in the world"' because they all owned 'detached houses in the suburbs'.[22]

Where you lived was also increasingly significant. Being a discerning consumer had become a hallmark of middle-class status by the 1990s. The government encouraged people to believe that free-market choice offered far greater rewards than public ownership and control over the utilities, hospitals and schools. By the mid-1990s, when the magpie generation had begun to have children, exercising choice over a child's secondary school was of great importance to middle-class parents. They were heavily influenced by government claims that comprehensive education was generally poor (even when this was not borne out by local schools), and by the Education Act of 1988, which made it possible for parents to exercise greater choice over which school their child attended. Many parents who aspired to climb the ladder believed that being a 'good' citizen and a 'good' parent meant making choices that would accrue as much material and cultural benefit to their family as possible.[23] For Paul Cosgrove and his wife, 'trying to be in the "best" area you can afford in terms of environment and schools' was vital.[24] These were not necessarily new aspirations, but the value placed on them had changed. By the 1990s the state had pushed responsibility for making 'good' choices on to individuals. Their discernment would, apparently, determine their destiny.

For those with limited qualifications, accent, demeanour and appearance remained important strategies for survival and for getting on. Like many gay men, Neil Black had learned early to lead a very private life. 'I . . . had to find strategies of my own', he explained, and believed this had made him very enterprising.[25] Once he had left home, he adopted the persona of the cosmopolitan graduate he'd like to have been. A decade later, in the early 1990s, living in a big city, Neil felt able to be more open about his sexuality. But at the same time, his lack of a degree became a problem, as managerialism in the NHS increased. It was difficult, if not impossible, for someone who entered public-sector work straight from school to reach the top of this new hierarchy. Increasingly, managers were recruited from outside, and were usually graduates.[26] Neil had been a social-care manager for several years when he was suddenly notified that he needed a degree in order to qualify for a pay rise. '[P]ersonnel asked me to bring in a copy of mine for the record. I never ever said I had one and just ignored the request'. The persona Neil had cultivated to distance himself from the closeted, working-class boy he had once been now worked in his favour. His employers 'thought I was a posh, well-educated poof' and, assuming he was a graduate, simply 'paid me the allowance.'[27] But Neil Black knew he was lucky: magpies who lacked a degree, let alone A levels, increasingly found it hard to get on. The post-war expansion of room at the top had come to an end.

This group had not achieved all or even most of what they wanted. Many were disappointed and frustrated by this. But unlike earlier generations, including the golden generation, they found it difficult to acknowledge this. They had been brought up to believe that hard work would pay off. They then found themselves in an adult world where this was far less true than it had been just a decade or two earlier, yet which was governed by politicians who claimed the poor only had themselves to blame. Many of these magpies stressed their imagination and resilience; their ability to roll with the bad times and make the best of what came their way. This also set them apart from parents who had been stuck in poverty, an unhappy marriage or a dead-end job. 'I cannot help but feel with everything on offer there must be a way to improve one's situation', was Paul Cosgrove's philosophy. He saw a silver lining in every cloud: even poor A level results, which pre-vented him going to the older university he'd hoped for, 'opened up' a 'world of polytechnics and colleges'.[28] Neil Black defined success as 'working hard and, if things don't work out, changing direction or tak-ing on new opportunities', even while he 'regretted' his lack of a uni-versity education, believing he 'would have been a very different person' if he had been able to study art. Like the magpies who were more content with how things turned out, this group stressed their ability to be imaginative and enterprising in the routes they took. 'Britain is very unfair', thought Neil, but 'it lets you alone most of the time to do what you want . . . you can descend into chaos or build your-self up as much as you like.'[29]

What helped these magpies to cope with their disappointments was their sense of entitlement to a decent standard of living. 'My own career hasn't exactly had a glittering trajectory', Paul Cosgrove observed. But although Paul believed it was important to work hard, he did not see unequal opportunities as the result of idleness or dependence on the state, as the ideology of the 1980s suggested he should. He thought it was 'a shame that there are limits on your mobil-ity according to what you can afford – the realising that there are just some areas you haven't the money to live in'.[30] Most did not believe that ambition could overcome the advantages of wealth or the prob-lems of discrimination. They were also keen to stress that success 'does not necessarily mean material wealth', as Paul Cosgrove put it.[31] Many were hostile to what Graham Knowles described as 'the middle-class attitude of must have the latest gadget or keep up with the Joneses'.[32] They suggested that status-consciousness had become more prevalent over their lifetimes as Britain became a more unequal place. And their dislike of this often betrayed a longing for more edu-cation, and creative or socially useful work, as well as prosperity. For some, these were all connected. Neil Black thought that achieving upward mobility would mean 'being able to afford nicer things . . . and live in a nicer place', but also getting more education and 'becoming more intelligent'.[33] This group were well aware that educational opportunity was still, in late twentieth century Britain, highly dependent on a person's background.

*

These magpies' belief that profound inequalities of power and wealth were barriers to their own success did not inspire many of them to try and change society in the way that members of the pioneer or golden generations had done. But for those who were downwardly mobile, or failed to realise their aspirations, it was an important psychic prop as their once promising prospects vanished in adulthood. Their conviction that the world offered them a little more than they'd received set them apart from many of those born after them.

PART VI

THATCHER'S CHILDREN
1972–1985
THE MILLENNIALS
1986–1999

Chapter Fifteen

THE PURSUIT OF EXCELLENCE
AND INEQUALITY

The children born between the early 1970s and the late 1990s were less likely to be upwardly mobile and more likely to be downwardly mobile than their parents or grandparents. Those born between 1972 and 1985 – Thatcher's children – were the first in four generations to be more likely to slide down the ladder than to ascend it. About 30 per cent of men and 35 per cent of women were upwardly mobile, but 35 per cent of men and 38 per cent of women were downwardly mobile. Those born after 1985 – the millennials – had an even greater chance of sliding down the ladder. Forty per cent of both men and women in this generation were downwardly mobile. While the same proportion apparently ascended the ladder, most of those who entered managerial and professional employment did not enjoy the security or autonomy that earlier generations had experienced. Their chances to enter skilled manual work, or secure and progressive clerical jobs, were also far lower than those of earlier generations.[1]

Many of those born since 1972 believed that they were to blame for sliding down the ladder. They grew up being told they could and should scale its heights. Every government since 1979 eschewed the earlier, post-war commitment to making Britain a more equal society. Instead, they emphasised the responsibility of individuals to work hard and compete in order to be successful in an increasingly unequal world. John Major, who replaced Margaret Thatcher as Conservative prime minister in 1990, made much of his own background as an upwardly mobile grammar-school boy. In 1997 Tony Blair's New Labour government came to power. The talk was of expanding opportunity rather than equality. In 2004 Labour adopted social mobility as an explicit policy objective. 'I want to see social mobility, as it did in the decades after the war, rising once again, a dominant feature of British life', Prime Minister Blair announced.[2] This commitment united all the governments that succeeded his: Gordon Brown's Labour administration of 2007–10, David Cameron's coalition government of Conservatives and Liberal Democrats between 2010 and 2015, and the Conservative governments of Theresa May and Boris Johnson that followed.

But these politicians presided over growing inequality and a decline in chances to climb the ladder. The two were connected: as the highest rungs on the ladder grew further apart from the rest, they became harder to reach. Between the 1990s and the 2010s the richest 5 per cent of people in Britain grew wealthier, while everyone else fell further behind.[3] Successive governments, together with those at the top of big business and the media, used the rhetoric of social mobility to justify this unequal status quo.

In 2001, Tony Blair declared that '[o]ur top priority was, is and always will be education, education, education . . . developing the talents and raising the ambitions of all our young people.'[4] Those aged under thirty in 2001 certainly grew up believing that school and – increasingly – university were their only route up the ladder. This chapter follows them through childhood and youth to examine why this goal was so important to them, and yet proved so hard to achieve.

*

Many of those born after 1971 wanted to do something very different from their parents. Those who grew up in areas of high unemployment were particularly keen to escape. Claire Torrington was born in the north-east of England in 1974. Her father had worked in the shipyards but after being made redundant in the early 1990s he became a salesman. Claire knew that a white-collar job did not necessarily mean a step up. Her father struggled on a zero-hours contract, which were increasingly used by employers keen not to commit to offering workers a set number of hours each week. This made daily life, and budgeting, hard to plan in the Torrington family. Claire's mother worked as a shop assistant. The family found it hard to make ends meet at times – there was no money for extras like school trips. Like many of Thatcher's children, Claire did not consciously aspire to change her social class in her youth. The language of social mobility had not yet entered the media and politics. But by her late teens Claire wanted 'to travel, to experience new things'.[5] Kenny Smith, born in 1978, had similar ambitions. He also grew up in the north-east. His parents, who were manual workers, experienced unemployment and long-term ill health. Other relatives and family friends who had tried to take the entrepreneurial route advocated by Margaret Thatcher 'lost their own businesses' in the recession that followed the stock market crash of 1987. Kenny hoped to become an actor or, failing that, a social worker.[6]

Such ambitions weren't new to these younger generations. But in the 1980s and 90s the children of many manual and service-sector workers felt an added pressure to realise their dreams. Their parents' trajectories were impossible to replicate as skilled manual work and secure clerical work declined. Many saw only a future of dead-end factory, shop or office jobs ahead of them if they did not climb the ladder. And they grew up under governments that claimed that high unemployment was, at least in part, the fault of assertive trade unions and a lack of initiative among those at the bottom of the ladder. Some of these younger people still claimed a pride in being working class. But this now meant – in Claire Torrington's words – 'not [being] wasteful with money' and 'working hard'.[7] They knew little of the older tradition of mutual help and solidarity for collective improvement. And they were keen to distance themselves from the scrounging benefit cheats who had populated political speeches and the tabloid press throughout their young lives. Claire Torrington attended a large, socially mixed comprehensive school. While she could not join those groups of more affluent children 'who went on fancy holidays', she also felt it was important to distance herself from her working-class peers. 'I knew I didn't want to be pregnant by sixteen and on benefits', she said.[8] Claire recognised this wasn't a dream most of her classmates harboured either, but the bleak future that confronted them, and her, apparently offered few other options. By the time Claire had passed all her GCSEs in 1991, she had decided that she would like to be a schoolteacher.

Many young people believed that having 'a career' would set them apart from the insecurity their parents had experienced. Social scientists who interviewed members of both these generations found that this desire for a 'career' was widespread. It was connected to young people's sense that manual and service-sector work could only offer them a patchwork of stop-gap jobs. Unlike many of the magpies, who were keen to try out different jobs and lifestyles, these younger generations craved the stability, security and also the status that a job in management or the professions could offer.[9] In the early 2000s sociologists asked teenagers in Tower Hamlets, one of London's poorest boroughs, about their aspirations. Most of them wanted what Neelam, a young British Bangladeshi woman, called 'high, fast jobs': professional or managerial posts. This was the only way that they could acquire the 'prestige' and wealth they wanted.[10]

These ambitions were not confined to the poorest children, nor to those in the areas worst hit by deindustrialisation. Both generations grew up in an unequal world that rewarded only the few at the top. Tessa Parr was born in 1972 in London. Her parents were from working-class families in the East End, but both got clerical jobs, enabling them to buy their first home in Kent in the early 1980s. But when the recession hit ten years later, Tessa's father lost his job and had to claim unemployment benefit – a 'humiliating' experience. Tessa's parents managed to keep their home but only by long hours and years of hard work, her mother as a waitress and then as a nurse, and her father as a salesman. In their early seventies they were still working hard: the millstone of their mortgage dashed their hopes of retirement. As a teenager, Tessa considered herself 'lucky to grow up so close to London where unemployment was less of a problem than in other parts of the country'. However, she did not want to work as a bank clerk – the job most readily available to young women who left school at sixteen – or to scrimp and save as her parents had done in order to afford a house. That meant she needed 'a career'. And this meant getting to university. In 1990, Tessa became the first in her family to get A levels and go into higher education. She chose to study speech therapy, both because of 'personal interest' and because it would lead to a job.[11] By the time she graduated, 30 per cent of eighteen-year-olds were going to university, and their numbers continued to rise through the 1990s.

Tony Blair wasn't the first politician to declare that education would provide golden tickets to a better future. When they returned to government in 1979, the Conservatives presented Labour's commitment to comprehensive schools as letting down talented children and pledged to 'concentrate on social mobility for children in "downtown" schools'. Labour's emphasis on high-quality schools for all, enshrined in educational reforms of the 1960s and 70s, was ditched in favour of a stress on meritocracy that harked back to the 1950s. In 1982 the government introduced an 'assisted places' scheme to provide "'pupils from low-income families who are selected on merit alone"' the chance to attend a private school.[12] In 1988, the Education Reform Act forced schools to compete with one another for pupils – the most popular received more money. In 1992, John Major's Conservative government introduced school league tables, encouraging parents to judge institutions by their academic results. While Labour abolished the assisted places scheme when it returned to power in 1997, the government retained and encouraged parental choice over schools, continued to produce school league tables, and allowed private sponsors to take over 'failing' schools from local authorities.

Far from stimulating upward mobility, the educational reforms of the late 1980s and 90s increased social segregation in schools. In the 1980s, take-up of private education rose for the first time since the 1950s (although the numbers were still small: just 8 per cent of children attended a private school).[13] The assisted places scheme disproportionately benefited the children of relatively poorly paid professionals – vicars and teachers were particularly prominent. Fewer than 10 per cent of recipients were the children of manual workers.[14] Within the state sector, the 1988 Education Reform Act deepened inequality. By the mid-1990s, middle-class children were more likely to be educated in well-resourced schools, helped by covert school selection policies designed to attract children who were likely to perform well in examinations, and by parents' ability to chauffeur their children to schools a long distance from home.[15]

Although successive governments presented these reforms as responding to public demand, many parents regretted the changes. A survey conducted in Scotland found that parents found choosing schools confusing and time-consuming. Most compared the situation unfavourably with the 1970s when local authorities had allocated children to a school.[16] Researchers found that children in areas and in families where school choice was a matter of anxiety and concern picked up on these worries. They were particularly likely to see schooling as immensely important to their life chances.[17]

Among them was Lucy Young. Born in 1978, Lucy was the daughter of an upwardly mobile couple – her father was the print-worker-turned-computer technician who was able to buy the family's council house in the 1980s. Her parents decided against the local comprehensive school, instead sending Lucy to a highly selective grammar school a long bus ride from home. Like earlier generations of grammar-school pupils, Lucy was aware that the family's hopes rested on her. Homework was sacrosanct: 'mum felt that it was my job to do well at school and hers to cook [and] clean', she later wrote. Her school encouraged this attitude. 'We were heavily pressurised into courses that played to our strength so the school did well in the league tables', Lucy recalled. 'It was decided languages were my thing.'[18]

Lucy's education provided her with an excellent head start. She went on to study modern languages at a very reputable university. But Lucy's experience of school did not match up with politicians' claim that parents and children were able to exercise greater 'choice' as a result of the new marketplace in schools. In common with some of the grammar-school girls of older generations, Lucy experienced education as a process of dutifully following her school's advice, rather than developing independent passions or interests. She exercised choice in her social life, becoming involved in sports which gave her some freedom from school. When she came to decide which university to attend, she chose not to apply to Oxford or Cambridge, which she considered 'too much pressure'. Her sporting interests could only be pursued at a small number of institutions, and Lucy used this to justify her choice to her school and her parents.[19] Unlike some of the golden generation, who openly rebelled against elite ideas of education, Lucy saw her decision as a very individual choice to opt out of pressure and competition (notably, her hobby was a non-competitive pursuit). In this she was typical of her generation, many of whom adopted the language of 'choice' encouraged by successive governments since 1979, and especially since the late 1980s. They did not consider changing society; instead they saw their agency as limited to negotiating their place within it.

But many children did not wish to change their place in society. Those who attended comprehensive schools experienced less pressure than Lucy Young did. And children with parents in secure work often shared the magpies' belief that it would be easy to acquire the education and work they wanted. Samantha Bridges was born in south-east England in 1979. Her mother was a nurse; her father was a police officer but died when Samantha was very young. When Samantha was seven her mother married an accountant. Samantha believed that 'it was marrying him that made us middle class'. Samantha was happy at her local, socially mixed schools and large sixth-form college. Although no one in her family had a degree, by sixteen she looked forward to university as 'just the next step'.[20] And children who grew up in affluent middle-class households were keen to follow in their parents' footsteps and believed it would be possible to do so, regardless of schooling. Oscar Greene was born in 1986. His mother was a graduate – the first in her family to go to university – while his father, a university professor, came from a long line of university-educated professionals. Oscar attended a comprehensive school in London. He grew up knowing that 'we were born with advantage' and would go 'into middle-class jobs' without much difficulty.[21]

Oscar's relaxed view of his future was similar to that taken by many of the magpies, including children of public-sector administrators and professionals. But respondents to a Mass Observation directive on social mobility in 2016 suggested that this was not so widely shared among younger people. Among those born since 1972 – and especially the millennials – only the children of the highest-earning professions and managers, often employed in the private sector, confidently assumed they would follow in their parents' footsteps. Most of them, like Samantha Bridges and Oscar Green, had grown up in southeast England, reflecting the region's increasing concentration of high-earning professionals and businesspeople.

Children who grew up in areas and families affected by unemployment and poverty were more critical of their education. They had no family support to fall back on, and schooling was their means of escape. Some believed that their schools were not 'aspirational' enough, especially those who attended schools with an almost exclusively working-class intake. Researchers found that comprehensive schools often underestimated the potential of working-class pupils, particularly those that served predominantly working-class neighbourhoods.[22] Kenny Smith attended his local comprehensive in Sunderland in the 1980s, but he regretted the abolition of grammar schools, which he believed had offered 'a rare opportunity for children from underprivileged backgrounds'.[23] Black British children, and the sons and daughters of migrants, were particularly likely to end up in poorly resourced schools. Many endured racial discrimination from teachers and fellow pupils.[24] Those who did well often succeeded by making efforts to avoid racist teachers or those with low expectations of working-class children, and by studying alone.[25] Helen Abeda was among them. In 1989, aged eight, she came to Britain as a refugee with her mother and brother. While she enjoyed primary school, secondary school in South London 'was pretty bad . . . there were a lot of dangers . . . Gang violence, high pregnancy rates'. Helen was bullied for her hard work and enthusiasm. Classmates called her '"Bounty", black on the outside and white on the inside'. She described being 'picked on if you were able to answer questions'.[26] The researcher Heidi Safia Mirza found that many black women from working-class backgrounds had to be extremely self-reliant to progress in education, regardless of the type of school they attended.[27]

But despite these problems, many of Helen's generation did receive invaluable support from their schools and from the wider welfare state. Supportive teachers and mentors could help young people to negotiate racist environments.[28] For Helen Abeda, the staff at her local public library were also crucial. As an eight-year-old, she recalled, 'I would go to the library every single day after school . . . that was a way of, firstly survival, but also getting to know my new home.' When Helen went to secondary school she did her homework in the library. Enthusiastic teachers, and the librarians, encouraged her interest in the humanities, and helped her to achieve excellent GCSE and A level results. Poorly maintained schools, the low expectations of some teachers, and cramped council housing were obstacles that only the most self-motivated and hard-working student could overcome. But for young people like Helen, public services like libraries and schools could expand horizons and opportunities.

Helen Abeda was born in 1980. The millennials, born after 1985, had more access to the kind of support she benefited from. From 1997 until 2010, Labour's welfare programme reduced child poverty. The government's 'Every Child Matters' and Sure Start programmes, the abolition of the assisted-places scheme, increased investment in comprehensive schools and the introduction of a means-tested Educational Maintenance Allowance for sixteen-to-eighteen-year-olds, help to explain why child poverty fell between 1997 and 2010.[29]

But New Labour's philosophy was similar to that of the preceding Conservative administration in attempting to create meritocracy, rather than to overcome inequality. Like the Conservatives, New Labour believed that the free market – rather than a strong welfare state – was the best means of achieving this. Expanding employment was never mentioned and nor was narrowing wealth inequality – the emphasis was on helping working-class children acquire 'social' and 'cultural capital' through education and training.[30] New Labour claimed that low taxes on the wealthiest encouraged ambition and hard work. And Blair's governments continued to treat comprehensive education as a problem, particularly for brighter children. Decrying 'bog-standard comprehensives', New Labour encouraged schools to develop different specialisms and special programmes for gifted and talented children.[31]

But in fact, those born between the early 1970s and the late 1990s were *less* likely to complain that schools failed them than were older people who had attended pre-war elementary schools or post-war secondary moderns. While some were critical of teachers' low aspirations or discrimination, these younger generations were just as likely to complain that comprehensive education gave them unrealistically *high* expectations. 'They said I could be a theatre manager', recalled Kenny Smith. 'Yes, there's loads of call for those, especially in a recession!'[32] At the age of seventeen, Kenny had to leave school to care for his terminally ill father and disabled mother. Claire Torrington, meanwhile, 'felt like an outsider' at her comprehensive school, neither fitting in with children from middle-class homes nor her peers who expected to leave at sixteen. When Claire formed the idea that she might become a teacher – an aspiration encouraged by some of those who taught her – she encountered hostility at home. 'My parents accused me of wanting to be something I wasn't' and having 'ideas above my station', she recalled. By the time Claire was studying for A levels in the early 1990s, her father was unemployed and student grants were being replaced with loans. It was a 'very stressful' time, and in 1993, aged eighteen, Claire eventually acquiesced to her parents' decision that she could not go to university because of the expense. She left school after passing three A levels 'with relief' that the conflicts between family and education were over. But not going to university quickly became her 'biggest regret', and remained so into middle age.[33]

The focus on education as a means of self-advancement became more acute for Claire's generation because they had fewer alternatives. In the past, the arts and sport had provided chances for young people to develop and pursue interests, if not a career. Access was never as wide as it could have been, and only a tiny minority of working-class people had ever forged careers in these fields. But the success of some sportspeople, notably footballers, and of those working-class men who got into the media and the arts in the late 1950s and 60s, showed that, given the chance, many people were capable of excelling in these fields. And in the 1980s and 90s, recession and deindustrialisation encouraged people to look at other ways of realising their dreams. Generations of young men had dreamed of becoming professional footballers, and now this ambition was more attractive than ever. The creation of the Premier League in 1993, lucrative television contracts, and the floating of several football clubs on the stock market turned some top-flight footballers into millionaires and international celebrities. By 2010, half of all sixteen-year-olds said their career plan was to become a celebrity (though many were critical of the fact that celebrity status relied on appearance and charisma rather than hard work).[34] And while Conservative politicians claimed this as proof of laziness and an unjustified sense of entitlement,[35] these young people's ambitions were in fact more realistic than aspiring to become a City trader or a barrister. Professional footballers, pop stars and television stars were less likely to have been privately educated or to have attended Oxbridge than high-earning lawyers or bankers.[36] The desire for celebrity was underpinned by a very realistic sense of their limited prospects, and the role of luck in getting to the top.

But realising the dream of becoming a professional actor or sportsperson was becoming harder, especially for those from working-class backgrounds. From the 1980s, government funding for the arts and sport was cut and became concentrated on rewarding excellence. New Labour increased funding, but prioritised helping the most talented.

Nowhere was this more evident than in football. In 1997, New Labour relaxed Football Association (FA) rules on scouting young players, allowing the 'best' clubs to recruit and train the most talented. Previously, FA funding had gone to a wider mix of football clubs, including non-league clubs which provided community sports activities. Now FA funding was channelled into Premier League 'academies', which recruited children as young as five.

But experienced coaches questioned the emphasis on 'excellence'. Critics of football academies pointed out that their focus on strength and stamina left little space for the artistry that might 'thrill and inspire the fans', overlooking late developers and risk-takers.[37] The fear of rejection among those desperate to 'make it' stifled creativity. That fear grew as funding was concentrated on fewer clubs. Non-league football struggled, closing down career and recreational opportunities for those who failed to get into a Premier League team – the fate of more than 99 per cent of academy players.[38]

Among those affected was Ryan Craig. Born in 1995, Ryan was recruited to Coventry City's football academy aged just eight. He grew up in the shadow of the huge Longbridge car plant in south Birmingham, which closed two years after Ryan enrolled at Coventry City. Ryan's father, Adrian, believed this was his son's chance to make a different kind of future: 'It was a big commitment' – Ryan was required to train three nights per week and every weekend, which meant Adrian taking time off work to drive him around – 'but we decided we were prepared to make the effort to give Ryan the best possible chance.' But Ryan himself found the experience increasingly upsetting. 'It stopped being fun', he recalled. 'Sometimes they'd encourage you, but most of the time they just put you down.' He had no time for homework or family life: 'There didn't seem to be much free time'. By the time Ryan was eleven the training and travelling to matches were becoming too expensive and impractical for Adrian to manage, but the decision was taken out of the family's hands in a brutal fashion: Coventry let Ryan go with no notice. 'They're great when they want you', Adrian acknowledged, 'but as soon as they get rid of you, that's it. Goodbye'. Ryan was 'really sad' that his dream had ended without even the chance to say goodbye to his friends at the club.[39]

It became *harder* for working-class children, however talented, to get a chance. The Premier League clubs, which were determined to maximise profits, demanded parents pay for kit, travel and as many other costs as they could jettison. The notion that a club should contribute to the community life of its town or city had disappeared in the pursuit of talent and wealth. 'You used to recruit most players from inner cities', acknowledged Bryan Jones, director of Aston Villa's youth training academy between 1997 and 2014. 'Today, ours is a very middle-class academy.'[40]

The uncertain future affected boys and girls differently. In the late 1990s, a sociologist interrogated political claims that boys' low educational performance was due to 'white working-class culture' being insufficiently 'aspirational'. She was Diane Reay, the miner's daughter who had become a primary-school teacher after graduating in the 1960s. By the 1990s she had become a sociologist, helped by the expansion of polytechnics and the creation of women's studies and social-science courses there. Reay's research showed that, regardless of their social class, boys were socialised to believe that 'feminine' tasks and behaviours were worthless. This wasn't new, but the disappearance of older ways of being a working-class man – such as doing skilled manual work –made the future highly uncertain for boys.[41]

This had been true of the magpie generation, but these younger boys faced an additional pressure. The magpies had grown up in the wake of second-wave feminism, which had challenged rigid gendered roles for boys and girls, and in a welfare state which suggested, albeit implicitly, that caring for others was important. These younger generations grew up in a world where tasks considered feminine – caring for others and co-operating – were given no political or economic value, while the rapacious acquisition of wealth and power was lauded as achievement. Diane Reay found that many boys became disruptive or aggressive to suggest that they had what it took to succeed.[42]

Richard Campbell was among them. He was born in a small town in south-east England in 1995 to mixed-race parents. His white father was a carpenter, and his black mother worked as a shop assistant. Richard enjoyed secondary school, did well there and 'had a really good relationship with a couple of teachers'. But shortly before his GCSEs, Richard stopped studying. Despite his teachers' encouragement to aim for A levels, he could not see the point in a town where the only jobs available were poorly paid clerical or manual work. He 'went off the rails', became disruptive in class, and was eventually asked to leave.[43] At sixteen he entered the labour market with just a few poor GCSEs, moving from one poorly paid job to another.

Not all boys reacted like Richard, of course. Increasing numbers of young people aspired to go to university. An increasing range of white-collar and professional jobs like journalism, nursing and banking demanded a degree. And as universities expanded in the 1980s, more young people were aware of higher education as an option. In 2009 a study of pupils in their first year at secondary school found that an even higher proportion of those on free school meals (79 per cent) wanted to go to university than their peers (75 per cent).[44]

This helps explain why the proportion of young people going to university increased so dramatically as these two generations came of age. One-third of Thatcher's children and the millennials got a degree or were working towards one. For the children of manual and clerical workers a degree was particularly valuable – graduates from such backgrounds were far less likely to experience downward mobility than those who didn't go to university.[45]

Most of these children were unable to realise their aspirations. Children from wealthier homes remained far more likely to go to university than the rest. The huge increase in university students occurred largely in the wealthiest fifth of households. Twenty per cent of those born in the 1970s into these households went to university. But almost 50 per cent of those born into the richest fifth of households in the 1990s did so. By contrast, the proportion of manual and low-paid service-sector workers' children who attended university rose from 6 per cent among those born in the 1970s to 9 per cent among those born in the 1990s.[46]

Many parents and young people were deterred by the increasing cost of higher education. From 1988, the Conservative government progressively reduced student grants, replacing them with loans. In 1997, one of the New Labour government's first actions was to make university students pay a proportion of their tuition fees, arguing – contrary to the Robbins Report of 1963 – that higher education was essentially of benefit to the individual, not society. Parents, children and students were treated as consumers whose choices would determine whether or not they or their offspring climbed the social ladder or languished at the bottom. But for many families, university now meant the worrying prospect of lifelong debt.

Nevertheless, many young people decided that the gamble was worth it. And this was particularly true of girls. Their response to recession and growing inequality was different to boys'. In the 1990s their examination results improved, and an increasing proportion of them went to university. In 1979, 11 per cent of eighteen-year-old white men and 8 per cent of eighteen-year-old white women had gone to university. The same was true of 2 per cent of Bangladeshi or British Bangladeshi men, and 1 per cent of Bangladeshi or British Bangladeshi women (the ethnic group with the lowest proportion of university entrants). In 2001, 38 per cent of eighteen-year-old white men and women went to university, and 39 per cent of Bangladeshi or British Bangladeshi men and women. These increases were reflected in every other ethnic group, and were particularly striking among women.[47] A team of sociologists who followed young women born in the 1980s and 90s found that girls in both working-class and middle-class families worked hard and had very high expectations of themselves. In the uncertain world of the 1990s and 2000s, they recognised and responded to the need to achieve high grades to have a chance of a secure and satisfying job.[48]

But these researchers counselled against seeing this as a simple success story. They pointed out that women who climbed the ladder faced older pressures – to support their families, for example – and new pressures to enter careers that would pay off their student debts and achieve the security their families lacked.[49] Studies of young women who went to university have shown that, white or black, they had to be exceptionally determined, especially if they had to overcome parents' fears of debt, or the belief (particularly prevalent in Pakistani and Bangladeshi households where parents came from labouring families) that university was not appropriate for women.[50] Like many first- and second-generation migrants, Helen Abeda faced family pressure to pursue vocational studies. 'Although there was this appreciation of education, there were certain career paths that you had to choose', she recalled: 'medicine, law, accountancy, engineering.' This belief that education was for vocational purposes was encouraged by every government between 1979 and 2019, with funding for adult- and further-education courses increasingly contingent on them having a vocational bent, and higher education presented as a pathway to individual career success. But Helen, encouraged by a sixth-form teacher and the staff at her local library, wanted to pursue her growing interest in history, with no idea where this might lead. With their help she was accepted to a university several hundred miles from home. Helen found the experience 'very liberating'; she was able 'to set up a whole new life'. But she also suffered 'guilt' at being so far away from her family and unable to help them with money or care.[51] Helen's guilt was exacerbated by a secret she kept from her relatives until her graduation day in 2002: her degree was not in science, as they had thought, but in the humanities.

But simply getting to university was no longer enough in the competitive world of late-twentieth-century Britain. Central government funding of universities was reduced from the late 1980s, with successive administrations arguing that higher education should become a marketplace. In the early 1990s, the former polytechnics were encouraged to become universities, removing their local authority funding (which was slashed as an extra incentive to transition). John Major's government argued this would create a level playing field between all higher education institutions, and raise standards across the sector. Now they all had to compete for funds based on how many students they attracted and how much research they did. It sounded fair, but in reality the older universities, which had the greatest assets (Oxford and Cambridge were and are some of the largest landowners in Britain), had a huge advantage.

Increased competition for scarce funding encouraged the wealthiest institutions to pitch for a larger slice of the pie. In 1994 eighteen universities including Oxbridge and London constituted themselves as the Russell Group, a self-declared 'elite'.[52] Many of the former polytechnics had done pioneering work, broadening the curriculum and increasing the number of mature and part-time students during the 1970s and 80s; they had been the engines for upward mobility, not the older, highly selective institutions. But neither government nor the Russell Group had any interest in sharing resources equally. In an era when public funding to universities was declining, and institutions were encouraged to compete for students, 'anything that differentiates ourselves . . . is to our advantage', one senior Russell Group manager told the *Sunday Times*.[53] As a result, courses tailored to mature and part-time students began to decline.

For these younger generations, the value of a degree depended far more on the university which awarded it than had been true in the past. Oxbridge had always had a cachet, but now other divisions appeared. As the number of graduates increased, many employers accepted the claim that Russell Group universities were better than the rest; this was a cheap and easy means of filtering floods of applicants. Because professionals and managers were highly likely to have attended these institutions themselves, they accepted the new political common sense that these were the 'best' universities. By the time Thatcher's children were at university, those who attended Russell Group institutions were far more likely to become high-earning professionals and managers than other graduates.[54]

This was no meritocracy. Among these generations, less than 3 per cent of children from Britain's poorest families attended a Russell Group university, compared with almost 16 per cent of children from the wealthiest families.[55] The increase in working-class students' attendance at university was almost entirely concentrated in the former polytechnics; the increase in black students occurred almost exclusively in business and other vocational courses outside the Russell Group.[56]

Those who did get to elite universities did not always find the experience happy or successful. Even Samantha Bridges, from a relatively affluent home, found it hard to fit in at her Russell Group university after a happy time at her comprehensive school and sixth-form college. 'Studying was fine . . . but I did feel an outsider among the very wealthy students. I got a job at a shop in the town and made friends there.'[57] Working-class students had been a tiny minority among the golden generation, yet some of them had been able to make friends and enjoy university life. Samantha Bridges was from a more affluent home than many of them. But the prevailing political ethos made a difference. Inequality was no longer treated as a problem to be overcome. Being on a lower rung of the ladder was now widely represented as the fault of those who found themselves there, while being at the top was lauded as evidence of hard work and talent. And, in a profoundly unequal society with little room at the top – as Britain was by the 1990s – those on the uppermost rungs were keen to hang on to their privilege rather than to share it with others who might dislodge them from their perch. As a result, the strategies that Ferdynand Zweig had observed among some wealthy Oxford students in the early 1960s – creating cliques based on shared backgrounds within which they forged networks important to their future careers while denigrating the backgrounds of other students and avoiding social contact with them – were more widely and openly practised among these younger generations.[58]

Those researchers who tracked a number of girls as they grew up during the 1980s and 90s found that the pressure to succeed academically and professionally could exacerbate more long-standing demands for female perfection. The demonisation of single mothers in the 1990s and 2000s exacerbated the pressure on working-class girls to become beautiful, sociable and thin.[59] Conservative and New Labour governments cut benefits to single parents and made it harder for them to get council accommodation. In the early 2000s New Labour highlighted that those at the bottom of the ladder were more prone to ill health but suggested it was their 'responsibility' to improve their 'unhealthy living' – particularly obesity – which placed an 'increasing strain . . . on the NHS'.[60] Following this lead, the media caricatured overweight single mothers in tabloid exposés and television comedies. Girls of all social classes were highly receptive to messages from politicians and teachers that their personality and appearance would determine their future, in a world where collective strategies to improve everyone's lot – whether trade unionism or feminism – had been severely undermined.[61] Some reacted by developing severe anxiety, depression or an eating disorder.[62]

Among them was Karen Foot. Born in 1978, Karen was the daughter of a teacher and a social worker, both the first in their families to go to university and enter the professions. But as the relative earnings and security of public-sector workers fell in the 1980s, Karen compared her family with those of more affluent school friends and found them wanting. In her teens, she drove herself remorselessly to achieve the academic and social perfection she believed would offer her the 'proper, upper-middle-class life' that a 'good job' would give her. Aged sixteen, Karen developed an eating disorder. At eighteen, she experienced her 'failure' to win a place at Oxbridge – 'there was only one option, pass or fail' – as a profound judgement on her inability to fit into the class she aspired to join. In her view, the admissions interview assessed 'what sort of person you were, and it was at this I failed.'[63] In the 1960s, in some quarters, being 'authentic' to your roots had been valued. In the neoliberal world of the 1990s, being able to reinvent yourself was a valued skill.

Karen would really have liked to study creative writing or art, 'but no prestigious institution offered this'.[64] She was socially ambitious, seeing a Russell Group education as essential to acquiring the life she wanted. Being 'your best self', as she put it, meant being middle class: educated, hard-working, responsible, materially successful and at ease in the world. She accepted a place on a highly competitive degree course at a very prestigious Russell Group university.

Once at university, Karen made great efforts to socialise with wealthier students. She quickly made friends with a group of privately educated students with money and contacts. In her studies – she read for a humanities degree – and her spare time she worked hard to acquire that 'cultural capital' she believed was a prerequisite for members of the upper middle class: she spent some of her student loan on learning to play the piano.[65]

But Karen gradually realised that her new friends had something important in common that she could not replicate: wealth. She learned that 'having clothes for different occasions was important', not only fancy clothes for evenings out but 'clothes just for lounging around in on Sundays, whereas the working-class students would just wear the same clothes all the time'. Karen was already in debt and couldn't keep up. Not having the right clothes or accent 'was agony'.[66]

Researchers discovered that other students of Karen's generation experienced similar pressures at socially elite universities. Some survived by focusing on achieving academic success; others found students from similar backgrounds or with shared interests. But a significant number found the social pressures very hard to bear.[67] The cost of ambition could be high. Karen Foot fell into depression and began self-harming. She eventually left the university and completed her degree at a less prestigious institution 'which made me feel even more of a failure'. When she graduated she got a clerical job that didn't require a degree. Compared with her parents, she was downwardly mobile. Not everyone shared Karen's ambitions or was so bitterly disappointed if they did not achieve them. But in a society where only the very top rungs of the ladder promised security and fulfilling work, and in which material success was lauded, most people were vulnerable to feeling like failures even when they had in fact achieved a great deal.

Those who did experience upward mobility continued to be highly likely to do so via the welfare state and the public sector. Paula Norman was born in 1978 in a Scottish city. The granddaughter of miners, she grew up in children's homes and foster care. Like most young people in care she left school in her mid-teens with few qualifications and took a series of low-paid jobs. By her early twenties she had a young son. But in the 2000s, grants for single parents allowed her to go back to education and to get a university degree. Unlike Karen Foot or Samantha Bridge's, Paula's choice of university was dictated by proximity rather than prestige: she 'did not want to make my children move home and school.' But she did not choose her course for vocational reasons but because she 'loved' the subject (history). Despite being older and having children, Paula fitted into the social and cultural life 'very well' and greatly enjoyed her studies. After graduating, she became a lecturer at a further education college. For Paula, education and her new career were not about reinventing herself but had allowed her to choose how far she wanted to change her life and helped her to be 'a useful member of society' as a lecturer. 'I live on a council estate which I love... lots of my colleagues live close by', is how she described her life after graduation. 'I fit in well in the area and at work'.[68]

*

After 1979 successive governments claimed that education would create a meritocracy by fostering healthy competition and developing talent. It was certainly true that the expansion of higher education broadened the horizons and created new ambitions among these younger generations. But it was the expansion of comprehensive education in the 1970s, the retention of universal services like library provision through these generations' youth and – from 1997 – government investment in early years care that made it possible for increasing numbers of them to go to university. These services were far from perfect and could not overcome discrimination or create more room at the top. Older routes to satisfying or at least financially secure work were closing, and the manual skills associated with them no longer had any political or much economic value. The high achievements of many girls and of some black students were often gained at great personal cost. They masked discrimination in schools and the increasingly threadbare safety net of the welfare state. Social class continued to be the most reliable indicator of the educational qualifications the members of both these generations would achieve.

Politicians' stress on rewarding 'excellence', whether by feting the Premier League, promoting the Russell Group or focusing school resources on the so-called gifted and talented, did nothing to address the diminishing options available to those who weren't interested in academic study, or who lacked the money or support to pursue other paths. This focus also ignored that the upwardly mobile were helped most by universal provision in the form of libraries, comprehensive schools and university access courses. Most significant of all, the championing of a narrow version of 'success' meant that many jobs and services on which society depended were no longer adequately rewarded. The results of this for the job prospects of Thatcher's children and the millennials are the subject of the final chapter.

Chapter Sixteen

THE LADDER BROKEN

The changing world of work suggested more of those born since 1972 should have climbed the ladder than fallen down it. More than 7 per cent of workers were unemployed in the early 1990s, when Thatcher's children were leaving school, but unemployment fell rapidly from 1997. It remained low over the next twenty years. By 2008, 15 per cent of workers were managers, 14 per cent were in technical or professional support roles, and 12 per cent were professionals.

The younger generations were the beneficiaries. By 2011 almost half of Thatcher's children were in professional or managerial jobs – a far higher proportion than among the magpies.[1] Work classified as 'routine' or 'semi-routine' – everyone from care assistants to clerks – employed just 19 per cent of men and 20 per cent of women. We don't have comparable figures for the millennials, but they had similar trajectories, for the fastest-growing occupations between the 1990s and the 2010s were managerial, professional and technical jobs.

But these workers' income, job security and status tell a different story. By 1991 almost 50 per cent of male 'sales managers' were employed on 'flexible' contracts, a trend that continued over the next two decades.[2] Between the 1990s and the 2010s, expansion in management and the professions occurred in support roles and technical jobs that lacked the wealth and security previously associated with senior posts. In the 2000s 'job-title inflation' increased, especially in the financial services – such as insurance and accountancy – along with sales work and retail, where the proportion of low-paid managers rapidly rose.[3] And as heavy industry declined, very few jobs offered the kind of autonomy that earlier generations had associated with skilled manual work or with the profession.

As Thatcher's children and the millennials embarked on adult life, many of them believed that only by being upwardly mobile could they be successful. Politicians encouraged this. Older strategies for collectively improving people's lives were weakened or destroyed. Blair retained Thatcher's anti-trade union laws. Most workers had little recourse to collective bargaining and so, just as in the 1930s, many of them experienced a worsening in their working conditions and income.

The policy focus on social mobility intensified after the global financial crash of 2007–08. Instead of reshaping the economy to allow a collective uplift, Gordon Brown's Labour government redoubled efforts to increase social mobility for the talented few. In 2009 Brown convened a panel to investigate how access to the most lucrative professions could be made fairer, chaired by former New Labour minister Alan Milburn. The message was clear: bankers and financiers could pocket huge bonuses, even destabilise the global economy, and make the world a more unequal place; politicians would do little to intervene. The only acceptable route to make society fairer was by allowing a few more working-class people to climb to the top – even if, once there, their actions made life worse for those at the bottom.

Alan Milburn quickly made clear that he had no intention of interfering with the workings of business. In his preface to the panel's report, *Unleashing Aspiration*, Milburn summed up the prevailing political ethos – while calling for the government to 'equalise opportunities', he suggested that the real solution lay with 'individual drive and ambition'.[4]

Following the 2010 general election, the new Conservative and Liberal Democrat coalition government adopted Labour's goal of increasing upward mobility. The deputy prime minister, Liberal

Democrat Nick Clegg, declared that 'social mobility is the central social policy objective for the coalition government'.[5] The coalition renamed Gordon Brown's panel the Social Mobility and Child Poverty Commission. This made clear that the government believed that social mobility was the primary solution to hardship. The coalition cut social security benefits and New Labour initiatives that had reduced child poverty like Sure Start. People would no longer be saved from poverty by the state – they must save themselves, by climbing the ladder.

Yet upward mobility was increasingly difficult to achieve. The most lucrative and powerful jobs remained in the hands of the wealthy few. In 1987 73 per cent of barristers had been privately educated, a figure that had dropped by only 2 per cent by 2016. The proportion of medical professionals who were privately educated had risen over the same period from 51 per cent to 61 per cent.[6]

*

Among both Thatcher's children and the millennials, the worst off were those with no or few qualifications. They were most likely to be manual-workers' children. The number of secure manual and routine clerical jobs fell and were harder to come by if you didn't have A levels. On the lowest rungs of the ladder, those occupations that grew fastest were low-paid service jobs, including sales, care assistants and educational assistants. Many of these workers relied on temporary contracts in insecure posts demanding long hours, and were in the bottom quartile of wage earners.[7]

Escaping from such work was harder than it had been for the golden generation or the magpies. Those who left school at sixteen or eighteen lacked the chances to return to education that members of earlier generations had seized. In 2006 Labour's education minister, Alan Johnson, declared that the government would not fund further education courses with 'little value to the economy . . . so more plumbing, less Pilates [and] flower-arranging'.[8] This wiped out many of those arts and humanities courses that had brought many women back into education in the 1970s. Meanwhile, New Labour's introduction of university tuition fees hit mature students hard; getting into debt was a great deterrent to those who had their own children's future to consider. While enrolment in higher education rose during the 2000s, the number of mature students fell.[9] Then, in 2012, the coalition government hiked university fees threefold and abolished the existing system of student bursaries, replacing these with costly loans.[10] The proportion of part-time students (the most popular route taken by those aged over twenty-five) immediately fell by 35 per cent.[11]

Becoming self-employed was an increasingly popular means of escaping insecurity. After leaving school in the early 1990s, Claire Torrington, who had wanted to travel and to 'challenge' herself, worked her way up a private firm from secretary to middle manager – albeit on a series of temporary contracts. But in the mid-2000s Claire was made redundant. The financial crash of 2007–08 made it impossible for her to get a similar post. She and her husband eventually decided to start their own business in information technology. They joined an expanding group: self-employed people composed 12 per cent of the workforce in 2001 and 15 per cent by 2017. Many relied on a patchwork of jobs in which they were treated as an employee without the pensions, sick pay or holiday entitlement that employers were obliged to provide for permanent staff. Others, like Claire, became 'consultants' to firms or other self-employed people, a form of work that offered no guarantee of security and relied on relentlessly selling oneself and one's expertise.[12] Starting one's own business had always been hard work, but in an era of government cuts to welfare support, the safety net for those who took this step was threadbare, the risks daunting, and the rewards meagre for most.

For those born between 1972 and 1985, having a degree made a significant difference to their job prospects. Not all of them became professionals or managers – a degree was now a prerequisite for many clerical jobs as well. After graduating from her Russell Group university, Samantha Bridges became a clerk in the public sector. By her early thirties she was a senior administrator in a secure job with good future promotion prospects. She was not yet on a par with her stepfather – an accountant – but she was not far off.[13] Meanwhile, Karen Foot, who had taken a low-paid clerical job after graduating, was able to work her way up to a senior post in local government by her early forties.[14] These graduates in white-collar work were able to become home-owners by the age of forty, and had enough money and leisure time to pursue further study and enjoy holidays and hobbies. But a generation earlier, a degree would not have been a prerequisite for that kind of lifestyle.

While university made a difference to their prospects, it could not overcome other barriers. Class mattered, even among those who did get into an elite university. Annabel Hawkins was born to a wealthy family in the 1970s. At her boarding school, 'the best socially connected girls' were the most popular – a valuable lesson for life: 'you meet the right people and the hamster wheel of life begins'. After university, Annabel embarked on a career as a stockbroker, 'achieved initially by social contacts'. Annabel gained promotions and job tips through acquaintances made at '"season" events [and] society weddings' to which she was invited by 'my friends from private school'.[15] Manual-workers' children who got a Russell Group degree were significantly *less* likely to enter the professions or management than graduates whose parents were themselves professionals or managers, regardless of which university this latter group attended.[16] Selective education did not improve the chances of 'bright' working-class children to shine. Instead, it introduced barriers they struggled to overcome while making little difference to the chances of children born nearer the top of the ladder.

Politicians' emphasis on individual striving offered no robust challenge to such inequalities, nor to the discrimination that women or black people faced. In both generations, girls outperformed boys at school. Among the millennials, women did better than men at degree level. By the 2000s, British Indian and Chinese people, and black British women were outperforming white British university students.[17] But in the workplace, these educational differences counted for little. White British men remained more likely to enter managerial and professional posts than any other group.[18]

Where you lived also mattered. By the 2010s, the north–south divide had been replaced with a division between London – the centre of economic and political power – and the regions. This gap rapidly widened after the financial crash of 2007–08.[19] The coalition government's social mobility commissioner, Alan Milburn, praised London as the 'engine room' of social mobility and urged other cities to follow its example.[20] The assumption that London was a model that the provinces could copy was endorsed by the coalition government's intention to create a 'northern powerhouse' between Manchester and Sheffield.

This strategy was at best naive. It was true that large cities did offer greater opportunities to gain a university education, work in a range of jobs and accumulate wealth than small towns or rural areas. But in the 2010s, no city came close to having the kind of wealth and resources concentrated in London. Since 1979 successive governments had encouraged employers to prioritise profit over regional development or public services, and to invest in the stock market rather than their workforce. Financial services, long concentrated in London, had been allowed to grow unchecked, assisted by low rates of business taxation. Meanwhile, industrial and regional investment had declined. London had benefited at the regions' expense. And because of London's size and status as the capital, it made no sense to suggest other cities could follow its example.[21]

Those who lived in poorer regions were aware that they had only limited options unless they moved away. Kenny Smith, from Sunderland, was among them. He had left his comprehensive school at the age of eighteen to care for his invalid parents. In the late 1990s he returned to further education. But the introduction of university tuition fees in 1997, and the lack of social-care provision available for his mother, made university an impossible dream. Kenny's caring responsibilities also meant that he was unable to get the job in television or radio he'd hoped for, 'which seemed to be based more in London and Manchester'.[22]

Kenny's hunch was correct: breaking into the media was becoming harder, especially outside the capital. In this sector as in so many others, successive governments had encouraged free-market policies that benefited the very rich but closed routes for ambitious young people. In the 1980s Margaret Thatcher's governments had supported the growth of Rupert Murdoch's News International empire. In the 1990s John Major's government had cut funding to the BBC and regional ITV franchises, ostensibly to encourage greater competition and quality. These policies were upheld by New Labour and subsequent governments. But the result was the collapse of regional newspapers and television. Between 2005 and 2016 198 local newspapers closed as the country's big four media groups – Trinity Mirror, Newsquest, Local World and Johnston Press – cut costs in the face of declining advertising revenue.[23] Many blamed the rise of the Internet, but researchers and editors argued that this could have been a golden opportunity to develop the British media in new directions, if only government investment had been forthcoming. 'There used to be a career route for young reporters on local papers to move to nationals, bringing regional knowledge and a respect for their area', points out Dr Martin Moore, director of the Centre for the Study of Media, Communication and Power and a senior research fellow at King's College London.[24] By the 2000s, that route all but vanished. Its disappearance had serious implications not only for aspiring journalists like Kenny Smith, but also for local democracy. By the 2010s many districts, particularly in rural areas, had no newspaper or radio station scrutinising the workings of local government and businesses, or the impact of national policies or international finance, on their community.

Working-class graduates were more likely to have grown up in poorer towns and regions than their middle-class counterparts. They were aware that being socially mobile meant being geographically mobile, but often could not afford to move away from home. Debbie Morgan was born in 1980 in the Midlands. Her father was a civilian driver in the army and her mother was a cleaner. Debbie was a hard worker at her comprehensive school. Like many of her generation, she saw climbing the ladder not simply as a means of getting a more secure or fulfilling job or acquiring more money, but also to help her become 'a better version' of herself. Her youthful ambition to go to university was, she said, motivated by her conviction that 'I was going to have a real life, defined and purposeful'.[25]

In the 1990s, Debbie Morgan achieved her ambition when she became the first in her family to go to university. But when her mother became terminally ill Debbie returned home to look after her, and decided it would be cheaper and more practicable to complete her degree with the Open University. She loved studying, and graduated with first-class honours, more 'confident' about pursuing new challenges.[26]

But the chance to pursue these challenges never came. Student debt, and the need to work, obliged Debbie to stay at home – first in a midlands village and then in a former mining town in Wales – and get the first job that became available. Ten years after graduation she was a library assistant, a job she enjoyed but which did not require a degree and was increasingly insecure as public-spending cuts deepened in the 2010s. Funding for libraries was cut by £400 million between 2010 and 2019. More than 300 closed down and many more reduced their opening hours.[27] By 2016 Debbie was anticipating redundancy: 'I'll probably end up working in a supermarket', she predicted.[28] One year later, 37 per cent of graduates were employed in non-graduate jobs, generally clerical and service-sector posts.[29]

Even within the wealthiest cities, class background shaped people's prospects. London was no engine of social mobility. The capital was both the richest city in Britain and the most unequal. By 2010 40 per cent of London's children lived in poor households – twice as many as the national average.[30] The children of affluent families with connections certainly benefited from the concentration of wealth and opportunity in the capital. Oscar Greene, the son of a university professor, grew up in London. After moving away in the 2000s to study at a Russell Group university, he embarked on a career in publishing, 'which I was able to do because I could live in the family home in

London'.[31] Studies found that unpaid internships and work experience, informally arranged through family friends, were important conduits into the financial, advertising and legal sectors centred in London.[32] But Londoners from working-class backgrounds were no more likely to get the 'top' jobs than inhabitants of other areas of the country. London had become the most socially polarised city in Britain, but researchers found that a similar inequality of both wealth and opportunity characterised the largest provincial cities, too, including Bristol and Manchester. Their wealthy inhabitants lived in expensive neighbourhoods and had very different kinds of jobs to most local people. And they did not choose to let their wealth trickle down the ladder. Instead they worked hard to secure their own and their children's prospects by investing in their homes, education – these cities housed elite private schools as well as universities – and their own savings.[33] This was a perfectly understandable strategy in such an uncertain, unequal world. But it did not produce any engines of social mobility.

*

The financial crash of 2007–08, and the political response to it, made upward mobility even harder to achieve, and downward mobility more likely. Conservative, Liberal Democrat and New Labour politicians agreed that inequality was an essential incentive to hard work – as if idlers at the bottom of the ladder had precipitated the recession. But there was a crucial difference between the Labour governments of Tony Blair and Gordon Brown, and the coalition government elected in 2010. Labour believed that social mobility could go hand in hand with social policies designed to narrow social and economic inequality. But the Conservatives and Liberal Democrats were in favour of significant disparities in wealth, and saw social mobility strategies as replacements for social policies that were designed to prevent or minimise poverty and inequality.[34] In 2013 the Conservative mayor of London, Boris Johnson – an Old Etonian who would become prime minister six years later – made the case for focusing on social mobility rather than narrowing the gap between the rich and the poor. '[S]ome measure of inequality is essential for the spirit of envy and keeping up with the Joneses that is, like greed, a valuable spur to economic activity', he said. Johnson believed that talent would be best helped by competition, not social welfare: 'the harder you shake the pack the easier it will be for some cornflakes to get to the top'.[35] This understanding of the state's role as shaking things up and hoping for the best was very different from the carefully planned construction of the welfare state that had formed Labour's response to crisis back in 1945.

The consequences of the financial crash were tremendous for both Thatcher's children and the millennials. At first the situation did not seem as serious as the global crisis precipitated by the 1929 crash or the 1980s recession. Mass unemployment did not return, but the security and relative pay of manual, service-sector and many clerical workers declined while poverty increased. The coalition government cut New Labour policies designed to reduce poverty, claiming 'austerity' demanded this. By 2016 22 per cent of UK population were living in poverty – 55 per cent of them in households with at least one wage-earning adult.[36] But the government also cut the income tax paid by Britain's wealthiest people. Income inequality, which had grown since the late 1990s, rapidly increased. In 1998 the highest earners were paid forty-seven times the earnings of the lowest paid. In 2015 they were paid 128 times more. By then, the wealthiest 10 per cent owned 45 per cent of Britain's household wealth.[37]

None of this assisted upward mobility. In fact, reforms touted as assisting upward mobility primarily helped the wealthiest. The government encouraged more private providers to take over state schools, replacing local-authority comprehensives with privately run academies and free schools. In 2011 the Conservative education minister Michael Gove justified this by arguing that it would raise ambitions and results. 'There need be no difference in performance – none whatsoever – between pupils from disadvantaged backgrounds and those from wealthier homes', he claimed. 'A difficult start in life can be overcome, with hard work and good teaching'.[38] There was no need to regulate employers' recruitment, retention or promotion strategies. It was up to parents, teachers and children to make the effort to climb the ladder, and the private sector would help them to do so.

This strategy did not increase upward mobility in the 2010s – but it did help private schools to survive the economic crisis. Labour's investment in state education, and the financial crash, had caused the number of children who were privately educated to fall after 2008.[39] The coalition's educational reforms were inspired by the same desire to protect the private sector that had inspired the direct grant schools of the 1940s and the assisted places scheme of the 1980s. In the 2010s, establishing or contributing to academy schools and free schools enabled the private sector to benefit from state funding while retaining autonomy over admissions and curriculum. And by suggesting that private schools had much to teach the state sector, the coalition government undermined confidence in the latter, while giving a much-needed boost to the former.[40]

These reforms further eroded the conditions and status of teaching – the profession that had long been the destination of upwardly mobile graduates, especially women. Teachers lost much of their remaining autonomy, and their working conditions were eroded, for the owners of academy chains and free schools were able to employ untrained teachers, renegotiate contracts and reduce pay. In 2012 a Mass Observation survey revealed that many people agreed with the teachers' unions that their status and conditions had plummeted since the millennium.[41]

The withdrawal of state support also affected more lucrative professions. Doctors and lawyers had historically enjoyed a large degree of autonomy from the state but had nevertheless relied on government funding and support. But after the crash, the expense of a university training in law, medicine or academic research became a riskier investment as conditions in these professions declined. Cuts in legal aid of 37 per cent between 2007 and 2013 made it harder for aspiring barristers and solicitors to earn a living. Trainee barristers had to 'put in a minimum of sixty-hour weeks'.[42] The coalition government cut junior doctors' pay and eroded their job security and working conditions.[43] University lecturers and civil servants were expected to work longer hours for less pay and smaller pensions. Redundancies in the Civil Service rose from 2013, while increasing numbers of university staff were employed on temporary contracts. Even in the most long-standing professions, job security could no longer be taken for granted.

Doctors, lawyers and university professors complained about a lack of autonomy to innovate and govern themselves, as the managerialism that had hit the lower-paid professions in the late 1980s and 1990s was rolled out in their domains.[44] In the public sector, only those at the very top – university vice chancellors and senior managers, the directors of school academy chains and the CEOs of NHS hospital trusts – did well.

The decline in the pay and conditions of professionals affected the ambitions of both Thatcher's children and the millennials. Thatcher's children had grown up at a time when teaching and other public-sector professions had enjoyed good security, salaries and status. Many of them felt obliged to revise their ambitions, first in their teens if they were thwarted by the cost of higher education, and then by the decline in public-sector conditions in the twenty-first century. After being sacked from her managerial post in the private sector in the 2000s, Claire Torrington had wondered about going into teaching – her ambition since schooldays. The cost of a degree, and the increased hours, targets and pressure endured by teachers made her reluctantly decide that 'it was too much for me'.[45]

Older generations knew that just getting into a firm or a profession was only the first step: they'd have to work their way up from there. But by the 2000s, those among Thatcher's children who had got into administrative or professional jobs were discovering that the opportunities to progress were declining. This was a particularly dramatic change in the public sector, which had historically provided greater security and more training and educational opportunities than most private firms. Neither employers nor the government invested much in workplace training any more – employers in both the private and public sectors increasingly used graduate recruitment schemes to hire managers, which was cheaper than training existing employees. In the early 2000s, the New Labour government encouraged this practice by making degrees and even postgraduate qualifications mandatory for NHS staff, without offering a budget to cover their education. This encouraged the recruitment of recent graduates or the promotion of those staff who could afford to pay their way.[46]

Tessa Parr was among those affected. Having decided that she needed a degree in order to avoid the fate of her parents, who were still working to pay off their mortgage in their seventies, she had studied speech therapy at university in the 1990s. She then began work in the NHS as a speech therapist, and by 2000 she and her husband, also a public-sector professional, were settled in a prosperous Midlands city and were buying their first home. But in the 2000s Tessa's job became increasingly stressful. New Labour's reforms almost led to her demotion, for she lacked the master's degree that suddenly became a requirement for her post. It was 'humiliating to be seen as less valuable for the sake of a qualification'.[47] Then, from 2010, Tessa and her colleagues found their workload increased. The health budget had risen by an average of 7 per cent each year under the Labour governments of 2000 to 2010, but it rose by only 0.5 per cent per year between 2010 and 2015. At the same time, the government reduced the social care budget by £4.5 billion, placing extra pressure on the NHS.[48] In 2016 Tessa described her constant fear 'of my job being downgraded, or of being redeployed to a lower-paid job in a field I'm less interested in'.[49] Like many public-sector workers, Tessa did not have the luxury to aspire to further training or seek new challenges or promotions; she was constantly worried about tumbling down the ladder. She was one of the increasing number of workers reporting depression or stress – the most frequent causes of absence from work by 2011.[50]

The demise of further and adult education also reduced satisfying job opportunities in the public sector. By 2015 Karen Foot was living with her partner in a small northern town where they could afford to buy a house and for Karen to work part-time while she studied creative writing. She enrolled on a very competitive master's degree, which offered the prize of a contract with a literary agent to the student whose work was judged the best. Karen did well but when she didn't win the prize, 'I felt as if I'd failed, my old mistakes coming back to haunt me', she said.[51] She remained unsure how to pursue her writing ambitions. Thirty years earlier, Karen and her peers would have had more opportunities to teach in adult or further education, or to work in community arts. By the 2010s, only those judged the very best could pursue creative or artistic ambitions. This gave more power to those senior, established figures who defined 'excellence' in competitive fields like the arts and the media. It left little scope for newcomers to innovate or take risks.

For millennial graduates, background mattered even more than had been true in earlier generations. Those with parents in the professions or management were far more likely to go into those occupations than anyone else. These jobs continued to offer higher income and greater security than other workers enjoyed. But there were fewer such jobs to go round. Even in expanding sectors, like higher education, newly established positions offered less security and autonomy. After a few years in publishing, Oscar Greene decided to follow in his father's footsteps and become a university lecturer. By his early thirties he had a PhD but could only find work 'on the outskirts of academia', taking up temporary, zero-hours contracts to teach, 'because universities are catching up with the rest of the world in terms of their labour practices'. Universities were expanding, but they did so by increasing their temporary and hourly paid staff. In 2017 Oscar was one of almost a million people who were employed on zero-hours contracts and over 1.5 million on short-term contracts, many in white-collar and professional jobs.[52] He was able to survive thanks to low housing costs in his adopted city in northern England, a part-time clerical job and, crucially, 'because I have family to fall back on'.[53]

*

For the magpies, home ownership had offered stability and security as their prospects at work became more uncertain. Those born from 1972 grew up aspiring to own their own home. New Labour championed home ownership and reduced council housing, as did all successive governments. The housing market was almost entirely unregulated, and prices soared from the late 1990s, especially in south-east England. Television programmes like *Location, Location, Location* reinforced the notion that moving up the ladder by buying a home in an affluent area was a realisable and desirable aim. By 2017 councils owned just 7 per cent of housing while 63 per cent was owner-occupied.[54] An increasing proportion – 30 per cent by 2017 – was privately rented.

Few younger people made any money out of housing, though the media and politicians suggested the most entrepreneurial could do so. The most successful private landlords tended to be older people, who had bought their homes before prices rose dramatically in the late 1990s and had savings, a family inheritance or a large salary or business to draw upon.[55] Among them was Don Milligan, the Communist-turned-gay liberation activist who had moved to the Netherlands in the 1970s. He'd moved to London in the 1980s and got a clerical job for the Greater London Council, but after Margaret Thatcher abolished it in 1986, Don said, 'I began to look after myself; my politics didn't change, but . . . I was forty odd . . . I thought, "Oh my god, I'd better do something".' Don and his partner, Gary, decided to move to Manchester where property was cheaper. Alongside their day jobs – Gary as a university lecturer and Don as a self-employed 'trainer' for private companies, offering everything from study skills to computing knowhow – they began to buy and sell former council flats. Along the way, they invested in the stock market, buttressed by their property and their savings. By the mid-2000s Don owned a smart apartment in Manchester's city centre, a home in south-west England and significant assets in stocks and shares. 'I'm a washed-up utopian', he said, only half-joking – and one who still hoped for a different future. He believed that 'there is no grounds for why I should have more than anyone else' and was clear that 'government should tax me more . . .

I've got an unearned income, but of course somebody's earning it – it's just not me.'[56]

'Buy-to-let' did not allow many people to climb the ladder. In fact the processes that allowed a few landlords to make large amounts of money increased everyone else's precarity. Between 2008 and 2011, the richest fifth of people benefited from a fall in their average housing costs from just over £500 per month to just over £400. Everyone else's housing costs rose. They increased most in those cities where landlords owned the biggest shares of property, like Oxford, where the cost of a home rose from 9.8 times to 11.3 times the average salary in just one year between 2012 and 2013.[57]

Many of Thatcher's children made huge sacrifices to become home-owners. Doing so offered a security and status that they were unable to realise at work. For some, home-ownership was central to their dream of being upwardly mobile and defining themselves as middle class. Claire Torrington and her husband achieved their dream of owning a 'middle-class' home in their late thirties, when they bought a house on a suburban estate in their northern city. This 'big investment' in their future was 'our reward for being sensible and working hard'.[58] It was a form of security, and a sign that they had made it, despite their chequered working lives.

But fulfilling this aspiration did not always lead to happiness. Homeowners from working-class backgrounds were less likely to find work in the most lucrative and secure jobs, or to have family wealth to tide them over hard times. Like many members of her generation, Claire Torrington discovered that a large mortgage was a millstone rather than a guarantee of future security. She and her husband 'find ourselves wondering if we are doing things right, because we see our friends [going to] spa weekends, [having] long holidays and buying expensive designer goods'. Claire wasn't always reassured by the thought that 'a lot of these people are in debt' (credit-card arrears being less socially acceptable than a mortgage). She would have liked more fun – and the quiet neighbourhood they had chosen provided little. She confessed to having long periods 'when I hated living here'.

But like many of her contemporaries, Claire was certain that her inability to fit into this 'middle-class' lifestyle was a failing she must overcome, rather than a sign that the dream was not as alluring as politicians and television personalities suggested. She reminded herself that 'the house I live in now is unimaginable for a little girl like me from a working-class family', and that this defined her as upwardly mobile and successful.[59]

Others also found fitting into affluent neighbourhoods harder than they had anticipated. As in earlier generations, the work of negotiating a family's place in a new community fell on women. Tessa Parr and her husband had made 'an aspirational move' to their current home in the 2000s, by which time they had a young family. But Tessa found she didn't 'belong' in her expensive suburb: 'the snobbery is unbelievable'. She found the 'Boden-wearing, Bugaboo-pram-pushing set' very dull. 'I object to the assumption that everyone else is the same as them', she wrote in 2016. 'Those who [aren't] . . . are to be looked down on.'[60] Tessa was finding that exclusively affluent neighbourhoods in highly unequal societies tend to breed fear and suspicion of less wealthy outsiders, exhibited in gated communities, conspicuous consumption and in scrutinising and, if necessary, shaming newcomers who don't 'fit in'. Social scientists have shown that this encourages conformity in fashion, cafes, cars and home decoration, with everyone keen to show that they are entitled to their prized place there. But rising property prices, and the consumption of designer brands and artisan coffee, price some residents and local retailers out, bankrupting small businesses as coffee chains and retail complexes moved in. In turn, remaining residents can become disenchanted with the monocultural feel of their neighbourhood.[61] As her job security in the NHS diminished, Tessa increasingly found herself 'struggling to keep my teenagers in sliced bread, so somewhere that places a premium on artisan bread isn't somewhere that I can feel fully comfortable'.[62]

Research suggests that most people prefer living in neighbourhoods with some social mix.[63] That was true of these younger generations. By her thirties, Samantha Bridges had settled in a provincial town, outside the expensive south-east of England where she had grown up. She enjoyed living alongside 'middle-class *Guardian* readers, students, Eastern European people, and an Arabic population'.[64] But others felt they could not make this choice. Either socially mixed neighbourhoods weren't available, or they could not afford to live in them. Those who could often believed that moving into more expensive areas would benefit themselves and their children. Tessa Parr's consolation were the 'good schools' that might help secure her children's rung on the social ladder.[65]

For many of the millennials, home ownership was a distant dream. Home ownership rates among the under-twenty-fives halved between 1995 and 2015.[66] The large number reliant on temporary contracts, low-waged work or precarious posts in the professions were far more conscious of the places where they could not afford to live than those where they might aspire to buy a home. Those with the ability to make choices about where to live calculated that house prices, and the cost of travel and food, made south-east England prohibitively expensive. Graduates also felt they were forced out of London at a point when the most lucrative career opportunities were increasingly clustered there. Oscar Greene was 'only in the north-east because I couldn't afford to live down south'.[67]

*

After the financial crash, politicians' emphasis on home ownership as a means of acquiring security and even wealth diminished. There was no attempt to build more council housing or deal with rising house prices. Instead, politicians increasingly urged voters to achieve social mobility via education and employment.

They were assisted by a growing social mobility industry. Since the 2000s, an increasing number of charities, lobby groups and businesses focused on increasing social mobility. One of the most prominent was, and is, the Sutton Trust, which undertakes research, lobbies government and runs summer schools to encourage children from 'disadvantaged' areas to apply to university. City firms established leadership and mentoring programmes for young black people and those from working-class backgrounds.

The social mobility industry has disseminated the politicians' message that personal aspiration and ambition can overcome 'disadvantage'. Speakers for Schools, an initiative established by the journalist Robert Peston in 2011, gives state-school students 'access to leading figures . . . who can share inspiration on pursuing their ambitions and broaden their horizons'. Speakers for Schools believes that state-school students' 'lack of confidence' constrains their 'belief in what is possible for the future'.[68] The possibility that their low confidence might result from a very realistic assessment of their prospects is never considered.

Most of those within the social mobility industry agree with the chair of the UK's Social Mobility Awards, merchant banker Kenneth Olisa, that 'to improve social mobility, we must raise children's aspirations'.[69] They ignore the evidence that young working-class people have very high aspirations. During his work with poor households during the 2000s and 2010s, Sam Royston, head of policy and public affairs at the Children's Society, found that 'low ambition and lack of parental encouragement are 'not more prevalent in low-income families'.[70] The ambitions of the millennials, most of whom aspired to attend university, and go on to become professionals, celebrities or make a useful contribution to society, support his view.

The social mobility industry claimed – in the words of the Speakers for Schools website – to 'shake up the current system to change the status quo'.[71] But in the 2000s and the 2010s, none of those invested in this industry sought to remove the obstacles that prevent children from realising their ambitions. They offered no criticism of the ways that the Russell Group or private schools hoarded resources. They did not campaign against the preservation of wealth by the country's richest people; the speculation on housing which left so many people at the mercy of private landlords; or the lack of control of banks and the stock exchange against legal restrictions to trade unions' rights.

The only institutions that the social mobility think tanks, charities and organisations ever seriously sought to change were state schools. Throughout the 2000s and 2010s, the Sutton Trust's research focused on the disproportionately high number of privately educated people at Oxbridge and in the professions. But rather than propose the abolition of the private sector, the Sutton Trust's founder, businessman Peter Lampl, advocated a marketplace in schools and established his own academy in Liverpool. None of these social mobility initiatives promoted those policies that worked in the past – such as creating more room at the top in the post-war public sector and the expansion of comprehensive education in the 1970s. Yet there is no evidence that any of the initiatives pioneered by social mobility lobby groups or charities has increased upward mobility or even working-class people's entry into higher education.[72]

But the social mobility industry did help to create some new opportunities for upwardly mobile graduates. Charities and lobby groups sought to encourage 'diversity' at the top of firms and professions, as well as within universities. By the 2010s, some graduates owed their jobs to such initiatives. Helen Abeda was among them. After graduating in the early 2000s, she decided to pursue postgraduate research. She was able to gain her PhD by combining her studies with paid work on a scheme to encourage working-class and black students to attend university. In her thirties she got a full-time, permanent post at a Russell Group university, where she combined her research with directing schemes to assist upwardly mobile students. She was proud, she said, that 'a person from my background has come this far'.[73]

Richard Campbell's route into professional life had some similarities with Helen's. After leaving school aged sixteen with few qualifications, he was inspired to go to university by working in a care home in his late teens. 'Having responsibility for other people's lives', he said, encouraged him to believe that 'I'm not stupid, maybe I should actually do something with my life.' The realisation that he might make a difference to other people motivated him to get a degree. After graduating in the 2000s, Richard got a job fundraising for scholar-ships at a Russell Group university because he 'liked the idea of doing something that helped people'.[74] Richard was soon recruited to a more senior administrative role at an equally prestigious institution.

But the route up the ladder was far from straightforward. The social mobility and diversity industry claimed to introduce merito-cratic practices into management and the professions, but its success in this regard was negligible. Instead, institutions increasingly claimed a commitment to 'diversity' by making conspicuous a few people who were different to the white, male, middle-class majority, while doing nothing to tackle systemic discrimination.[75] Nor did these institutions have any interest in rewarding those workers in essential jobs like cleaning or catering who were disproportionately female and black. In fact, 'diversity' initiatives in large institutions like universities or local authorities often replaced older units dedicated to combatting race and sex discrimination.[76] They appeared as these organisations began to erode the conditions of these lower-paid staff, often outsourcing them to private firms.

Very often those appointed to posts designed to encourage 'diver-sity' found themselves in middle-ranking administrative posts or in middle-management roles. In both Helen Abeda's and Richard Campbell's cases, these jobs were far more lucrative, secure and senior than the work their parents did. But such jobs rarely offered progres-sion to the senior managerial or professional roles that some of the appointees would have preferred to occupy. Despite her PhD Helen Abeda did not have the university lectureship she'd wanted – instead she was an administrator. She was ambivalent about the fact that her background counted for as much as her research in her employment prospects. 'Sometimes it feels like: do they really want me? Or is it just the image I project?' Black women in senior roles are often expected to act as 'an exotic token, an institutional symbol, a mentor and . . . expert of all things to do with "race"', writes the researcher Heidi Safia Mirza. This 'emotional and professional burden' hampers their prospects of getting into the jobs they really want.[77] Helen Abeda was expected to do the outreach work that the academic professionals in her workplace did not want to do. She had few prospects to develop her research, which would allow her to compete for lectureships. 'I've never really had the advantages that most [lecturers] have had', she explained, 'yet you're being asked to be a representative.'[78] The diversity industry did create some new jobs, but left the professions and senior echelons of management untouched.

In their work, both Helen Abeda and Richard Campbell felt a pressure to conceal some of the obstacles that they had encountered. It was acceptable to talk about their families' or schools' low aspirations or limited knowledge of university, but less permissible to discuss the discrimination they faced within their institutions. Helen was clear that the success story her employers wanted her to tell – that anyone could do anything if they were bright and had ambition – was only a partial truth. 'I go into schools and I try to tell them, here's how you do it, but without saying "it is easy", because it is not, you do meet prejudice.' As researchers have noted, 'widening participation initiatives, aimed primarily at raising working-class "desire to participate", fail to address questions regarding "ability to participate"'. A study of working-class teenagers found that they 'constructed their ability to participate within a notion of economic and social risk', whereas diversity and social mobility initiatives 'draw on a meritocratic discourse, identifying "ability to participate" [in higher education] solely in terms of academic achievement'.[79] Helen Abeda was not alone in wondering if the focus on celebrating 'diversity' by employing some prominent black women allowed her employer to ignore how class affected people's chances. Networks for black people in her field were dominated by those from wealthier families. While she was glad that 'their voices are being heard', she 'drew back from it. Because . . . class plays into it . . . that's been a bit of a struggle to cope with.'[80]

These social mobility and diversity workers experienced intense pressure to conform to the culture of the institutions they joined. Either they became a token, conspicuous by their difference, or they sought to fit in. Richard Campbell took the latter route. He had found going to university a culture shock, but it was when he began work that he 'really started to change'. As he explained, 'my job was to work with donors and prospective donors' – wealthy people – and colleagues 'from very middle-class backgrounds'. As Richard's work shifted from social mobility strategies to fundraising, he realised that there was no kudos in being either black or working class. For two years, he said, 'I did quite a lot of work on ... the way that I spoke, the types of topics that I would read up on and have conservations about ... I started reading the *Financial Times*.' Although Richard's job was concerned with widening access to higher education, the notion that universities might need to radically change their culture and practices was unthinkable. The increasing reliance on wealthy donors to fund scholarships and resources, caused by declining government investment, encouraged universities to create the kind of environment that these donors – many of them white, wealthy men who had made their money in business and finance, not fields renowned for championing equality – would approve of. Richard believed that 'it's important to fit in because you don't want people to look at you and think, "Oh, what's he doing here?"' – as many of his managers and business contacts might do about a young black man with a regional accent.[81]

Unlike Helen, Richard was able to 'pass' as white. He said that he knew he had succeeded in climbing the social ladder when 'I noticed people consider me to be white ... Back home, on the council estate, I was the black kid. But now ... if I'm in a business meeting in London, they assume that I am white, because of how I dress, how I behave.' One acquaintance was 'embarrassed' to discover Richard's mother was black.[82] Being black and successful, like being working class and successful, was incompatible in the minds of those managers and professionals with whom Richard now mixed.

The social mobility and diversity industry had failed to challenge the working patterns and hierarchies that ensured most people ended up at the bottom of the ladder. While ethnic and social difference could be celebrated as evidence of 'diversity', the emphasis was always on raising people's aspirations, resolutely ignoring the limited room at the top. As Helen Abeda and Richard Campbell found, their colleagues and employers were far less comfortable in dealing with social class than with race, since its very existence testifies to structural inequalities of power and wealth. As the scholars Walter Benn Michaels and Adolph Reed point out, the way to tackle class inequalities is not to celebrate a person's culture or background, but to seek to destroy social class by creating a more equal society.[83] Overturning the status quo was less attractive to employers, politicians and the social mobility industry than celebrating 'diversity'.

*

Those born since 1972 worried more about sliding down the ladder than the magpies or the golden generation had done. They were aware that the lack of a robust welfare state, and the decline in the conditions and pay of manual and many clerical jobs, made life on the lowest rungs very hard. They were also more anxious than the magpies about the need to climb the ladder. Thatcher's children in particular believed that people should strive to be upwardly mobile, and that achieving this was down to them. Tessa Parr was 'not sorry for people who think the state owes them everything . . . there is not a bottomless pit of money to go round'.[84] Intolerance to claimants of social security benefits actually increased during the 2000s, because of New Labour's emphasis on personal responsibility.[85] Those who aspired to upward mobility but did not achieve it tended to blame themselves. Kenny Smith thought that he had failed to get a degree or a satisfying career because he had not been determined enough to follow his dream. 'You have to be true to yourself to make the most of yourself . . . if you want something enough you can make it happen', he wrote in 2016. It was hard to see how Kenny could have made his dreams come true without deserting his family responsibilities. He had no intention of doing so – but in the competitive world of the twenty-first century, caring had little political or economic value. There was, Kenny knew, no reward for being a 'nice guy'.[86] Those who had begun life in more affluent circumstances, but had failed to achieve the upward mobility they wanted, often cited a lack of knowledge and cultural capital as having held them back. 'Posh people have more options – the rest of us only know what our parents do', as Karen Foot put it.[87] To Karen and many of her contemporaries, the deficiencies of their families and schools were at least partially to blame for their lack of opportunities.

Those who had climbed the ladder ascribed this to their own hard work and talents. Unlike the golden generation and the magpies, they tended not to see the welfare state as in any way responsible. Jason Somerville was born in 1978. His parents were private-sector clerical workers, who brought Jason up to be competitive and entrepreneurial. He wanted to make money, and at eighteen decided it would be more 'savvy' to train as an accountant in local government, 'paid for by my employer', than get into debt at university. At the same time, Jason moved 'from strange relationship to strange relationship . . . always with men that could give me something' – money, gifts and knowledge of the middle-class life he aspired to. In his early thirties Jason became a self-employed accountant, but this only partly achieved his goal: 'I didn't consider myself to be a middle-class person'. His earnings did not allow him to realise his dream of living in one of the most expensive neighbourhoods in northern England alongside 'head teachers, doctors and barristers'. What made the difference was prostitution. Like many socially mobile people, Jason prided himself on being a good mixer, and on being able to fit into the social class he wished to join. Living in an expensive neighbourhood defined him as socially equal to his clients: 'I attract the men who want someone "a bit posh" with a nice house and nice clothes, who can talk to them at their level', he said. Being able to attract such men reinforced Jason's belief that he could now 'describe myself . . . as being middle class'.[88]

But selling your body is very different to selling products – it has particular risks attached to it and suggests that people can be bought and sold like goods.[89] Jason Somerville himself recognised this. Hard work and intelligence – both attributes he believed he had in spades – weren't enough to sustain his lifestyle. 'Reinvent yourself, I've had to', was his advice to those living on the ladder's lowest rungs, a phrase that indicated the effort he'd made to turn himself into an attractive commodity.[90] Jason wasn't alone in using prostitution to try to achieve his dreams. In 2015, a small study of thirty-one university students who worked as prostitutes found that most undertook the work to pay for basic living expenses, few made more than the amount they needed to get by, and most felt unsafe while they were working.[91] This wasn't the autonomy and self-fulfilment that so many members of earlier generations had hoped that climbing the ladder would bring them. In the early twenty-first century, the mantra of social mobility justified treating everything and everyone as if they had a price – the acquisition of wealth was a laudable sign of ambition and effort.

The political mantra of individual responsibility and aspiration provided no means of challenging sex or class inequality. Many of Thatcher's children believed that citing discrimination was at best a futile admission of defeat, and at worst an excuse for personal failings. Claire Torrington's ambitions had been stymied by the prohibitive cost of a university education and the lack of permanent, secure jobs for school leavers. But she attributed her 'failure' to become a teacher or a senior manager to her family's 'low aspirations' and her own 'lack of confidence'.[92] This kind of blame took a huge toll. When Claire was made redundant in her early thirties, she did not blame her employer, but instead became depressed and had a nervous breakdown, overwhelmed by her powerlessness and sense of failure. A decade later, she continued to suffer from anxiety and stress.

Nevertheless, by the mid-2010s, most of those born since 1972 did agree that Britain was an 'unfair' place. They did not necessarily want an entirely equal society, but blamed the Conservative Party for creating a chasm that even the most ambitious could not cross. 'The Conservatives take the view that if people work hard enough then there's no excuse for poverty, but they forget the advantages that they start life with – wealth, good education, connections', believed Kenny Smith.[93] 'Politics has once again become the remit of the rich and privileged, especially under the current government', wrote Claire

Torrington in 2016. By the 2010s, both generations believed that the most significant division in society was not between the working and the middle classes. Most concurred with Debbie Morgan that 'there's a big chasm between wealthy people and normal people' and, regardless of their own jobs and income, they rated themselves as 'normal'.[94]

Thatcher's children in particular weren't sure what could be done about this. Those who could afford to sometimes asserted their 'choice' to opt out of the rat race to the top. They tended to be graduates from middle-class backgrounds who had embarked on their career before the financial crash. Lucy Young, who became a library manager in the city where she'd attended university, described her adopted home as 'the graveyard of ambition . . . jobs are full of over-qualified people because we'd all rather live in a nicer area with a lower-paid job than in a high-profile job' in London. This group often presented their life-style – in provincial towns, away from the south-east of England where many of them had grown up – as a positive choice rather than a neces-sity. They often clamed to enjoy a better quality of life than that of friends or acquaintances in corporate law and the financial services – 'belonging to them looks like too much hard work', said Samantha Bridges.[95] They glossed over those aspects of life over which they had very little control – including their inability to afford to live in south-east England, the area from which most of them came.

Despite the contribution that bankers had made to the financial crisis and the recession that followed, few of Thatcher's children criticised wealthy financiers and businesspeople for what they did. Most of them thought that what bankers did had little impact on their own lives. The important thing was to allow people to choose a range of careers and lifestyles, including those that did not focus on accruing great wealth, and to enable them to live comfortably if they worked hard.

But the younger of Thatcher's children, and especially the millen-nials, were more likely to blame both government and big business for inequality and for limited mobility. Most of them had begun their working lives after the crash of 2007–08. Some had experienced downward mobility, while others feared that they would. They argued that inequality was caused by a small elite, whose strategies to preserve wealth and power in their own hands limited everyone else's opportunities. Jenny Ward, born to working-class parents in 1987, had graduated during the financial crisis of 2008. She recognised that however ambitious people were, 'there aren't the jobs available'. Ten years later she had a master's degree, but remained a poorly paid healthcare assistant in northern England.[96] Jenny and many of her contemporaries agreed that this state of affairs was sustained by – in the words of Oscar Greene – 'the rich and the rules they put in place to make it expensive enough being poor that you can never work your way out'.[97] Many of them were directly affected by the erosion of conditions in the professions and the public sector. They recognised that those at the top of the ladder worked to reproduce their power over others and their wealth. And they considered this unacceptable in one of the wealthiest countries in the world.

For these younger people, social mobility was not a solution to inequality. And in arguing their case, they drew on perspectives that had found wider popularity since the financial crash. Over the next decade, books like Kate Pickett's and Richard Wilkinson's *The Spirit Level*, Danny Dorling's *Inequality and the 1%*, and Owen Jones's *Chavs: The demonization of the working class* and *The Establishment* became surprise bestsellers. These researchers revealed a Britain divided between a small wealthy elite and everyone else. They also showed that the existence of a wealthy elite didn't create greater opportunity, but instead caused the growing poverty and insecurity that everyone else experienced. Rather than believing that Britain's salvation lay in helping a few new faces claw their way to the top, these writers and scholars questioned whether the ladder was really the best means of organising society. Their research showed that more equal societies tended to enjoy greater happiness, better health, higher educational attainment, more innovation and less social tension.

There were other signs of growing public scepticism towards individualistic ambition, competition and wealth acquisition. Since 2000, the profile of trade union members had changed. As the number of male manual work declined, women and black workers became a more significant proportion of trade unionists. Between 2010 and 2015 union membership in the private sector increased (though it remained very low – 14 per cent of workers in the private sector were unionised by 2015 compared with more than half of public-sector workers). And a rising proportion of trade unionists were found in the professions. While union density was very low compared with the 1970s – just 6 million workers, or 26 per cent of the workforce, belonged to a union in 2010 compared with more than 13 million, or 53 per cent, in 1979 – unions were appealing to workers in expanding sectors.[98] They were also becoming more left wing. The early 2010s saw the election of several left-wing union leaders, including Len McCluskey, born in 1950, who failed his eleven-plus, became a dockworker, and in 2011 became leader of Unite – a successor of the TGWU and the second-largest trade union in Britain.

Then, in 2015, the Labour Party held a leadership contest. Left-winger Jeremy Corbyn was the surprise winner, and Party membership rocketed to over half a million – making Labour the largest democratic party in Europe. Two years later, in the general election of 2017, Corbyn's Labour Party defied all media predictions to destroy the Conservatives' majority. Labour pledged to act 'for the many, not the few' by increasing public investment and treating education as a social benefit, not an individual choice or asset – notably by abolishing university tuition fees. The Party's manifesto rejected the promise of social mobility in favour of promising greater opportunity for everyone. In 2010, Labour's manifesto had mentioned 'social mobility' five times and 'aspiration' six times. In 2017 'social mobility' did not appear in Labour's manifesto and 'aspiration' only once, to describe a collective desire for secure homes which was used to justify plans to increase council housing. Jeremy Corbyn's Labour Party didn't promise great riches, but instead collective uplift – 'a fairer' Britain where 'we will measure our economic success not by the number of billionaires but by the ability of our people to live richer lives . . . the creation of wealth is a collective endeavour'.[99]

Labour achieved the biggest electoral swing to the Labour Party since Attlee's landslide victory in 1945. Although the Conservatives hung onto power, in a confidence-and-supply arrangement with the Democratic Unionist Party, Labour won the majority of votes cast by those born since 1972. Pollsters assume that people become more likely to vote Conservative once they reach forty – as many of Thatcher's children had done by 2017. Yet a larger proportion of them voted Labour than they had done in the general elections of 2010 and 2015.[100]

Labour didn't win in 2017, and lost badly in the next general election, two years later, which was fought on the issue of Brexit, four years after Britain had narrowly voted to leave the European Union. The Conservative promise to respect that result offered a different route to greater control over one's life and society. Fear of the future and of poverty may well have influenced those who associated deindustrialisation and the rise of poorly paid work with the European Union and immigration. Many voters who backed the Tories were based in former mining communities, coastal towns with unaffordable housing and low-wage economies, and towns that had never recovered from the recession of the 1980s. Nevertheless, Labour gained the majority of the millennials' votes, and about 37 per cent of Thatcher's children voted for them too – a larger proportion than voted Conservative.[101] Labour's message of greater equality made sense to a majority of younger voters. But regardless of how they cast their ballot, many of the electorate clearly hoped for radical change.

Underpinning this desire was huge discontent with the status quo – even desperation. By 2020, getting to the top was harder than ever. Exhortations to be more aspirational, like the schemes peddled by the social mobility industry, had not increased upward mobility. Insecurity had grown since the 1980s and was exacerbated by the financial crash of 2007–08 and the political response to it. By the 2010s, even the most lucrative professions no longer offered the certainty and autonomy they once had. There was less room at the top. And life in the middle or the bottom was getting harder, especially for the young. The negotiating power of manual and administrative workers had been eroded. Their security was diminishing, their share of the country's wealth declining. House prices continued to rise. The welfare state no longer provided much of a safety net for those who found themselves sick, unemployed or under-paid. Younger people's hopes of climbing the ladder were increasingly overshadowed by their fear of sliding down it.

Conclusion

WE CAN REPLACE THE LADDER
WITH A BRIGHTER FUTURE

As a promise of a better society, social mobility has failed. Policies designed to encourage the talented to ascend to the top have not resulted in a meritocratic ladder. Instead, twenty-first-century Britain is more akin to the 'greasy pole' criticised by the Workers' Educational Association in the 1900s. At the top sits a tiny group of wealthy and powerful people, who have spent the last few decades stripping the world of its resources and destabilising the global economy to make themselves richer and more powerful still. Far below is everyone else, clinging tight, occasionally jostling to inch their way slightly higher, but all too often sliding further down.

There is no point lamenting the loss of the ladder, which was never meritocratic. But the experiences and hopes of the people in this book do offer inspiration for a better future.

We don't need to waste time raising people's ambitions. Idleness and low aspiration have never explained the lack of upward mobility. Presented with greater opportunities, most people grasped them – especially if they had the reassurance of a welfare state safety net to catch them if they fell. Most of those who wanted to climb the ladder were inspired not by a desire to get rich but by a wish for economic security and the control over their lives and choices that offered. Many wanted to make a useful contribution to society; some aspired to shape their country's future.

Climbing a few rungs up the ladder rarely delivered these dreams. We need to create a future that will, because we require imaginative thinking, big ambitions and hope to tackle the pressing problems of the twenty-first century, including climate change, pandemics like COVID-19, automation and an ageing population.

The labour movement pioneers of the early twentieth century and the leftists of the 1970s remind us that an unequal hierarchy of wealth and power is only one model for organising society. They envisioned egalitarian alternatives that are worth pursuing. I end this book with some thoughts about how this could be realised. Implementing these suggestions would require greater social and economic equality, policies for equitable raising of money (through taxation but also through borrowing), democratic ownership of businesses and services, and regulation of the housing and financial markets. Proposals for how to achieve these goals have been developed by the economist Ann Pettifor and social scientists like Kate Pickett, Richard Wilkinson and Danny Dorling.[1] I focus here on how, within such a framework, we could replace social mobility with a commitment to equality and innovation, and on the benefits this would bring.

Universal, free, non-selective education from the cradle to the grave

Education and training don't create opportunity, but they do determine who is able to take advantage of it. Education needs to be free, universal and democratic: learners, teachers and teaching assistants, lecturers and tutors, caretakers and canteen staff, and the communities in which they work, should help decide what is taught and how it is delivered. Community schools, colleges and universities can be brought under the aegis of local education authorities composed of elected representatives, along the lines of the Greater London Council's Inner London Education Authority before Margaret Thatcher abolished it in 1988.

All educational institutions should be funded by the state, and universities should become more democratically accountable, by being obliged to have, as a majority of their governing bodies (at present stuffed with potential and actual benefactors and grandees), staff and students from their own institution and representatives of local trade unions and the local council. The Russell Group should receive no special favours from government; nor should any other interest group. University, school and college admissions should be transparent and open to consultation and debate with students, teaching unions and political representatives.

Adult education has long been the poor relation of the education system, and must become its centrepiece. There is no reason anyone should feel they have missed their chance by sixteen or eighteen. We should enable those with some life experience to return to education to develop the knowledge and skills they need. When there's been a chance to do so, thousands of people have taken it up. But adult and further education should not narrowly focus on preparing people for specific jobs. Doing so has proved costly and ineffective because jobs and technology change so fast. It is also short-sighted when we need people who can create solutions to the national and global crises we face, not fit into pre-existing slots. People should be able to learn about all kinds of subjects, along the lines of the original Workers' Educational Association, to encourage creativity and innovation.

Recognising that education is far more important than simply examination or test results, we should abolish league tables and review whether examinations are really necessary at any level. Because the debate over education has for so long assumed that the most elitist institutions are the 'best', the practices of those establishments are often unquestioningly approved. A recent Sutton Trust report argues that 'careful consideration should be given to the setting of homework, fostering and nurturing aspiration, high-quality . . . careers advice . . . encouraging successful alumni to return and talk about their experiences'.[2] Yet none of these strategies has increased upward mobility over the past 140 years. In fact there is increasing evidence that homework, setting in 'ability' groups, and the imposition of school uniform hamper attainment by sapping children's enthusiasm for learning and encouraging them to judge themselves failures before they're out of their teens.[3] Our education system should nurture imaginative thinkers who can create a better society, not rote learners who can leap through outdated hoops.[4]

We should focus on providing a good education for everyone, rather than developing 'specialist' centres or different schools for different 'abilities'. Allocating children a place at the school closest to their home recognises that any other form of selection is simply social elitism. We have no reliable way of measuring intelligence or aptitude. Attempts to do so have reproduced the privileges of the few and deprived many people of the chance to develop their interests and skills.

Allocating a child a place at her local school would also remove that huge obstacle to opportunity – parental choice. We have seen that in every generation, a small but significant group of parents have sought educational advantage for their child by choosing or buying a school place for them. These agonised decisions involve a huge amount of time and work by parents, especially by mothers. Yet their choices are influenced by ill-informed fear about working-class children's ability to damage the prospects of their wealthier peers. In the 1990s researchers found that 'there is certainly *an element* of class discrimination in the perception of, and response, to schools', though they discovered that such fears were groundless –middle-class children perform well at socially mixed schools.[5]

It's understandable that parents are anxious for their children when there is so little room at the top. But there are good reasons why parents should not be given 'choice' about the school they send their child to. Economists and sociologists have argued that 'reducing choice [could] actually increase outcomes if instead these parents are limited to working with schools to drive up standards'.[6] As we have seen, comprehensive education was extremely popular with all parents, regardless of social class, when politicians invested money and confidence in it.

For similar reasons, we must open up private schools to everyone. There is no reason why a few people should be able to buy resources that have relied on state subsidy. We can start by abolishing all state support for private education. Since the financial crash of 2007–08, private education has been in crisis. Throughout recent history, governments have bailed private schools out of successive crises by offering them generous subsidies. The only times that the private sector has shown any inclination to open its doors a little wider have been when it is struggling to survive. The post-war direct grant scheme, the assisted places of the 1980s and 90s and the academy and free-school programmes of the 2010s have all offered the private sector huge support. Currently, private schools receive about £200 million of taxpayers' money every year.[7] Yet this is a sector that has never fully accepted the professionalisation of teaching – many private schools employ large numbers of untrained staff and fail to recognise trade unions.

It would be sensible to impose VAT on private-school fees to recoup some of the public money spent on this sector, and to end the charitable status of private schools. Without state subsidy, these schools can take their chance in the free market they claim to support. Of course, any private school wishing to join the state sector and provide comprehensive, free education would be allowed to do so, on condition that its staff reach the standards required of state-school teachers.

Some will denounce the ending of parental 'choice' as totalitarian. But the rationale for placing high standards for all over unlimited choice for the few is in fact already enshrined in law. Although Britain has private medical provision, the medicines and treatments that can be offered are strictly regulated; we do not allow shops to stock food that does not reach certain hygiene standards; and we do not allow people to circumvent the adoption system by simply buying a child. We understand that wealth does not necessarily lead people to make the best choices for themselves or for society as a whole. In fact, as we have seen, the wealthier people are, the more likely they have been to make short-term, ill-informed choices that offer limited immediate gains for themselves but can greatly harm everyone else.

Reward work for its social value and expand socially useful work

Attempts to increase upward mobility into the professions have focused on encouraging socially elite, lucrative professions to broaden their recruitment pool voluntarily. This strategy has failed. Many professionals argue that they need to recruit exceptionally well-qualified people, regardless of background. It is difficult to argue that anyone facing surgery, for example, should be more concerned with their surgeon's family background than their capabilities. As a result, the emphasis on opening up the professions always shifts to scrutiny of educational access, which in turn leads to the kind of education marketplace outlined above – one in which professionals themselves, desperate to preserve their privileges for their children, use their resources to get them into schools and universities that are well regarded by other professionals (because they attended them in the past). In turn, these children's pathway into the professions is smoothed by the contacts and financial help their parents can offer them.

What constitutes a profession is, as we have seen, highly subjective. Those who work in the most lucrative and long-standing professions tend to be wealthy, well connected and have a vested interest in maintaining the status quo. Less than a hundred years ago, surgeons sought to bar women from their profession. Today, the surgeons we have are not necessarily those who are the most motivated or best qualified – they are recruited from a small pool of entrants. And although all of us want a highly qualified doctor, what this means has changed over time. We now know that life experience and empathy help to make good doctors – and so medical schools have introduced accelerated courses for mature students, and teach students about how to establish a rapport with patients, in the knowledge that this can speed recovery.[8]

What is *not* considered a profession is also subjective. The COVID-19 pandemic of 2020 highlighted that we desperately need workers in occupations that are currently characterised by long hours, little

security and poor pay. Supermarket staff, paramedics, hospital cleaners and social care workers are essential to our society. Yet they are
offered few material rewards and little scope for training or further
education. Many are paid below the minimum wage.[9] Staff sickness
and turnover rates are very high in the social care sector. 'Coronavirus
has forced us to rethink who we value and how', wrote the *Financial
Times* correspondent Sarah O'Connor in April 2020. 'Some of the
workers we have left to languish in low-paid and insecure jobs are the
very ones we cannot live without'.[10]

We therefore have some jobs that are highly desirable but to which
entry is conditional on leaping social barriers, and others – equally
demanding and at least as necessary – which often don't pay people
enough to live on. We can break this cycle by recognising that the
value of a job is neither objective nor best decided by the marketplace.
Unchecked, those who can do well in the free market will value short-
term profits over long-term planning and development. This is why
private providers of social care pay their staff low wages, despite the
obvious need for high-quality care of older and vulnerable people, and
why university vice chancellors accept salaries of hundreds of thousands of pounds while employing increasing proportions of their staff
on insecure, temporary contracts, despite the increase in student
numbers.

Political decisions determine a job's value, with those who have
more political power able to argue that their work should be highly
regarded. Value is expressed economically, through monetary payment and benefits like pensions. It would be possible to use income or
wealth tax to narrow inequality, and these are measures worth implementing (though beyond the scope of this book).[11] But those doing
socially useful work should be paid well and enjoy good benefits.
There is no objective reason why a banker or vice chancellor should
be paid more than a home help.

Since the 1980s employers and politicians have argued that offering 'respect' or 'training' can overcome the lack of value implied by
low wages and uncertain prospects. But simply affording workers

greater 'respect' through the provision of workplace 'charters' or 'contracts' of behaviour does not address the problem of low-paid, insecure work. Nor does offering these workers 'training' or repackaging low-paid jobs as 'apprenticeships' or as 'internships'. This form of low-paid work was traditionally used in the professions and in skilled manual trades to exclude those who could not afford to work for a pittance at the beginning of their careers. This remains true today – and such posts no longer guarantee a permanent job. This form of work increases employers' profits with no gain for anyone else.

We should also make it possible and desirable for workers to move between jobs and try out new career paths in midlife or later. Too often, people's social and economic position has been fixed by their mid-thirties, partly because changing course at that stage can be very risky or expensive. Those who are forced to do so, by immigration, divorce or unemployment, often travel down the social ladder into poverty.

Since the 1980s, neoliberal politicians have suggested that we need 'flexible' workers. In fact, we need an integrated workforce with flexible jobs. This would mean assessing jobs according to the skills required and working out which sectors might benefit from exchanges and swaps. If a government decided to acquiesce to popular demand and take back the railways into public ownership, it would make sense for railway workers to be seconded to the Civil Service to advise on the process and learn something about their new employers. It would also make sense for civil servants to spend a stint of their career working in the railways in order to understand the challenges of that sector.

This kind of proposal seems radical only because, at the moment, senior civil servants or doctors are paid more, and have a higher social status, than train drivers. If we evaluated jobs on the basis of their social contribution then we would be likely to construct a far more equitable hierarchy of jobs. We need to interrogate what skills different jobs really require. The designation of 'professions' and 'skilled' work was, as we have seen, too often a means of preserving the privileges of the few at the expense of the many.

We should also foster democracy in workplaces. Both the political right and elements of the political left have championed self-help and self-reliance, but dismissed trade unionism or co-operative working practices as offering unfair favours to employees. But being able to help oneself and others depends on having the opportunities to do so, rather than relying on managers or the state to intervene. Co-operative methods of working encourage people to innovate and work together to create ventures that benefit a large constituency. In the early part of the twentieth century the Co-op movement showed how this could be done. In the 1970s, initiatives like community law centres were run co-operatively and proved immensely popular. Today there are plenty of models of co-operative working that are highly successful. At Unicorn Grocery in Manchester, a large, vegan supermarket, more than eighty co-workers collectively own and run the store. Everyone – whatever their qualifications or experience – takes a turn at cleaning the toilets, serving customers, and participating in the working groups that make decisions about all aspects of the store, and all are paid the same. Unlike many corporate supermarkets, Unicorn's revenue has increased since the financial crash, in part, its co-workers believe, because of their conviction that organic, vegan produce can appeal to a very large customer base if it is affordable. Unicorn's imaginative, adventurous approach is directed by an equitable vision of society that seeks to distribute benefits to a large constituency of workers and customers, rather than focusing on short-term profits.[12]

A progressive government would repeal the anti-trade union legislation of the 1980s – an important first step to ensuring that all workers are able to negotiate with employers on their wages and conditions. This would help make workers integral to planning and organising work. Government could offer surety for bank loans designed to develop socially valuable and equitable ways of working in every sector.

Employers sometimes claim that if any of this was enacted they'd leave for higher salaries and profits overseas. We should call their bluff. Many employers are reliant on government for contracts, bailouts and subsidies (the banks being a prime example). Many rely on public institutions, like universities, for research and development. If a few employers or highly paid CEOs do emigrate, then this book has shown we have a large number of talented, determined people who would be able to replace them – assuming that we need the large number of managers and directors that our economy supports. We probably don't.

Spread opportunity across the country

The concentration of well-paid jobs in south-east England means opportunities are far more limited for those who live elsewhere. Attempts to replicate London's reliance on financial speculation – for example, through creating a 'northern powerhouse' centred on Manchester – are flawed, because all the northern cities together cannot generate the wealth of the City of London.[13] And, as we have seen, the City has not encouraged social mobility, let alone equality; speculation increases the wealth of a few rather than giving opportunity to the many. London is one of the most socially segregated and unequal cities in the world.

Communities should be able to draw on their own experiences and foster their talents to create new ways of doing things. In the 1950s and 60s, a few working-class people got a foothold in regional newspapers and television. They undertook welcome innovations in the arts and the media. If national television and broadcasters and newspaper proprietors are obliged to invest in the regions, we can create a media that is more in touch with events and concerns in the country at large. This might mean that events such as the Brexit vote of 2016, or Labour's popularity in the 2017 General Election, come as less of a surprise to broadcasters, editors and politicians. To build a media driven by our needs, rather than by the profit motive, small groups or individuals should not be allowed to create media empires. This would also fill a gap that international rivals to the BBC can't address.

Government funding of the arts, sport and media should be used to encourage mass participation across the country. The ability of more people to create and distribute music, film and photography via smartphone and Internet technology should be celebrated and supported by directing some of the government funding received by the BBC and the arts at regional training programmes, arts groups emphasising opportunities for all, and grants for social media and artistic start-ups. To break down the artificial division between 'community' arts and sport and 'professional' initiatives, space on BBC TV and radio, on the BBC's Internet platform and in national galleries, museums and the National Theatre should be given to community-based groups and new initiatives.

We must also revitalise local government. In the 1920s and 30s, some local authorities offered bold visions for the future which challenged the edicts of national government. Their strategies for housing, healthcare and education were tailored to local needs. Since the 1980s, cuts to local government and the privatisation of utilities, schools and housing have robbed councils of their powers. These need to be returned to them.

But councils also need to become more democratic than they were in the past. Established before the age of mass democracy, many councils operated as cabals of local dignitaries, and even those visionary twentieth-century authorities like Herbert Morrison's London County Council favoured governance by the expert few for the good of the many. The frustrations of the 1970s and, more recently, the vote for Brexit, demonstrate that people want more democratic ways of governing their communities and workplaces. That means local democracy. Governance by small cliques and council cabinets should end. Councils should become less concerned with sporadic online 'consultations' and more focused on encouraging people to participate directly in deciding where money should be spent, involving more people in the planning and delivery of services. This means engaging with community campaigners rather than with private investors and lobby groups.

Focus policy on women

Reorganising society around the goals of human fulfilment and environmental sustainability is essential if the human race is to survive, let alone flourish. The social mobility industry assumes that everyone can and should aim for a career, in which work takes centre stage, competition is motivation, individual achievement is the goal and acquiring wealth or power is the reward. But most useful work has never been done this way. Everyone owes their life to the unselfish act of mothering. Giving birth was a dangerous activity for most of the generations we've examined, and mothering an expensive and onerous task. Yet a majority of women did become mothers and many invested ambition, as well as time and love, in their children. The men who succeeded in reaching a higher rung usually owed their achievements to the support of their mothers or wives. Women's experiences remind us that humanity relies on co-operation and love, not competition and greed.

The experience of women – 51 per cent of the population – undermines the assumption that social mobility can somehow benefit everyone. Women are subject to sex-based discrimination because of their potential or actual role as mothers. In a capitalist society, this means that those who are concerned to acquire wealth treat women primarily as reproducers of workers whose labour can generate profit or, at the top of the ladder, as the reproducers of wealth and privilege. Male mobility has relied on women remaining at the bottom to do the dirty work of cleaning and caring.

However society is organised in future, we must recognise the costs associated with women's unpaid labour and the discrimination they face in the workplace and in wider society. This means consulting women on what education and training they would like. Women who take time to look after others should be offered not only 'retraining' for work, but education and leisure, as well as a state pension offering a comfortable standard of living.

There is of course no reason why women should take on the lion's share of caring work if they don't want to. We've seen that motherhood and marriage were not unalloyed joys for women; many understandably resented sacrificing their own chance of education, independence, a career or leisure for husbands and children. More socialised childcare and reducing working hours for both men and women would help. This would make clear that we value caring for others at least as much as we value people's contribution to the workforce. It would also be of economic benefit: we know that shorter working hours can raise productivity and improve people's health, leading to fewer absences from work.[14]

Our children should grow up knowing that girls are as capable as boys, and migrants and black British people as capable as those who are white and British-born. This has not been achieved by the social mobility and diversity industries because they fail to address the causes of sexist and racist discrimination. In the early twentieth century, and again in the 1970s, feminists argued powerfully against gender stereotyping. We have seen how such stereotypes have constrained women's opportunities throughout the past 140 years. It is time to rediscover the campaigns of 1970s feminists, who argued that both sexist and racist discrimination can be overturned.

Redistribute political power

Women's experience shows that simply achieving greater economic equality is not enough. Discrimination based on sex and race continued even in the post-war decades when, economically, Britain was more equal than ever before. Having a few extra women at the top of the ladder has not offered much to most other females, and often involves those tokenistic figures at the top in a great deal of emotional and practical work as they act as ambassadors for 'diversity' or as mentors to other women.

For women to flourish, we need to redistribute political power. This will help men as well. Revitalising democratic institutions like trade unions and local government will allow people at the grass roots to make decisions about their communities and workplaces. But women's voices will only be heard if feminist groups play a full role in policymaking. Because the status quo has rarely benefited them, women have been more imaginative than men in their visions of a different, better society. They have emphasised creativity, social welfare and education. We have seen how influential some feminists, such as Ellen Wilkinson, were in creating and implementing transformative social policies over the past century.

Policymakers should distrust research that ignores or marginalises women – as much social mobility research does – and provide them with far greater opportunities to participate in planning a more equal society.

Choose life not work

Much of this book has focused on work, because this is where most people climbed or fell down the ladder. But there is no reason why we should organise life around work. Many economists and politicians warn that our ageing population and increasing automation in our workplaces will cause rising unemployment and poverty.[15] But history shows there is nothing inevitable about this. The debate about the impact that technology will have on our lives is nothing new – back in the 1930s Henry Durant published *The Problem of Leisure*, about how best to educate people for the huge swathes of free time that new production techniques would offer everyone.[16] By the 1970s, many educators, journalists and politicians from across the political spectrum accepted that the 'age of universal leisure' was approaching.[17]

Following three decades of a fairly robust welfare state and near-full employment, many commentators in the 1970s assumed that most people would be able to benefit from automation. They knew that they were living in one of the richest countries in the world, which was at that point becoming a more equal place. They remind us that automation could bring great rewards. It is up to us to harness technology for our needs, while considering the needs of the planet on which all of our lives depend.

*

The programme of change set out here may sound too ambitious. But we've seen that transformation can occur, sometimes with extraordinary rapidity. In 1940 few people would have dreamed that they'd have free healthcare, secondary schools for all, university grants and a political commitment to full employment within a decade. It took confidence to vote for this in 1945, and hard work to deliver it. Politicians, local-government planners, engineers, nurses, teachers, welfare workers, hospital cleaners and school caretakers all made it happen. If Labour could erect an unprecedentedly ambitious welfare state at the end of a crippling world war, then the fifth richest nation of the early twenty-first century can initiate the kind of reform proposed here – as leading economists agree.[18]

But having the will to enact change is crucial. In this history, transformation was always initiated and implemented by people outside Parliament as well as within it. Our power to act in new ways has grown, thanks to the Internet, more education, and because we can learn from the mistakes and achievements of the past. The activists of the 1970s established grass-roots initiatives and used networks of activists and trade unionists to find allies and share good practice. They used strikes and lobbying to make politicians listen to them. Some of their legacies – including law centres – survive today. While they are weaker today, trade unions still exist, while new campaigning and research organisations committed to furthering equality have emerged. Just as in the past many people found it more effective to focus on a single issue, albeit connected to a wider vision of the future – whether by fighting for women's rights, working-class education, or workers' bargaining power – so there are ways of doing so today.

In the past, movements for change were internationalist in outlook, inspiration and alliances. In the era of Brexit, the UK has, perhaps understandably, become more parochial. But the solutions to some of our problems may be found in other societies. Britain is one of the most unequal countries in the world.

There is much work to do if we are to succeed, and many obstacles that weren't faced by earlier generations of reformers. But we have something they don't. Back in 1945, the architects of the welfare state, those who voted for it and the millions whose work ensured it flourished had no knowledge of whether they would succeed. We know that they did. They created a society that was more equal, and showed this did not lead to economic disaster but instead to improvements in everyone's living standards. Their investment in caring for others, their representation of ordinary people in the arts and culture, their innovations in science, academia and beyond, shattered the myth peddled that state welfare made people idle. And those who had claimed only a few people were capable of benefiting from an advanced education have been proven wrong by every generation since the Second World War.

Back in 1945, no one knew this would happen. But we now know that it did, and using that knowledge we can do even better as we respond to the Covid-19 crisis and its aftermath. People voted for Brexit because they wanted more control over their lives and their communities. Many looked back to a past of imperial glory and hierarchy that, in reality, offered few benefits to the majority. But they were also invoking a time when trade unions were stronger, local government more powerful, and the welfare state something to be proud of. We can and should build on that story.

We certainly have the talent. Those who got a chance to shine in the past did so. Their ideas, energy and skills smashed preconceptions about what people of their class or sex or race were capable of, and showed the world that they were worth more than life on the lowest rung. The tenacity of the dream of climbing the social ladder points to one of the tragedies of the last century: the enduring horror of poverty. But it also points to another survivor: hope.

ACKNOWLEDGEMENTS

This book owes its existence to too many people to mention here by name, and I hope they know how much I appreciate their advice, ideas and support. Particular thanks are due to Jim Hinks, Laura Paterson, Andrea Thomson and Eve Worth for research assistance; the staff at the Bodleian Libraries, Oxford; the trustees and staff of the Mass Observation Archive and The Keep, Brighton; the archivists of Lloyds Bank plc and Manchester High School for Girls; Lynette Cawthra and the rest of the staff and volunteers at the Working Class Movement Library; Carol Dyhouse, Steph Lawler, Stephen Machin, Diane Reay and Mike Savage. I'm grateful to my colleagues at St Hilda's College, Oxford, and Oxford University History Faculty for their support, especially Mike Newell, Senia Paseta, Ruth Percy and Hannah Smith. The Oxford University John Fell Fund generously supported my research.

The book could not have been written without those people who kindly agreed to be interviewed, and those who responded to the Mass Observation 2016 directive on social mobility. It was a pleasure and a privilege to learn from them.

My terrific agent, Rachel Calder, brought compassion and incisive criticism to the project from start to finish. Becky Hardie's belief in the book and her astute editorial skills were invaluable. She and the rest of the team at Chatto turned the manuscript into a book with skill, enthusiasm and imagination. Huge thanks to all of them.

Andy Davies requires a book of acknowledgements all to himself for his advice, enthusiasm and support, which were unstinting from the heady days of planning the project to the despatch of proofs during the Covid-19 pandemic. I hope he will settle for love, gratitude and a reading for Course You Can Malcolm at FC United of Manchester.

Snakes and Ladders is dedicated to Sheila Forbes who asked the question that prompted me to write it, and who has tirelessly supported women in their careers and beyond.

LIST OF ILLUSTRATIONS

Plate Section I

Plate Section II

1. Labour Party election poster, 1945 (© People's History Museum / National Labour History Archive)
2. Aneurin Bevan, the founder of the NHS, is toured around the Park Hospital, Davyhulme, Lancashire, 1947 (© Richard Splash / Alamy Stock Photo)
3. Trainee teachers at Wynyard Hall in County Durham (© Irene (Georgeson) Simpson as seen in her article 'Lessons in Education 1: Wynyard College': https://www.craxford-family.co.uk/themeblue/ness16irene1.php)
4. Winchester College pupils, 1952 (© Popperfoto / Contributor)
5. Social scientists including Michael Young, Phyllis Willmott, Peter Willmott and Richard Titmuss, 1958 (Churchill Archives Centre, WLMT 1/13 © Estate of Phyllis Willmott)
6. Female clerical workers, 1948 (© picturethepast.org.uk / Nottingham Local Studies Library)
7. A Bradford Bangladeshi family, c. 1960 (© Bradford Museums and Galleries)
8. Harold Wilson meets the Beatles, 1964 (© Hulton Deutsch / Contributor)
9. Teacher and pupils at Clissold Comprehensive School, 1973 (© Bill Cross / Associated Newspapers / Shutterstock)
10. Ruth Hirst with fellow Ruskin College students, 1969 (© Ruth Todd)
11. Members of the Association of Scientific, Technical and Management Staff at the TUC International Women's Year Rally, London, 1975 (© TUC Library Collections at London Metropolitan University)
12. Schoolgirls in Coventry learning to use computers, 1987 (© Hulton Deutsch / Contributor)
13. Labour Party general election leaflet, 1987 (© the People's History Museum/National Labour History Archive)
14. Conservative Party election poster, 1979 (reproduced by permission of the Conservative Party Archive Trust)
15. The Patel family outside their corner shop in London, 2004 (© Richard Splash / Alamy Stock Photo)
16. Inequality in London in the 2000s (© Jack Taylor / Stringer)
17. Protestors who were part of the campaign that prevented Essex County Council from closing a third of the county's libraries (© Save Our Libraries Essex)

Every effort has been made by the publishers to trace the holders of copyright. Any inadvertent omissions of acknowledgement or permission can be rectified in future editions.

NOTE ON SOURCES

The social mobility statistics in this book are derived from numerous studies that use different methodologies but broadly agree about the general patterns of social mobility. John H. Goldthorpe first devised the class schema now used by many social mobility researchers, and Goldthorpe, Catriona Llewellyn and Clive Payne, *Social Mobility and Class Structure in Modern Britain*, Oxford University Press, 1980 was my starting point. Most subsequent research follows Goldthorpe in using occupation as the major determinant of a person's social position, including Erzsebet Bukodi et al., 'The mobility problem in Britain: new findings from the analysis of birth cohort data', *British Journal of Sociology*, vol. 66, no. 1, 2015, pp. 93–117; and Anthony Heath and Clive Payne, 'Social Mobility', in Albert H. Halsey, ed., with Josephine Webb, *Twentieth-Century British Social Trends*, Macmillan, 2000. Most of the people whose experiences appear in this book also understood occupation as the major determinant of their social status, if not of their social class. As I explain in the introduction, often people distinguished status from class.

Paul Lambert, Kenneth Prandy and Wendy Bottero's, 'By Slow Degrees: Two Centuries of Social Reproduction and Mobility in Britain', *Sociological Research Online*, vol. 12, no. 1, 2007, pp. 1–26, is helpful because unusually, it includes women as well as men. These researchers prioritise occupation in their coding of people's social class, but they also consider family networks that extend further than the parent–child relationship which is focused on by most other researchers. Their twentieth-century sample is relatively small, and so is only used here where other studies bear out their conclusions, or where the personal testimonies in this book support their findings on women. The statistics on women offered in this book are taken from Heath and Lambert et al when dealing with generations up to the Breakthrough Generation. Statistics on women in later generations are generally taken from Bukodi et al and from Blanden and Machin.

As economists, Jo Blanden and Stephen Machin use income, rather than occupation, to assess social mobility in late twentieth and early twenty-first century Britain; see their *Recent changes in intergenerational mobility in Britain: Report for Sutton Trust*, Sutton Trust, 2007. This resonates with the two youngest generations to appear in this book (those born between 1972 and 1999), who grew up and began work during the period Blanden and Machin cover. As the nature of many occupations changed, they focused more on wealth and consumption as means to measure, and achieve, social mobility. In the final chapters of the book that discuss these generations, I draw primarily on Blanden and Machin's statistics. However, while these studies are all invaluable, the statistics offered in this book should be taken as a guide to developments, rather than as absolutes. For reasons discussed in the introduction, women's mobility in particular is hard to measure. This book argues that social mobility cannot be understood entirely or even primarily as a set of statistics, not least because class relations change over time in ways that defy consistent measurements across generations. It is an experience, defined by relationships between people in specific times and places, and inflected by aspirations and expectations.

Many of the personal testimonies used in this book come from respondents to a Mass Observation directive on social mobility which I designed in 2016. All directives issued by Mass Observation since 1981 can be accessed online at http://www.massobs.org.uk/mass-observation-project-directives. Responses can be consulted by permission of the archivists at The Keep in Brighton. Each respondent has a unique reference number so they can be tracked through different directives.

Mass Observation's writers range in age from their teens to their nineties, and live across Britain. About 68 per cent of them are women. About one-third are or were employed in manual or routine clerical jobs, and two-thirds in administrative, associate professional or professional jobs. Mass Observers therefore aren't socially representative of Britain as a whole, but many of them are upwardly mobile.[1]

I've also used interviews conducted by me or researchers I've employed. To avoid cluttering the text with notes, I give details below of those interviewees who are quoted in the book (all transcripts are in my possession). I have also drawn on many archived, published and unpublished personal testimonies which are listed in the notes.

Interviewees

Helen Abeda, interviewed by Andrea Thomson
Ian Beesley, interviewed by the author
Richard Campbell, interviewed by Andrea Thomson
Sue Cohen, interviewed by Laura Paterson
June Hannam, interviewed by Jim Hinks
Dee Johnson, interviewed by Andrea Thomson
Don Milligan, interviewed by Jim Hinks
Lyn O'Reilly, interviewed by Jim Hinks
Wendy Pettifor, interviewed by the author
Darren Prior, interviewed by the author
Paul Salveson, interviewed by Jim Hinks
Anthea Samson, interviewed by Laura Paterson
Ruth Todd (née Hirst), interviewed by the author
Alan Watkins, interviewed by Hilary Young

I've given pseudonyms to many of the interviewees and to all the respondents to Mass Observation directives.[2] In the past, when I've written books about working-class history, I've found that most people are very happy to be identified by name. This has not been the case here. The upwardly mobile were particularly wary of being named. Some have been obliged to conceal their background from employers, neighbours or friends. Those who are critical of current policy on social mobility, or their own employers' attitudes towards social mobility, are often wary of expressing their views openly. This also helps explain why many people, including some in public life, refused (often reluctantly) to speak to me. I hope they feel this book explains why social mobility has involved, and continues to involve, pain and concealment – even for many of its apparent success stories.

NOTES

Introduction

1 See the Note on Sources at the end of this book for more information on the social mobility statistics used throughout this book.
2 This point is developed further in Mike Savage et al., *Social Class in the 21st Century*, Penguin, 2015, pp. 33–6.
3 See the Note on Sources at the end of the book for more information.
4 For more details of Mass Observation's origins and the writers themselves see Mike Savage, *Identities and Social Change in Britain since 1940: The politics of method*, Oxford University Press, 2010. For more on Mass Observation's founders see 'History of Mass Observation', http://www.massobs.org.uk/about/history-of-mo, and Tom Jeffrey, 'Mass Observation: A short history', http://www.massobs.org.uk/occasional-papers, both consulted 15 August 2019.
5 For a review of comparative studies and the pitfalls in using them see Albert Simkus, 'Comparative Stratification and Mobility', *International Journal of Comparative Sociology*, vol. 22, no. 1, 1981. On European social mobility see Andrew Miles and David Vincent, eds., *Building European Society: Occupational change and social mobility in Europe 1840–1940*, Manchester University Press, 1993. Information on recent global trends in social mobility is available from The Equality Trust, 'Equality Trust Research Digest: Social Mobility', 2012, https://www.equalitytrust.org.uk/sites/default/files/research-digest-social-mobility-final.pdf, consulted 12 January 2019; see also Richard Wilkinson and Kate Pickett, *The Inner Level. How more equal societies reduce stress, restore sanity and improve everyone's well-being*, Penguin, 2018, pp. 176–8.
6 Wilkinson and Pickett, pp. 195–8.

Chapter One: The Fight for Opportunity

1 Samuel Smiles, *Self-Help; with illustrations of character and conduct*, London, 1859, accessed online at Project Gutenberg, https://www.gutenberg.org/ebooks/935, pp. 1, 4.

2 Andrew Miles, *Social Mobility in Nineteenth and Early Twentieth-Century England*, Macmillan, 1999.

3 Guy Routh, *Occupations of the People of Great Britain 1801–1981*, Macmillan, 1987, pp. 10–16. All subsequent information on demography and occupations is taken either from Routh or from the decennial censuses of England and Wales (occupation and population tables) and of Scotland (occupation and population tables).

4 Ibid.

5 Quoted in Jonathan Rose, *The Intellectual life of the British Working Classes*, Yale University Press, 2010, p. 216.

6 Mike Savage and Andrew Miles, *The Remaking of the British Working Class, 1840–1940*, Routledge, 1994, pp. 28–9.

7 Quoted in Derek Gilliard, 'Education in England: A history', chapter 6, http://www.educationengland.org.uk/history/chapter06.html.

8 Quoted in ibid.

9 Sidney Webb, 'The Workers' Political Programme', Fabian Society, 1891, p. 9.

10 Quoted in Jane Martin, 'Mary Bridges and Education Reform, 1890–1920', *Women's History Review*, vol. 13, no. 3, 2004, p. 475. See also Jane Martin, *Making Socialists: Mary Bridges Adams and the fight for knowledge and power, 1855–1939*, Manchester University Press, 2010.

11 Rose, chapter 5.

12 Quoted in Alan Bullock, *The Life and Times of Ernest Bevin*, vol. 1, Heinemann, 1960, p. 10.

13 William John Edwards, *From the Valley I Came*, Angus & Robertson, 1956, p. 139.

14 Jack Braddock and Jessie Braddock, *The Braddocks*, Macdonald, 1963, pp. 7–8.

15 Ibid., p. 10.

16 Edwards, p. 139.

17 Albert Mansbridge, *An Adventure in Working Class Education: Being the story of the Workers' Education Association, 1903–1915*, Longmans, Green & Co., 1920, p. 28.

18 Quoted in D. J. Booth, 'Albert Mansbridge's Formative Years: A Reappraisal', *Journal of Educational Administration and History*, vol. 6, no. 2, 1974, pp. 10–17.

19 The details of Mansbridge's life given here are drawn from Mansbridge, *An Adventure in Working Class Education*, and from Mark Smith, 'Toynbee Hall, adult education and association', http://infed.org/mobi/toynbee-hall-adult-education-and-association-2/, consulted 18 February 2018.

20 Mansbridge, p. 31.
21 Workers' Educational Association, *Tutorial Classes*, WEA, c.1920, p. 1.
22 Ibid.
23 An Old Student, 'Looking Backwards', *Rewley House Papers*, February 1929, p. 70.
24 Anon., 'The History of the Tunstall II Tutorial Class: 1913–14', *Rewley House Papers*, March 1935, pp. 346–7.
25 Edward Palmer Thompson, 'William Morris: a lecture to the William Morris Society', 1959, https://www.marxists.org/archive/thompson-ep/1959/william-morris.htm, consulted 8 January 2020.
26 Valerie Quinney, 'Workers' Education: A Confrontation at Ruskin College', *American Journal of Education*, vol. 92, no. 1, 1983, pp. 52–78.
27 Plebs League, *The Burning Question of Education: Being an account of Ruskin College dispute, its causes and consequences*, Plebs League, c.1909, p. 8.
28 Jack Lawson, *A Man's Life*, Hodder & Stoughton, 1932, p. 96.
29 Edwards, p. 122.
30 Lawson, p. 106.
31 Lawson, p. 105.
32 Quoted in Anon., 'History of the Tunstall II Tutorial Class', pp. 346–7.
33 Edwards, pp. 104, 128.
34 Roger Lewis, *Leaders and Teachers: Adult education and the challenge of labour in South Wales, 1906–1940*, University of Wales Press, 1993, p. 34.
35 Tom Mann, *The Way to Win*, Barrier Daily Truth Press, 1909; see also Tom Mann, *Tom Mann's Memoirs*, The Labour Publishing Company, 1923.
36 Eric Taplin, *Near to Revolution: The Liverpool General Strike of 1911*, Bluecoat, 1994.
37 Alison Oram, *Women teachers in state schools in England and Wales 1900–1939*, PhD thesis, London School of Economics, 1996, p. 351.
38 Ellen Wilkinson, 'Ellen Wilkinson', in the Countess of Oxford and Asquith, ed., *Myself When Young by Famous Women of Today*, Muller, 1938, p. 406.
39 Information on England and Wales is from the censuses of 1901 and 1911. All information on Scottish education and comparisons with other countries is taken from Robert David Anderson, *Education and Opportunity in Victorian Scotland: Schools & Universities*, Edinburgh University Press, Edinburgh, 1989, and Robert David Anderson, *Education and the Scottish People, 1750–1918*, Clarendon Press, 1995, especially chapter 9.
40 Wilkinson, 'Ellen Wlkinson', in the Countess of Oxford and Asquith, ed., pp. 406–7.
41 Gilliard, chapter 7, http://www.educationengland.org.uk/history/chapter07.html, consulted 9 November 2016.
42 Wilkinson, 'Ellen Wilkinson', in the Countess of Oxford and Asquith, ed., p. 406.

43 Ibid.
44 Ibid., p. 410.
45 Ibid.
46 Jose Harris, *Private Lives, Public Spirit: Britain 1870–1914*, Penguin, 1994, pp. 238–9.
47 Quoted in Clair Glynis Roberts, 'Lesbian Identities – a comparison of two sets of female friends in the early twentieth century', PhD thesis, University of Hull, 2003, https://hydra.hull.ac.uk/assets/hull:11507a/content, p. 83. See also Tierl Thompson, *Dear Girl: The diaries and letters of two working women (1897–1917)*, Women's Press, 1997.
48 Quoted in Rose, p. 217. On the influence of Isadora Duncan on British feminists, see Lucy Delap, *The Feminist Avant-Garde*, Cambridge University Press, 2007, pp. 40–41.
49 'A caste system in schooling is a bad thing', *Manchester Guardian*, 20 March 1911.
50 On middle-class students see William Whyte, *Redbrick: a social and architectural history of Britain's civic universities*, Oxford University Press, 2015, pp. 145, 205–6. About 1 per cent of university students were the children of manual workers: see Hartmut Kaelble, *Social Mobility in the 19th and 20th Centuries. Europe and America in Comparative Perspective*, Berg, 1983, pp. 67–8; Kaelble differentiates between 'artisans' and 'workers' but the addition of artisans would mean an increase of less than 1 per cent in this figure.
51 Workers' Educational Association, *The Choice Before the Nation. Some Amendments to the Education Bill*, WEA, 1918, pp. 6–7, 26.
52 John Whitehouse, House of Commons Debate, 18 July 1916, cc. 869–984, Hansard, cc. 968–9.
53 Workers' Educational Association, *The Choice Before the Nation*, p. 28.
54 Quoted in *Yorkshire Herald*, 8 March 1915, and reprinted in Workers' Educational Association, *Child Labour and Education: During the war and after*, WEA, 1915, p. 15.
55 Col. Meysey Thompson, Board of Education: Class IV., House of Commons Debates, 18 July 1916, *Hansard*, vol. 84, cc. 933–4. Meysey Thompson was a Liberal Unionist MP. The Liberal Unionists had merged with the Conservative Party in 1912 and he went on to stand as a Conservative candidate in the 1918 general election.
56 Workers' Educational Association, *The Choice Before the Nation*, pp. 10, 13.
57 Lindsay Paterson, 'The Significance of the Education (Scotland) Act, 1918', *Scottish Affairs*, vol. 27, no. 4, 2018, pp. 401–24; The Consultative Committee on Secondary Education with special reference to grammar schools and technical high schools, *Report*, HMSO, 1938, p. 88.
58 Lawson, p. 71.
59 G. F. Brown, 'Working Class Adult Education', in A. H. Thornton and M. D. Stephens, eds., *The University in its Region: The extramural contribution*, University of Nottingham, 1977, p. 53.
60 Ibid.

61 Ibid.

62 Lawson, p. 65.

63 Braddocks, pp. 86, 89.

64 Jose Harris, 'Labour's social and political thought', in Duncan Tanner, Pat Thane and Nick Tiratsoo, eds., *Labour's First Century*, Cambridge University Press, 2000, pp. 13, 14.

65 Marjory Todd, *Snakes and Ladders: an autobiography*, Longmans, 1960, p. 109.

66 Jennie Lee, *My Life with Nye*, Cape, 1980, pp. 47 and 59.

67 On the labour movement's and the Labour Party's relationship with the state, see Ralph Miliband, *Parliamentary Socialism: A study in the politics of Labour*, Allen & Unwin, 1961, and Harris, 'Labour's social and political thought', pp. 12–29.

68 Sheila Fitzpatrick, 'The Russian Revolution and Social Mobility', *Politics and Society*, vol. 13, no. 2, 1984.

Chapter Two: White Collars

1 Quoted in Jonathan Rose, *The Intellectual Life of the British Working Classes*, Yale University Press, 2010, p. 402.

2 Gregory Anderson, 'The Social Economy of Late-Victorian Clerks', in Geoffrey Crossick, ed., *The Lower Middle Class in Britain*, Croom Helm, 1977, p. 113.

3 Guy Routh, *Occupations of the People of Great Britain 1801–1981*, Macmillan, 1987, pp. 20–4.

4 Sir Stafford Northcote and Sir Charles Trevelyan, *Report on the Organisation of the Permanent Civil Service*, HMSO, 1854, pp. 4, 7.

5 Mike Savage, *Gender and Bureaucracy*, Blackwell, 1992, p. 42; Katherine Stovel, Mike Savage and Peter Bearman, 'Ascription into Achievement: Models of Career Systems at Lloyds Bank, 1890–1970', *American Journal of Sociology*, vol. 2, no. 2, 1996.

6 Quoted in Lee Holcombe, *Victorian Ladies at Work: Middle-class Working Women in England and Wales, 1850–1914*, David & Charles, 1973, p. 166.

7 Unless otherwise specified, all information on John Gray's personal life and family is taken from the censuses of Scotland for 1871, 1881, 1891, 1901 and 1911, and birth, marriage and death certificates, all consulted via Scotland's People: https://www.scotlandspeople.gov.uk.

8 This and all further information that follows about the Bank of Scotland is taken from Bank of Scotland, Staff Report Books, 1893–1908, 1/270A/ 7–8; Bank of Scotland, Branch Salaries, 1896–1937, GB 1830BOS/8/2/1/2/ 15–20, Lloyds Banking Group plc Archive, Edinburgh.

9 Andrew Miles, *Social Mobility in Nineteenth and Early Twentieth-Century England*, Macmillan, 1999, and Andrew Miles, 'How open was late nineteenth-century British society? Social mobility and equality of opportunity, 1839–1914', in Andrew Miles and David Vincent, eds., *Building*

European Society: Occupational change and social mobility in Europe, 1840–1940, Manchester University Press, 1993; Jason Long, 'The surprising social mobility of Victorian Britain', *European Review of Economic History*, vol. 17, no. 1, 2013, p. 10.

10 Stovel, Savage and Bearman; Anderson, 'The Social Economy of Late-Victorian Clerks', pp. 358–399 in Crossick, ed., p. 113.

11 All information on Scottish education and comparisons with other countries is taken from Robert David Anderson, *Education and Opportunity in Victorian Scotland: Schools & Universities*, Edinburgh University Press, Edinburgh, 1989 and Robert David Anderson, *Education and the Scottish People, 1750–1918*, Clarendon Press, 1995, especially chapter 9.

12 T.C. Smout, *A Century of the Scottish People 1830–1950*, Collins, 1986, pp. 209–30.

13 Interview with Frank Benson, transcript held at Trevor Lummis and Paul Thompson, Family Life and Work Experience Before 1918, 1870–1973, UK Data Service, SN:2000.

14 The Censuses of Scotland for 1871, 1881, 1891 show various young relatives living with the Grays.

15 Interview with Robert Ferguson, transcript held at Trevor Lummis and Paul Thompson, Family Life and Work Experience Before 1918, 1870–1973, UK Data Service, SN:2000.

16 For example, *Review of the Incorporated Association of Headmasters*, February 1908. Also see Jerry White, *London in the Nineteenth Century: 'A human awful wonder of God'*, Jonathan Cape, 2007, pp. 170–1.

17 Miles, 'How open was late nineteenth-century British society? Social mobility and equality of opportunity, 1839–1914', in Miles and Vincent, eds., p. 22, and Dudley Baines and Paul Johnson, 'In search of the "traditional" working class: Social mobility and occupational continuity in interwar London', *Economic History Review*, vol. 52, no. 4, 1999, p. 704.

18 Interview with Robert Ferguson, transcript held at Trevor Lummis and Paul Thompson, Family Life and Work Experience Before 1918, 1870–1973, UK Data Service, SN:2000.

19 Interview with James Luke, transcript held at Trevor Lummis and Paul Thompson, Family Life and Work Experience Before 1918, 1870–1973, UK Data Service, SN:2000.

20 Quoted in Anderson, *Education and Opportunity in Victorian Scotland*, p. 225.

21 Charles Booth, *Life and Labour of the People of London*, 2nd series: Industry, vol. 3, 1903, p. 274.

22 Quoted in Stovel, Savage and Bearman, p. 363.

23 Anderson, 'The Social Economy of Late-Victorian Clerks', in Crossick, ed., p. 114; Stovel, Savage and Bearman, p. 364.

24 Booth, p. 274.

25 Stovel, Savage and Bearman, p. 363.

26 Interview with Caradog Ludwig, transcript held at Trevor Lummis and Paul Thompson, Family Life and Work Experience Before 1918, 1870–1973, UK Data Service, SN:2000.

27 George Gissing, *The Diary of a Nobody*, J.W. Arrowsmith, 1892; this comic novel was initially serialised in *Punch* in 1888–9.

28 Anwyn Moyle with John F. McDonald, *Her Ladyship's Girl: A Maid's Life in London*, Simon & Schuster, 2014, p. 121. For more on domestic servants and their skills see Selina Todd, *The People: The rise and fall of the working class 1910–2010*, John Murray, 2014, chapter 1.

29 Interview with Caradog Ludwig, transcript held at Trevor Lummis and Paul Thompson, Family Life and Work Experience Before 1918, 1870–1973, UK Data Service, SN:2000.

30 For other examples of upwardly mobile men who behaved in this way see Carolyn Steedman, *The radical soldier's tale: John Pearman, 1819–1908*, Routledge, 1988, and Rose, chapters 1 and 2.

31 Victor Sawdon Pritchett, *A Cab at the Door*, Slightly Foxed, 2013, p. 161.

32 Richard Church, *Over the Bridge: An Essay in Autobiography*, Heinemann, 1955, pp. 220–1.

33 James McBey, *The Early Life of James McBey*, Canongate, 1993, pp. 86–92.

34 Herbert Morrison, *Herbert Morrison: An Autobiography*, Odhams Press, 1960, p. 42.

35 Various editions of *Town Talk* quoted in A. J. Hammerton, 'Pooterism or Partnership? Marriage and Masculine Identity in the Lower Middle Class, 1870–1920', *Journal of British Studies*, vol. 38, no. 3, 1999, p. 298.

36 Mike Savage et al., *Property, Bureaucracy and Culture: Middle-class formation in contemporary Britain*, Routledge, 1992, pp. 51–3.

37 On this pattern in insurance firms see Timothy Alborn, 'Quill-Driving: British Life-Insurance Clerks and Occupational Mobility, 1800–1914', *Business History Review*, vol. 81, no. 1, 2008, p. 48.

38 Guy Routh, *Occupations and Pay in Great Britain 1906–1979*, Macmillan, 1980, p. 104.

39 Booth, p. 275.

40 Interview with James Luke, transcript held at Trevor Lummis and Paul Thompson, Family Life and Work Experience Before 1918, 1870–1973, UK Data Service, SN:2000.

41 McBey, pp. 50, 95–6.

42 Booth, p. 276.

43 Interview with Alan Rees, transcript held at Trevor Lummis and Paul Thompson, Family Life and Work Experience Before 1918, 1870–1973, UK Data Service, SN:2000.

44 Quoted in Michael Heller, 'London Clerical Workers 1880–1914: The search for stability', PhD thesis, University College London, 2003, p. 317.

45 Ibid., pp. 316–18.

46 'Neurasthenia', *Lancet*, 30 April 1904, p. 1220; Francis Creed, 'Life Events and Appendicectomy', *Lancet*, 27 June 1981, pp. 1381–85.

47 Heller, pp. 111–12.
48 Pritchett, p. 161.
49 McBey, p. 61.
50 Thomas Stearns Eliot, 'The Waste Land', Poetry Foundation, https://www. poetryfoundation.org/poems/47311/the-waste-land. *The Waste Land* was first published in 1922.
51 There are very few studies of this because social mobility research has focused on occupation and income. Here I have drawn on an early pioneering study by Jerzy Berent, 'Social Mobility and Marriage', in David Glass, ed., *Social Mobility in Britain*, Routledge & Kegan Paul, 1954, chapter 12, and Ursula Benz and Colin Mills, 'Social Class Origin and Assortative Mating in Britain, 1949–2010', *Sociology*, vol. 52, no. 6, pp. 1217–36.
52 On clerks' desire to marry other clerks see Diana Gittins, *Fair Sex: Family Size and Structure, 1900–39*, Hutchinson, 1982, pp. 80–6.
53 Stovel, Savage and Bearman, p. 363.
54 Alan McKinlay, 'Banking, Bureaucracy and the Career: the Curious Case of Mr Notman', *Business History*, vol. 55, no. 3, 2013, pp. 431–47.
55 Ibid.
56 John H. Goldthorpe, Catriona Llewellyn and Clive Payne, *Social Mobility and Class Structure in Modern Britain*, Oxford University Press, 1980, chapter 8.
57 Gissing, pp. 18, 22.
58 Mass Observation Archive: Replies to June 1939 Directive on Class, DR 1016.
59 Ibid.
60 Gareth Stedman Jones, *Languages of Class: Studies in English Working Class History, 1832–1982*, Cambridge University Press, 1983, p. 187. For a terrific critique of such commentators, including Geoffrey Mortimer, *The Blight of Respectability*, London University Press, 1897, and Thomas William H. Crosland, *The Suburbans*, John Long, 1905, see Michelle Johansen, 'The Public Librarian in Modern London (1890–1914): The case of Charles Goss at the Bishopsgate Institute', PhD thesis, University of East London, 2006, pp. 11–14; and Michelle Johansen, '"The Supposed Paradise of Pen and Ink": Self-education and social mobility in the London Public Library (1880–1930)', *Cultural and Social History*, published online 5 February 2019, https://www.tandfonline.com/doi/full/10.1080/14780038.2019.1574047, consulted 28 March 2019.
61 Simon Gunn, 'Class, Identity and the Urban: The middle class in England c.1790–1950', *Urban History*, vol. 31, no. 1, 2004, p. 41.
62 Eleanor Gordon and Gwyneth Nair, *Public Lives: Women, family and society in Victorian Britain*, Yale University Press, 2004, pp. 15–22.
63 Gittins, pp. 89–93; Simon Szreter and Kate Fisher, *Sex before the Sexual Revolution: Intimate life in England 1918–1963*, Cambridge University Press, 2010, pp. 193–4.
64 Mass Observation Archive: Replies to June 1939 Directive on Class, DR 1061.

65 James Hinton, 'Nella Last, née Lord', *Oxford Dictionary of National Biography*, https://ezproxy-prd.bodleian.ox.ac.uk:2095/10.1093/ref:odnb/73539; Nella Last, Richard Board and Suzie Fleming, *Nella Last's War: the diaries of Housewife, 49*, Profile 2006; Nella Last, Patricia Malcolmson and Robert Malcolmson, *Nella Last's Peace: the post-war diaries of Housewife, 49*, Profile, 2008.

66 'The Life of the New Poor', *Daily Mail*, 17 October 1919, p. 6. See also 'The New Poor', *Daily Mail*, 24 October 1919, p. 5, and 'Plight of the New Poor', *Daily Telegraph*, 24 December 1919, p. 12.

67 Workers' Educational Association, *Education for Trade Unionists – a call to action*, WEA, c.1929, p. 1; William Emrys Williams and Archie Edward Heath, *Learn and Live: The consumer's view of adult education*, Methuen, 1936, pp. 19–22.

68 Stovel, Savage and Bearman, pp. 358–99.

69 Quoted in Raphael Samuel, *Theatres of Memory: past and present in contemporary culture*, Verso, 2012, p. 206.

Chapter Three: Crashing Down the Ladder

1 Barry Eichengreen, 'Unemployment in interwar Britain', papers for the Institute for Research on Labor and Employment, University of California Berkeley, 1988. Further unemployment statistics and information are taken from this source unless otherwise specified.

2 Arthur Lyon Bowley and Margaret H. Hogg, *Has Poverty Diminished?*, P. S. King and Son, 1925, pp. 19-23.

3 Quoted in Julia Lafferty, 'The Spanish Flu Pandemic 1918-1919', The Hackney Society, 12 April 2020, http://www.hackneysociety.org/page/the_spanish_flu_pandemic_191819, consulted 22 July 2020. See also Robert Hume, '"Far too little, too late": what happened when Spanish Flu hit Britain a century ago?', *BBC History Magazine*, January 2018, https://www.historyextra.com/period/first-world-war/spanish-flu-britain-how-many-died-quarantine-corona-virus-deaths-pandemic/, consulted 22 July 2020.

4 Harold Perkin, *The Rise of Professional Society in England since 1880*, Routledge, 1989), pp. 78–101.

5 William Whyte, *Redbrick: a social and architectural history of Britain's civic universities*, Oxford University Press, 2015, pp. 180–2.

6 Albert H. Halsey, 'Schools', in Albert H. Halsey, ed., *British Social Trends since 1900: A guide to the changing social structure of Britain*, Macmillan, 1988, pp. 163–4.

7 Gill Sutherland, 'Education' in F.M.L. Thompson, ed., *The Cambridge Social History of Britain 1750–1950. Volume 3: Social Agencies and Institutions*, Cambridge University Press, 1990, p. 167; Harold Perkin, 'The Pattern of Social Transformation in England', in K. H. Jarausch, ed., *The Transformation of Higher Learning 1860–1930: Expansion, diversification,*

social opening and professionalisation in England, Germany, Russia, and the United States, University of Chicago Press, 1983, p. 209.

8   'Unemployed Ex-Soldiers', *Manchester Guardian*, 2 October 1920, p. 9.

9   'Pin Money women. None Employed by the Manchester Corporation', *Manchester Guardian*, 27 October 1920, p. 7.

10   Tameside Local Studies Library, Manchester Studies collection, tape 28, interview with Mrs E. Cleary.

11   Anon., 'A Skilled Wire Drawer', in Hugh Lancelot Beales and Richard Stanton Lambert, eds., *Memoirs of the Unemployed*, Victor Gollancz, 1934, p. 181. Arthur Rigg is a pseudonym.

12   For an excellent account of the trade unions in this period see Mary Davis, 'The Union Makes Us Strong: TUC History Online', http://www.unionhistory.info/timeline/1918_1939.php, consulted 18 October 2019. On the challenge that unemployment posed to the craft unions see also Alastair J. Reid, *United We Stand: a history of Britain's trade unions*, Penguin, 2005, pp. 294–303.

13   Anon., in Beales and Lambert, eds., p. 180.

14   William Temple and the Pilgrim Trust, *Men Without Work: A report made to the Pilgrim Trust*, Cambridge University Press, 1938, p. 21.

15   Ibid., p. 92.

16   Charles Webster, 'Healthy or Hungry Thirties?', *History Workshop Journal*, vol. 13, no. 1, 1982, pp. 110–29.

17   Hubert Llewellyn Smith, *The New Survey of London Life and Labour*, vol. 3, P. S. King and Son Ltd, 1932, pp. 78–96; David Caradog Jones, *The Social Survey of Merseyside*, vol. 1, Liverpool University Press, 1934, pp. 156–60; Percy Ford, *Work and Wealth in a Modern Port: Southampton*, Allen & Unwin, 1934, pp. 114–16; Benjamin Seebohm Rowntree, *Poverty and Progress: A second social survey of York*, Longman, 1941, pp. 30–1; Herbert Tout, *The Standard of Living in Bristol*, Arrowsmith, 1938, p. 21.

18   On unemployment relief see John Stevenson and Chris Cook, *The Slump: Britain in the Great Depression*, Longman, 2010, pp. 77–80.

19   Quoted in John Field, *Learning through Labour: Training, unemployment and the state 1890–1939*, University of Leeds Studies in Continuing Education, 1992, p. 64.

20   Walter Brierley, 'Frustration and Bitterness – a Colliery Banksman', in Beales and Lambert, eds., p. 90.

21   John Brierley, *The Road from the Means Test: A son remembers his Derbyshire novelist father and his own time in khaki*, Swift, 1996, p. 28.

22   Mike Savage et al., *Property, Bureaucracy and Culture: Middle-class formation in contemporary Britain*, Routledge, 1992, p. 48.

23   Ibid., pp. 47–8.

24   Paulo Di Martino, 'Legal institutions, social norms and entrepreneurship in Britain (c.1890–c.1939)', *Economic History Review*, vol. 65, no. 1, 2012, pp. 120–43. It is impossible to fully identify how many individual bankrupts owned businesses, but Di Martino points out that the proportion of

aristocrats and professionals declared bankrupt declined during these years, while the proportion of small shopkeepers, proprietors of small businesses, manual and clerical workers increased.

25 Selina Todd, 'Digitisation of R. Brown's Orientation to Work and Industrial Behaviour of Shipbuilding Workers 1968–1969; Manual Workers' Questionnaires', UK Data Service, SN: 6586, CL01.

26 Llewellyn Smith, vol. 3, pp. 78–96; Caradog Jones, vol. 1, pp. 156–60; Ford, pp. 114–16; Rowntree, pp. 30–1 and Tout, p. 21. See Andrew Davies, *Leisure, gender and poverty: Working-class culture in Salford and Manchester, 1900–1939*, Open University Press, 1992, pp. 14–29 for a discussion of measurements of poverty. While some of these surveys recorded lower levels than 20 per cent, using Rowntree's measurements – probably the most accurate of any of the interwar surveys – suggests at least 20 per cent experienced poverty.

27 Tout, pp. 25–6.

28 Edward Wight Bakke, *The Unemployed Man. A social study*, Nisbet, 1933, p. 164.

29 Rowntree, pp. 27, 158–9; Selina Todd, *Young women, work, and family in England, 1918–1950*, Oxford University Press, 2005, chapter 2.

30 Peter Scott, *Triumph of the South: A regional economic history of early twentieth century Britain*, Ashgate, 2007, pp. 203–28.

31 Mike Savage, 'Trade unionism, sex segregation and the state: Women's employment in "new industries" in interwar Britain', *Social History*, 1988, vol. 13, no. 2.

32 Ibid.

33 Arthur McIvor, *A History of Work in Britain 1880–1950*, Palgrave, 2001, p. 55.

34 Manchester Juvenile Employment Bureaux, *Advice to Boys and Girls about to Leave School*, Manchester Juvenile Employment Bureaux, c.1933, p. 1.

35 William Temple and the Pilgrim Trust, p. 21; Judy Giles, *Women, Identity and Private Life in England, 1900–50*, Macmillan, 1995, pp. 31–63.

36 Guy Routh, *Occupations of the People of Great Britain 1801–1981*, Macmillan, 1987, pp. 20–1.

37 Frances Widdowson, *Going Up into the Next Class*, Hutchinson and the Women's Research and Resources Centre, 1983, p. 26. The history of women's education in the nineteenth and early twentieth centuries that follows is drawn from Widdowson and from Peter Cunningham and Philip Gardner, *Becoming Teachers: texts and testimonies, 1907–1950*, Woburn Press, 2004.

38 Carol Dyhouse, 'Going to University in England between the Wars: access and funding', *History of Education*, vol. 31, no. 1, 2002, pp. 1–14.

39 Ibid., p. 2.

40 Jean Floud, 'The Educational Experience of the Adult Population of England and Wales as at July 1949', in D. V. Glass, ed., *Social Mobility in Britain*, Routledge, 1954, p. 107.

41 Carol Dyhouse, 'Women Students and the London Medical Schools, 1914–39: The Anatomy of a Masculine Culture', *Gender and History*, vol. 10, no. 1, 1998, pp. 110–32.

42 Alison Oram, *Women Teachers and Feminist Politics, 1900–1939*, Manchester University Press, 1996, p. 26.

43 For an account of women's struggle to enter the interwar professions see Pat Thane, 'Afterword: challenging women in the British professions', *Women's History Review*, 2019, advance access, pp. 6–10.

44 Dolly Smith Wilson, 'Fighting the "damnable triumph" of feminism: battles between teachers' unions in interwar Britain', *Gender and Education*, 2007, vol. 19, no. 6, p. 670.

45 Mary Birkinshaw, *The Successful Teacher: an occupational analysis based on an enquiry conducted among women teachers in secondary schools*, Hogarth Press, 1935, pp. 67–8.

46 Ibid., p. 73.

47 Ibid., p. 34.

48 On the importance of the Sex Disqualification (Removal) Act in this regard see Mari Takayanagi, '"Sacred Year or Broken Reed": The Sex Disqualification (Removal) Act 1919', *Women's History Review*, vol. 29, no. 4, 2020, pp. 563–82.

49 Birkinshaw, p. 35.

50 'Students in British universities', *Nature*, no. 160, 20 December 1947, p. 861; Carol Dyhouse, *Students: A Gendered History*, Routledge, 2006, pp. 98–9.

51 Brian Abel Smith, *A History of the Nursing Profession*, Heinemann, 1960, p.153.

52 Ibid., p. 36.

53 Quoted in Ibid., p. 135.

54 E. A. McLaughlin from the recollections of Mrs F. E. Creswell, *Autobiography of Nurse Knowles: the experiences of a nurse in training in Liverpool, 1928–31*, Minerva Press, 1997, p. 12.

55 Ray Strachey, *Our Freedom and its Results*, Hogarth Press, 1936, p. 149.

56 Edith Hall, *Canary Girls and Stockpots*, WEA Luton Branch, 1977, p. 40.

57 Brian Abel Smith, *A History of the Nursing Profession*, Heinemann, 1960, p. 282; E. A. McLaughlin from the recollections of Mrs F. E. Creswell, *Autobiography of Nurse Knowles: the experiences of a nurse in training in Liverpool, 1928–31*, Minerva Press, 1997, p. 13.

58 Quoted in James Nott, *Going to the Palais: a social and cultural history of dancing and dance in Britain, 1918–1960*, Oxford University Press, 2015, p. 35.

59 Quoted in ibid., p. 41.

60 Joan L. Harley, 'Report of an enquiry into the occupations, further education and leisure interests of a number of girl wage-earners from elementary and central schools in the Manchester district, with special reference to the influence of school training on their use of leisure', M. Ed. Dissertation, University of Manchester, 1937, p. 41.

61   Harold L. Smith, 'The Womanpower Problem in Britain During the Second World War', *Historical Journal*, vol. 27, no. 4, 1984, p. 926.

62   Vera Brittain, *Women's Work in Modern England*, Douglas, 1928, p. 58.

63   Kate Murphy, *Behind the Wireless: a history of early women at the BBC*, Macmillan, 2016, p. 160. The following discussion of the BBC draws on this rich and excellent history for context.

64   Mass Observation Archive: Replies to June 1939 Directive on Class, Directive Respondent (DR) 1086.

65   Mass Observation Archive: Replies to June 1939 Directive on Class, and July 1939 Directive on Clothes.

66   Mass Observation Archive: Replies to June 1939 Directive on Class, DR 1086.

67   Savage et al, pp. 143–9.

68   Mass Observation Archive: Replies to June 1939 Directive on Class, DR 1086.

69   'Love on the Dole', *Times Literary Supplement*, 29 June 1933.

70   John Brierley, p. 28.

71   Ibid., p. 85.

Chapter Four: The Technocrats

1   Ross McKibbin, *Parties and People: England 1914–1951*, Oxford University Press, 2010, chapter 2; Alison Light, *Forever England: femininity, literature and conservatism between the wars*, Routledge, 1991.

2   See for example 'Ancestral Lands for Sale', *Daily Express*, 29 September 1920, p. 4.

3   'Scholarship Boys', *Daily Telegraph*, 18 November 1925, p. 10.

4   Diana Athill, *Life Class: The selected memoirs of Diana Athill*, Granta, 2010, pp. 160–1.

5   Herbert Morrison, *Herbert Morrison: An Autobiography*, Odhams Press, 1960, p. 144.

6   Quoted in Paul Foot, 'Portrait of an Appalling Man', *International Socialism*, February 1974, p. 27.

7   Morrison, p. 173.

8   For more on Mass Observation's founders see 'History of Mass Observation', http://www.massobs.org.uk/about/history-of-mo and Tom Jeffrey, 'Mass Observation: A short history', http://www.massobs.org.uk/occasional-papers, both consulted 15 August 2019.

9   For more details of Mass Observation's origins and the writers themselves, and for an excellent account of their commitment to a technocratic identity that has greatly influenced my own interpretation of these testimonies see Mike Savage, *Identities and Social Change in Britain since 1940: The politics of method*, Oxford University Press, 2010.

10   Mass Observation Archive: Replies to June 1939 Directive on Class, DR 1130.

11 Where possible when discussing Mass Observers I also give their mother's current or former occupation. Most Mass Observers did not mention this, which demonstrates the importance of their father's job in shaping their own social status.

12 Mass Observation Archive: Replies to June 1939 Directive on Class, DR 1130.

13 Mass Observation Archive: Replies to June 1939 Directive on Class, DR 1108.

14 George Ernest May and the Committee on National Expenditure, *Report*, 1931, HMSO, p. 191.

15 Ruth Durant, *Watling: A Survey of Social Life on a New Housing Estate*, P. S. King and Son Ltd, 1939, pp. 67–8.

16 Ibid., p. 178.

17 David Parker, '"This gift from the gods"? Hertfordshire and the 1936 Education Act', *History of Education*, June 1996, vol. 25, no. 2, pp. 165–80, 178.

18 Brian Simon, *The Politics of Educational Reform*, Lawrence and Wishart, 1974, p. 252.

19 William Emrys Williams and Archie Edward Heath, *Learn and Live: The consumer's view of adult education*, Methuen, 1936, p. 179.

20 Mass Observation Archive: Replies to June 1939 Directive on Class, DR 1018.

21 Mass Observation Archive: Replies to June 1939 Directive on Class, DR 1108.

22 Mass Observation Archive: Replies to June 1939 Directive on Class, DR 1016.

23 Carol Dyhouse, 'Family Patterns of Social Mobility through Higher Education in England in the 1930s', *Journal of Social History*, vol. 34, no. 4, 2001, pp. 817–42.

24 Mass Observation Archive: Replies to June 1939 Directive on Class, DR 1021.

25 National Union of Students quoted in Sarah Barnes, 'England's Civic Universities and the Triumph of the Oxbridge Ideal', *History of Education Quarterly*, vol. 36, no. 3, 1996, p. 279. See also William Whyte, *Redbrick: a social and architectural history of Britain's civic universities*, Oxford University Press, 2015, pp. 206–8.

26 Mass Observation Archive: Replies to June 1939 Directive on Class, DR 1021.

27 Peter Mandler, 'The Two Cultures', *Twentieth Century British History*, vol. 26, no. 3, 2010, p. 404.

28 Mass Observation Archive: Replies to June 1939 Directive on Class, DR 1108.

29 Mass Observation Archive: Replies to June 1939 Directive on Class, DR 1021.

30 Mass Observation Archive: Replies to June 1939 Directive on Class, DR 1018.

31 Mass Observation Archive: Replies to June 1939 Directive on Class, DR 1108.
32 Ibid. and Mass Observation Archive: Replies to June 1939 Directive on Class, DR 1130.
33 Mass Observation Archive: Replies to June 1939 Directive on Class, DR 1130.
34 Mass Observation Archive: Replies to June 1939 Directive on Class, DR 1108.
35 Mass Observation Archive: Replies to June 1939 Directive on Class, DR 1018.
36 See for example Mass Observation Archive: Replies to June 1939 Directive on Class, DR 1270.
37 Mass Observation Archive: Replies to June 1939 Directive on Class, DR 1108.
38 Mass Observation Archive: Replies to June 1939 Directive on Class, DR 1021.
39 Mass Observation Archive: Replies to June 1939 Directive on Class, DR 1018.
40 Durant p. 60.
41 Alfred Adler, *What Life Should Mean to You*, Allen & Unwin, 1931, reproduced in Heinz and Rowena Ansbacher. eds., *The Individual Psychology of Alfred Adler*, Harper and Row, 1956, chapter 4, section 3.
42 Mass Observation Archive: Replies to June 1939 Directive on Class, DR 1130.
43 Mass Observation Archive: Replies to June 1939 Directive on Class, DR 1108.
44 Williams and Heath, pp. 11–14.
45 Mass Observation Archive: Replies to June 1939 Directive on Class, DR 1130.
46 Ibid.

Chapter Five: The Meritocratic War

1 Quoted in Labour Party, *The War and the Workers*, Labour Party, 1940, p. 12.
2 Geoffrey Field, *Blood, Sweat and Toil: Remaking the British working class, 1939–1945*, Oxford University Press, 2011, pp. 29–30.
3 Mass Observation Archive: Replies to Spring 2016 Directive on Social Mobility, S2083.
4 Alex Turner, 'Memories of a World War Two evacuee', http://www.bbc.co.uk/history/ww2peopleswar/stories/72/a2740772.shtml, consulted 1 September 2018.
5 Albert H. Halsey, *No Discouragement: An autobiography*, Macmillan, 1996, pp. 30–1.
6 Mass Observation Archive: FR 886, 'Civilian Attitudes to the Navy', September 1941, p. 2.

7   The National Archives, WO 163/161, 'Army Morale and Efficiency By a Private in the Black Watch', December 1942, p. 2.

8   C. B. Otley, 'The Educational Background of British Army Officers', *Sociology*, vol. 7, no. 2, 1973.

9   Imperial War Museum (IWM), Documents 7938, Private Papers of Captain J. C. Banks, MS of untitled memoirs, p. 3.

10   Halsey, *No Discouragement*, pp. 31, 32. See also Paul Brickhill, *Reach for the Sky*, Cassell, 2002, p. 172.

11   Mass Observation Archive: FR 832, Eleventh Weekly Report, August 1941, p. 8.

12   Henry Michael Denne Parker, *Manpower: A study of wartime policy and administration*, HMSO, 1957, pp. 324–5.

13   The National Archives, HW 64/73, Recruitment to Bletchley, Memo A.D. (A), 8 April 1943.

14   Quoted in Field, p. 89.

15   Ibid., p. 100.

16   Ian S. Gazeley, 'The levelling of pay in Britain during the Second World War', *European Review of Economic History*, 2006, vol. 10, no. 2, pp. 175–204.

17   Mass Observation Archive: FR 839, 'Manchester Industrial Atmosphere', August 1941, p. 2.

18   Ibid., p. 1.

19   Phyllis Willmott, *A Green Girl*, Peter Owen, 1983, p. 109.

20   Phyllis Willmott, *Coming of Age in Wartime*, Peter Owen, 1988, p. 21.

21   Ibid., p. 85.

22   *Woman's Own*, 3 April 1942, p. 8.

23   Tom Harrisson, ed., *War Factory: A Report by Mass Observation*, Gollancz, 1943, p. 31.

24   Quoted in Harold L. Smith, *Britain in the Second World War: A social history*, Manchester University Press, 1996, p. 44. See also Mass Observation (for the Advertising Service Guild), *People in Production: An Enquiry into British War Production*, Penguin, 1942, pp. 112–32.

25   Mass Observation, *People in Production*, pp. 23–5, 187–201.

26   Parker, pp. 324–5.

27   David Edgerton, *Warfare State: Britain 1920–1970*, Cambridge University Press, 2006, p. 217.

28   Parker, p. 330.

29   The National Archives, PREM 4/8/7, Sixteenth Report from the Select Committee on National Expenditure on Organisation and Control of the Civil Service', October 1942, p. 10.

30   Roger Victor Clements, *Managers: A study of their careers in industry*, Allen & Unwin, 1958, p. 154.

31   John Scott Fulton, Alfred H. Halsey and Ivor Crewe, *The Civil Service*, HM Treasury, vol. 3, part 1, 1969, pp. 36, 52.

32   Mass Observation, *People in Production*, p. 106.

33   The National Archives, LAB 8.584, Women's Consultative Committee, Minutes of Meeting, 8 October 1941, p. 2.

34   Mass Observation, *People in Production*, p. 133.

35   Brian Abel Smith, *A History of the Nursing Profession*, Heinemann, 1960, p. 170.

36   Brenda McBryde, *A Nurse's War*, Chatto & Windus, 1979, pp. 12, 39–40.

37   Abel Smith, p. 283.

38   'Students in British universities', *Nature*, no. 160, 20 December 1947, p. 861; Carol Dyhouse, *Students: A Gendered History*, Routledge, 2006, pp. 98–9.

39   Pat Thane, 'Girton Graduates: Earning and learning, 1920s–1980s', *Women's History Review*, vol. 13, no. 2, 2004, p. 356.

40   The National Archives, HW 64/73, Recruitment to Bletchley, 'Outstanding vacancies', 16 April 1942.

41   Fulton, Halsey and Crewe, pp. 20–3.

42   Ibid.

43   Parker, pp. 420–2; John Leopold, *Human Resources in Organisations*, Pearson Education, 2002, p.5; Angela Woollacott, 'Maternalism, professionalism and welfare supervisors in World War One', *Women's History Review*, 1994, vol. 3, no. 1, pp. 48–9.

44   Mass Observation Archive: FR 722, 'Social Welfare and the Blitzed Towns', June 1941, pp. 1–2, 7–8.

45   Mass Observation Archive: FR 26, 'Women's Organisations in Wartime', February 1940, p. 28.

46   William Utting, 'Cooper, Joan Davies', *Oxford Dictionary of National Biography*, https://ezproxy-prd.bodleian.ox.ac.uk:2095/10.1093/ref:odnb/71955.

47   Interview with Margaret Stacey, held at Paul Thompson, Pioneers of Social Research, 1996–2012, UK Data Service, SN: 6226.

48   Ibid.

49   On unemployment see Angus Calder, *The People's War. Britain 1939–1945*, Granada, 1971, p. 372.

50   Gazeley, pp. 175–204.

51   Mass Observation Archive: FR 737, 'Change in Clothing Habits', June 1941, p. 3.

52   Mass Observation Archive: FR 857, 'Post-war Jobs', September 1941, p. 16.

53   Mass Observation Archive: FR 569, 'Airmen', February 1941, p. 5.

54   The National Archives, WO 32/10464, Training: General, Minute 1A, Common Reception Centres for Basic Training and Selection of Army Class Intake, 1943, p. 1.

55   The National Archives, WO 163/61, War Office morale report, August–October 1942, p. 1.

56   The National Archives, WO 163/161, 'Army Morale and Efficiency By a Private in the Black Watch', December 1942, pp. 1, 3.

57 Edward Smithies, *Aces, Erks and Backroom Boys: Aircrew, Ground Staff and Warplane Builders Remember the Second World War*, Cassell, 2002. Also see Martin Francis, *The Flyer: British culture and the Royal Air Force, 1939–1945*, Oxford University Press, 2008, p. 49.

58 Quoted in Jeremy Crang, *The British Army and the People's War*, Manchester University Press, 2000, p. 9.

59 The National Archives, WO 277/19, Personnel Selection 1939–1945, Colonel B. Ungerson, 'Personnel Selection', p. 52.

60 Jan Pahl and Raymond Pahl, *Managers and their Wives: A study of career and family relationships in the middle class*, Allen Lane, 1971, p. 99.

61 Mass Observation Archive: Replies to Spring 2016 Directive on Social Mobility, S2207.

62 Imperial War Museum, Private Papers of Captain Peter Gorb, 'My Phoney War', unpublished MS, p.7.

63 Crang, p. 37.

64 Mass Observation Archive: FR 757, 'General Picture of WAAF Life', June 1941, p. 1.

65 Willmott, *Coming of Age*, pp. 105, 110.

66 E. M. Hutchinson, 'Williams, Sir William Emrys', *Oxford Dictionary of National Biography*, https://ezproxy-prd.bodleian.ox.ac.uk:4563/10.1093/ref:odnb/31838.

67 Richard Hoggart, *Life and Times*, Chatto & Windus, 1988, p. 60.

68 Halsey, *No Discouragement*, p. 35.

69 Mass Observation Archive: FR 1451, 'Reconstruction', October 1942, pp. 42, xv.

70 Mass Observation Archive: FR 1282, 'Class Consciousness and Class Unconsciousness', May 1942, p. 15.

71 Mass Observation Archive: FR 1451, 'Reconstruction', October 1942, p. 32; see also p. 41.

72 William Henry Beveridge and the Inter-departmental Committee on Social Insurance and Allied Services, *Social Insurance and Allied Services: Report* (Beveridge Report), HMSO, 1942, https://archive.org/stream/in.ernet.dli.2015.275849/2015.275849.The-Beveridge_djvu.txt, consulted 8 December 2019.

73 Arthur Greenwood, Prohibition of fees in schools maintained by local education authorities and in young people's colleges, House of Commons Debates, 28 March 1944, *Hansard*, vol. 398, cc. 1298.

74 Pat Thane, 'Michael Young and Welfare', *Contemporary British History*, vol. 19, no. 3, 2005, p. 297.

75 Conservative Party manifesto 1945, http://www.conservativemanifesto.com/1945/1945-conservative-manifesto.shtml, consulted 8 March 2020.

76 Labour Party, 'Let Us Face the Future', manifesto, 1945, http://www.labour-party.org.uk/manifestos/1945/1945-labour-manifesto.shtml, consulted 8 March 2020.

77 Ibid.

78 Halsey, *No Discouragement*, p. 35.

Chapter Six: Room at the Top

1 Phyllis Willmott, *Coming of Age in Wartime*, Peter Owen, 1988, p. 153.

2 Mass Observation Archive: FR 2059, 'Do the Factory Girls want to Stay Put or Go Home?', March 1944, pp. 5–6.

3 David Glass, ed., *Social Mobility in Britain*, Routledge & Kegan Paul, 1954, p. 25.

4 Ibid., p. 20.

5 Pat Thane, 'Labour and welfare', in Duncan Tanner, Pat Thane and Nick Tiratsoo, eds., *Labour's First Century*, Cambridge University Press, 2000.

6 Peter Reese, *Homecoming Heroes: An account of the reassimilation of British military personnel in civilian life*, Leo Cooper, 1992, p. 199.

7 Quoted in Pete Grafton, *You, You and You!: The people out of step with World War Two*, Pluto Press, 1981, p. 148. John Stafford is a pseudonym.

8 Quoted in Jane Hubbard, ed., *We Thought it was Heaven Tomorrow*, Yorkshire Art Circus, 1985, pp. 15–16. Eddie Jackson is a pseudonym.

9 Albert H. Halsey, *No Discouragement: An autobiography*, Macmillan, 1996, p. 36.

10 Suzanne Mettler, *Soldiers to Citizens: the GI Bill and the Making of the Greatest Generation*, Oxford University Press, 2005. Thanks to Ruth Percy for bringing this to my attention.

11 Mass Observation Archive: Replies to Spring 2016 Directive on Social Mobility, M5643.

12 Quoted in Barbara J. Smith, *Doors of Opportunity: Bognor Regis Emergency Teacher Training College*, University of Chichester, 2014, p. 74.

13 P. H. J. H. Gosden, *Education in the Second World War: A study in policy and administration*, Methuen, 1976, pp. 123, 130.

14 Ministry of Education, *Challenge and Response: An account of the Emergency Training Scheme for the Training of Teachers*, Pamphlet 17, HMSO, 1950, pp. 161–2.

15 Quoted in Barbara J. Smith, p. 76.

16 Imperial War Museum, 17208, Private Papers of R. W. Pye, MS by Richard Pye, n.d., p. 63.

17 William Taylor, *The Secondary Modern School*, Faber & Faber, 1963, p. 203.

18 Gareth L. Williams et al., *The Academic Labour Market: Economic and social aspects of a profession*, Elsevier Scientific, 1974, p. 30.

19 Imperial War Museum, 17208, Private Papers of R. W. Pye, p. 86.

20 Richard Hoggart, *Life and Times*, Chatto & Windus, 1988, p. 96.

21 Ibid.

22 Raymond Williams, 'An Open Letter to WEA Tutors', 1961, in John McIlroy and Sallie Westwood, eds., *Border Country. Raymond Williams in Adult Education*, National Institute of Adult Continuing Education, 1993, p. 223.

23   John Scott Fulton, Albert H. Halsey and Ivor Crewe, *The Civil Service*, HM Treasury, vol. 3, part I, 1969, p. 35.

24   Gosden, pp. 123–4.

25   Fulton, Halsey and Crewe, p. 36.

26   Kit Russell, 'The Morale of the Social Workers', *Report on the Annual Conference of the Association of Social Workers, 1959*, Association of Social Workers, 1960, pp. 14–15. See also Phyllis Willmott, 'Russell, née Stewart, Katherine Frances', *Oxford Dictionary of National Biography*, https://doi.org/10.1093/ref:odnb/70246.

27   Mark Abrams, 'British Standards of Living', *Current Affairs*, no. 63, September 1947, pp. 12–13.

28   John Burnett, *A Social History of Housing, 1815–1985*, Routledge, 1986, p. 277.

29   Quoted in Claire Langhamer, 'The Meanings of Home in Post-war Britain', *Journal of Contemporary History*, vol. 40, no. 2, 2005, p. 348.

30   Mass Observation Archive: FR 3073, 'Middle Class – Why?', December 1948, pp. 20, 25.

31   Ibid., p. 25; see also pp. 1–2, 20 and 26.

32   Ibid., p. 25.

33   See for example Mass Observation Archive: FR 3075, 'A Report on the Present-Day Cost of Living', January 1949, p. 20; Kathleen Box, 'The Cinema and the Public, 1946', *The Social Survey*, NS106, HMSO, 1946, pp. 1–2., and Ferdynand Zweig, *Labour, Life and Poverty*, Gollancz, 1948, pp. 48–9.

34   Nella Last, Patricia and Robert Malcolmson, *Nella Last in the 1950s*, Profile, 2010, p. 72.

35   Charles Vereker and John Barron Mays, *Urban Redevelopment and Social Change*, Liverpool University Press, 1961, p. 87.

36   Archive of the University of Liverpool, Household Surveys of Liverpool, Crown Street Survey 1955–1956, D416/a/4.

37   Quoted in 'Mr Morrison Warns His Party', *Manchester Guardian*, 29 May 1947, p. 5.

38   Quoted in 'Easing the Middle Class Burden', *Daily Mirror*, 24 January 1950, p. 2.

39   Ben Jackson, 'Citizen and Subject: Clement Attlee's Socialism', *History Workshop* Journal, vol. 86, no. 1, 2018, pp. 291–8, and Pat Thane, 'Michael Young and Welfare', *Contemporary British History*, vol. 19, no. 3, 2005, pp. 293–8.

40   Abrams, p. 13.

41   Pat Thane, 'Family Life and "Normality" in Post-war Britain', in R. Bessel and D. Schumann, eds., *Life After Death. Approaches to a Cultural and Social History During the 1940s and 1950s*, Cambridge University Press, 2003, p. 194.

42   Mass Observation Archive: FR 3109, 'Some Comments on the National Health Survey', April 1949, p. 6.

43 Mass Observation Archive: Replies to March 1947 Directive on Clement Attlee, and June 1947 Directive on the Conservative Party, DR 1108.
44 Quoted in Kevin Theakston, 'The oratory of Winston Churchill', in Richard Hayton and Andrew S. Crines, eds., *Conservative Orators: from Baldwin to Cameron*, Manchester University Press, 2015, p. 40.

Chapter Seven: The Melodrama of Social Mobility

1 Albert H. Halsey, *No Discouragement: An autobiography*, Macmillan, 1996, p. 55.
2 Jean Floud, 'Sociology and Education', *Sociological Review*, vol. 4, no. 1, 1956, p. 60. See also Stephen J. Ball, 'Floud (née McDonald), Jean Esther', *Oxford Dictionary of National Biography*, https://ezproxy-prd.bodleian.ox.ac.uk:2095/10.1093/ref:odnb/106355.
3 Jean Floud, 'Edward Shils (1910-1995)', *Minerva*, vol. 34, no. 1, 1996, p. 85. See also Jean Floud, 'Teaching in the Affluent Society', *British Journal of Sociology*, vol. 13, no. 4, 1962, pp. 299–308.
4 Halsey, *No Discouragement*, p. 50.
5 Ibid., p. 57.
6 Dennis Marsden, 'Sociology Research Worker', in Ronald Goldman, ed., *Breakthrough. Autobiographical Accounts of the Education of Some Socially Disadvantaged Children*, Routledge & Kegan Paul, 1968, p. 122.
7 Brian Jackson and Dennis Marsden, *Education and the Working Class*, Penguin, 1962, p. 16.
8 Mark Abrams, *Teenage Consumer Spending in 1959*, LPE, 1959.
9 Kit Hardwick, *Brian Jackson. Educational innovator and social reformer*, Lutterworth Press, 2003, p. 22.
10 Richard Hoggart, *The Uses of Literacy*, Penguin, 1957, p. 294.
11 Edward Palmer Thompson, 'At the Point of Decay', in Thompson, ed., *Out of Apathy*, Stevens, 1960, p. 4.
12 Anthony Crosland, *The Future of Socialism*, Jonathan Cape, 1956, pp. 73–4.
13 Michael Young, *The Rise of the Meritocracy 1870-2033*, Penguin, 1958, pp. 116, 121–2, 135–6, 189–90.
14 Edward Palmer Thompson, 'The New Left', *New Reasoner*, no. 9, May 1959, p. 15.
15 Hoggart, *The Uses of Literacy*, p. 302.
16 Dai Smith, 'Foreword', in Raymond Williams, *Border Country*, Parthian, 2006, p. ix.
17 Albert H. Halsey and Jean E. Floud, 'English Secondary Schools and the Supply of Labour', in Albert H. Halsey, Jean E. Floud and Charles Arnold Anderson, *Education, Economy and Society*, Free Press, 1961, p. 87. See also Jean E. Floud, *Social Class and Educational Opportunity*, Heinemann, 1956.
18 Jackson and Marsden, pp. 249–51.
19 Raymond Williams, *Culture and Society, 1780–1950*, Penguin, 1961 (first published 1958) p. 317.

20   Jackson and Marsden, pp. 249–51.
21   Gareth L. Williams, *The Academic Labour Market*, Elsevier, 1974, pp. 29–30.
22   Halsey, *No Discouragement*, p. 131.
23   Anthony Crosland quoted in Maurice Kogan, *The Politics of Education. Edward Boyle and Anthony Crosland with Maurice Kogan*, Penguin, 1971, pp. 190–1.
24   Gareth L. Williams, pp. 29–30.
25   Albert H. Halsey and Martin Trow, *The British Academics*, Faber & Faber, 1971, p. 323.
26   Colin Bell, *Middle Class Families: Social and geographic mobility*, Routledge & Kegan Paul, 1968, p. 8.
27   Hoggart, *The Uses of Literacy*, p. 37.
28   Halsey and Floud, 'English Secondary Schools and the Supply of Labour', p. 87; Jackson and Marsden, pp. 30–6, 73.
29   John H. Goldthorpe, Catriona Llewellyn and Clive Payne, *Social Mobility and Class Structure in Modern Britain*, Oxford University Press, 1980, p. 288.
30   Halsey, *No Discouragement*, p. 60.
31   Richard Hoggart, *Life and Times*, Chatto & Windus, 1988, p. 67.
32   Ann Oakley, *Father and daughter: Patriarchy, gender and social science*, Policy Press, 2014, p. 120.
33   Halsey, *No Discouragement*, p. 51.
34   Margaret Stacey, *Tradition and Change: A study of Banbury*, Oxford University Press, 1960.
35   Interview with Margaret Stacey, held at Paul Thompson, Pioneers of Social Research, 1996–2012, UK Data Service, SN: 6226.
36   Ibid.
37   Peter Mandler, 'The Two Cultures', *Twentieth Century British History*, vol. 26, no. 3, 2010, p. 404.
38   Michael Fogarty, Isobel Allen and Patricia Walters, *Women in Top Jobs, 1968–1979*, Heinemann, 1981, pp. 40, 72, 104.
39   Phyllis Willmott, *Coming of Age in Wartime*, Peter Owen, 1988, pp. 143, 169.

Chapter Eight: A Managerial Revolution?

1   Roger Victor Clements, *Managers: A study of their careers in industry*, Allen & Unwin, 1958, p. 157.
2   Richard Parry, 'United Kingdom Public Employment: Patterns of change 1951–1976', *Studies in Public Policy*, Centre for the Study of Public Policy, University of Strathclyde, p. 12.
3   Jan Pahl and Raymond Pahl, *Managers and their Wives: A study of career and family relationships in the middle class*, Allen Lane, 1971, p. 153.
4   Ibid., p. 264.

NOTES

5   Rosemary Stewart, *Management succession: The recruitment, selection and promotion of managers*, Acton Society Trust, 1956, p. 8.
6   Pahl and Pahl, p. 69.
7   Labour Party, *Industry and Society*, Labour Party, 1957; Terence Higgins, *The second managerial revolution*, Conservative Party, 1965; for a critique see 'The Insiders', *Universities and Left Review*, 1958, no. 3.
8   David Glass, ed., *Social Mobility in Britain*, Routledge & Kegan Paul, 1954, p. 20.
9   John H. Goldthorpe et al., *The Affluent Worker in the Class Structure*, Cambridge University Press, 1969.
10 Interview no. 42, Affluent Worker in the Class Structure 1961–1962, Part one – the Luton Study, Box 8, UK Data Archive, SN: 7944.
11 Clements, pp. 68, 81.
12 Mass Observation Archive: Replies to Spring 2016 Directive on Social Mobility, P1009.
13 Clements, p. 69.
14 John F. Wilson and Andrew W. Thomson, *The Making of Modern Management: British management in historical perspective*, Oxford University Press, 2006, p. 119.
15 Stewart, p. 74.
16 Clements, p. 68.
17 Ibid., pp. 73, 81.
18 Ibid., p. 73.
19 Ibid., pp. 73, 81 and Stewart, pp. 55–6.
20 Wilson and Thomson, p. 119; Nick Tiratsoo, '"Cinderellas at the Ball": Production managers in manufacturing, 1945–80', *Contemporary British History*, vol. 13, no. 3, 1999, pp. 105–20.
21 Clements, p. 87.
22 Gareth L. Williams et al., *The Academic Labour Market: Economic and social aspects of a profession*, Elsevier Scientific, 1974, p. 35.
23 Clements, p. 84.
24 Stewart, pp. 55–6.
25 Margaret Stacey, *Tradition and Change: A study of Banbury*, Oxford University Press, 1960, p. 33.
26 Tiratsoo, pp. 105–20.
27 Stewart, p. 74.
28 Colin Bell, *Middle Class Families: Social and geographic mobility*, Routledge & Kegan Paul, 1968, p. 23.
29 Stewart, p. 56; I. C. McGivering et al., *Management in Britain: A general characterization*, University of Liverpool, 1960, pp. 58–62.
30 Stewart, p. 29; Clements, p. 68.
31 Clements, p. 69.
32 Pahl and Pahl, pp. 258–61.
33 Bell, p. 40.
34 McGivering et al., pp. 58–62.

35 Bell, p. 40.
36 Ibid., p. 30.
37 Stewart, p. 63.
38 Guy Routh, *Occupations and Pay in Great Britain 1906–1979*, Macmillan, 1980, p. 156; Ian Gazeley, 'Manual Work and Pay, 1900–1970', in Nicholas F. R. Crafts, Ian Gazeley and Andrew Newell, eds., *Work and Pay in Twentieth Century Britain*, Oxford University Press, 2007, pp. 70–4.
39 Pahl and Pahl, pp. 99, 259.
40 David V. Donnison, 'The Movement of Households in England', *Journal of the Royal Statistical Society*, Series A, 1961, p. 60.
41 Bell, pp. 1–12.
42 Pahl and Pahl, pp. 95–9; quote from p. 99.
43 Bell, p. 23.
44 Ibid., p. 30.
45 Ibid., p. 32.
46 Ibid., p. 39.
47 Ibid., p. 31.
48 Pahl and Pahl, p. 200.
49 Ibid., p. 216.
50 Ibid., p. 193.
51 Mass Observation Archive: Replies to Autumn 2014 Directive on Working Families, J2891.
52 Pahl and Pahl, p. 193.
53 Mass Observation Archive: Replies to Spring 2016 Directive on Social Mobility, P1009.
54 Pahl and Pahl, p. 189.
55 Clements, p. 85.
56 Ibid.
57 Mass Observation Archive: Replies to Spring 2016 Directive on Social Mobility, H1745.
58 Quoted in Bell, p. 94.
59 Ibid., pp. 94–5.
60 Mass Observation Archive: Replies to Spring 2016 Directive on Social Mobility, P1009.
61 Clements, p. 109.
62 Pahl and Pahl, pp. 261–2.
63 Stacey, p. 141.
64 Pahl and Pahl, p. 57.
65 Stacey, p. 172.
66 Mass Observation Archive: Replies to Spring 2016 Directive on Social Mobility, M3412.
67 Clements, p. 69.
68 Pahl and Pahl, p. 106.
69 Interview no. 27, Paul Thompson, Families, Social Mobility and Ageing, UK Data Archive, SN: 4938.

70 Clements, p. 157.
71 Pahl and Pahl, p. 50.
72 Clements, p. 84.
73 Ibid., p. 92, and Pahl and Pahl, p. 99.
74 Bell, p. 23.
75 Pahl and Pahl, p. 216.
76 Ibid., p. 262.
77 Interview with Ray Pahl, held at Paul Thompson, Pioneers of Social Research, 1996–2012, UK Data Archive, SN: 6226.

Chapter Nine: Moving On, But Not Moving Up

1 Kathleen Paul, *Whitewashing Britain: Race and citizenship in the post-war era*, Cornell University Press, 1997, p. 90. See also Ceri Peach et al., 'Immigration and Ethnicity', in Albert H. Halsey, ed., with Josephine Webb, *Twentieth-Century British Social Trends*, Macmillan, 2000, chapter 4.
2 A. J. Hammerton and Al Thomson, *Ten Pound Poms: Australia's invisible migrants*, Manchester University Press, 2005, pp. 65, 214.
3 Reginald Appleyard, *The Ten Pound Immigrants*, Boxtree, 1988, p. 61.
4 Quoted in Linda McDowell, 'Workers, migrants, aliens or citizens? State constructions and discourses of identity among post-war European labour migrants in Britain', *Political Geography*, vol. 22, no. 8, 2003, p. 10.
5 Students and dependants brought the number of European migrants to Britain up to about 475,000 between 1945 and 1951, though many of these stayed for less than three years. Sheila Patterson, *Dark Strangers*, Penguin, 1965, p. 62. On other figures see Paul, p. 90.
6 I don't distinguish between 'migrants' and 'refugees' because the two categories overlap. As this chapter makes clear, migration was encouraged by circumstances beyond the migrant's control, whether political instability, racial discrimination or a lack of economic opportunity at home.
7 Interview with Sue Cohen by Laura Paterson, 2016.
8 Ibid.
9 'Your Opportunity – The Case for the Foreign Maid', *Housewife*, February 1939, p. 5.
10 Quoted in McDowell, 'Workers, migrants, aliens or citizens?', p. 11.
11 Tony Kushner, 'An Alien Occupation – Jewish Refugees and Domestic Service in Britian, 1933–1948', in W. E. Mosse, ed., *Second Chance: Two Generations of German-Speaking Jews in the United Kingdom*, JCB Mohr, 1991, pp. 553–78.
12 Quoted in Linda McDowell, 'Narratives of family, community and waged work: Latvian European Volunteer Worker Women in post-war Britain', *Women's History Review*, vol. 13, no. 1, 2004, p. 35.
13 Quoted in ibid.

14   Interview with Sue Cohen.
15   McDowell, 'Workers, migrants, aliens or citizens?', p. 11.
16   Interview with Sue Cohen.
17   Ibid.
18   Ibid.
19   Quoted in 'Journeys to Cheshire', Cheshire, Halton and Warrington Race and Equality Centre, http://chawrec.org.uk/what-we-do/journeys-to-cheshire/, consulted 23 May 2017.
20   Bradford Local Studies Library, Bradford oral history collection, B34, interview transcript, pp. 18, 26.
21   Ibid.
22   Appleyard, p. 57.
23   Imperial War Museum, Documents 1350, Private Papers of Miss P. Y. Lin, questionnaire no. 7.
24   Appleyard, pp. 56–8; Mark Peel, *Good Times, Hard Times: The past and the future in Elizabeth*, Melbourne University Press, 1995, pp. 108–12; Imperial War Museum, Documents 1350, Private Papers of Miss P. Y. Lin, questionnaire nos. 7, 68, 74, 92.
25   OECD, Population with Tertiary Education, 2015: https://data.oecd.org/eduatt/population-with-tertiary-education.htm, consulted 31 July 2017.
26   T.J. Hatton, 'Emigration from the UK, 1870–1913 and 1950–1998', *European Review of Economic History*, vol. 8, no. 2, 2004, pp. 149–69.
27   Patterson, p. 66.
28   Ibid.
29   'Why 492 West Indians came to Britain', *Manchester Guardian*, 23 June 1948, https://www.theguardian.com/century/1940–1949/Story/0,,105104,00.html, consulted 8 January 2020.
30   Mikkel Rytter, *Family Upheaval: Generation, mobility and relatedness among Pakistani migrants in Denmark*, Berghahn Books, 2013, p. 53.
31   The Birmingham Black Oral History Project, 'Land of Money' transcribed interviews, interview with Carlton Duncan, http://www.bbohp.org.uk/node/21, consulted 22 March 2019.
32   'Why 492 West Indians came to Britain', *Manchester Guardian*, consulted 9 February 2019.
33   The Birmingham Black Oral History Project, 'Land of Money' transcribed interviews, interview with Zahoor Ahmed, http://www.bbohp.org.uk/node/21, consulted 22 March 2019; J. H. Taylor, *The Halfway Generation: A Study of Asian Youths in Newcastle upon Tyne*, NFER Publishing, 1976, pp. 17, 45.
34   Taylor, p. 20.
35   Shaila Srinivasan, *The South Asian Petty Bourgeoisie in Britain: An Oxford case study*, Avebury, 1995, p. 30.
36   I use the term 'black' where referring to experiences of racism, oppression and the challenging of oppression that were shared by different national and/or ethnic groups, while recognising that those differences – like those

of class and sex – are important. In the words of Pragna Patel, one of the founders of Southall Black Sisters: 'the secular term "black" was ... vital in the UK in challenging racism and in forging a common cause between Asian and Afro-Caribbean women . . . For us, it has come to symbolise unity across difference'. Pragna Patel, '50 Years of Women's Liberation in the UK', speech given on 1 February 2020, University College London, https://womansplaceuk.org/2020/02/03/50-years-of-womens-liberation-in-the-uk-pragna-patel/, consulted 8 March 2020.

37 Political and Economic Planning, *Racial Discrimination*, PEP, 1954, p. 8.
38 Ibid., p. 9.
39 The Birmingham Black Oral History Project, 'Land of Money' transcribed interviews, interview with Carlton Duncan, http://www.bbohp.org.uk/node/21, consulted 22 March 2019.
40 The Birmingham Black Oral History Project, 'Land of Money' transcribed interviews, interview with Nurul Hoque, http://www.bbohp.org.uk/node/21, consulted 22 March 2019.
41 Bradford Local Studies Library, Bradford oral history collection, C39, interview transcript, p. 2.
42 Interview with Avtar Singh Jouhl, *International Socialism*, no. 164, 2019.
43 The Birmingham Black Oral History Project, 'Land of Money' transcribed interviews, interview with Avtar Singh Jouhl, http://www.bbohp.org.uk/node/21.
44 Bradford Local Studies Library, Bradford oral history collection, C39, interview transcript, p. 3.
45 Interview with Avtar Singh Jouhl, *International Socialism*.
46 Pnina Werbner, *The Migration Process: Capital, gifts and offerings among British Pakistanis*, Berg, 1990, pp. 50–1.
47 Interview with Avtar Singh Jouhl, *International Socialism*.
48 Ibid.
49 'Immigrant solidarity shown in strike by Indian workers', *Guardian*, 21 December 1965, p. 4.
50 Quoted in Donald Hyslop et al., *Here to Stay: Bradford's South Asian Communities*, City of Bradford Metropolitan Council, c.1994, p. 37.
51 Srinivasan, p. 77.
52 Quoted in Hyslop et al., pp. 23, 27.
53 Quoted in ibid., p. 10.
54 Quoted in ibid., p. 27.
55 John Berger, 'Past Seen from a Possible Future' in Geoff Dyer, ed., *John Berger: Selected Essays*, Bloomsbury, 2001, pp. 238–45.
56 Quoted in Hyslop et al., p. 37.
57 The Birmingham Black Oral History Project, 'Land of Money' transcribed interviews, interview with Carlton Duncan, consulted 22 March 2019.
58 Patterson, p. 66.

Chapter Ten: But Only Some Shall Have Prizes

1 Erzsebet Bukodi et al., 'The mobility problem in Britain: new findings from the analysis of birth cohort data', *British Journal of Sociology*, vol. 66, no. 1, 2015, pp. 93–117. This study demonstrates that those born in the mid-1940s were most likely to experience upward mobility.
2 Guy Routh, *Occupations of the People of Great Britain 1801–1981*, Macmillan, 1987, and censuses of 1951, 1961 and 1971.
3 Mass Observation Archive: FR 1269, 'Post-war Education', May 1942, pp. 1–2, 10.
4 Peter Darvill, *Sir Alec Clegg: A biographical study*, Able, 2000, p. 240.
5 Quoted in ibid.
6 Quoted in Labour Party, *Annual Conference Report 1946*, Labour Party, p. 122.
7 The Consultative Committee on Secondary Education with special reference to grammar schools and technical high schools, *Report*, HMSO, 1938, p. xxxiv.
8 The Committee of the Secondary Schools Examination Council, *Report on Curriculum and Examinations in Secondary Schools*, HMSO, 1943, pp. 17, 37.
9 The National Archives, ED 152/202, Yorkshire: West Riding, letter from A. E. Parsons to Alec Clegg, 25 January 1949, p. 5.
10 Darvill, p. 240.
11 Ministry of Education, *The Nation's Schools: Their plan and purpose*, HMSO, 1945, pp. 15–16.
12 The National Archives, ED 152/125, Northumberland, 'Northumberland development plan', c.1948.
13 The National Archives ED 34/165, Mr A. J. Irvine [Lab, Liverpool Edge Hill] Parliamentary Question, House of Commons, 29 November 1951.
14 Glen O'Hara, *Governing Post-war Britain*, Palgrave, 2012, p. 160.
15 Jean E. Floud, *Social Class and Educational Opportunity*, Heinemann, 1956, pp. 77, 143.
16 'Right School – and right teacher – for the brilliant child', *Manchester Guardian*, 18 October 1949, p. 5.
17 Floud, *Social Class and Educational Opportunity*, pp. 77, 143. For an example of an eleven-plus paper see 'Pens down, no cheating', *Telegraph*, 27 June 2008, https://www.telegraph.co.uk/news/features/3637048/Pens-down-no-cheating-you-may-now-start-your-own-11-plus-exam.html, consulted 1 March 2019.
18 Brian Jackson and Dennis Marsden, *Education and the Working Class*, Penguin, 1962, p. 93.
19 Lorna Sage, *Bad Blood*, Bloomsbury, 2000, pp. 20–1. See also Jacky Brine, 'The everyday classificatory practice of selective schooling: A fifty-year retrospective', *International Studies in Sociology of Education*, vol. 16, no. 1, 2006, p. 39.

20 Ministry of Education, *The Nation's Schools: Their plan and purpose*, HMSO, 1945, p. 26.
21 The National Archives, CSC 5/466, Use of intelligence tests, 'Weighting of Intelligence Tests in Normal Competitions', 1949; 'Cost of intelligence tests used in Executive and Clerical Class Competitions', 1951; 'Effect of practice and coaching on performance in intelligence tests', MS 1952.
22 The National Archives, CSC 5/466, Use of intelligence tests, memo to 'Mr Murray', 8 April 1952.
23 'Education Test Abolished', *The Times*, 20 November 1952, p. 2.
24 Peter Mandler, 'Educating the Nation I: The Schools', *Transactions of the Royal Historical Society*, vol. 24, 2014, pp. 5–28.
25 Jan Pahl and Raymond Pahl, *Managers and their Wives: A study of career and family relationships in the middle class*, Allen Lane, 1971, p. 65.
26 The National Archives, ED 152/130, Oxfordshire, minute from Helen Asquith, 19 March 1955.
27 Gregory Baldi, 'The Politics of Differentiation: Education Reform in Postwar Britain and Germany', PhD thesis, Georgetown University, 2010, pp. 12–16, 187–92.
28 Richard Austen Butler, Baron Butler of Saffron Walden, *The Difficult Art of Autobiography*, Clarendon Press, 1968, p. 132.
29 Mass Observation Archive: FR 1269, 'Post-war Education', May 1942.
30 Donald P. Leinster-Mackay, *The Rise of the English Prep School*, Falmer Press, 1984, pp. 278–9.
31 Ibid.
32 Roy Todd, letter to the author, 14 October 2015.
33 Central Advisory Council for Education (England), *15 to 18*, HMSO, 1959, vol. 2, p. 36.
34 Ibid.
35 Mass Observation Archive: Replies to Spring 2016 Directive on Social Mobility, H1745.
36 Jackson and Marsden, pp. 150, 161.
37 Central Advisory Council for Education, *15 to 18*, vol. 2, p. 36.
38 Ibid., vol. 1, p. 64.
39 Mass Observation Archive: Replies to Spring 2016 Directive on Social Mobility, E743.
40 The National Archives, ED 152/192, Yorkshire: West Riding, Report by HM Inspectors on Cockburn High School, May 1949, p. 3.
41 James William Bruce Douglas, *The Home and the School*, MacGibbon & Kee, 1964, p. 118.
42 Brian Simon, *Intelligence Testing and the Comprehensive School*, Lawrence and Wishart, 1953, p. 21.
43 Mass Observation Archive: Replies to Spring 2016 Directive on Social Mobility, E743.
44 Jackson and Marsden, pp. 110–20.
45 Ibid., pp. 67–70.

46   Mass Observation Archive: Replies to Spring 2016 Directive on Social Mobility, W2322.

47   Albert H. Halsey and Jean E. Floud, 'English Secondary Schools and the Supply of Labour', in Albert H. Halsey, Jean E. Floud and Charles Arnold Anderson, *Education, Economy and Society*, Free Press, 1961, p. 87.

48   Jackson and Marsden, pp. 113, 114, 117.

49   'Lord Bragg: depression at 12 left me frightened every day', *Telegraph*, 5 July 2014, http://www.telegraph.co.uk/culture/culturenews/10948207/Lord-Bragg-Depression-at-12-left-me-frightened-every-day.html, consulted 5 April 2018. For an excellent study of the emotional impact of attending grammar school see Jackson and Marsden, pp. 110–20.

50   Frank Musgrove, *The Migratory Elite*, Heinemann, 1963, p. 126.

51   Central Advisory Council for Education, *15 to 18*, vol. 1, p. 230.

52   Halsey and Floud, 'English Secondary Schools and the Supply of Labour', p. 88.

53   Jackson and Marsden, p. 150.

54   Margaret Forster, *Hidden Lives: A family memoir*, Penguin, 1996, p. 173.

55   Jackson and Marsden, p. 150.

56   Mass Observation Archive: Replies to Spring 2016 Directive on Social Mobility, W2322.

57   Mass Observation Archive: Replies to Spring 2016 Directive on Social Mobility, E743.

58   Central Advisory Council for Education, *15 to 18*, vol. 1, p. 228.

59   Political and Economic Planning, Michael Forgarty et al., *Women and Top Jobs: An interim report*, PEP, 1967, p. 10.

60   Committee on Higher Education, *Higher Education: Report of the Committee appointed by the Prime Minister under the Chairmanship of Lord Robbins* (Robbins Report), HMSO, 1963, pp. 7–8.

61   Ibid.

62   Darvill, p. 239.

63   Ibid.

64   Jackson and Marsden, p. 122.

65   Ibid., p. 250.

66   Interview with Sue Cohen.

67   See Mary Evans, *A Good School. Life at a Girls' Grammar School in the 1950s*, Women's Press, 1991.

68   Ibid. By the 1960s this attitude was changing in some schools, partly because of parental pressure. See Mary Ingham, *Now We Are Thirty*, Methuen, 1982, pp. 83 and 100.

69   Central Advisory Council for Education, *15 to 18*, vol. 1, pp. 227–8.

70   'Students in British universities', *Nature*, no. 160, 20 December 1947, p. 861; Carol Dyhouse, *Students: A Gendered History*, Routledge, 2006, pp. 98–9.

71   Committee on Higher Education, *Higher Education* (Robbins Report), Appendix A, p. 63.

72   Interview with Anthea Samson by Laura Paterson, 2016.

73 Mass Observation Archive: Replies to Spring 2016 Directive on Social Mobility, W2322.

74 Ferdynand Zweig, *The Student in the Age of Anxiety*, Heinemann, 1963, pp. 67–8.

75 Ibid., pp. 21, 29, 81, 150.

76 Penny Darbyshire, 'Where Do English and Welsh Judges Come From?', *Cambridge Law Journal*, vol. 66, no. 2, 2007, pp. 378–9.

77 Committee on Recruitment to the Dental Profession, *Report*, HMSO, 1957, p. 16; British Medical Association, *Recruitment to the Medical Profession*, BMA, 1962, p. 122; John Scott Fulton, Albert H. Halsey and Ivor Crewe, *The Civil Service*, HMSO, vol. 3, part 1, 1969, pp. 20–3.

78 British Medical Association, p. 122.

79 Mass Observation Archive: Replies to Spring 2016 Directive on Social Mobility, W2322.

80 Mass Observation Archive: Replies to Spring 2016 Directive on Social Mobility, D1602.

81 Mass Observation Archive: Replies to Spring 2016 Directive on Social Mobility, S3035.

82 Mass Observation Archive: Replies to Spring 2016 Directive on Social Mobility, B1771.

83 Floud, *Social Class and Educational Opportunity*.

84 Labour Party, *New Britain*, Labour Party, 1964.

85 Albert H. Halsey, 'Further and Higher Education', in Albert H. Halsey, ed., with Josephine Webb, *Twentieth-Century British Social Trends*, Macmillan, 2000, pp. 224, 227.

86 Richard Parry, 'United Kingdom Public Employment: Patterns of change 1951–1976', *Studies in Public Policy*, Centre for the Study of Public Policy, University of Strathclyde, p. 8.

87 Ian Gazeley, 'Manual Work and Pay, 1900–1970', in Nicholas F. R. Crafts, Ian Gazeley and Andrew Newell, eds., *Work and Pay in Twentieth Century Britain*, Oxford University Press, 2007, p. 72.

88 Maurice Kogan, *The Politics of Education. Edward Boyle and Anthony Crosland with Maurice Kogan*, Penguin, 1971, p. 22.

Chapter Eleven: The Ladder Shaken

1 'The Extremists', *Daily Mirror*, 20 January 1971, p. 12.

2 Paul Baker, 'Portrait of a Protest', *New Society*, vol. 12, no. 318, 31 October 1968, pp. 631–4. For the tabloids, see for example 'The inside page', *Daily Mirror*, 1 November 1968, p. 11.

3 'The lessons to be learned', *Daily Mirror*, 1 June 1972, p. 8.

4 Albert H. Halsey, 'Further and Higher Education', in Albert H. Halsey, ed., with Josephine Webb, *Twentieth-Century British Social Trends*, Macmillan, 2000, p. 227, and Paul Bolton, 'Education: historical statistics',

Note SN/SG/4252, House of Commons Library, 2012, https://dera.ioe. ac.uk/22771/1/SN04252.pdf, consulted 13 April 2018, p. 20.

5   Interview with June Hannam by Jim Hinks, 2017.
6   Interview with Don Milligan by Jim Hinks, 2017.
7   Interview with Lyn O'Reilly by Andrea Thomson, 2017.
8   Ruth Todd, 'Ruskin College 1967–1969', *North East History*, vol. 47, no. 1, p. 152.
9   Interview with Lyn O'Reilly.
10 Interview with Don Milligan.
11 Diane Reay, 'Social mobility, a panacea for our times', *British Journal of Sociology of Education*, vol. 34, nos. 5–6, 2013, p. 670.
12 Todd, p. 152.
13 Reay, p. 670.
14 Interview with June Hannam.
15 Reay, p. 671.
16 Todd, p. 152.
17 British Library, Sound Archive, Oral History of British Photography, interview with Andrew Dewdney.
18 Ibid.
19 Interview with Don Milligan.
20 Interview with Lyn O'Reilly.
21 Interview with June Hannam.
22 Conversation with the author, 2015.
23 Interview with June Hannam.
24 Interview with Wendy Pettifor by the author, 2016.
25 Interview with Don Milligan.
26 Interview with Wendy Pettifor.
27 Leslie Woodhead, 'Memories of Granadaland', Granadaland conference at Manchester Metropolitan University, May 2016.
28 Michael Apted quoted in Richard Brooks, 'Seven Ups and Downs', *Observer*, 12 July 1998, review section, p. 2.
29 Tony Warren, *I was Ena Sharples' Father*, Duckworth, 1969, p. 10.
30 Hunter Davies, *The Beatles, Football and Me. A Memoir*, Headline Review, 2006, p. 165.
31 Ibid., p. 95.
32 'The Beatles meet the MP from Beatlepool', *Daily Mirror*, 20 March 1964, p. 16.
33 Interview with Andrew Dewdney.
34 Interview with Paul Salveson by Jim Hinks, 2017.
35 Jo Stanley, 'To Celeb-rate and Not to Be-moan', in Pat Mahony and Christine Zmroczek, eds., *Class Matters: 'Working-class' women's perspectives on social class*, Taylor & Francis, 1997, p. 181.
36 Interview with Don Milligan.
37 Ibid.
38 Todd, pp. 153–4.

39 Interview with Paul Salveson.
40 Reay, p. 672.
41 Interview with June Hannam.
42 Interview with Paul Salveson.
43 Interview with Ian Beesley by the author, 2016.
44 Todd, p. 154.
45 Interview with Don Milligan.
46 Interview with June Hannam.
47 Peter Mandler, 'The Two Cultures Revisited: The Humanities in British Universities since 1945', *Twentieth Century British History*, vol. 26, no. 3, 2015, p. 411.
48 Interview with June Hannam.
49 J. Ritchie et al., *The Employment of Art College Leavers*, SS 448, OPCS, Social Survey Division, 1972, p. 25.
50 Interview with Ian Beesley.
51 Interview with Paul Salveson.
52 Interview with Ian Beesley.
53 Interview with Paul Salveson.
54 Interview with June Hannam.
55 Interview with Paul Salveson.
56 Ritchie et al, p. 23.
57 Todd, p.155, and private information.
58 Reay, p. 672.
59 Interview with Lyn O'Reilly.
60 Interview with Andrew Dewdney.
61 Chris Wrigley, *British Trade Unions, 1945–1995*, Manchester University Press, 1997, p. 30.
62 William Brown, 'Industrial Relations and the Economy', in Roderick Floud and Paul Johnson, eds., *The Cambridge Economic History of Modern Britain,* Cambridge University Press, 2004, p. 403.
63 Leo Panitch, *Social Democracy and Industrial Militancy: The Labour Party, the trade unions, and incomes policy, 1945–1974*, Cambridge University Press, 1976, p. 217.
64 Interview with Lyn O'Reilly.
65 Interview with Wendy Pettifor.
66 Interview with June Hannam.
67 David Adelstein, 'The Roots of the British Crisis', in Alexander Cockburn and Robin Blackburn, eds., *Student Power: Problems, diagnosis, action,* Penguin, 1969, p. 78.
68 Raymond Williams, 'Different sides of the wall', *Guardian*, 26 September 1968.
69 Huw Beynon, *Working for Ford*, Penguin, 1973, pp. 70–1, 191.
70 An excellent account of this economic crisis and its global context is given in Ann Pettifor, *The Production of Money. How to Break the Power of Bankers*, Verso, 2017, pp. 89–92.

71 Interview with June Hannam.
72 Stanley, p. 177.
73 Interview with June Hannam.
74 Interview with Don Milligan.
75 Interview with Paul Salveson.
76 Interview with Don Milligan.
77 Reay, p. 672.
78 Interview with June Hannam.
79 Interview with Lyn O'Reilly.
80 Glen O'Hara, *Governing Post-war Britain*, Palgrave, 2012, p. 164.
81 R. E. A. Mapes, *Geographic mobility among two cohorts of teachers in Reading and Stoke-on-Trent*, SSRC, 1975, pp. 68–71.
82 Interview with June Hannam.
83 Interview with Lyn O'Reilly.
84 Peter Kandler quoted in Helene Curtis and Mimi Sanderson, eds., *The Unsung Sixties: Memoirs of social innovation*, Whiting & Birch, 2004, p. 156.
85 Interview with Wendy Pettifor.
86 Todd, pp. 156–7.
87 Interview with Wendy Pettifor.
88 Interview with Andrew Dewdney.
89 Interview with Ian Beesley.
90 Interview with Andrew Dewdney.
91 Chris Wrigley, *British Trade Unions Since 1933*, Cambridge University Press, 2002, p. 30.
92 Tony Benn, *Arguments for Socialism*, Penguin, 1980.
93 Labour Party, *Let Us Work Together*, manifesto, February 1974, http://www.labour-party.org.uk/manifestos/1974/feb/1974-feb-labour-manifesto.shtml, consulted 6 March 2019.
94 Eve Worth, 'The Welfare State Generation: Life Histories of Women Born in Britain c.1938–1952', DPhil thesis, University of Oxford, 2018, p. 99. See also Eve Worth, 'Women, Education and Social Mobility in Britain during the Long 1970s', *Cultural and Social History*, vol. 16, no. 1, 2019, pp. 67–83.
95 Stanley, p. 176.
96 Labour Party, *Let Us Work Together*.
97 Ian Gazeley, 'Manual Work and Pay, 1900–1970', in Nicholas F. R. Crafts, Ian Gazeley and Andrew Newell, eds., *Work and Pay in Twentieth Century Britain*, Oxford University Press, 2007, p. 72.
98 Interview with Dee Johnson by Andrea Thomson, 2017.
99 Interview with Wendy Pettifor.
100 Interview with Lyn O'Reilly.
101 Interview with June Hannam.
102 Interviews with Don Milligan and Lyn O'Reilly. See also interview with Andrew Dewdney.

103 Reay, pp. 672–3.
104 Interview with Andrew Dewdney.
105 Archive of the University of Liverpool, Household Surveys of Liverpool, Household Surveys of Liverpool Wards, 1979, D719.
106 Interview with Lyn O'Reilly.
107 Gazeley, p. 72.
108 Peter Kandler quoted in Curtis and Sanderson, eds., p. 156.

Chapter Twelve: Money, Money, Money

1 Quoted in 'A bitter touch of class', *Daily Mail*, 10 January 1980, p. 15.
2 'Maggie will sweep Jim out with the tide', *Daily Express*, 8 February 1979, p. 9; 'Good news for anyone who wants that touch of class', *Daily Express*, 8 February 1979, p. 9.
3 'Opinion', *Daily Express*, 10 September 1979, p. 8.
4 Margaret Thatcher interviewed in the *Sun*, 28 February 1983, https://www.margaretthatcher.org/document/105089, consulted 6 February 2019.
5 Ian Gazeley and Andrew Newell, 'Unemployment', in Nicholas F. R. Crafts, Ian Gazeley and Andrew Newell, eds., *Work and Pay in Twentieth Century Britain*, Oxford University Press, 2007, pp. 237–38; Duncan Gallie, 'The Labour Force', in Albert H. Halsey, ed., with Josephine Webb, *Twentieth-Century British Social Trends*, Macmillan, 2000, p. 316.
6 A. B. Atkinson, 'Distribution of Income and Wealth', in Albert Halsey with Webb, pp. 360–6; Richard Wilkinson and Kate Pickett, *The Spirit Level: Why greater equality makes societies stronger*, Penguin, 2010, chapter 12.
7 'A bitter touch of class', *Daily Mail*, 10 January 1980, p. 15.
8 Keith Waterhouse, 'The Cowboy Tendency', *Daily Mirror*, 17 January 1980, p. 11.
9 Chris Rhodes, *Manufacturing: statistics and policy*, House of Commons Briefing Paper, HMSO, 2017, p. 7.
10 Interview with Alan Watkins by Hilary Young, 2008.
11 Ibid.
12 Jane Ritchie, *Thirty Families: Their living standards in unemployment*, HMSO, 1990, p. 22.
13 Gallie, 'The Labour Force', in Halsey, ed., with Webb, pp. 316–17, and for details of women's employment see Jean Martin and Ceridwen Roberts, *Women and Employment A Lifetime Perspective*, HMSO, 1984.
14 Patrick Heady and Malcolm Smyth, *Living Standards during unemployment: A survey of families headed by unemployed people – carried out by Social Survey Division of OPCS on behalf of the Department of Social Security*, HMSO, 1989, vol. 1, p. 36. See also Jonathan Gershuny and Catherine Marsh, 'Unemployment in Work Histories', in Duncan Gallie, Catherine

Marsh and Carolyn Vogler, eds., *Social Change and the Experience of Unemployment*, Oxford University Press, 1994, p. 114.

15 Quoted in Ritchie, *Thirty Families*, p. 39.

16 Quoted in ibid., p. 40.

17 Gallie, 'The Labour Force', in Halsey, ed., with Webb, p. 316.

18 Mass Observation Archive: Replies to Autumn 2014 Directive on Working Families, D2585.

19 Ritchie, p. 8.

20 Interview with Alan Watkins.

21 Ritchie, p. 8.

22 Interview with Alan Watkins.

23 Martin and Roberts, p. 148.

24 Ibid.

25 Margaret Thatcher, speech to Conservative Party Conference, 10 October 1986, https://www.margaretthatcher.org/document/106498, consulted 2 November 2018.

26 Quoted in David Thomas, *Alan Sugar: The Amstrad Story*, Century, 1990, p. 30.

27 Richard Branson, *Losing My Virginity*, Virgin, 1998, p. 485.

28 For more on Branson's career and how successive governments saved him from poor investments or business decisions see Tom Bower, *Branson: Behind the Mask*, Faber & Faber, 2014.

29 Ray Forrest and Alan Murie, 'Accumulating evidence. Housing and family wealth in Britain', in Forrest and Murie, eds., *Housing and Family Wealth. Comparative International Perspectives*, Routledge, 1995, p. 60.

30 Quoted in Forrest and Murie, 'Accumulating evidence. Housing and family wealth in Britain', in Forrest and Murie, eds., *Housing and Family Wealth. Comparative International Perspectives*, Routledge, 1995, p. 60.

31 Alan Holmans, 'Housing', in Halsey, ed., with Webb, pp. 487–9.

32 Selina Todd, *The People: The rise and fall of the working class 1910–2010*, John Murray, 2014, pp. 319–20.

33 Forrest and Murie, 'Accumulating evidence. Housing and family wealth in Britain', in Forrest and Murie, eds., p. 60.

34 Ray Forrest and Alan Murie, *Moving the Housing Market*, Aldershot, 1990, p. 61.

35 Gershuny and Marsh, 'Unemployment in Work Histories', in Gallie, Marsh and Vogler, eds., p. 114.

36 Danny Dorling, *Inequality and the 1%*, Verso, 2015, p. 103.

37 Ibid.

38 Mass Observation Archive: Replies to Spring 2016 Directive on Social Mobility, S5563.

39 Ibid.

40 Mass Observation Archive: Replies to Spring 2016 Directive on Social Mobility, D1602.

41 Mass Observation Archive: Replies to Spring 2016 Directive on Social Mobility, H2639.

42 Mass Observation Archive: Replies to Spring 2016 directive on *Social Mobility*, E743.
43 Ibid.
44 Ibid.
45 Mass Observation Archive: Replies to Spring 2016 Directive on Social Mobility, H2639.
46 Mass Observation Archive: Replies to Spring 2016 Directive on Social Mobility, D1602.
47 The historian Eve Worth has produced a groundbreaking and illuminating study of this group and the observations in this chapter owe a great deal to discussions with her. See Eve Worth, 'The Welfare State Generation: Life Histories of Women Born in Britain *c*.1938–1952', unpublished DPhil, University of Oxford, 2018.

Chapter Thirteen: DIY Society

1 Interview with Darren Prior by the author, 2017.
2 Labour Party, *Let Us Work Together*, manifesto, February 1974, http://www.labour-party.org.uk/manifestos/1974/feb/1974-feb-labour-manifesto.shtml, consulted 6 March 2019.
3 Albert H. Halsey, 'Further and Higher Education', in Albert H. Halsey, ed., with Josephine Webb, *Twentieth-Century British Social Trends*, Macmillan, 2000, p. 239.
4 Labour Party, *Let Us Work Together*.
5 Mass Observation Archive: Replies to Spring 2016 Directive on Social Mobility, S3779.
6 Interview with Darren Prior.
7 Mass Observation Archive: Replies to Spring 2016 Directive on Social Mobility, E5014.
8 Richard Wilkinson and Kate Pickett, *The Inner Level. How more equal societies reduce stress, restore sanity and improve everyone's well-being*, Penguin, 2018, chapter 5.
9 Mass Observation Archive: Replies to Spring 2016 Directive on Social Mobility, E5577.
10 'Tracey Thorn: "Not everything you do is cool"', *Observer*, 27 January 2019, https://www.theguardian.com/music/2019/jan/27/tracey-thorn-another-planet-a-teenager-in-suburbia-interview, consulted 15 July 2019.
11 Tracey Thorn, *Bedsit Disco Queen: How I grew up and tried to be a pop star*, Virago, 2013, p. 31.
12 Mass Observation Archive: Replies to Spring 2016 Directive on Social Mobility, E5577.
13 Mass Observation Archive: Replies to Spring 2016 Directive on Social Mobility, S3779.
14 Mass Observation Archive: Replies to Spring 2016 Directive on Social Mobility, E5014.

15 Halsey, 'Further and Higher Education', in Halsey, ed., with Webb, p. 231.
16 Thorn, *Bedsit Disco Queen*, p. 70.
17 Mass Observation Archive: Replies to Spring 2016 Directive on Higher Education, E5577.
18 Halsey, 'Further and Higher Education', in Halsey, ed., with Webb, p. 230; Judith Smith, 'Mature Learners: A synthesis of research', Higher Education Academy, 2008, https://www.heacademy.ac.uk/system/files/wp_mature_learners_synthesis_on_template_updated_090310.pdf.
19 Interview with Darren Prior.
20 'Elitism in Britain – breakdown by profession', *Guardian*, 28 August 2014, https://www.theguardian.com/news/datablog/2014/aug/28/elitism-in-britain-breakdown-by-profession, consulted 4 June 2017.
21 Linda McDowell, *Capital Culture: Gender at Work in the City of London*, Blackwell, 1997, pp. 50–57.
22 'Elitism in Britain – breakdown by profession', *Guardian*, 28 August 2014.
23 Nick Leeson, *Rogue Trader*, Sphere, 2015, online edition (no page numbers).
24 Ibid.
25 Nicola Horlick, *Can You Have It All?*, Pan, 1998, p. 86.
26 Quoted in Chris Carter and Crawford Spence, 'Being a Successful Professional: An Exploration of Who Makes Partner in the Big Four', *Contemporary Accounting Research*, vol. 31, no. 4, 2014, p. 972; see also Louise Crewe and Annie Wang, 'Gender Inequalities in the City of London Advertising Industry', *Environment and Planning A: Economy and Space*, vol. 50, no. 3, 2018, pp. 671–88.
27 'Can the Asians recivilise our inner cities?', *Daily Mail*, 28 July 1993, p. 8.
28 Yajoun Li and Antony Heath, 'Class Matters: A Study of Minority and Majority Social Mobility in Britain, 1982–2011', *American Journal of Sociology*, vol. 122, no. 1, 2016, pp. 162–200.
29 Julia Chinyere Oparah, *Other Kinds of Dreams: Black women's organisations and the politics of transformation*, Routledge, 1998, p. 155; Helen Connor et al., 'Why the Difference? A Closer Look at Higher Education Minority Ethnic Graduates', Department of Education and Skills, Research Report no. 552, 2004, p. 43.
30 J. H. Taylor, *The Halfway Generation: A Study of Asian Youths in Newcastle upon Tyne*, NFER Publishing, 1976, p. 68. See also Shaila Srinivasan, *The South Asian Petty Bourgeoisie in Britain: An Oxford case study*, Avebury, 1995, p. 115.
31 Aneez Esmail et al., 'Acceptance into medical school and racial discrimination', *British Medical Journal*, vol. 310, no. 6978, 1995, pp. 501–2.
32 Connor et al., p. 103.
33 Carolina V. Zuccotti, 'Do Parents Matter? Revisiting Ethnic Penalties in Occupation among Second Generation Ethnic Minorities in England and Wales', *Sociology*, vol. 49, no. 2, 2015, pp. 229–51.
34 Connor et al., pp. 76, 79.

35 Bradford Local Studies Library, Bradford oral history collection, C6, interview transcript.
36 Ibid.
37 Taylor, p. 69.
38 Srinivasan, p. 114.
39 Ian Gazeley and Andrew Newell, 'Unemployment', in Nicholas F. R. Crafts, Ian Gazeley and Andrew Newell, eds., *Work and Pay in Twentieth Century Britain*, Oxford University Press, 2007, p. 236.
40 Hazel Atashroo, 'Beyond The "Campaign for a Popular Culture": Community Art, Activism and Cultural Democracy in 1980s London', PhD thesis, University of Southampton, 2017, p. 47.
41 Geoff Dyer, *Working the Room: essays and reviews 1999–2010*, Canongate, 2015, pp. 323 and 336.
42 Morrissey, *Autobiography*, Penguin, 2013, p. 140.
43 Interview with Darren Prior.
44 Thorn, p. 31.
45 Ibid., p. 30.
46 'Fearsome trader moved markets but feared maths', *Guardian*, 28 February 1995, https://static.guim.co.uk/sys-images/Guardian/Pix/pictures/2015/2/15/1424024214589/The-Guardian-28-February–001.jpg, consulted 7 June 2017.
47 Margaret Thatcher, speech to the 1922 Committee, 19 July 1984, https://www.margaretthatcher.org/document/105563, and interview with *Woman's Own*, 23 September 1987, https://www.margaretthatcher.org/document/106689, both consulted 8 August 2018.
48 Mass Observation Archive: Replies to Spring 2016 Directive on Social Mobility, E5577.
49 Interview with Darren Prior.
50 Mass Observation Archive: Replies to Spring 2016 Directive on Social Mobility, E5577.
51 Leeson (no page numbers).
52 Mass Observation Archive: Replies to Spring 2016 Directive on Social Mobility, E5577.
53 'Head teachers and governors face lessons in management', *Financial Times*, 7 September 1988, p. 10. Quote from Kenneth Baker is also from this article.
54 Interview with Darren Prior.
55 Carter and Spence, pp. 972–5.

Chapter Fourteen: Rat Race

1 Mass Observation Archive: Replies to Spring 2016 Directive on Social Mobility, A4127.
2 Ibid.

3   Mass Observation Archive: Replies to Spring 2016 Directive on Social Mobility, A3623.

4   Mass Observation Archive: Replies to Spring 2008 Directive on Your Lifeline, A4127.

5   Ibid.

6   Claire Wallace, *For Richer, For Poorer: Growing Up In and Out of Work*, Tavistock Publications, 1987; Jonathan Gershuny and Catherine Marsh, 'Unemployment in Work Histories' in Duncan Gallie, Catherine Marsh and Carolyn Vogler, eds., *Social Change and the Experience of Unemployment*, Oxford University Press, 1994.

7   For other examples see Wallace, *For Richer, For Poorer*.

8   Mass Observation Archive: Replies to Spring 2008 Directive on Your Lifeline, A4127.

9   Mass Observation Archive: Replies to Spring 2016 Directive on Social Mobility, A3623.

10   Ibid.

11   Shirley Dex and Andrew McCullough, *Flexible Employment: The future of Britain's jobs*, Blackwell, 1999, p. 31.

12   Mass Observation Archive: Replies to Spring 2016 Directive on Social Mobility, A3623.

13   Mass Observation Archive: Replies to Summer 2012 Directive on School, Teachers and Siblings, E743.

14   Local Government Training Board, *Survey of Manpower and Qualifications within Social Service Departments in England and Wales and Social Work Departments in Scotland*, HMSO, pp. 6–7.

15   Elisabeth Al-Khalifa, 'Management by Halves', in Frances Widdowson and Hilary De Lyon, eds., *Women Teachers: issues and experiences*, Open University, 1989, p. 87.

16   Interview with June Hannam by Jim Hinks.

17   Mass Observation Archive: Replies to Spring 2016 Directive on Social Mobility, S3035.

18   'Margaret Thatcher interview for the *Sun*, 28 Feb 1983, https://www.margaretthatcher.org/document/105089, consulted 6 February 2019.

19   Mass Observation Archive: Replies to Spring 2016 Directive on Higher Education, D4736.

20   Ibid.

21   Mass Observation Archive: Replies to Spring 2016 Directive on Social Mobility, A4127.

22   Mass Observation Archive: Replies to Spring 2016 Directive on Social Mobility, D4736.

23   Diane Reay, 'A useful extension of Bourdieu's conceptual framework?: Emotional capital as a way of understanding mothers' involvement in their children's education', *Sociological Review*, vol. 48, no. 4, 2000, pp. 579–80; Diane Reay, 'Doing the dirty work of class? Mothers' work in support of their children's schooling', *Sociological Review*, vol. 53, no. 2, supplement, 2005, pp. 104–15.

24 Mass Observation Archive: Replies to Spring 2016 Directive on Social Mobility, D4736.
25 Mass Observation Archive: Replies to Spring 2016 Directive on Social Mobility, A3623.
26 Mike Savage et al, *Social Class in the 21st Century*, Penguin, 2015, pp. 227–9.
27 Mass Observation Archive: Replies to Spring 2016 Directive on Social Mobility, A3623.
28 Mass Observation Archive: Replies to Spring 2016 Directive on Social Mobility, D4736.
29 Mass Observation Archive: Replies to Spring 2016 Directive on Social Mobility, A3623.
30 Mass Observation Archive: Replies to Spring 2016 Directive on Social Mobility, D4736.
31 Ibid.
32 Mass Observation Archive: Replies to Spring 2016 Directive on Social Mobility, D4127.
33 Mass Observation Archive: Replies to Spring 2016 Directive on Social Mobility, A3623.

Chapter Fifteen: The Pursuit of Excellence and Inequality

1 Social Mobility and Child Poverty Commission, *State of the Nation in 2015*, HMSO, 2015, p. 2.
2 'Blair pledges "opportunity society"', *Guardian*, 11 October 2004, https://www.theguardian.com/politics/2004/oct/11/labour.uk, consulted 5 July 2017.
3 Danny Dorling, *Inequality and the 1%*, Verso, 2015, p. 6.; Jonathan Cribb et al., *Living Standards, Poverty and Inequality in the UK: 2013*, Institute of Fiscal Studies, 2013.
4 Tony Blair, quoted in 'Full text of Tony Blair's speech on education', *Guardian*, 23 May 2001, https://www.theguardian.com/politics/2001/may/23/labour.tonyblair, consulted 4 September 2018.
5 Mass Observation Archive: Replies to Autumn 2014 Directive on Working Families, R5429.
6 Mass Observation Archive: Replies to Spring 2016 Directive on Social Mobility, N5744.
7 Mass Observation Archive: Replies to Spring 2016 Directive on Social Mobility, R5429. See also Mass Observation Archive: Replies to Spring 2016 Directive on Social Mobility, S5774; Mass Observation Archive: Replies to Spring 2016 Directive on Social Mobility, A4127.
8 Mass Observation Archive: Replies to Spring 2016 Directive on Social Mobility, R5429.
9 See for example Debbie Humphry, 'Moving On? Experiences of Social Mobility in a Mixed-Class North London Neighbourhood', DPhil thesis, University of Sussex, 2014, pp. 174–6; Louise Archer and Merryn

Hutchings, '"Bettering Yourself"? Discourses of Risk, Cost and Benefit in Ethnically Diverse, Young Working-Class Non-Participants' Constructions of Higher Education', *British Journal of Sociology of Education*, vol. 21, no. 4, 2000, pp. 555–74.

10   Fauzia Ahmad, *South Asian Women and Employment in Britain*, Policy Studies Institute, 2003, p. 15.

11   Mass Observation Archive: Replies to Spring 2016 Directive on Social Mobility, T4715.

12   'Thatcher cool on swing to Labour', *Guardian*, 2 May 1979.

13   Paul Bolton, 'Education: historical statistics', Note SN/SG/4252, House of Commons Library, 2012, https://dera.ioe.ac.uk/22771/1/SN04252.pdf.

14   A.D. Edwards et al., *The State and Private Education: an evaluation of the Assisted Places Scheme*, Falmer, 1989, pp. 2, 4, 112, 161–5.

15   Sharon Gerwitz et al., *Markets, Choice and Equity in Education*, Open University Press, 1995, pp. 25–37.

16   John E. C. McBeath, *Talking about Schools: Surveys of parents' views on school education in Scotland*, HMSO, 1989, pp. 3 and 10.

17   Diane Reay and Dylan William, '"I'll Be a Nothing": Structure, Agency and the Construction of Identity through Assessment', *British Educational Research Journal*, vol. 25, no. 3, 1999, pp. 343–54.

18   Mass Observation Archive: Replies to Spring 2016 directive on Social Mobility, S5563.

19   Ibid.

20   Mass Observation Archive: Replies to Spring 2016 directive on Social Mobility, S4002.

21   Mass Observation Archive: Replies to Spring 2016 Directive on Social Mobility, J5734.

22   Diane Reay, *Miseducation. Inequality, education and the working classes*, Policy Press, 2017, pp. 110–14.

23   Mass Observation Archive: Replies to Spring 2016 Directive on Social Mobility, N5744.

24   Reay, *Miseducation*, pp. 110–14.

25   Heidi Safia Mirza, 'Race, Gender and IQ', *Race, Ethnicity and Education*, vol. 1, no. 2, 1998, pp. 109–26.

26   Interview with Helen Abeda by Andrea Thomson, 2019.

27   Mirza, pp. 109–26.

28   Ibid.

29   Richard Wilkinson and Kate Pickett, *The Inner Level: How more equal societies reduce stress, restore sanity and improve everyone's well-being*, Penguin, 2018, p. 181.

30   Sharon Gerwitz, 'Cloning the Blairs: New Labour's programme for the re-socialization of working-class parents', *Journal of Education Policy*, vol. 16, no. 4, 2001, pp. 365–78; Diane Reay, 'Tony Blair, the promotion of the "active" educational citizen, and middle-class hegemony', *Oxford Review of Education*, Vol. 34, no. 6, 2008; Katharine Burn and Ann Childs,

'Responding to poverty through education and teacher education initiatives', *Journal of Education for Teaching*, vol. 42, no. 4, 2016.

31 Quoted from Alastair Campbell, 'The day of the bog-standard comprehensive is over', speech, Labour Party Spring Conference, Glasgow, 2001.

32 Mass Observation Archive: Replies to Spring 2016 Directive on Social Mobility, N5744.

33 Mass Observation Archive: Replies to Spring 2016 Directive on Social Mobility, R5429.

34 'Fame the career choice for half of sixteen-year-olds', *Independent*, 17 February 2010, https://www.independent.co.uk/news/education/education-news/fame-the-career-choice-for-half-of-16-year-olds-1902338.html; Kim Allen and Heather Mendick, 'Young people's uses of celebrity: Class, gender and "improper" celebrity', *Discourse*, vol. 34, no. 1, 2013, pp. 77–93.

35 '*X Factor* culture fuelled the UK riots, says Iain Duncan Smith', *Guardian*, 9 December 2011, https://www.theguardian.com/uk/2011/dec/09/x-factor-culture-fuelled-riots, consulted 6 May 2018.

36 Philip Kirkby, *Leading People 2016*, Sutton Trust, 2016; Mike Savage et al., *Social Class in the 21st Century*, Penguin, 2015, p. 247; Sam Friedman and Daniel Laurison, 'Breaking the "Class" Ceiling? Social Mobility into Britain's Elite Occupations', *Sociological Review*, 2015, vol. 63, no. 2, pp. 259–89.

37 Quoted in Chris Green, *Every Boy's Dream. England's Football Future on the Line*, A. & C. Black, 2009, p. 69.

38 Ibid., p. 71.

39 Quoted in ibid., pp. 65–6 and 147.

40 Quoted in ibid., p. 74.

41 Diane Reay, 'Shaun's Story: Troubling discourses of white working-class masculinities', *Gender and Education*, vol. 14, no. 3, 2002, pp. 221–34.

42 Ibid.

43 Interview with Richard Campbell by Andrea Thomson.

44 Diane Reay, 'Social mobility, a panacea for our times', *British Journal of Sociology of Education*, vol. 34, nos. 5–6, 2013, p. 668.

45 Savage et al., pp. 227–9.

46 Social Mobility and Child Poverty Commission, *State of the Nation in 2015*, HMSO, 2015, p. 6.

47 Paul Bagguley and Yasmin Hussain, 'Negotiating Mobility: South Asian Women and Higher Education', *Sociology*, vol. 50, no. 1, 2016, p. 50; Helen Connor et al, *Why the Difference?: A closer look at higher education minority ethnic students and graduates*, DfES Publications, 2004, p. 43.

48 Valerie Walkerdine et al., *Growing Up Girl: Psychosocial explorations of gender and class*, Palgrave, 2001, pp. 34–8.

49 Ibid.

50 Bagguley and Hussain; Louise Archer and Merryn Hutchings, '"Bettering Yourself? Discourses of Risk, Cost and Benefit in Ethnically Diverse, Working-class Non-Participants' Constructions of Higher Education', *British Journal of Sociology*, vol. 21, no. 4, 2000, pp. 555–74.

51 Interview with Helen Abeda.

52 'Exclusive: University Elite Plans Breakaway Top League', *Observer*, 9 October 1994, p. 1. The Russell Group named themselves after the London hotel in whose bar they first met. By 2020 twenty-four universities were in the Russell Group.

53 'An Ivy League begins to take root', *Sunday Times*, 11 September 1994, p. 8.

54 Savage et al., pp. 245–7.

55 Martin Harris, Director of Fair Access, 'What more can be done to widen access to highly selective universities?', April 2010 http://dera.ioe.ac.uk/1055/1/Sir-Martin-Harris-Fair-Access-report-web-version.pdf, p. 110.

56 Bagguley and Hussain, p. 51.

57 Mass Observation Archive: Replies to Spring 2016 Directive on Higher Education, S4002.

58 On the rise of narcissism, contempt for those who are poorer and conspicuous consumption among younger generations see Wilkinson and Pickett, chapters 3 and 7.

59 Walkerdine et al., pp. 45–7.

60 'Tony Blair's speech on healthy living', *Guardian*, 26 July 2006, https://www.theguardian.com/society/2006/jul/26/health.politics, consulted 5 July 2017.

61 Walkerdine et al., pp. 181–2.

62 Ibid., introduction and pp. 181–2.

63 Mass Observation Archive: Replies to Spring 2016 Directive on Higher Education, M5113.

64 Ibid.

65 Ibid.

66 Ibid.

67 Diane Reay, Gill Crozier and John Clayton, '"Strangers in Paradise"?: Working-class Students in Elite Universities', *Sociology*, vol. 43, no. 6, 2009.

68 Mass Observation Archive: Replies to Spring 2016 directive on Social Mobility, M3055.

Chapter Sixteen: The Ladder Broken

1 Frank Buscha and Patrick Sturgis, 'Declining social mobility? Evidence from five linked census in England and Wales 1971–2011', *British Journal of Sociology*, vol. 69, no. 1, 2018.

2 Shirley Dex and Andrew McCullough, *Flexible Employment: The future of Britain's jobs*, Macmillan, 1997, p. 31.

3 Mike Savage et al., *Property, Bureaucracy and Culture: Middle-class formation in contemporary Britain*, Routledge, 1992, pp. 70–1.

4 Alan Milburn, Panel on Fair Access to the Professions, *Unleashing Aspiration: The Final Report of the Panel on Fair Access to the Professions*, HMG, 2009, p. 5.

5   'Nick Clegg insists education reform will encourage social mobility', *Guardian*, 23 November 2010, https://www.theguardian.com/education/2010/nov/23/nick-clegg-education-reform-social-mobility, consulted 6 March 2016.

6   Philip Kirkby, *Leading People 2016*, Sutton Trust, 2016; see also 'Elitism in Britain – breakdown by profession', *Guardian*, 20 August 2014, https://www.theguardian.com/news/datablog/2014/aug/28/elitism-in-britain-breakdown-by-profession, consulted 4 June 2017.

7   Daniel Oesch and Jorgé Rodriguez Menes, 'Upgrading or polarization? Occupational change in Britain, Germany, Spain and Switzerland, 1990–2008', *Socio-Economic Review*, no. 9, no. 3, 2011, p. 513.

8   Quoted in 'Johnson: fund more plumbing and less Pilates', *Guardian*, 7 June 2006, https://www.theguardian.com/education/2006/jun/07/furthereducation.uk1, consulted 13 June 2017.

9   John Butcher, 'There has been a massive drop in the number of mature students studing at UK universities', *The Conversation*, 12 September 2017, http://theconversation.com/there-has-been-a-massive-drop-in-the-number-of-mature-students-studying-at-uk-universities-83180, consulted 12 April 2018.

10   Muhammad Rakib Ehsan and David Kingman, *Escape of the wealthy. The unfairness of the English student finance system*, Intergenerational Foundation, 2019.

11   Robert Gilchrist et al., *Potential Mature Students: Recruitment to HE*, Department of Education and Skills, Research Report no. 385, 2002, https://dera.ioe.ac.uk/4706/1/RR385.pdf.

12   Mass Observation Archive: Replies to Spring 2016 Directive on Social Mobility, R5429; see also Oesch and Menes.

13   Mass Observation Archive: Replies to Spring 2016 Directive on Social Mobility, S4002.

14   Mass Observation Archive: Replies to Spring 2016 Directive on Social Mobility, M5113.

15   Mass Observation Archive: Replies to Spring 2016 directive on Social Mobility, M3055.

16   Mike Savage et al., *Social Class in the 21st Century*, Penguin, 2015, pp. 245–7.

17   Yaojun Li and Anthony Heath, 'Class Matters: A Study of Minority and Majority Social Mobility in Britain, 1982–2011', *American Journal of Sociology*, vol. 122, no. 1, 2016, pp. 162–200; Heidi Safia Mirza, 'Race, Gender and IQ', *Race, Ethnicity and Education*, vol. 1, no. 1, 1998, pp. 109–26.

18   Carolina V. Zucotti, 'Do Parents Matter? Revisiting Ethnic Penalties in Occupation among Second-Generation Ethnic Minorities in England and Wales', *Sociology*, vol. 49, no. 2, 2015, pp. 229–51.

19   Savage et al., *Social Class in the 21st Century*, pp. 267–70.

20   Sam Friedman and Lindsey Macmillan, 'Is London Really the Engine-Room? Migration, Opportunity Hoarding and Regional Social Mobility in the UK', *National Institute Economic Review*, vol. 240, no. 1, 2017.

21 Savage et al., *Social Class in the 21st Century*, pp. 267–70.
22 Mass Observation Archive: Replies to Spring 2016 Directive on Higher Education, N5744.
23 Stephen Armstrong, *The New Poverty*, Verso, 2017, p. 152.
24 Quoted in ibid, p. 153.
25 Mass Observation Archive: Replies to Spring 2016 Directive on Social Mobility, C5706.
26 Ibid.
27 'Council funds for libraries, museums and galleries cut by nearly £400m', *Independent*, 25 January 2019, https://www.independent.co.uk/news/uk/home-news/libraries-museums-arts-galleries-funding-recourses-county-council-network-cnn-social-care-a8741271.html, consulted 30 January 2019.
28 Mass Observation Archive: Replies to Spring 2016 Directive on Social Mobility, C5706.
29 Office of National Statistics, 'Percentage of graduates in non-graduate roles, parts of the UK, 2015–2017', *Annual Population Survey*, ONS, 2018, https://www.ons.gov.uk/employmentandlabourmarket/peopleinwork/employmentandemployeetypes/adhocs/008381percentageofemployedgraduatesinnongraduaterolespartsoftheuk2015to2017.
30 Danny Dorling, *Inequality and the 1%*, Verso, 2015, p. 107.
31 Mass Observation Archive: Replies to Spring 2016 Directive on Social Mobility, J5734.
32 Social Mobility Commission, *Time for Change: An assessment of government policies on social mobility, 1997–2017*, HMSO, 2017, p. 4; Louise Crewe and Annie Wang, 'Gender Inequalities in the City of London Advertising Industry', *Environment and Planning A: Economy and Space*, vol. 50, no. 3, 2018, pp. 671–88.
33 Savage et al., *Social Class in the 21st Century*, chapter 8.
34 Katharine Burn and Ann Childs, 'Responding to poverty through education and teacher education initiatives', *Journal of Education for Teaching*, Vol. 42, no. 4, 2016.
35 Quoted in 'Boris Johnson evokes Thatcher spirit with greed is good speech', *Guardian*, 27 November 2013, https://www.theguardian.com/politics/2013/nov/27/boris-johnson-thatcher-greed-good, consulted 5 June 2016.
36 Carla Ayrton et al., *Monitoring poverty and social exclusion 2016*, Joseph Rowntree Foundation, 2017.
37 Social Mobility Commission, *Time for Change*, p. 5.
38 Quoted in Diane Reay, 'Social mobility, a panacea for our times', *British Journal of Sociology of Education*, vol. 34, nos 5–6, 2013, p. 667.
39 Paul Bolton, 'Education: historical statistics', Note SN/SG/4252, House of Commons Library, 2012, https://dera.ioe.ac.uk/22771/1/SN04252.pdf.
40 On the impact of recession on private school rolls after 2007, see 'Demand for state schools rises as recession hits', *Guardian*, 19 December 2008,

https://www.theguardian.com/education/2008/dec/18/schools-private-recession, consulted 5 March 2018; 'Recession forces many to give up private schools', *Telegraph*, 23 November 2008, and 'Eton headmaster: Private schools "may close"', *Telegraph*, 27 January 2009. On the attraction of academisation for private schools, see 'Liverpool College to scrap fees after opting for academy status', *Liverpool Echo*, 26 June 2012, https://www.liverpoolecho.co.uk/news/liverpool-news/liverpool-college-mossley-hill-scrap-3343064, and 'Private schools should join multi-academy trusts, says ISC chair', *Schoolsweek*, 7 November 2017, https://schoolsweek.co.uk/private-schools-should-join-multi-academy-trusts-says-isc-chair/, consulted 17 March 2018.

41 Mass Observation Archive: Replies to Summer 2012 Directive on School, Teachers and Pupils.

42 Anon., *The Secret Barrister: Stories of the law and how it's broken*, Macmillan, 2018, pp. 210–11.

43 Social Mobility Commission, *Time for Change: An assessment of government policies on social mobility, 1997–2017*, HMSO, 2017, p. 79.

44 See responses to Sir Jeremy Haywood's piece 'Our Vision for a Brilliant Civil Service and What it Means for You', Civil Service official blog, https://civilservice.blog.gov.uk/2016/06/16/our-vision-for-a-brilliant-civil-service-and-what-it-means-for-you/, consulted 7 September 2018; Stefan Collini, *What Are Universities For?*, Penguin, 2012, and Stefan Collini, 'Voters should be enraged by higher education profiteering', *Guardian*, 6 June 2017.

45 Mass Observation Archive: Replies to Spring 2016 Directive on Social Mobility, R5429.

46 Sara McCafferty and Harry Hill, 'Another Change Agenda: Reflections on "Agenda for Change"', *Public Policy and Administration*, vol. 30, no. 2, 2015.

47 Mass Observation Archive: Replies to Spring 2016 Directive on Social Mobility, T4715.

48 'The Conservatives' underfunding of the NHS made crisis inevitable', *New Statesman*, 3 January 2018, https://www.newstatesman.com/politics/uk/2018/01/conservatives-underfunding-nhs-made-crisis-inevitable, and Kings Fund, 'How much has been spent on the NHS since 2005?', https://www.kingsfund.org.uk/projects/general-election-2010/money-spent-nhs, both consulted 18 March 2018.

49 Mass Observation Archive: Replies to Spring 2016 Directive on Social Mobility, T4715.

50 Selina Todd, *The People: the rise and fall of the working class 1910–2010*, John Murray, 2014, p. 349.

51 Mass Observation Archive: Replies to Spring 2016 Directive on Social Mobility, M5113.

52 Social Mobility Commission, *Time for Change*, p. 2.

53 Mass Observation Archive: Replies to Spring 2016 Directive on Social Mobility, J5734.

54 Ministry of Housing, Communities and Local Government, Dwelling Stock Estimates, England: 2017, https://assets.publishing.service.gov.uk/government/uploads/system/uploads/attachment_data/file/710382/Dwelling_Stock_Estimates_2017_England.pdf/.

55 Dorling, p. 103.

56 Interview with Don Milligan by Jim Hinks.

57 Dorling, pp. 103–5.

58 Mass Observation Archive: Replies to Spring 2016 Directive on Social Mobility, R5429.

59 Ibid.

60 Mass Observation Archive: Replies to Spring 2016 Directive on Social Mobility, T4715.

61 Richard Wilkinson and Kate Pickett, *The Spirit Level: Why greater equality makes societies stronger*, Penguin, 2010, chapters 6 and 13; Richard Wilkinson and Kate Pickett, *The Inner Level: How more equal societies reduce stress, restore sanity and improve everyone's well-being*, Penguin, 2018, chapter 9.

62 Mass Observation Archive: Replies to Spring 2016 Directive on Social Mobility, T4715.

63 Rebecca Tunstall and Ruth Lupton, *Mixed Communities*, Department for Communities and Local Government, 2010.

64 Wilkinson and Pickett, *The Inner Level*, chapter 9; Mass Observation Archive: Replies to Spring 2016 Directive on Social Mobility, S4002.

65 Mass Observation Archive: Replies to Spring 2016 Directive on Social Mobility, T4715.

66 Social Mobility and Child Poverty Commission, *State of the Nation in 2015*, HMSO, 2015, p. v.

67 Mass Observation Archive: Replies to Spring 2016 Directive on Social Mobility, J5734.

68 https://www.speakers4schools.org/about-us/, consulted 20 July 2019.

69 'Kenneth Olisa: "To improve social mobility, we must raise children's aspirations"', *Guardian*, 9 October 2018, https://www.theguardian.com/society/2018/oct/09/kenneth-olisa-social-mobility-raise-childrens-aspirations, consulted 20 July 2019.

70 Quoted in Armstrong, p. 27.

71 https://www.speakers4schools.org/about-us/.

72 Danny Dorling, 'Who should and who shouldn't come up to Oxford as an undergraduate', 8th Annual Access Lecture, University College Oxford, 2017, http://podcasts.ox.ac.uk/8th-annual-access-lecture-2017, consulted 8 January 2020.

73 Interview with Helen Abeda by Andrea Thomson.

74 Interview with Richard Campbell by Andrea Thomson.

75 Walter Benn Michaels, 'The Trouble with Diversifying the Faculty', *Liberal Education*, vol. 1, no. 1, 2011, pp. 14-19; Floya Anthias and Cathie Lloyd, 'Introduction', in Anthias and Lloyd, eds., *Rethinking anti-racisms: from theory to practice*, Routledge, 2003; Pragna Patel, 'Back to the

Future. Avoiding Déjà Vu in Resisting Racism' in Anthias and Lloyd, eds., pp. 128–48; Pragna Patel, 'Faith in the State? Asian Women's Struggle for Human Rights in the UK', *Feminist Legal Studies*, vo. 16, no. 9, 2008, pp. 9–36; Adolph Reed, 'The Limits of Anti-racism', *Left Business Observer*, no. 121, September 2009.

76   Pragna Patel, 'Women Migrants and Faith Organisations: Changing Regimes of Gender, Religion and Race in London', *Feminist Review*, vol. 97, no. 1, 2011, pp. 142–50.

77   Heidi Safia Mirza, 'Transcendence over Diversity: Black Women in the Academy', *Policy Futures in Education*, vol. 4, no. 2, 2006.

78   Interview with Helen Abeda.

79   Louise Archer and Merryn Hutchings, '"Bettering Yourself? Discourses of Risk, Cost and Benefit in Ethnically Diverse, Working-class Non-Participants' Constructions of Higher Education', *British Journal of Sociology*, vol. 21, no. 4, 2000, p. 569.

80   Interview with Helen Abeda.

81   Interview with Richard Campbell.

82   Ibid.

83   Walter Benn Michaels, 'What Matters', *London Review of Books*, vol. 31, no. 16, 27 Aug 2009; Adolph Reed, Jr., 'Antiracism: a neoliberal alternative to a left', *Dialectical Anthropology*, vo. 42, no. 2, 2018; Adolph Reed, Jr., 'Socialism and the Argument against Race Reductionism', *New Labor Forum*, vol. 29, no. 2, 2020.

84   Mass Observation Archive: Replies to Spring 2016 Directive on Social Mobility, T4715.

85   Helene Snee and Fiona Devine, 'Fair Chances and Hard Work? Families making sense of inequality and opportunity in 21st century Britain', *British Journal of Sociology*, vol. 69, no. 4, 2018, pp. 1134–54.

86   Mass Observation Archive: Replies to Spring 2016 Directive on Social Mobility, N5744.

87   Mass Observation Archive: Replies to Spring 2016 Directive on Social Mobility, M5113.

88   Mass Observation Archive: Replies to Spring 2016 Directive on Social Mobility, D5740.

89   Julie Bindel, *The Pimping of Prostitution. Abolishing the Sex Work Myth*, Palgrave Macmillan, 2017.

90   Mass Observation Archive: Replies to Spring 2016 Directive on Social Mobility, D5740.

91   Tracey Sagar et al., 'The Student Sex Work Project: Research Summary', 2015, http://www.thestudentsexworkproject.co.uk/wp-content/uploads/2015/03/TSSWP-Research-Summary-English.pdf, consulted 6 March 2020, p. 22.

92   Mass Observation Archive: Replies to Spring 2016 Directive on Social Mobility, R5429.

93   Mass Observation Archive: Replies to Spring 2016 Directive on Social Mobility, N5744.

94 Mass Observation Archive: Replies to Spring 2016 Directive on Social Mobility, C5706. See also Savage et al., *Social Class in the 21st Century*, pp. 59–61.

95 See also Mike Savage et al., *Globalization and Belonging*, Sage, 2005 pp. 94–9, 104–5, 203.

96 Mass Observation Archive: Replies to Spring 2016 Directive on Social Mobility, H5589.

97 Mass Observation Archive: Replies to Spring 2016 Directive on Social Mobility, J5734.

98 James Achur, *Trade Union Membership 2010*, Department for Business, Innovation and Skills, 2011, p. 3.

99 Labour Party, *For the Many, Not the Few*, Labour Party manifesto 2017.

100 Ipsos MORI, 'How Britain voted in 2010, 2015 and 2017', https://www.ipsos.com/ipsos-mori/en-uk/how-britain-voted-2015, consulted 20 January 2020.

101 Ipsos MORI, 'How Britain voted in 2019', https://www.ipsos.com/ipsos-mori/en-uk/how-britain-voted-20159, consulted 20 January 2020.

Conclusion: We Can Replace the Ladder With a Brighter Future

1 For books that delve into these areas, or discuss how to pay for what I outline here, see Richard Wilkinson and Kate Pickett, *The Spirit Level: Why greater equality makes societies stronger*, Penguin, 2010; Richard Wilkinson and Kate Pickett, *The Inner Level: How more equal societies reduce stress, restore sanity and improve everyone's well-being*, Penguin, 2018; Ann Pettifor, *The Production of Money. How to Break the Power of Bankers*, Verso, 2017 and Tony Benn, *Arguments for Socialism*, Penguin, 1980.

2 Abigail McKnight, 'Downward mobility, opportunity hoarding and the "glass floor"', Sutton Trust, 2015, p. 40.

3 Susan Hallam, *Homework. The Evidence*, Institute of Education, 2004, pp. 30–2.

4 For an excellent discussion of how a National Education Service might be created see Melissa Benn, *Life Lessons: The case for a national education service*, Verso, 2018.

5 Sharon Gerwitz et al., *Markets, Choice and Equity in Education*, Open University Press, 1995, pp. 32, 34.

6 McKnight, p. 40; Gerwitz et al, pp. 30–50.

7 Robert Verkaik, speaking at the launch of Private School Policy Reform, Mechanics Institute, Manchester, 19 September 2019.

8 Mainul Haque, 'Importance of empathy among medical doctors to ensure high-quality healthcare level', *Advances in Human Biology*, vol. 92, no. 1, 2019, pp. 104–7; Sarah Brien and George Lewith, '"Why are you doctors?"

The importance of care and compassion', *Clinical Medicine*, vol. 1, no. 3, 2001, pp. 223–6; Wilkinson and Pickett, *The Inner Level*, pp. 83–7.

9   Lindsay Judge and Nye Cominetti, 'From Rights to Reality. Enforcing Labour Market Laws in the UK', Resolution Foundation, 2019, https://www.resolutionfoundation.org/publications/from-rights-to-reality/, consulted 20 January 2020.

10   'It is Time to Make Amends to the Low-Paid Essential Worker', *Financial Times*, 1 April, 2020.

11   Wilkinson and Pickett, *The Inner Level*, pp. 244, 246, 255.

12   'Our Values', Unicorn Grocery, https://www.unicorn-grocery.coop/our-co-op/our-values/, consulted 12 March 2018, and 'Co-operatives', a talk by members of Unicorn Grocery Co-op, Chorlton Park Labour Party political education session, 19 October 2016.

13   Mike Savage et al., *Social Class in the 21st Century*, Penguin, 2015, p. 267.

14   Anna Thomas, 'Why working fewer hours would make us more productive', *Guardian*, 9 November 2015, https://www.theguardian.com/sustainable-business/2015/nov/09/fewer-working-hours-doctors-eu-negotiations, consulted 21 January 2020.

15   'Robots threaten 15 million UK jobs, says Bank of England's chief economist', *Guardian*, 12 November 2015, https://www.theguardian.com/business/2015/nov/12/robots-threaten-low-paid-jobs-says-bank-of-england-chief-economist, consulted 22 March 2019; Adair Turner, speech to the shadow chancellor's State of the Economy conference, 19 May 2018, https://www.john-mcdonnell.net/economic-conferences/state-of-the-economy-2018/, consulted 22 March 2019.

16   Henry William Durant, *The Problem of Leisure*, Routledge, 1938.

17   'Turbulent Welsh Waters', *Country Life*, 27 September 1973, p. 844; *Microelectronics, Productivity, and Employment*, OECD, 1981; a good survey of pessimistic and optimistic views in the 1970s debate is provided by A. E. Cawkwell, 'Information technology and work', *Journal of Information Science*, vol. 6, no. 4, 1983, pp. 123–35.

18   Pettifor, chapter 8. See also Wilkinson and Pickett, *The Spirit Level*, chapter 16.

Note on Sources

1   For more on the profile of Mass Observers, see 'Mass Observation Project Database', http://database.massobs.org.uk, consulted 15 August 2019.

2   This is a requirement of using Mass Observation data. I have also changed names of places, institutions and job titles where this is necessary to protect the identities of those generous enough to share their stories with me.

INDEX

INDEX

Conservative Party, 18–19, 346
  Baldwin government, second (1924–9), 39, 76, 80, 92
  Cameron government (2010–16), 300, 322–3, 324, 326, 329–32
  child labour and, 34–5
  Churchill government (1951–5), 137, 141, 191, 198–9
  City Technology Colleges, 291
  Eden government (1955–7), 191
  education and, 96, 194,
  Education Act (1902), 19
  general election (1918), 62–3, 74
  general election (1922), 39, 91
  general election (1945), 127
  general election (1951), 137, 141
  general election (1955), 157
  general election (1959), 147
  general election (1970), 238
  general election (1979), 247–8
  general election (2017), 349–50
  General Strike (1926), 39, 76
  Heath government (1970–74), 234, 235
  hereditary rights and, 19
  inflation and, 163, 235
  Johnson government (2019–), 300
  Macmillan government (1957–63), 145, 191, 207, 210, 213
  Major government (1990–97), 300, 303, 315, 327
  May government (2016–19), 300
  private enterprise and, 140, 146, 156, 163, 249, 268, 272, 283, 301
  privatisation, 255, 256, 257, 258, 273
  public sector marketization, 281–2
  Robbins' Report (1963), 207–8, 313
  secondary-school scholarships and, 96
  Spens Committee (1933–8), 194
  technological innovation and, 149
  Thatcher government (1979–90), 247–63, 273, 280–82, 291, 301, 303, 313, 327, 354
  unemployment and, 73, 74, 75, 80
  Unemployment Act (1922), 75
Cooper, Joan, 117, 135
Corbyn, Jeremy, 349–50
Coronation Street, 224
Cosgrove, Paul, 291–2, 293, 294–5
Coutts bank, 256, 273–4
Coventry City FC, 310
COVID-19 pandemic (2019–20), 4, 5, 354, 358–9, 368
Craig, Ryan, 310
Crosland, Charles Anthony 'Tony', 146–7, 148, 150, 157, 214
Czechoslovakia, 232, 235

Daily Express, 248, 250
Daily Mail, 63, 250–51, 275
Daily Mirror, 91, 225
Davies, Ann, 166–7, 202
Davies, Hunter, 224
democracy, 125, 126, 233
Democratic Unionist Party (DUP), 350
depression, 317, 318
Dewdney, Andrew, 220–21, 225, 231, 239–40, 245
do it yourself, 268, 270, 279
Dobson, Barry, 204–5, 210
Dockers' Union, 26
doctors, *see* medicine, careers in
domestic servants, 50–51, 79
Donovan Commission (1968), 234
Dorling, Danny, 348, 354

downward mobility, 8
  breakthrough generation (1920–34), 110, 137, 197, 203, 204–5
  fear of, 63, 91, 137, 263, 344, 351
  golden generation (1935–55), 191, 201–2, 203, 204–5, 249–55, 263
  magpie generation (1956–71), 267, 285–96
  millennial generation (1986–99), 299, 329, 344, 348
  precarious generation (1900–19), 69, 70, 75, 79, 83, 86, 88, 92, 197
  shame and, 8, 78, 271
  Thatcher's children (1972–85), 299, 312, 319, 329, 344, 348
Duncan, Carlton, 181, 182, 187–8
Duncan, Isadora, 32
Dunkirk evacuation (1940), 109
Dupree, Jack, 229
Durant, Henry, 366
Durham University, 207, 224
Durham, County Durham, 25
Dyer, Geoff, 278

East Anglia University, 208
East Denholm, Scottish Borders, 66
East India Company, 42
eating disorders, 230, 317
education, 2, 3, 5, 6, 9, 354–7
  breakthrough generation (1920–34), 105–7, 118, 122–5, 131–5, 142–6, 148, 158, 160–61
  golden generation (1935–55), 9, 191–215, 220, 226–36, 256
  magpie generation (1956–71), 267–73, 276, 278, 280, 282, 283, 287, 292, 293
  millennial generation (1986–99), 300, 307, 312–20, 324, 325, 330–31, 332
  pioneer generation (1880–99), 16, 18, 20, 22–7, 29–31, 33–7, 45–6
  precarious generation (1900–19), 73–4, 81–3, 86, 92, 93–8
  Thatcher's children (1972–85), 300, 302, 303–6, 309, 312–20, 323–5, 326, 328, 332, 333–4
Education Act
  1902 19, 29
  1918 35–6, 63, 82
  1944 122, 132, 145, 192
  1988 293
Education (Scotland) Act
  1872 45
  1918 35, 192
  1945 192
Education and the Working Class (Willmott and Young), 144, 151
Education Reform Act (1988), 303, 304
Educational Maintenance Allowance, 308
Edwards, John, 20, 21, 25–6
Edwards, Mary, 165–6
elections
  1906 general election, 19, 27
  1910 general elections, 28–9
  1918 general election, 62
  1922 general election, 39, 75, 91
  1934 LCC election, 93
  1945 general election, 5, 38, 127, 192
  1951 general election, 137, 141
  1955 general election, 157
  1959 general election, 147
  1966 general election, 214
  1970 general election, 238

INDEX

Hall, Amanda, 270, 272, 273, 280–81, 285, 287, 288, 289
Hall, Edith, 84–5
Halsey, Albert, 132, 142–5, 149, 150, 153, 196, 205, 213
  ABCA lecturer, 124
  doctorate, 148
  Floud, relationship with, 143, 148, 153
  Liverpool lecturer, 152
  LSE, studies at, 131, 142
  Oxford lecturer, 150
  RAF service, 107, 108, 127
Halsey, Margaret, 152
Hampson, John, 89
Hankey, Maurice Pascal Alers, 1st Baron, 113
Hannam, June, 218–19, 221–2, 226–9, 233, 235–7, 244, 259–60, 290
Hannington, Wal, 78
Harris, Chris, 269, 285–6
Harris, Jose, 38
Harrisson, Tom, 125
Hawkins, Annabel, 325
Heath, Edward, 234, 235, 241
Henderson, Arthur, 34
higher education
  breakthrough generation (1920–34), 109, 113–19, 122, 124, 131–4, 136, 149–55
  golden generation (1935–55), 208, 213, 217, 226–36, 242
  magpie generation (1956–71), 271, 272, 280, 282, 292
  millennial generation (1986–99), 324, 325, 332
  precarious generation (1900–19), 73–4, 81, 83, 86, 97–8, 100
  pioneer generation (1880–99), 23–6, 30, 35, 36, 46
  Thatcher's children (1972–85), 305–6, 309, 312–20, 324, 326, 328, 332, 333–4
Hilton, Jack, 88
Hirst, Ruth, 218, 219, 220, 222, 226, 227, 230, 239
Hitler, Adolf, 101, 105
Hodges, Ann, 61, 62, 95, 97
Hoggart, Richard, 124, 134, 144–6, 148–9, 151–2, 204, 218, 231, 233
homosexuality, 236, 259, 288–9, 294
Hookway, E. J., 26
Hoque, Nurul, 183
Horlick, Nicola, 274–5
Horn, Carol, 168
House of Commons, 4
House of Lords, 4, 28
housing
  breakthrough generation (1920–34), 127, 137, 145, 154, 155, 176, 183, 184
  golden generation (1935–55), 208, 218, 219, 257–9, 263
  magpie generation (1956–71), 293
  millennial generation (1986–99), 338
  pioneer generation (1880–99), 36, 62, 63
  precarious generation (1900–19), 77, 85, 91, 94, 99
  Thatcher's children (1972–85), 335–8
Housing Act (1919), 63
Housing Act (1982), 257
Howard's End (Forster), 41, 50
Hull University, 134, 272
Hundal, N. S., 185–6

ICI, 92, 178
immigrants, 365
  breakthrough generation (1920–34), 172, 173–8, 180–88

golden generation (1935–55), 209
magpie generation (1956–71), 275–77
millennial generation (1986–99), 313
Thatcher's children (1972–85), 306, 313, 325
income inequality, 6, 77, 214, 231–2, 243, 245, 250, 330
Independent Labour Party (ILP), 17, 18, 21, 30, 36, 38, 53
India, 70, 180, 181, 275–7
Indian Workers' Association (IWA), 184, 185
industrialisation, 42
inequality, 1, 3, 5, 6, 11, 359
  breakthrough generation (1920–34), 119, 127, 147, 150, 155
  golden generation (1935–55), 196, 201, 231, 239
  magpie generation (1956–71), 296
  millennial generation (1986–99), 329, 330, 346
  pioneer generation (1880–99), 18
  precarious generation (1900–19), 93, 100
  Thatcher's children (1972–85), 300, 308, 313, 316, 325, 344, 347–8
Inequality and the 1% (Dorling), 348
inferiority complex, 100
inflation, 163, 235
influenza epidemic (1918–19), 71
Inner London Education Authority, 354
innovation, 6, 8, 208
Institute of Community Studies, 144, 154–5
Institute of Education, 153
Institute of Personnel Management, 116
intelligence, 123
  as hereditary, 196, 213
  school selection and, 148–9, 194, 196, 197
  tests, 122, 123, 197
International Marxist Group, 234–5
International Monetary Fund (IMF), 247
International Socialists, 234
Ireland, 173, 180, 183
ITV, 223, 327

Jackson, Brian, 144, 145, 146, 149, 151, 197, 203, 205, 208
Jackson, David, 122
Jackson, Eddie, 131
Jamaica, 173, 180, 181, 187
James, Eric, 196
Japan, 70, 234
Jennings, Philip, 94, 95, 97, 98–9, 140, 141
Jewish people, 174–7, 209
Jim Crow laws, 222
job-title inflation, 321
Johnson, Alan, 323
Johnson, Alexander Boris, 300, 329–30
Johnson, Dee, 243–4
Johnston Press, 327
Jones, Bryan, 311
Jones, Chris, 216–17
Jones, Owen, 348
Jouhl, Avtar Singh, 183–5

Kandler, Peter, 238, 246
Kaur, Jodha, 276–7
Keele University, 73, 150, 151, 208, 210
Kemp, Peter, 94, 97, 98, 100
Kenya, 276
Khan, Yasmina, 186
King, Martin Luther, 232
King's College London, 327
Knowles, Freda, 84

INDEX